Mao's China

The Transformation of Modern China Series
James E. Sheridan, General Editor

The Fall of Imperial China
Frederic Wakeman, Jr.

China in Disintegration
The Republican Era in Chinese History, 1912–1949
James E. Sheridan

Mao's China
A History of the People's Republic
Maurice Meisner

Intellectuals and the State in Modern China
A Narrative History
Jerome B. Grieder

Chinese Foreign Policy *
A Conceptual History
Mark Mancall

* In preparation.

Mao's China

THE PEOPLE'S REPUBLIC OF CHINA

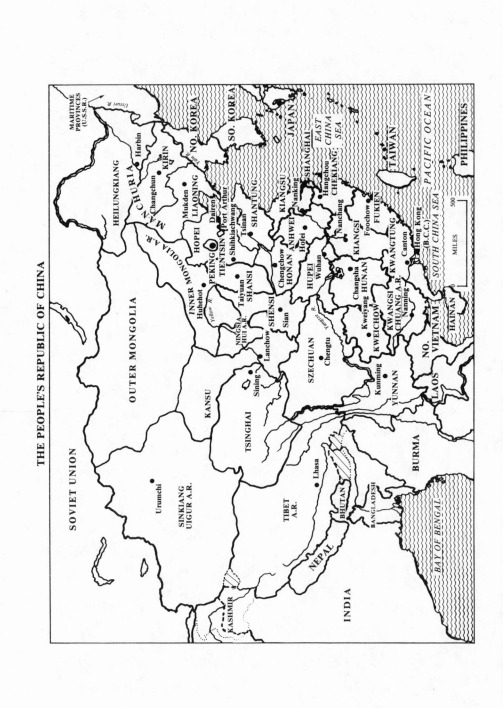

Mao's China

A History of
the People's Republic

Maurice Meisner

THE FREE PRESS
A Division of Macmillan Publishing Co., Inc.
NEW YORK

Collier Macmillan Publishers
LONDON

The Free Press
A Division of Macmillan Publishing Co., Inc.
866 Third Avenue, New York, N. Y. 10022

Collier Macmillan Canada, Ltd.

First Free Press Paperback Edition 1979

Library of Congress Catalog Card Number: 76–51566

Printed in the United States of America

printing number   paperback
5   6   7   8   9   10

Printing number   hard cover
5   6   7   8   9   10

Library of Congress Cataloging in Publication Data

Meisner, Maurice J.
   Mao's China.

   (The Transformation of modern China series)
   Includes bibliographical references and index.
   1.   China—History—1949–1976.   I.   Title.
DS777.55.M455   951.05   76–51566
ISBN 0–02–920820–3
ISBN 0–02–920810–6 pbk.

To LAURI

Contents

Part Four: The Thermidorean Reaction, 1960–1965

Part Five: The Cultural Revolution and Its Aftermath

Preface

Karl Marx had a taste for historical paradox. In 1850, a century before the birth of the People's Republic of China, he indulged in a bit of fanciful speculation:

> When in their imminent flight across Asia our European reactionaries will ultimately arrive at the Wall of China, at the gates that lead to the very stronghold of arch-reaction and arch-conservatism, who knows if they will not find there the inscription:
> République Chinoise,
Liberté, Egalité, Fraternité.[1]

Westerners today fly to China in ever increasing numbers—and by jet aircraft—and now find inscribed on Chinese walls not only the radical democratic slogans of the French Revolution but also the socialist and communist slogans of Karl Marx. The land that in Marx's time was known as "the Celestial Empire," and which Marx (in his less paradoxical moments) called a "living fossil," is now not only a republic but a "people's republic," and on its gates one finds the inscription: "Consolidate the Dictatorship of the Proletariat!" No one could have predicted (and Karl Marx certainly never made the prediction) that the most modern of revolutionary doctrines of the "advanced" Western world would find its deepest roots in the most ancient and archaic land of "backward" Asia.

Historians long have pondered this paradox. Marxism, after all, rests on the assumption that socialism presupposes capitalism. It is a doctrine that teaches that only a highly developed capitalist economy creates the industrial prerequisites that makes socialism a real historical possibility—and, at the same time, produces the modern proletariat, the social agent destined to make that possibility a historical reality. Yet in precapitalist China contemporary disciples of Marx carried out the greatest of modern revolutions, and did so by harnessing the forces of peasant revolt.

Chinese Marxists, of course, were not the first to make the attempt to build socialism in an economically backward land. The first Marxist revolution took place in Russia, the most backward country in Europe, and the Russian Bolsheviks (quite contrary to their original expectations) were soon forced to confine their revolutionary efforts to a single country largely lacking the Marxist-defined material and social preconditions for socialism. The social results of those efforts are now apparent, and they offer little comfort and even less inspiration for those who envision a socialist future for mankind. Chinese Marxists came to power three decades later through a different revolutionary route in a far more backward land—and over the past quarter of a century they have forged a novel post-revolutionary path, the ultimate social results of which cannot yet easily be predicted. This book is a history of that unique attempt to construct a socialist society in the world's most populous country.

That era formally began on the first day of October of 1949 when Mao Tse-tung stood high on the Gate of Heavenly Peace in Peking to announce the establishment of the People's Republic of China. The date is historically important but the event was historically anti-climactic. The peasant soldiers of the People's Liberation Army had marched into Peking and other cities many months before the official proclamation of the new state, there to be greeted by an urban population who had played little part in the long revolutionary struggle. The decisive battles of the revolution had taken place earlier, in the vast rural hinterlands far removed from ancient Chinese capitals and modern Chinese cities. The conquest of the cities and the establishment of the People's Republic in Peking was not so much the time of revolution as it was the military and political consummation of more than two bitter decades of an historically unique revolutionary civil war. The heroic and crucial era of the revolution lay in the past and new revolutionary dramas, still wholly unforeseen by the victors of 1949, had yet to begin.

Nonetheless October 1, 1949 is a symbolically important date in Chinese and world history. If revolutions involve the violent destruction of political institutions that allow new societies to emerge, then what Chinese Communists celebrate on the first day of October is a revolution no less significant than the great French Revolution of 1789 and the Russian October Revolution of 1917, no less momentous in the scope of its political destructiveness, no less important in opening the way for a new and unprecedented course of social development, and no less great in its worldwide impact. But unlike the French and Russian Revolutions, there is no single political act that suddenly changed the historical direction. There is no one dramatic revolutionary event as decisive as when the Parisian masses stormed the Bastille, or when the Russian Bolsheviks seized power during the "ten days that shook the world." For Chinese revolutionaries there was no Bastille to storm and no Winter Palace to capture. The peculiarities of the modern Chinese historical environment posed very different and far more difficult revolutionary tasks. When the People's Republic was officially proclaimed on October 1, 1949, the battles that destroyed the old order already had been fought and won. It was not a time of revolutionary violence in Peking but a day when revolutionaries turned rulers could look back and reflect upon the many years of struggle and sacrifice that had brought them to power—and also look forward to the hopefully peaceful tasks of developing their nation. The embryos of the new state and society had gradually come into being during the long decades of revolutionary violence that had destroyed the old regime, and it was that prior process of both revolutionary destruction and creation that was consecrated on October 1, 1949. And on that date, for more than a quarter century, Chinese leaders have stood on that same ancient Gate of Heavenly Peace to celebrate National Day, the official anniversary of the birth of "new China."

But a history of the People's Republic cannot begin with that official holiday. Revolutions produce new societies but not *ex nihilo*. While Mao Tse-tung once declared China to be a "blank" sheet of paper on which dedicated men could write any new revolutionary words they wished, the historical slate cannot so easily be wiped so clean. For the historical truth of revolutionary matters, as Marx observed a century before his Chinese disciple proclaimed the revolutionary virtues of being "poor and blank," is that while men make their own history "they do not make it just as they please . . . under circumstances chosen by themselves, but under circumstances directly encountered, given and transmitted from the past."[2] The Chinese Revolution and the People's Republic are the products of particular circumstances and experiences inherited and transmitted from China's past. The new order did not suddenly emerge full-blown from Minerva's head in 1949, as that still popular (but very misleading) phrase, "the Communist takeover," might suggest. And those who prepared and brought about that revolution were not alien intruders; they were the products of a specific Chinese historical situation as well as the makers of a new Chinese history. To understand the history they made after 1949, it is necessary to understand something of the historical conditions from which they came.

Hence Part One of this book is a general inquiry into the Chinese historical environment from which Chinese Marxist revolutionaries emerged and an account of the conditions they encountered and transformed. Parts Two to Five attempt to relate and assess the history of what now can be called "the Maoist era," from the time Mao Tse-tung announced the birth of the new state in 1949 to his death on September 9, 1976.

My aim is not to discuss that history as a case study in the process of "modernization," for the aim of the founders of the People's Republic was to make China both modern *and* socialist. Rather the chapters that follow treat the history of the People's Republic in the perspective of the Chinese Communists' own Marxist goals and standards. To view the Chinese Communists simply as "nationalists" or "modernizers" neither does justice to their aims and efforts nor does it allow a sufficiently high and rigorous standard of judgment to assess their successes and failures.

In preparing this volume, I have become painfully aware of the difficulties and dangers of writing contemporary history. The closer one is to an historical era, and particularly to a revolutionary era that has yet to come to an end, the more difficult it is to recognize its significant features. What seems vitally important today may appear inconsequential tomorrow. And in attempting to write a history of the People's Republic, one suffers from both an overabundance and an absence of data. I only hope that I have not left out too much that is historically important or included too much that will prove to be trivial.

Much of what appears in these pages is based on the labors of many scholars who have worked and written on recent Chinese history. My debt to them is only inadequately acknowledged by references to their works in the notes and the bibliography. I trust they will forgive me for using their work to arrive at interpretations they may not share.

For reading the entire manuscript and offering mountains of incisive criticisms and suggestions, I am especially grateful to James Sheridan, Sylvia Glagov, Robert Marks, Lynn Lubkeman, Howard Temin, and Lorraine Meisner. I regret that I have not been able to answer all the questions they and others have raised. I deeply appreciate the many forms of assistance provided by the faculty and staff of the Department of History at the University of Wisconsin, Madison. For generosity of time and spirit, a special debt is owed to Cecile Henneman, Helen Hull, and Carrie Marks.

Notes

1. Karl Marx "Revue," in Karl Marx and Friedrich Engels, *Werke* (Berlin: Dietz Verlag, 1964), 7:222.
2. Karl Marx, "The Eighteenth Brumaire of Louis Bonaparte," in Karl Marx and Frederick Engels, *Selected Works* (Moscow: Foreign Languages Publishing House, 1950), p. 225.

Part One

The Revolutionary Heritage

Western Imperialism and the
Weakness of Chinese Social Classes

THE HISTORY OF REVOLUTION in modern China begins in the mid-nineteenth century with a Christian peasant rebellion that failed, and climaxes, although it is by no means the revolutionary conclusion, with a Marxist-led peasant revolution that succeeded in mid-twentieth century. Significantly, the ideologies of both the Taiping Rebellion of 1850–1865 and the Communist revolution, nearly a century later, were drawn not from the millennial Chinese tradition, but from modern Western intellectual sources. Hung Hsiu-ch'uan, leader of the massive Taiping Rebellion that very nearly overthrew the reigning Manchu dynasty, was a self-proclaimed disciple of the Christian god (and, he believed, the younger brother of Jesus Christ) while Mao Tse-tung, in his particular fashion, was a modern disciple of Karl Marx. However much their respective ideologies were "Sinified" and adapted to Chinese historical conditions (and there was much in the way of adaptation in both cases), neither Hung nor Mao presented himself as a Chinese sage in a Chinese tradition of sages. Instead, both appeared on the Chinese historical scene as iconoclasts, bearers of new social visions and prophets of new social orders based on universal truths derived from Western intellectual and political traditions.

Reflected in the borrowing of Western ideologies to serve Chinese revolutionary ends is the central role of Western imperialism in molding the history of modern China. And one role that imperialism played was profoundly revolutionary, albeit unintentionally so. Imperialism was revolutionary not only in a social and economic sense but also culturally and intellectually. Imperialism not only undermined the old Confucian order—thus making a revolution possible and indeed necessary—it pro-

3

vided, as a by-product, new ideas and ideologies which turned the modern Chinese revolutionary process against the traditions and institutions of the Chinese past. Chinese revolutionaries used Western tools and ideas not only to rid China of the foreign imperialist yoke but also to throw off the yoke of the Chinese tradition. New visions of the future precluded a Confucian-based social order as well as a Western-dominated China. The rejection of the Chinese cultural–historical past proclaimed in the Taiping version of radical Christian egalitarianism struck an iconoclastic chord that still reverberates more than a century later in the People's Republic.

In view of the general historical picture of China as the land of petrified tradition, portraying Chinese in their "response to the West" as virtually immobilized because of their conservative attachment to traditional Confucian social and cultural values, it is well to keep in mind that modern Chinese revolutionary history began in an iconoclastic fashion and generally has retained this character. The rejection of the Chinese cultural–historical heritage proclaimed in the Taiping version of radical Christian egalitarianism ushered in a strongly anti-traditional impulse that was to be taken up in different fashions by later revolutionary movements, especially by the iconoclastic intelligentsia of the May Fourth era, from whose ranks emerged the founders and early leaders of the Chinese Communist Party.

However much a conservative defense of traditional cultural values may have inhibited conservative Chinese attempts at "modernization" (and more than culture was involved in the failure of Chinese conservatives to change China), there is little evidence to support the widespread assumption that modern Chinese revolutionary change can be understood in terms of the survival of traditional patterns of thought and behavior. Chinese revolutionaries tended to adopt what were perceived to be the most radical ideas and ideologies the West had to offer, and to derive from those ideas and ideologies radical visions of a future that demanded a complete and fundamental break with the ways of the past. The revolutionary concern was always with the plight and future of China; yet the aim was not to revitalize old Chinese traditions but to find ways to bury them.

Yet ideas and ideologies alone do not create revolutionary situations, much less revolutions. It was the modern Chinese social situation that was potentially revolutionary, making revolutionary ideas (and iconoclastic impulses) historically dynamic forces. Again, in the crucial social realm, foreign imperialism played a decisive role. But it was a contradictory role, both revolutionary and counterrevolutionary, one which created a modern revolutionary situation and yet, at the same time, inhibited the consummation of a modern revolution. Imperialism, as Karl Marx predicted, served as "the unconscious tool of history" in creating conditions for a social revolution in China and, indeed, in all of the precapitalist societies of the non-Western world upon which it impinged. However vile the motives which actuated it and however brutal the methods which characterized it, imperialism was a necessary historical force in breaking apart stagnant and tradition-bound societies seemingly incapable of moving into modern history on their own. For Marx imperialism was a force that "batters down all Chinese walls," one that "compels all nations, on pain of extinction, to adopt the bourgeois mode of production; it compels them to introduce what it calls civilization into their midst, i.e., to become bourgeois themselves. In one word, it creates a world after its own image."[1]

But Marx was too sanguine about the ultimate socioeconomic effects of imperialism in China. To be sure, the nineteenth-century Western onslaught did indeed batter down the walls of the old Chinese empire, humiliating China through repeated wars and the unequal treaties imposed in their wake, and contributing to the disintegration of the traditional political structure. And the introduction of modern Western capitalist forces of production undermined and transformed much of the traditional economic order, particularly in and around the treaty ports where foreign political and military power held sway. Yet the new Chinese world was not refashioned in the image of the Western bourgeois world, as Marx had anticipated. Modern capitalism in China, introduced under foreign imperialist auspices, retained an alien character and developed only in limited and distorted form. A modern Chinese bourgeoisie emerged, but it was a numerically small and economically weak class, and one which remained largely dependent upon the forces of foreign imperialism which had given birth to it. Moreover, it was primarily a commercial and financial bourgeoisie, and not an industrial one, largely serving as intermediaries between the Chinese market and the capitalist world market. In a semicolonial country where the modern sector of the economy was dominated by the imperialist presence, it is hardly to be expected that the fledgling Chinese bourgeoisie could have been anything more than an extension of foreign capitalism, however much individual members of that class may have nurtured nationalist resentments against foreign domination. Quite naturally and inevitably, a small and weak bourgeoisie—especially one engaged more in commerce and finance than in industry—was accompanied by a diminutive and ill-formed urban proletariat. When the imperial regime fell in 1911, there were no more than 1,000,000 industrial workers in a land of 400,000,000 people—and most of these worked in small shops lacking mechanical power. Drawn mostly from the peasantry, rather than from the traditional urban artisans, the workers retained strong ties to their native villages and to peasant traditions. These factors, coupled with the numerical paucity of the working class, militated against the development of a modern sense of proletarian class consciousness.

The modern Chinese social structure was thus marked by the feebleness of the modern social classes: a weak bourgeoisie and an even weaker proletariat. But it was not only the modern classes who were puny; the modern Chinese historical situation was fundamentally characterized by the weakness of *all* social classes. For the emergence of the bourgeoisie and proletariat, both of which remained embryonic and undeveloped, was accompanied by a decline in the power and prestige of the traditional ruling gentry-landlord class. While imperialism undermined the foundations of the imperial bureaucratic state with which the gentry was so closely intertwined, gentry-landlord proprietors found it more profitable to continue to exploit peasants in the traditional parasitic fashion—and the fashion became increasingly parasitic as traditional opportunities for bureaucratically obtained wealth (and traditional bureaucratic and Confucian moral checks on exploitation) declined along with the disintegration of the old political order. Because of lack of vision, opportunity, and capital, relatively few members of the old ruling class turned to modern commerce and industry or modern forms of commercial agriculture. The traditional Chinese gentry thus remained mostly traditional in a post-traditional Chinese social and intellectual world; from its ranks did not emerge any "modernizing elite" (as there did in late nineteenth-century Japan) capable of promoting economic development or exercising political power. Although the gentry remained economically and politically dominant on the local rural level until the Communist revolution, it was an increasingly weak and parasitic class, morally and intellectually bankrupt, and incapable of political expression on a national level.

The decay of the gentry was a major factor in preventing the reformation of the old imperial order from within, and thus hastened the coming of a revolutionary situation. That factor, coupled with the absence of a viable bourgeoisie and a strong centralized state, precluded China from following what Barrington Moore has termed "the conservative route to modernization," similar to that pursued by Meiji Japan. The attempt was made, of course. Following the suppression of the Taiping Rebellion and the humiliations of the Opium Wars, conservative "self-strengtheners" sought to "modernize" China in order to defend the empire from the foreign imperialist threat from without and to preserve the old Confucian sociopolitical order within. But it was a feeble effort. Its futility was revealed in the crushing defeat China suffered in 1895 at Japan's hands and in the last years of the century when China was virtually partitioned into a half-dozen colonies. The moribund dynasty lingered on for another decade, and departed quietly from the historical scene in the quasi-revolution of 1911.

The disintegration and collapse of the imperial order, for which the gentry had provided the social base for so long, hastened, in turn, the decline of the gentry in modern times. The end of the empire removed the political symbols of Confucian ideology that traditionally had sanctified the dominant position of the gentry in Chinese society and deprived the members of that class of the bureaucratic network upon which they had been so long dependent for wealth and political protection. The gentry limped into the twentieth century as a dying landlord class, capable of little more than pursuing the most ruthless traditional forms of socioeconomic exploitation, unchecked by traditional political or moral sanctions. The peasants who were the victims of that exploitation eventually were to have the opportunity to repay gentry-landlord ruthlessness in kind, although in a different way—in the ruthlessness of an agrarian social revolution that, in the end, was to eliminate the gentry as a social class in the mid-twentieth century.

For the moment, it is important to take note of a different historical result of the gentry's decay: the tendency, in modern China, for political and military power to become divorced from social and economic power. It is generally the historical case, at least in Western historical experience, that the decline of the power and prestige of a once dominant social class is accompanied by the ascendency of a new social class. Much of our thinking about the rise and decline of social classes, about the relationship between economic and political power in general, and about revolution, is dominated by categories derived from modern Western historical experience. A most prominent part of our historical consciousness is the transition from feudalism to capitalism, an epoch that saw the emergence of new capitalist forces of production and exchange, the undermining of the power of the aristocracy, and the rise of the modern bourgeoisie to social and political dominance.

Yet in modern China this was not precisely the historical case. While the decline of the gentry can be attributed in large measure to the impact of Western imperialism, no social class associated with new capitalist forces of production and exchange arose to assume the dominant position in Chinese society that the gentry was forced to abandon. As noted, the modern Chinese bourgeoisie and industrial proletariat were both extraordinarily weak classes. Products of Western capitalism, they were but pale reflections of their Western counterparts.

There remained, of course, the peasant masses who constituted the great majority of the Chinese population. But peasant life remained traditional in an era when the traditional Chinese order was disintegrating; new economic forces increased the already staggering burdens the peasants bore, adding new forms of exploitation to increasingly oppressive traditional forms, but without changing the old agrarian socioeconomic structure or traditional modes of life and thought. By virtue of the very nature of its localized and self-sufficient economic existence, the peasantry was a weak social class, provincial in outlook and without the means to politically articulate its grievances and interests on the national political scene. As in traditional times, modern Chinese society rested on the foundation of peasant labor, but for most of modern Chinese history peasants had little to do or say about the social and political direction that China followed. The Chinese peasantry had the potential for effective political action—and, indeed, for revolution—but it was not a potential that could be realized on its own accord; it required the leadership, organization, and ideology provided by members of other classes to make Chinese peasants modern historical actors and not simply the victims of modern history. As a class by itself, the peasantry was politically impotent as well as without social or economic power.

What was crucial, however, was the decline and decay of the land-lord-gentry, the class that had been dominant in Chinese society for more than two millennia, coupled with a modern bourgeoisie that was too embryonic to establish itself as a truly independent social class. An increasingly parasitic gentry survived the fall of the old imperial order in 1911 only because the Chinese bourgeoisie was unable (and, indeed, unwilling) to attempt to remove it.

Here we find the social basis for a modern Chinese historical phenomenon of crucial importance: the relative independence of political power from social and economic power. In a situation in which no social class was dominant, in which all were weak, political power tended to be increasingly independent of social class and to dominate society in general. This tendency is apparent in the growth of regionalist political–military power bases during the latter half of the nineteenth century; in the virtually immediate collapse (except in name) of the presumably bourgeois-type republic established by the Revolution of 1911 and the consequent dictatorship of the militarist Yuan Shih-k'ai (c. 1912–1916), and the subsequent full-blown emergence of warlordism over the following decade. Independent political power based on military force was characteristic not only of these traditional-type vestiges lingering on to condition the political life of the twentieth century, but also was characteristic of China's modern political parties, the Kuomintang and the Chinese Communist Party (CCP). Neither the history of the Kuomintang nor the history of the CCP can be understood simply in terms of political parties representing or expressing the interests of particular social classes. To be sure, both parties became involved in various ways with various social groups and their interests. But while landlords and the commercial and financial classes of the coastal cities became attached to the Kuomintang, it was not simply a party of landlords and bankers; the "bankers of Shanghai" were always as dependent on the military and political power of Chiang Kai-shek as he and his party were on the economic support of the urban monied classes. And while the CCP came to power on the basis of massive peasant support and participation, it did not become a peasant party in the process of the rural-based revolution it headed; it was a party that was to prove to be a good deal more revolutionary than the peasants whose support was decisive for its revolutionary victory. Both modern political parties operated in a historical situation in which politics and policies were not so much determined by social-class interests but one in which the holders of political and military power determined the direction of social development and the fate of social classes.

It was a modern Chinese phenomenon that held special revolutionary potential as well as one with conservative historical implications. The conservative manifestations are apparent in the emergence of semi-independent provincial power bases toward the end of the Ch'ing dynasty; in the warlord satrapies of the twentieth century; and in the Kuomintang regime after 1927. In all these cases, political power served not to change Chinese society but to preserve existing socioeconomic relationships, especially in the countryside. The revolutionary potential was to manifest itself in the emergence of an intellectual–political elite that was to give the revolutionary movement a more radical thrust than its social class support might otherwise have warranted.

Note

1. Karl Marx and Frederick Engels, "Manifesto of the Communist Party" (1848), in *Selected Works* (Moscow: Foreign Languages Publishing House, 1950), pp. 36–37.

2

The Defection of the Intellectuals

ALTHOUGH TAIPING PEASANT REBELS in the mid-nineteenth century had been the first to mount a revolutionary challenge to the dominance of the gentry and the entire Confucian sociopolitical order, the modern history of the Chinese revolution did not truly begin until near the turn of the century when members of the gentry began to turn against the Confucian values and ways of their own class. More precisely, in the 1890s a small but highly significant number of the sons of the traditional landlord–bureaucratic elite began to lose confidence in the utility (and eventually in the moral validity) of Confucian values and traditional institutions. Influenced by Western ideas and at the same time acutely aware of the inability of the old regime to respond effectively to the increasingly grave threat foreign imperialism posed to the very existence of China, they became intellectually alienated from traditional values and beliefs. And intellectual alienation was soon to lead to social and political alienation. Unwilling to uncritically accept traditionally sanctified values, some proved unwilling to succeed their fathers as social leaders and political rulers in the old system. A portion of young gentry-scholars, the sons of the traditional ruling elite, set themselves adrift from their social class moorings and formed the nucleus of a new strata in Chinese society—a modern intelligentsia from whose ranks were to emerge the leaders of modern revolutionary movements. It was the sons of the gentry—in effect, defectors from their class—who were to provide the ideology and leadership for a revolution that eventually was to destroy the gentry as a social class.

It was not, as is often suggested, the traditional prestige of the scholar in China that made intellectuals so politically important in twentieth-century history, but rather the specific conditions of the modern Chinese historical environment. In a situation characterized by massive social and cultural disintegration, by incredible political chaos, a situation in which all social classes were weak and none dominant, an intelligentsia could operate as a virtually autonomous force and decisively influence the course of historical development.

But intellectuals could not make history on their own. Having cut their ties to their own social class, they became socially independent but remained politically and historically impotent. Only when the intelligentsia felt the need and perceived the opportunity to tie themselves to other social classes, to become the political spokesmen expressing the social and economic discontents of the impoverished masses and to direct their activities into new forms of political action—it was only then that the intelligentsia was able to appreciate and seize upon the potentialities for revolutionary change that the modern Chinese historical situation offered; it was only then that they were able to take advantage of the opportunity to fashion social reality in accordance with their ideas, ideals, and visions. The seeds of the modern Chinese revolution were sown in the 1890s, when the sons of the gentry lost their belief in their moral right to succeed their fathers as rulers and emerged as an independent social stratum. But the modern Chinese revolution, properly speaking, did not begin until three decades later when the history of the intelligentsia became intertwined with the history of the masses.

This crucial historical relationship only began to be forged in the 1920s, with the emergence of a specifically Marxist-oriented segment of the intelligentsia. That intelligentsia, however, did not suddenly appear on the Chinese historical scene as a result of any simple act of instant enlightenment produced by the example of the Russian Bolshevik Revolution and the concurrent arrival of the theories of Marx and Lenin. Those who were to found and lead the CCP found the Marxist revolutionary message enlightening because they perceived in that message a solution to the crisis of Chinese society. But the manner in which they perceived the Chinese situation and the manner in which they understood and applied Marxism to attempt to resolve that situation were influenced profoundly by pre-existing intellectual predispositions.

Nationalism and Iconoclasm

A curious combination of nationalism and cultural iconoclasm is one of the more striking characteristics of the history of the modern Chinese intelligentsia. It is hardly surprising that Chinese intellectuals should be highly nationalistic, for nationalism (and, indeed, an incipient anti-imperialism) was inherent in the very historical conditions from which the intelligentsia emerged and developed. It was not fortuitous that the first significant political actions of modern intellectuals came at a time when a more aggressive foreign imperialism threatened China with territorial dismemberment and colonization. In 1895 imperial China was humbled by the military might of a modernizing Japan. And that was the year Sun Yat-sen launched the first of his abortive anti-Manchu revolutionary adventures. And, more significantly, the year K'ang Yu-wei organized some 1,300 younger members of the scholar-gentry elite to protest the Peking government's capitulation to Japan and to advocate far-reaching institutional changes seen as necessary for China's national survival. The event signaled the beginning of the defection of the intellectuals from the old order; it reflected not only widespread dissatisfaction with the traditional system among substantial numbers of the most prominent sons of the ruling class but also their reluctance to take their assigned bureaucratic places in a system in which they had lost confidence. By the mid-1890s, China was no longer the land of complacent Confucian scholars cherishing a comfortable belief in the moral superiority of Chinese civilization in the face of impending national disaster.

In the following years, during the frenzied drive to divide China into spheres of influence for foreign colonization, the political activities of the intellectuals assumed new forms and a greater urgency. Their efforts culminated in the heroic but ill-fated "Hundred Days' Reform" of 1898, the famous coup that attempted to change China from the top but was aborted by a counter-coup that placed China back where it was—in the hands of corrupt bureaucrats and a decaying gentry ruling class.

What was reflected in the political activities and influential writings of the disaffected intellectuals of the 1890s was a new nationalist commitment to China as a nation-state in a world dominated by predatory imperialist nation-states. The overriding concern was not to preserve a particular Chinese culture or a particular Chinese social order (although some tried to salvage as much of the tradition that seemed salvageable) but rather to build a strong Chinese state and society that could survive and prosper in a hostile international arena. It was a concern that conditioned the intellectual understanding and political uses of all new ideas and ideologies, not excluding the internationalist creed of Marxism.

While the emergence of an ardently nationalistic intelligentsia was in a sense dictated by modern Chinese historical circumstances, it is not so easy to understand why the nationalist quest was accompanied by strongly iconoclastic impulses. Nationalism, after all, generally demands a valued national past and it is the general proclivity of nationalists to celebrate and glorify their particular historical and cultural heritage, yet this was not so for modern Chinese nationalism. The tendency was to discard traditional values and culture as unsuitable for China's survival, and later to condemn them as the source of China's problems.

Yen Fu and Liang Ch'i-ch'ao, the major spokesmen for the first generation of the modern Chinese intelligentsia that emerged around the turn of the century, arrived at the conclusion that the basis of modern nation-state power was not simply the material accomplishments of the West but dynamic Western ideas and values that had given rise to those accomplishments—the ideas of struggle and progress, the values conducive to the release of individual human energies for dynamic economic growth and the conquest of nature. And these ideas and values, presented as Western, were offered for Chinese adoption because it was to the absence of such ideas and values in the Confucian tradition that the intelligentsia attributed China's modern economic and political weakness.

From declaring the tradition unsuitable to modern national ends, it was but a short step to condemning it as morally deficient as well. As the plight of China deepened, and as the need to explain and find solutions for that plight grew, it was an easy and logical step to take, foreshadowed by the brand of nationalism expounded in the writings of Liang Ch'i-ch'ao and Yen Fu. While an iconoclastic rejection of tradition was hardly the nationalist result that Liang or Yen wanted or anticipated, their search for the source of power in the modern world had led them to a fundamental intellectual break with the past, a break they were unable or unwilling to fully recognize. By establishing the preservation and power of the state as the nationalist criterion for judging the value of all ideas and institutions, they imparted two essential messages with essentially iconoclastic implications: one was the conviction that the values necessary for national strength in the modern world were to be sought in the wisdom of Western theories and ideologies, which had provided foreign powers with their economic and political predominance; and the second, logically flowing from the first, was the necessity to discard traditional Chinese beliefs and values that could not serve the overriding interests of national power.

An iconoclastic rejection of the cultural past was thus latent in the very origins of nationalism in China, even though those earliest nationalists retained a deep emotional tie to traditional Confucian moral values. That iconoclastic potential would be expressed in the most forceful fashion by the younger intelligentsia in the second decade of the century. Exposed to a wider range of modern Western ideas, their ties to traditional values and culture became increasingly tenuous. But what gave their anti-traditionalism its special intensity were the political events of the first two decades of the new century. The fall of the monarchy (the symbol of the Confucian moral order) in the Revolution of 1911 deprived traditional values of their final claim to legitimacy, yet political opportunists cynically manipulated elements of the Confucian tradition for purely reactionary purposes, using them as props for a decadent society and the corrupt bureaucrats and militarists who parasitically hovered over it. This continued association of Confucianism with social and political conservatism opened the floodgates to a fiercely iconoclastic assault against the entire traditional cultural heritage, a force that has yet to spend itself in today's Marxist China.

This nationalistic cultural iconoclasm received its fullest and most politically significant expression in the years 1915–1919, in what came to be known as the New Culture Movement, a movement calling for a completely new Chinese culture, based on the total destruction of the traditions and values of the past. The call for China's first cultural revolution was sounded by an ardent young Francophile, Ch'en Tu-hsiu, who returned to China in 1915, from a self-imposed exile in Japan, to found the periodical *Hsin ch'ing-nien* (*New Youth*)—and to make certain his iconoclastic intentions were sufficiently clear he later gave it a French title as well, *La Jeunesse*. In 1921 this passionate devotee of modern French democracy and culture became the first leader of the Chinese Communist Party.

It is difficult to overestimate the importance of the intellectuals who coalesced around the *New Youth*, for their writings molded the beliefs and attitudes of a whole generation of young students who were to achieve political prominence after the May Fourth incident of 1919 and who were to become the leaders of the modern Chinese revolution. Among their avid readers and followers was the youthful Mao Tse-tung who was influenced profoundly by the views presented in the pages of *New Youth*—and whose first published writing (an essay stressing the importance of "physical culture") appeared in that periodical in 1917. One of the enduring influences that *New Youth* conveyed to the young Mao and his contemporaries was the notion that a complete cultural and moral transformation was the primary prerequisite for meaningful social reform and political action. It was not a renovation of traditional culture they wanted, for most saw little or nothing in the Chinese past worth preserving or renovating. What they demanded was the total annihilation of all the culture, values, traditions and customs of the past and their replacement by a wholly new culture based on the Western democratic and scientific values they so admired. The bitter and sarcastic attacks leveled against Confucianism and the merciless condemnation of all traditional values that filled the pages of *New Youth* reflected not simply the view that the tradition was outmoded and useless but a feeling that it was morally corrupt as well and perhaps always had been so.

This virulently iconoclastic rejection of the traditions of the Chinese past was accompanied by an ardent faith in the Chinese youth of the present. The youth were to be the bearers of a new culture and a new morality (and thus the agents for the emergence of a new and young Chinese society) for young people were perceived to be relatively uncorrupted by old traditions and hopefully not yet infected by a diseased culture and a sick society. More amenable to new ideas and values than their elders, the youth were seen as the agents of the cultural transformation upon which the salvation of the nation was dependent.

Another striking feature of the *New Youth* intellectuals—and, indeed, generally characteristic of the modern Chinese intelligentsia—was an extraordinary faith in the power of ideas to change social reality, an enduring assumption that changes in values and consciousness must necessarily precede social, economic, and political changes. No doubt it is a general proclivity of intellectuals to emphasize (and overemphasize) the importance of ideas, particularly their own, but the intensity and consistency of this tendency in twentieth-century Chinese history (for which Maoism offers contemporary confirmation) seems quite unparalleled and suggests some general predisposition to stress the role of consciousness in determining the direction of historical development.

New Youth was not a Marxist periodical—not at least before Ch'en Tu-hsiu became a convert to Marxism in late 1919. But it eventually produced Marxists, once political events compelled many of its contributors and readers to abandon their Western liberal beliefs. From the editorial board of *New Youth* came two professors from Peking University, Ch'en Tu-hsiu and Li Ta-chao, the cofounders of the CCP. And the early party membership was largely composed of their young student followers, nurtured on the ideas conveyed in the pages of that extraordinary periodical. The leaders of the Chinese Communist movement—and later the leaders of the People's Republic—sprung from this early group of young revolutionary activists, most notably, of course, Mao Tsetung, Li Ta-chao's onetime library assistant at Peking University and political disciple. To their newly found Marxist faith they brought many of their earlier intellectual predispositions, nationalism, cultural iconoclasm, and a voluntaristic faith in the power of ideas to shape social reality.

These various beliefs were not easy to reconcile. The crucial role attributed to ideas and consciousness went far beyond the bounds of Marxist theory. An ardent nationalism was hardly in tune with the profoundly internationalist content and aims of Marxism, or wholly compatible with the Marxist demand for class struggle and social revolution. And nationalism further clashed with an iconoclastic rejection of China's cultural and historical heritage. Throughout the history of the Chinese Communist movement these conflicting beliefs gave rise to tensions that were to have profoundly important political implications—and they remain essentially unresolved problems in the People's Republic today. In new forms and under vastly different historical circumstances, the problems and tensions that were generated by the pre-Marxist cultural revolution of 1915–1919 were again to appear in the Maoist-inspired Cultural Revolution of recent years. Centrally involved in both was an iconoclastic assault against the traditions of the past, the problem of reconciling iconoclastic impulses with nationalist feelings, an enduring belief in the power of human consciousness to fashion social reality, and an abiding faith in youth as the agents of moral regeneration. A young Mao Tse-tung was the intellectual product of the first cultural revolution, and an aging Mao was the political promoter of the second.

The desertion of the intellectuals received its most extreme expression in the New Youth era of 1915–1919. The totalistic iconoclasm of the new intellectuals was a reflection of social rootlessness as well as an intellectual rejection of the traditions and institutions of the past. Iconoclasm was also an affirmation of their social independence, for the emergent intelligentsia formed a new strata in Chinese society not tied to, nor the spokesman for, any social class. Thus from the dying gentry class emerged an autonomous intelligentsia committed to building a new social order which precluded the continued existence of the class from which they had defected.

Yet the intelligentsia lacked the means to change Chinese society in accordance with the models derived from the modern West. For the counterpart to their autonomous status was their social isolation and political powerlessness. The modern Western bourgeois ideas and institutions they admired and advocated struck few responsive chords in warlord-dominated China. The modern Chinese bourgeoisie, the natural carriers of modern liberal ideas, failed to promote democracy and constitutional government, for it was too weak and disfigured a class to carry an independent ideology.

Thus the intellectuals found themselves as much isolated in the modern cities as they were intellectually and physically separated from the backward countryside. Social isolation and political impotency gave rise to restlessness, frustration, and a growing need to find roots in Chinese society. The strident calls for cultural transformation were not only their intellectual prescription for the ills of China but also a reflection of social and political loneliness, the inability to effect the changes they desired. Not until the dramatic events of 1919 transformed the Chinese political situation did the intelligentsia's circumstances change. For many, that transformation led to disillusionment with Western liberalism, and provided for some a new Marxist faith which offered the opportunity for effective political action and the promise for an end to social isolation.

The May Fourth Movement and the Origins of the Chinese Communist Party

The events leading to a fusion of China's "rootless" intellectuals and the oppressed masses began on May 4, 1919. On that day, which marks the true beginning of the modern Chinese revolution, more than 3,000 university students in Peking demonstrated against the decision of the Western democracies at the Versailles peace conference to transfer the former German imperialist concessions in Shantung province to Japan as war booty. The protest culminated in attacks on the homes and offices of ministers of the Peking government who were in the pay of the Japanese. The violent clashes with the police and the subsequent arrests served only to inflame nationalist resentments against both a weak and corrupt Chinese government and against the foreign governments which for so long had exploited and humiliated China. Demonstrations grew larger and more militant and rapidly spread to virtually all the major urban centers.

The political significance of the movement was that it did not remain a student movement. The student activists were soon joined by many of their professors at Peking University and, elsewhere, by industrial workers and merchant associations. The cities of China were swept by massive popular demonstrations, strikes, antiforeign boycotts, and sometimes violent confrontations with the authorities. The May Fourth incident catalyzed the political awakening of a society which for so long had seemed inert and dormant. A massive wave of popular anti-imperialism engulfed the cities, and the country (if not yet the countryside) was seething with political as well as intellectual ferment.

The dramatically new political situation radically politicized a significant number of the intellectuals. Many who had regarded themselves as liberal cosmopolitans emerged as militant nationalists, defending the country against the menace of foreign imperialism. Many who had rejected political participation because they attributed the plight of China to fundamental deficiencies in the culture and values of the Chinese people, for which political measures offered only superficial solutions, now began to favor immediate political action to save the nation from the external threat and to resolve the grave social and economic crises that threatened from within. The new spirit of political activism permeating the urban areas offered the hope that the masses could be organized for effective action and that the intellectuals could be effective in leading them. Concurrently, the intellectuals' views of the West underwent a rapid and dramatic transformation. The bitter nationalist resentments aroused by the fateful decision at Versailles, coupled with growing nationalist political activism at home, led to a rapid erosion of the faith that the "advanced" Western nations would instruct China in the principles of democracy and science. The foreign teachers were now perceived as oppressors, and the old image of a Western world providing progressive models for the regeneration of China was replaced by a new image of a West made up of cynical and aggressive imperialist states, threatening the very survival of China. Having rejected traditional Chinese intellectual and political values, the intellectuals still looked to the West for guidance; but they now began to look more to Western socialist theories, which were themselves critical of the West as it was, in place of the conventional Western liberal ideologies, which sanctioned the existing capitalist-imperialist order.

It was from this new political and intellectual environment created in the wake of the May Fourth incident that a portion of the Chinese intelligentsia began to turn to the example of the Russian Revolution and the Marxist promise of worldwide revolutionary transformation. Hitherto, the Bolshevik victory of 1917 had elicited much interest in Chinese intellectual circles but had found few Chinese converts. As faith in Western democracy eroded and with the internal political awakening offering new hopes for effective and immediate action on the Chinese scene, the Bolshevik message offered both a new intellectual faith and a new political model. Marxism was seen as the most advanced intellectual product of the modern West, but one that rejected the Western world in its capitalist form and its imperialist relationship with China. The latter was most forcefully demonstrated through the nationalist appeals of the Leninist theory of imperialism (which offered the colonial and semicolonial lands a crucial international revolutionary role) and the new Soviet government's renunciation of old czarist imperialist privileges in China. To become a Marxist was one way for a Chinese intellectual to reject both the traditions of the Chinese past and Western domination of the Chinese present. And to embrace the Russian Revolution and become a Communist was a way to find a program for concrete political action to transform Chinese society—and a way to find a place for the Chinese nation in what was perceived to be an international process of revolutionary change.

Although the early Chinese converts to Marxism were inspired by the vision of international revolution that the Bolshevik Revolution seemed to herald, they had come to that new socialist vision through a profoundly nationalist route. Just as two decades earlier the modern Chinese intelligentsia had emerged out of a long process of nationalist alienation from traditional Chinese values, so now the new Marxist intelligentsia grew out of nationalist disillusionment with the Western bourgeois democratic ideologies. The immediate threat of foreign imperialism and a consequent nationalist concern with the fate and future of China were central in both cases. In the Marxist case, nationalism was to be turned to social revolutionary ends, but the nationalist origins of Marxism in China were to remain to condition the manner in which the new doctrine was to be interpreted and employed. It was a necessary condition, for China was a land that required national independence as well as social revolution—and the two tasks were to prove inseparable.

It was on the basis of the nationalist and politically activist impulses generated by the May Fourth Movement, combined with the chiliastic expectations of an imminent international revolutionary upheaval inspired by the writings of Lenin and Trotsky, that the new Chinese converts to Marxism undertook the task of organizing a communist party. The foundations for what was to be the Chinese Communist Party were laid in 1920, when young Marxist activists established a variety of small Communist groups (under a variety of names) in the major cities of China. Similar groups were organized by radical Chinese students studying abroad in Paris, Tokyo, and Berlin. The national party itself did not formally come into existence until July 1921, when twelve delegates from the different groups met at a secret congress that opened in a girl's boarding school in Shanghai and, after a police raid, concluded its deliberations in a houseboat near Hangchow. Assisted by a representative from the newly formed (and Moscow-based) Third International (Comintern), the congress adopted standard Leninist methods of organization and proclaimed orthodox Marxist–Leninist aims.

The new party was small in number, youthful in composition, and its members inexperienced in revolutionary practice and Marxist theory. The founding congress could claim to represent a total of only fifty-seven members. In a land which lacked a socialist political tradition, there was little on which to build the new organization; the party was led by Ch'en Tu-hsiu and Li Ta-chao who recruited most of their followers from their own students. In a country lacking a Marxist social-democratic intellectual tradition, it was inevitable that both leaders and followers would have only a superficial knowledge of the Marxist theory that was to guide their revolutionary activities. It did not seem a promising beginning.

The Abortiveness of Bourgeois and Proletarian Revolution

THE PERIOD FROM 1921, when the Chinese Communist Party was founded, to 1927, when Chiang Kai-shek launched the bloody counterrevolution that very nearly destroyed the Chinese Communists, was marked by two revolutionary failures. One was the failure of a bourgeois-democratic revolution, or what was sometimes called "the national revolution." The other was the failure of China's nascent urban working class to bring about a socialist reordering of society, although they made a valiant attempt to do so in the great revolutionary upsurge of 1925–1927. The two abortive revolutions were to have momentous consequences. For the failures of the 1920s largely removed both the bourgeoisie and the proletariat from the revolutionary scene; and, after 1927, moved the revolution from the cities to the countryside, where Maoism was to grow and the revolutionary victory of 1949 was to be forged.

When the young intellectuals who comprised the new CCP began their organized revolutionary activities in 1921, they believed that their main task was to organize the Chinese proletariat for a socialist revolution that would be part of the international process of socialist transformation that Marx had prophesied and which the Russian Revolution seemed to herald. The results of those early efforts to build a mass working-class movement were by no means insignificant. The organization of industrial workers in the large cities, as well as miners and railroad workers in more remote areas, proceeded rapidly. Workers' strikes proliferated—and were often motivated by political considerations and nationalist resentments as well as demands for tolerable living and working conditions.

Within a few years young Communist activists could claim a national labor federation representing half-a-million workers, and marshal hundreds of thousands for militant May Day demonstrations.

Yet the Communists soon learned that, in a country ruled and plundered by marauding warlord armies, it was naked military power that was crucial in determining the direction of political events, and labor unions and other mass organizations could be repressed and crushed more easily than they could be built. Visions of a socialist revolution within China, if not abandoned, had to be postponed. And the Communists also soon learned that the promised world revolution similarly had been postponed. When the anticipated socialist revolutions failed to materialize in the industrialized countries of Western Europe, and as the Soviet Union remained the lone and lonely socialist state in a hostile capitalist world order, both Russian national interests and the logic of Leninist revolutionary strategy dictated that the Chinese revolutionary process was in its bourgeois-democratic stage and that the prospects for a socialist revolution lay well in the future—for the possibility of the latter always had been predicated on an international revolutionary explosion, which the Russian Bolshevik Revolution had failed to ignite. The new and pessimistic Soviet assessment of the revolutionary situation in China —and in the world—was communicated to the leaders of the CCP in 1922 by representatives of the Moscow-based Third International (Comintern). The new Chinese converts to Marxism reluctantly received the disheartening message. But both the political authority of Moscow and political conditions in China demanded that the Chinese Communists accept the view that the revolution would be confined to bourgeois limits. The CCP was to ally itself with the Kuomintang. The old revolutionary party, still headed by Sun Yat-sen and revitalized by the political activism of the May Fourth Movement, had achieved a tenuous political–military base in and around the city of Canton. The alliance was designed to achieve the twin goals of national unification and national independence, that is, the elimination of warlord separatism and foreign imperialism. It was an alliance in which the CCP was to be very much the junior partner. The Communists were to recognize the Kuomintang as the leader of the bourgeois or "national" revolution and they were to join that party as individual members in a united front. The alliance was formally consummated in January 1924. To the Kuomintang at Canton there flowed Soviet arms, money, and military and political advisers—for the purpose of building a modern army that eventually would move northward to unify and liberate the country. To the Communists, Moscow offered moral encouragement and political advice.

In retrospect, one is struck by how narrow a definition Comintern ideologists gave the Marxist concept of a "bourgeois-democratic" revolution—at least insofar as China was concerned. A bourgeois revolution, according to Marxist theory, is a political transformation that sweeps away the obsolete institutions and forms of state left over from the old feudal (or "precapitalist") socioeconomic order and replaces them with new political institutions favorable to the interests of the bourgeoisie and to the growth of capitalist production and property relationships. Central to this process is genuine national unification—the establishment of a centralized government with a uniform code of laws, a single national currency, and a uniform system of taxation; in short, the abolition of all the vestiges of feudal separatism and the creation of modern politico-legal conditions conducive to the growth of a national market and to the further development of capitalist production. The process was also to include, at least ideally, the formation of a democratic and parliamentary republic, the form of state power most appropriate for the class dominance of the bourgeoisie. Furthermore, it was assumed that a bourgeois revolution would permit some degree of freedom for the political activities of other social classes, especially the growing proletariat; and would abolish remaining feudal socioeconomic relationships that shackled the peasantry, thus hastening the growth of capitalism in the countryside.

In its specifically Leninist form, a bourgeois-democratic revolution in Asia and the Middle East came to include a nationalist revolution to throw off the foreign imperialist yoke. It also came to include a much greater emphasis on the antifeudal social revolution in the countryside— and, partly to compensate for the weakness of the indigenous bourgeoisie, a far greater political role for the proletariat and especially for the peasantry in the "bourgeois" phase of the revolutionary process.

Yet the "bourgeois" revolution that the Kuomintang–CCP alliance was designed to carry out was conceived as a much more limited affair. Beneath the facade of the revolutionary rhetoric of the time, the concept was redefined to include no more than the leaders of the Kuomintang were willing to accept. And this boiled down to two aims: national unification and national independence. Only lip service was paid to the idea and ideal of a democratic parliamentary republic; indeed, it was implicitly assumed from the beginning that China's new political order would be an essentially military one. And quite explicitly excluded, or at least postponed, was an antifeudal social revolution in the countryside. China's "bourgeois-democratic" revolution, in short, was to be no more than a purely nationalist revolution.

A successful nationalist revolution was, of course, desperately needed. The 1911 Revolution had done little more than remove the anachronistic monarchy. Its political result was neither a strong state nor a democratic one, but rather increased political chaos and fragmentation in the dark age of warlordism that came in its wake. It left undisturbed the web of imperialist political and economic impingements that had made China so dependent on the foreign powers, just as it left untouched the existing internal social structure and especially traditional rural socioeconomic relationships and gentry-landlord dominance in the countryside. By the 1920s, national unification and national independence had become almost universal demands among the politically conscious elements of Chinese society, uniting much of the traditional ruling class with the modern social classes and political parties. And for the leaders of an isolated and beleaguered Soviet Union, being driven inexorably to Stalin's doctrine of "socialism in one country" and now deeply involved in internal Chinese politics, a nationalist revolution that would produce a friendly Chinese regime was the immediate and overriding aim.

But China needed more than a purely nationalist revolution and more was being demanded. New social classes and groups had appeared on the political scene to give the "national revolution" a radical thrust that went far beyond the limited aims upon which the Kuomintang–Communist alliance was based. In the cities the new Chinese working class began to revolt against the injustices of early industrialism. In the countryside peasants organized (and were being organized) to overthrow the dominance of the traditional landlord class. And a radical intelligentsia, now politicized and politically organized in modern parties, stood eager and able to lead a mass revolutionary movement. These forces could not be confined within the narrow limits of a "national" revolution or even a "bourgeois-democratic" one more broadly defined, as the great revolutionary upsurge of 1925–1927 was to demonstrate.

The Revolution of 1925–1927

The alliance with the Kuomintang provided Communist revolutionaries with wider access to Chinese society and the powerful forces of revolution latent within it. Communists, working under the banner of the Kuomintang, renewed their efforts to organize increasingly rebellious workers and peasants. Over the years 1924–1927, the mass revolutionary movement in both town and countryside, partly organized and partly spontaneous, grew with unprecedented rapidity and moved in ever more radical social directions. It was the mass movement that gave China's two modern political parties the enormous strength they so quickly acquired during those years and provided the alliance between them with its extraordinary dynamism. But the increasingly radical character of the popular movement created political tensions and intensified social conflicts that undermined the political united front and resulted in the near destruction of the CCP.

The radical and militant phase of the revolution was signaled by the May Thirtieth Movement of 1925. During the early months of 1925, the

city of Shanghai—the center and symbol of the foreign imperialist presence—was swept by a wave of workers' strikes. In one instance, a Chinese worker was shot to death by a Japanese foreman. On May 30 workers and students staged a demonstration of protest, which culminated in
the foreign-governed International Settlement, when British-commanded
police dispersed the demonstrators, killing 12 of their number. The incident had an explosive effect, setting off a succession of strikes, demonstrations, antiforeign boycotts in all the major cities and a new massive
wave of anti-imperialism throughout the country. The most notorious
clash between Chinese and foreigners occurred in the foreign settlement
in Canton on June 23 when British and French troops killed 50 Chinese
demonstrators and wounded many more. The Canton massacre provoked a general strike by Chinese workers in Hong Kong, crippling the
colony and British trade for 16 months, and a nationwide boycott against
British goods. In a dramatic expression of political militancy, 100,000
Chinese laborers migrated from the British colony to Canton to form the
Hong Kong–Canton Strike Committee, which became one of the main
centers of the growing revolutionary movement.

The militant mass movement that emerged in the summer of 1925—
which was to grow with such extraordinary rapidity and force over the
next two years—was never a purely nationalist movement and could not
be confined to strictly anti-imperialist aims. Powerful nationalist resentments fueled the revolutionary movement, to be sure, and the resentments were exacerbated in the course of the movement by the spectacle
of foreigners killing Chinese on Chinese soil. But the workers were also,
and perhaps primarily, driven to revolt by the horrendous conditions of
work and life brought by early capitalist industrialism. Workers living in
foreign-dominated cities and laboring in foreign-owned or foreign-oper-
ated factories saw exploitation intimately connected with foreigners. It
was this combination of socioeconomic oppression and foreign oppression that gave the workers' movement its special militancy.

The urban working-class movement of 1925–1927 was accompanied
by the rise of a no less militant peasant movement in the countryside. In
addition to a resurgence of peasant protest and revolt through traditional
forms, primarily secret societies and banditry, there appeared new and
modern rural organizations, the peasant associations. Composed mostly
of poorer peasants, and in large measure the product of the ideas and
organizing activities of young revolutionary intellectuals, the new organizations posed an increasingly radical threat to dominance of the
gentry. By mid-1925, half-a-million peasants had joined the new associations and unions in Kwangtung, the province where Canton and the main
military–political base of the allied Kuomintang–Communist forces were
located. Within two years, membership in the Kwangtung peasant organizations had quadrupled and the peasant associations had spread rap-

idly to other provinces. Nationalist and antiforeign sentiments were involved, but the motive force was an elemental demand for social justice and economic survival.

The mass movement sparked by the May Thirtieth incident had an immediate and dramatic effect on both the Kuomintang and the CCP. The dynamism of the popular movement in both town and countryside, in large measure, enabled the Kuomintang to consolidate its power in Canton and expand it from there. Following the death of Sun Yat-sen in March 1925, Chiang Kai-shek was establishing himself as the political leader of the Kuomintang by virtue of his control of the Russian-trained Nationalist Army and by the end of the year had extended Kuomintang control to all of Kwangtung and portions of neighboring provinces. The long-awaited Northern Expedition to unify the country began in the summer of 1926, and warlord armies crumbled before its advance. The popular revolutionary movement aided the new army in its striking victories, while the continuing military successes of Chiang's forces gave further impetus to the workers and peasants.

Just as the May Thirtieth Movement led to a spectacular growth in the power of the Kuomintang, so it led to a no less dramatic increase in the power and influence of its Communist allies. The CCP began with less than 100 members in 1921, and had grown to no more than 500 by 1924. At the end of 1925, and on the basis of the mass radicalization of the preceding 6 months, the party could claim 20,000 members—and by early 1927 its membership had almost tripled to a total of 58,000. Its auxiliary organizations were even larger, particularly the Socialist Youth Corps which attracted and organized ever increasing numbers of militant students and young workers. Moreover, Communist activists, primarily responsible for the organization of industrial unions and peasant associations, exercised an enormous influence within the new mass organizations, albeit under the banner of the Kuomintang. And Communists held important positions within the Kuomintang itself, in the National government based in Canton, and in Chiang Kai-shek's new army.

The successes of the mass movement that gave the Kuomintang–CCP alliance its extraordinary political dynamism eventually undermined the political basis of the alliance and soon tore it asunder, leading to the suppression and virtual destruction of the CCP. Once the forces of popular revolution were set in motion they acquired a life of their own that could not be confined within the narrow limits of a "national revolution." Urban workers struck not only at the factories and enterprises owned by foreigners, but those owned and operated by the Chinese bourgeoisie as well; the working-class movement threatened not only foreign property and privileges but property rights in general. In the countryside, the peasant movement attacked not foreign overlords, but the power of Chinese landlords and rural elites. From the mass nationalist movement there thus arose the threat of social revolution—and it threatened classes and groups that formed the social basis of the Kuomintang: the urban bourgeoisie whose ties to, and dependence upon, the Kuomintang were solidified in direct proportion to the rising threat of social revolution; and the officer corps of Chiang Kai-shek's army, whose members, in large part, were the sons of the landed gentry, a class now threatened by the growing forces of agrarian revolution. With the interests of the propertied classes increasingly intruded upon, the Kuomintang, save for its minority "left wing," emerged more and more as the party of property and social order.

As the Nationalist Army moved northward during the latter half of 1926, the workers' and peasant organizations grew to massive proportions, ever more radical in aims and methods, and increasingly social revolutionary in character, especially in the countryside. Even the most radical Communists were astonished by the sudden surge and power of the largely spontaneous movement from below. The sense of astonishment (and the feeling of exhilaration) runs throughout Mao Tse-tung's now famous report on the peasant movement in Hunan, a document written in February 1927 in which Mao described the spontaneous revolutionary activities of the peasantry as a force as natural and elemental as "a tornado or tempest, a force so extraordinarily swift and violent that no power, however great, will be able to suppress it."[1]

But social revolution was incompatible with the terms of the Kuomintang–Communist alliance. And the Stalinist message from Moscow, duly conveyed to Chinese Communist leaders through the agency of the Comintern, was to restrict the radicalism of the masses, and to preserve the political alliance at all costs. Thus the leaders of the Chinese party found themselves in the embarrassing and agonizing position of attempting to limit popular radicalism rather than to promote it, to dampen the flames of revolution rather than to place themselves at the head of the insurgent masses. Not all Communists heeded Moscow's "advice," nor could they have enforced Comintern directives even had they wished to do so, for the popular revolution (particularly in the countryside) had acquired a momentum of its own that was beyond the power of any party to control. Although many individual Communists encouraged and attempted to organize and lead the movement, the party as a whole remained confused and immobilized. The result was that the rebellious masses were left defenseless and largely leaderless in face of the organized forces of counterrevolution preparing to suppress them.

During the early months of 1927 the mass revolutionary movement reached its apogee, while the Nationalist Army was demonstrating its military supremacy in its victorious march through the provinces of South and Central China. The tension between the purely nationalist aims of the Kuomintang and the social-revolutionary aspirations of the masses was nearing its breaking point. The break came when Chiang Kai-shek had ac-

quired the military power (and the financial backing of the higher bourgeoisie of Shanghai) to destroy the mass movement—and to cast off his
Russian patrons and Communist allies. The counter-revolution began in
Shanghai in April. On March 21–22 a Communist-led working-class uprising had succeeded in seizing control of Shanghai, and the victorious insurgents awaited the arrival of the approaching Nationalist Army. Chiang
and his forces entered the city without opposition on March 26, and they
were welcomed as liberators. The liberators soon turned executioners. Before dawn on April 12, armed units of the infamous Green Gang and other
underworld secret societies, together with selected units of the regular
Nationalist Army, attacked the headquarters of Communist and radical
trade-union organizations, inaugurating a bloodbath that virtually destroyed both the CCP and the workers' movement in China's largest city
and the main center of the organized radical movement. From Shanghai,
the repression was carried to all of the areas south of the Yangtze under
Kuomintang control and within reach of the Nationalist Army, extending
north to warlord areas not yet under the administration of the Nationalist
government. In an orgy of counterrevolutionary violence—which in scope,
scale and brutality was unprecedented and is as yet unmatched in twentieth-century revolutionary history—Chiang turned his Soviet-built army
to the task of destroying all radical mass organizations as well as the Chinese Communist Party. Trade unions and student organizations were an-
nihilated in the cities, but nowhere was the slaughter greater than in the
suppression of the peasant associations in the countryside. Organizations
that had mobilized tens of millions of peasants were brutally smashed, and
within a few months had vanished from the political scene, leaving few
traces of the great agrarian revolution that had risen so swiftly, promising
to transform the Chinese countryside. Those killed in the Revolution of
1925–1927 numbered in the hundreds, but the White Terror of 1927–1930
took a toll of human lives that must be counted in the hundreds of
thousands.

The Chinese Communist Party itself was virtually extinguished. Its organizational structure was quickly shattered in a series of lightening blows
struck by the Nationalist Army, and its ranks were decimated further in a
series of belated and desperate attempts to reverse the counterrevolutionary tide, the last of which was the Canton Commune and its bloody
suppression in December 1927; it was to prove the last Communist revolutionary stand in the cities of China. At the beginning of 1927 the Chinese
Communist Party was a powerful organization with a membership of
58,000. By the end of the year no more than 10,000 remained, and they
were scattered, disorganized, demoralized, and leaderless. Some Communists defected, but most had been killed in battle or summarily executed. Those who survived the carnage fled to the more remote areas of
the countryside, there to attempt to begin the revolution anew.

The Communists learned bitter lessons from their crushing defeat, and the lessons were to guide their revolutionary strategy in the years that followed. First and foremost among these was the recognition that in the modern Chinese historical situation military power was decisive in determining the outcome of political and social-class struggles. It was the military superiority of the Kuomintang that had defeated the revolution in 1927, and that elemental fact of Chinese political life was a lesson not lost on the leaders of the CCP. From it grew the now famous Maoist maxim that "political power grows out of the barrel of a gun." The maxim had been practiced by Chiang Kai-shek before Mao expounded it, but Mao was to learn to be a better practitioner of the lesson that Chiang had imparted to him. The Communists now knew that they had to build their own army and that the revolution would of necessity take the form of a military struggle. Many also had learned that Moscow was not the sole repository of revolutionary wisdom, at least not in so far as the Chinese revolution was concerned, for it was that peculiar "united front" strategy formulated in Moscow that had led them to defeat and disaster. United-front strategies were by no means rejected, but the Chinese Communists were now determined to maintain their own political and military independence. And there arose a new appreciation of the revolutionary potentialities of the peasantry. In part, this was a matter of necessity, for the party was no longer able to operate effectively in the Kuomintang-ruled cities; in part, it was to be a new revolutionary preference. In any case, the Communists were no longer bound to the orthodox Marxist–Leninist dogmas on the revolutionary limitations of peasants.

The events of 1927 marked the failure not of one revolution but of two: the workers' movement in the cities and the peasant movement in the countryside. The urban proletarian movement had been socialist in nature, or at least potentially so, for it was a revolt against both indigenous and foreign capitalism, and was aimed at the abolition of private property. The socialist potential went unrealized, but it was not historically inevitable that this should have been so. The proletariat constituted only a small minority of the Chinese population, but not an insignificant one. By the mid-1920s the number of industrial workers employed in large-scale enterprises had grown to approximately 2,000,000 and they were highly concentrated and strategically placed in the modern sector of the Chinese economy. To this must be added a far greater number of urban semiproletarians, the perhaps 10,000,000 Mao Tse-tung once termed "the city coolies," who swelled the ranks of the urban revolutionary movement.[2] The Chinese industrial proletariat proper was not far smaller than its Russian counterpart in 1917.[3] Nor was it any less politically militant. Indeed, few working-class movements anywhere in the twentieth century matched the revolutionary energies, the organizational initiative, the extraordinary heroism, and the spirit of self-sacrifice and dedication to the revolutionary cause which the Chinese proletariat displayed. Moreover, the urban work-ing-class movement developed in a situation that in many respects was highly favorable for revolution. With all social classes weak, political power fragmented, and a militant proletarian movement accompanied by a powerful agrarian revolution, the possibility of a successful revolution based upon a worker–peasant alliance was not beyond the realm of pos-sibility. What was lacking was not the objective preconditions for revolu-tion but rather its subjective prerequisites. A politically immature and inexperienced Communist party allowed itself to become shackled to the policies of the Comintern and dependent on the actions of the Kuomin-tang. From its ranks emerged no leader with the boldness and vision of a Lenin or a Trotsky to seize upon the possibilities that the revolutionary situation offered. The Chinese Communist leaders did not lead the masses but, however reluctantly and unwittingly, accepted and pursued foreign-made policies that led the mass movement to its disastrous end. The dis-asters that befell both the workers' movement and the Chinese Communist Party in 1927 were in no sense historically inevitable. It was not preor-dained that the Russians should have created a modern Chinese army and placed that army in the hands of a man who was to use it to crush the Chinese revolution. That tragic historical irony came about not because of the weakness of the mass movement but because of the weaknesses and limitations of its leaders—and ultimately because the critical decisions and policies were formulated in Moscow. It was not to be the last time that the perceived national interests of the Soviet state were to collide with the real interests of the Chinese revolution.

Yet what did happen in 1927, even though it did not necessarily have to happen, was crucial in determining the future and nature of the revolu-tion. The liquidation of the workers' movement and Communist power in the cities proved irreversible. When the Communist revolution revived in the years after the debacle of 1927 it did so in the form of a peasant-based revolution in the more remote rural areas. The urban proletariat, so blood-ily suppressed in 1927, remained politically quiescent for the next two decades, and the Communists were not to regain power in the urban areas until their victorious peasant armies marched into the cities in 1949.

If the socialist revolutionary potential of 1927 went unrealized, the bourgeois revolution proved abortive as well. To be sure, the victorious northward march of the Kuomintang armies in 1927–1928 did manage to achieve a semblance of national unification, albeit upon the ruins of the mass movement. But the new Nationalist government at Nanking pro-vided no impetus and little opportunity for modern capitalist development in the cities, where its power was based; and sought to maintain the social status quo in the countryside, where it was content to rest its authority on the existing local power of the traditional gentry-landlord elite. Even as a purely nationalist revolution, the triumph of the Kuomintang was superficial and incomplete, for "national unification" was based less upon the elimination of warlordism than on various and tenuous alliances with the more powerful warlord armies of North China. And "national independence" meant arriving at an accommodation with the imperialist powers and a continued dependence on foreign economic influences. The bourgeois revolution thus remained unfinished, and the task of completing it fell to the Communists.

Notes

1. Mao Tse-tung, "Report of an Investigation into the Peasant Movement in Hunan," in *Selected Works of Mao Tse-tung* (London: Lawrence & Wishart, 1954), 1:21–22.
2. Mao Tse-tung, "Analysis of the Classes in Chinese Society" (1926), in *Selected Works* (1954), 1:19.
3. On the eve of the Bolshevik Revolution, the Russian industrial proletariat numbered about 3,000,000.

4

The Maoist Phase of the
Revolution and the Yenan Legacy

A RADICALLY NEW PHASE of the Chinese Communist Revolution began in-conspicuously in October of 1927 when Mao Tse-tung led the remnants of a defeated military force to Chingkangshan, a remote mountain region and old bandit hideout bordering on the provinces of Hunan and Kiangsi. There Mao proceeded to build a tiny military base by recruiting peasant vagabonds and uniting his troops with those of several local bandit lead-ers. In the spring of 1928 the forces at Chingkangshan were augmented by the arrival of 1,000 rebel soldiers led by Chu Teh, who was to become the commander of what was to become the Red Army and Mao's comrade in arms during the twenty-one years of revolutionary warfare that were to follow.

It was in the Chingkangshan border area that the Maoist strategy of a rural-based revolution had its origins. From 1928 to 1931, the Maoist forces learned to employ the tactics of guerilla warfare upon which their survival was dependent. The "Mao–Chu Army" grew through the recruit-ment of local peasants and through the appeals of a radical program of land redistribution, and eventually secured military predominance in southern Kiangsi, where, in 1931, the Chinese Soviet Republic was established.

If Mao had embarked on an independent course of agrarian revolution, such was not the case for the Chinese Communist movement as a whole. During the years when Mao was consolidating a rural base in Kiangsi, other Communists following directives from Moscow were leading small peasant-rebel armies in attacks on the cities. But a demoralized working class failed to respond to Communist revolutionary appeals. The end of 1930 marked the end of Communist hopes to regain their old proletarian bases. What remained of the defeated Communist forces gravitated to the Kiangsi area or retreated to a dozen smaller rural Soviet bases mostly located along the upper reaches of the Yangtze River. For the next ten years a bitter internal conflict would rage between Comintern-supported Chinese Communist leaders and Maoists for control of the party and the Red Army. The battles were to be fought in the isolated rural areas where the revolution and the revolutionaries were now confined—and the terrain was to prove favorable to Mao.

The Chinese Soviet Republic, formally proclaimed in November 1931, with its capital at the town of Juichin in Kiangsi Province, was to survive three years. The Communists established a functioning governmental apparatus, administering a territory of about 15,000 square miles inhabited by approximately 3,000,000 people. The central Soviet area was augmented by a dozen or so smaller rural Soviets, with a total population of about 6,000,000. And the Red Army grew into a formidable fighting force of 300,000.

The history of the Chinese Soviet Republic was brief, and the experiment ended in failure, but the historical experience was by no means insignificant. The Communists had established a sizable and functioning civilian governmental apparatus in Kiangsi, and, although the government fell, those who survived its fall emerged as experienced political administrators as well as seasoned revolutionaries. The principles of guerilla warfare that Mao Tse-tung and Chu Teh originated at Chingkangshan were developed and tested on a far greater scale during the early 1930s. Perhaps most important, the Communists learned essential lessons about the preconditions for the political and social mobilization of the peasantry. They learned that the first prerequisite for agrarian revolution was the military predominance of the Red Army and the security it guaranteed, for peasants were willing to sacrifice to change the conditions under which they lived but not in situations they perceived to be hopeless and feared retribution from the forces of counterrevolution. They also learned that radical policies of wholesale social leveling which threatened the productive middle peasants were politically and economically counterproductive in a situation that demanded a broad base of popular support in a rural society existing on a subsistence level. And they learned that meaningful and lasting land reform could not be imposed from above by bureaucratic decree but had to be accomplished through the organization and participation of peasants within each village.

Just as Lenin once described the 1905 Russian Revolution as a "dress rehearsal" for the 1917 October Revolution, so the short-lived Kiangsi Soviet was a "rehearsal" for what proved to be the decisive Yenan period of the Chinese revolution. But it was a rehearsal that was performed at a terrible cost for both the Communists and their peasant supporters. In 1934 the Chinese Soviet Republic began to crumble under the onslaught of Kuomintang armies, and in the autumn of that year the Communists abandoned their base in Kiangsi and embarked upon that extraordinary year-long journey to the North that was to become known and celebrated as the Long March.

The Political and Psychological Significance of the Long March

In October 1935 Mao Tse-tung led what remained of the First Front Army through the last lines of enemy soldiers guarding Mount Liu-p'an Kansu Province and entered northern Shensi Province. In that remote and primitive area of China's vast and sparsely populated Northwest, Communist revolutionaries from many provinces were to find refuge. It was a precarious haven, but one that would provide sufficient time and opportunity to establish a new base area from where the revolution could begin once again.

Of the approximately 100,000 men and 50 women (80,000 soldiers and 20,000 administrative party cadres) who embarked from Kiangsi on the night of October 15, 1934, only about 8,000 survived the torturous trek to arrive with Mao in Shensi, just south of the Great Wall. Among the many dead, left along that circuitous route through the treacherous mountains, rivers, and marshes of western China, were many of Mao's closest friends and comrades and one of his brothers, Mao Tse-t'an, killed in one of the many bloody battles fought with pursuing Kuomintang troops and warlord armies along the way. Among the missing—and never to be found— were two of Mao's children, who remained behind with sympathetic peasant families in Kiangsi, along with many other children too young to undertake the 6,000-mile march.

Measured by any standard of human accomplishment, and quite apart from one's political persuasions, few would disagree with Edgar Snow's assessment that the Long March was "an Odyssey unequaled in modern times."[1] But the heroism and great human drama of the epic should not be allowed to obscure the fact that it was born out of political failure and the prospect of military catastrophe and ended in a near military disaster. Having successfully withstood Chiang Kai-shek's first four "encirclement and annihilation" campaigns (1930–33), the Communists had neither the economic or military resources to resist the new "blockhouse" strategy that Chiang's imported German military advisers had devised for the fifth campaign.

Abandoning the Chinese Soviet Republic and leaving the peasants who had supported them to the terrible reprisals of the Kuomintang marked a political defeat of very considerable magnitude. And the fact that the largest part of the Red Army was destroyed during the ordeals of the next year can hardly be seen as a victory. The exhausted survivors of the Long March who reached Shensi celebrated little more than the sheer (and fantastic) fact that they had managed to survive.

Yet the Long March was the prelude to what proved to be the victorious period of the Chinese Communist Revolution, and in that sense it was an event filled with momentous political and psychological implications. Politically, it was the time when Mao Tse-tung achieved effective control of the Chinese Communist Party, a position of influence and authority which had eluded him during the Kiangsi period as his power was eroded by the Comintern-supported "Twenty-eight Bolsheviks," a group of young Chinese Communists trained at Sun Yat-sen University in Moscow to do Stalin's bidding in China. It was not until January 1935, during the course of the Long March, that the power of the Twenty-eight Bolsheviks was broken and Mao emerged as chairman of the party's politburo. His leadership was not to go unchallenged in later years, but he now was sufficiently in control of the party (and enough of the army) to pursue his own revolutionary strategy in his own way. The incubus of the Comintern finally had been thrown off, and Mao had achieved political supremacy in defiance of Stalin. It was an event unprecedented in the history of Communist parties during the Stalinist era. Thus the Long March brought Mao to a position of supreme leadership in the Chinese Communist Party and brought the revolutionaries he led to a relatively secure geographical position—one where they could make good their vow to fight the Japanese and thereby mobilize Chinese nationalist sentiments for both patriotic and revolutionary ends.

The psychological effects of the Long March are much more intangible. For Mao, at least, the experience served to reinforce his voluntaristic faith that men with the proper will, spirit, and revolutionary consciousness could conquer all material obstacles and mold historical reality in accordance with their ideas and ideals. For those who survived the ordeal—and for those who were inspired by the story of their survival—the experience, however bitter it was at the time, gave rise to a renewed sense of hope and a deepened sense of mission. Men must be able to hope before they can act; they must possess not only ideals and a sense of mission, but hope and confidence that they will be able to realize their ideals and their mission through their own actions. More than any other event in the history of Chinese Communism, it was the Long March—and the legendary tales to which it gave rise—that provided this essential feeling of hope and confidence, the faith that determined men could prevail under even the most desperate conditions. And more than any other individual, it was Mao Tse-tung who radiated and inspired this confidence in the future. It was a confidence not only in those deemed capable of molding the future in accordance with Communist hopes but also in the values regarded as essential to the eventual realization of those hopes. The now familiar Maoist virtues of unending struggle, heroic sacrifice, self-denial, diligence, courage, and unselfishness were values espoused not by Mao alone but carried and conveyed by all of the veterans of the Long March, for these were the values they practiced and had come to regard as essential to their own survival and to the survival of the revolution to which they had devoted their lives. These ascetic values lay at the core of what later came to be celebrated as "the Yenan spirit."

Many more died during the Long March than survived it, and this fact alone made its peculiar contribution to "the Yenan spirit." The survivors' consciousness that they had lived while so many more had perished lent a sacred character to their revolutionary mission and gave rise to an almost religious sense of dedication. Later, Mao found it "odd" that he had survived and commented that "death just did not seem to want him."[2] The Long March, both in reality and later symbolically, was the supreme and ultimate test of survival amidst death. For Mao, the experience undoubtedly contributed enormously to the perception of himself as a man of destiny who would lead his followers to the completion of their revolutionary mission. And if others did not necessarily share Mao's special sense of destiny, they had shared similar experiences, suffered equally heavy personal losses, and had acquired a similar sense of being survivors. This psychological legacy went into the making of Yenan Communism and manifested itself in a very special commitment to carry on the revolutionary struggle, for only in that way could one justify the incredible sacrifices which had been made and prepare for those yet to be made.

The mere fact of survival thus became a matter of enormous psychological significance. It also was a matter of great political consequence, for it was testimony not only to the validity of the mission, but also to the policies and wisdom of the leader. Indeed, the cult of Mao Tse-tung, it seems not improbable to suggest, was born out of the Long March, for Mao was the prophet who had led the survivors through the wilderness. And if Shensi was not the promised land, later revolutionary successes were to fulfill his prophecies and vindicate his policies. Although one does not find in the Yenan period anything resembling the more extreme forms of the worship of Mao and his "thought" witnessed in recent years, a certain mystique and sense of awe had already begun to develop around his name and his person. As early as 1937 Edgar Snow reported that Mao had acquired the reputation of "a charmed life."[3]

In celebrating the heroism of the Long March, contemporary Chinese accounts present the event as a great victory which guaranteed the inevitable victory of the revolution. Victory did not seem so inevitable at the time, however. While what remained of the First Front Army celebrated their survival, they had little else to celebrate. In assessing the situation in 1936, Mao was a good deal more candid than later writers:

> Except for the Shensi–Kansu border area, all revolutionary bases were lost, the Red Army reduced from 300,000 to a few tens of thousands, the membership of the Chinese Communist Party was reduced from 300,000 to a few tens of thousands, and the Party organizations in Kuomintang areas were almost entirely wiped out. In short, we received an extremely great historical punishment.[4]

To be sure, Mao attributed the disaster to the ideological and political errors of his recently vanquished party opponents and duly expressed confidence in ultimate victory and in the new strategy he proposed to achieve that victory. But his appraisal of Communist fortunes at the conclusion of the Long March was bleak and accurate.

The military forces under Mao's control in Shensi were augmented in late 1935 by several thousand Communist partisans who had been engaged in guerilla warfare in the Northwest since 1931 under the leadership of Liu Chih-tan, a Whampoa graduate and former Kuomintang officer whose heroic exploits had earned him something of a Robin Hood reputation among the peasants of his native Shensi. In addition, several thousand other Communist troops who had abandoned a small base area in Hunan Province reached Shensi in September 1935, several weeks prior to Mao's arrival. In 1936 these forces were joined by the remnants of two other armies; the army under the command of Ho Lung, who had been operating in Hunan, and the troops led by Chang Kuo-t'ao and Chu Teh who had broken off from the main line of the Long March and finally arrived by way of Sinkiang. Yet by late 1936 the Red Army in Shensi numbered no more than 30,000, a pitifully small force compared to the pursuing Kuomintang and hostile warlord armies allied with Chiang Kai-shek.

The Yenan Era and Peasant Revolution

If the Communist military position in 1936 was precarious at best, the social-economic environment in which they now found themselves was hardly any more promising. Northern Shensi was one of China's most poor and backward areas. Centuries of erosion had made its lands barren and unfertile, capable of supporting only a relatively small and an extremely impoverished population; "a very poor, backward, underdeveloped, and mountainous part of the country," Mao Tse-tung remarked to a recent foreign visitor who had toured the province.[5] And to Chou En-lai in 1936, it seemed a most inauspicious place to revive the revolution. "Peasants in Shensi are extremely poor," he then complained, "their land very unproductive. . . . The population of the Kiangsi Soviet numbered 3,000,000 whereas here it is at most 600,000. . . . In Kiangsi and Fukien people brought bundles with them when they joined the Red Army; here they do not even bring chopsticks; they are utterly destitute."[6]

And what of Yenan itself, the now sacred city to which pilgrimages are made to view the historic revolutionary places, especially the austere wooden houses and the cave dwellings where Mao and others lived and worked during that legendary decade? Although an ancient city, founded some 3,000 years ago, it could not claim a particularly distinguished history. As Chinese civilization moved southward over the centuries, Yenan became a remote and unknown frontier town, used mostly as an advanced military outpost to defend the northern borders against nomadic invaders from central Asia. It was little more than a dreary and impoverished market town of perhaps 10,000 people when it was occupied by Communist troops at the end of 1936 and established as the administrative capital of what was to be called the Shensi–Kansu–Ningsia Border Region. The wretched poverty and backwardness of the entire area was reflected in the bleakness of Yenan. The town's now famous museums and shrines exhibit no ancient glories but are the products of a modern revolutionary history—and, in a sense, are the result of an accident of history. "We didn't pick it" was Mao's terse reply to a sympathetic American writer who once politely praised Yenan's harsh climate.[7]

But it is Yenan the time, not Yenan the place, that Chinese celebrate. Yet how did the time become one to celebrate when the place was so unfavorable? How did a ragged force of revolutionaries, isolated in an area so remote and so lacking in material resources, grow within a decade into a powerful army of more than a million men and acquire the massive peasant support upon which to base its momentous victory?

For those inclined to ponder the role of "accidents" in history, the Japanese invasion of China is undoubtedly a most intriguing case. Were it not for the Japanese attempt to conquer China in 1937, it can plausibly be argued, the conditions essential to the Communist victory may never have occurred. Yenan would have remained an obscure and unheralded market town in a remote Chinese province, unknown to Chinese and foreigners alike. No one in Peking today would be celebrating the "Yenan spirit" and no foreign "China watchers" would be deliberating the implications of the "Yenan syndrome."

The Japanese invasion undermined the foundations of the Kuomintang regime, for the Nationalists were driven from the major cities from which they derived their major sources of financial and political support. For the Kuomintang, the ravages of war resulted in incredible economic chaos and bureaucratic corruption—and, eventually, in almost total demoralization. More importantly, such administrative authority as the Kuomintang had managed to exercise in the countryside was largely destroyed. The gentry, upon whom that fragile authority had rested, either fled the rural areas or were left militarily and politically defenseless. At the same time, the Communists, already experienced in working in the villages among the peasantry and adept at guerilla warfare, were given access to vast areas of the countryside. For while the Japanese invaders were able to occupy the cities, they did not have the manpower to effectively control the countryside, where Communist guerilla bases multiplied rapidly during the war years. The retreat of Kuomintang military forces to the west in the face of invading Japanese armies, and the concurrent collapse of Nationalist governmental authority in much of China, allowed the Communists to break out of their remote sanctuary in Shensi and expand their military and political influence through vast areas of the countryside in northern and central China. Although the increasingly powerful Yenan base area remained the political and ideological center of the revolution, Communist cadres operated in many parts of rural China, gaining the political support of tens of millions of peasants and organizing many for guerilla warfare behind Japanese lines. The gradual growth of peasant-supported Communist political and military nuclei in many parts of China during the war years was to prove decisive when the civil war with the Kuomintang resumed with full fury in 1946.

Much of the enormous popular support the Communists gained during the war years was based on patriotic appeals for national resistance to the foreign invaders. The new mantle of modern Chinese nationalism had replaced the old "mandate of Heaven" as the symbol of political legitimacy in twentieth-century China. The nationalist credentials which the Kuomintang leaders lost—at first by their seeming unwillingness to defend the nation against the Japanese threat and then by their obvious inability to do so—were in large measure inherited by the Communists. During the war years, Yenan was not only the revolutionary center but also (for increasing numbers of Chinese) the symbol of Chinese nationalist resistance to the Japanese invaders. From the cities many thousands of students and intellectuals migrated to Yenan to join the Communist (and now also the nationalist) cause—and there, first at the Northwest Anti-Japanese Red Army University, many were trained, and ideologically "remolded," to become political, administrative, and military cadres for the rapidly expanding Communist base and guerilla areas.

The Japanese occupation not only intensified the economic crisis in the countryside but gave rise to the most bitter antiforeign sentiments among the peasants which the Communists were able to transform into a modern mass nationalist movement and utilize for revolutionary political ends. This new political opportunity was greatly facilitated by the ruthless policies pursued by the Japanese invaders—the brutal and indiscriminate military forays into the villages of north and central China, where Japanese soldiers could plunder and punish but could not hold and occupy. In those areas in which the Communists were able to gain access, the mobilization of the peasant masses on the basis of an anti-

Japanese nationalist program contributed enormously to the military and political successes of the Yenan period.

In view of the strong tendency to interpret Chinese Communism as a species of Chinese nationalism, or to view the revolution as a case of a new elite riding to power on a fortuitous wave of mass nationalism, it is important to keep the whole phenomenon of "peasant nationalism" in proper historical perspective. The Chinese peasant's sense of identification with China as a political entity and peasant resistance to foreign intruders and invaders were not phenomena which suddenly appeared in 1937. Both are age-old features of Chinese history. Even armed peasant resistance to modern imperialist incursions has a long history, dating back to the Opium War of 1839–1842. It would be highly misleading to either overestimate the spontaneous origins of the peasantry's precisely modern sense of national consciousness or to underestimate the role of Communist cadres in instilling that sense of modern nationalism. The Communists were ardent Chinese nationalists long before 1937 and they played a crucial role in transforming the elemental antiforeign response of the peasantry to the Japanese invaders into a modern nationalist response. By forging bonds of solidarity between peasants from various localities and regions, the Communists created a nationwide resistance movement and imbued it with a sense of national mission that otherwise would have been absent. In large measure, the Communists brought nationalism to the countryside; they did not simply reflect it.

Furthermore, neither the nationalistic appeals of the Communist Party nor the emergence of a mass nationalist movement made the social-economic grievances of the peasantry any less pressing or Communist promises of agrarian reform any less appealing. Precisely the opposite seems to have been the case in most areas where the Communists achieved their greatest successes in organizing and mobilizing peasant support. The war intensified the already horrendous economic burdens of the peasantry and thus increased the attractiveness of the Communist program for land reform. To be sure, the official land policy of the Yenan period was a relatively moderate one by Kiangsi standards. Instead of the outright expropriation and division of landlord holdings, a program for reductions in rents and interest rates was adopted, partly to conform to the terms of a tenuous wartime alliance with the Kuomintang but more importantly as an attempt to enlist the support of landlords and rich peasants as well as the masses of poor and middle peasants in the struggle against the Japanese invaders. But the reduction of rent to no more than one-third the crop and the elimination of the many extralegal means through which landlords and bureaucrats traditionally exploited peasants were hardly unappealing measures to those who had been subjected to the most merciless forms of social and political, as well as economic, oppression.

Moreover, the officially "moderate" agrarian policies were by no

means universally followed. In many cases large landholdings were distributed among land-hungry peasants, especially in areas where landlords
fled with retreating Kuomintang armies. Where the gentry-landlord elite
remained, collaboration between Chinese landlords and Japanese occupiers was not uncommon; in exchange for political services performed—
the traditional gentry function of "social control"—the Japanese allowed
the gentry their traditional economic privilege of exploiting the peasantry. In such cases, the landlord appeared to the peasant not only in his
old role as economic oppressor but also in the new role as national traitor.
Traditional hatred of the landlord because of socioeconomic reasons was
intensified by new nationalist resentments, and the Communists appealed
to both simultaneously, promoting class as well as national struggle.

Expropriation and division of gentry landholdings was a highly popular policy in much of the countryside—and where it occurred, and where
the Communists had sufficient military predominance to guarantee the
security of the peasants and their newly acquired land, the party won
over masses of loyal peasant followers. Conditions and policies of course
varied greatly from area to area. In some areas, social revolution was
sacrificed to obtain the support of all rural classes in the interests of
national unity; in others, radical land policies proved more effective; and
in some areas, neither nationalist nor socioeconomic appeals were effective. But even where the officially moderate land policies were pursued,
traditional agrarian relationships were profoundly transformed: the local
political power of the gentry elite was broken, its social authority and
prestige gravely undermined, and such reduced economic power as it
still held was dependent on the grace of the new holders of political-
military power in the local areas—the military and political cadres of
the Chinese Communist Party. In the areas under Communist control in
the Yenan era, the undermining and sometimes the destruction of the
power of the gentry-landlord class, the ruling elite of Chinese society
for 2,000 years, marked the beginning of the first genuine social revolution in Chinese history since the establishment of the imperial order in
221 B.C.

The Japanese invaders made their particular and unintended contribution to that revolutionary process by removing the Kuomintang
army and bureaucracy from much of China, thereby permitting the Communists to organize the peasantry for both nationalist and social revolutionary ends. The invasion did not by itself create a revolutionary situation—for that already existed—but it did much to intensify that situation
and even more to provide new opportunities for revolutionary action.
But "revolutionary situations," however mature, do not by themselves
create revolutions. Only revolutionaries make revolutions, and only when
they are able to appreciate the potentialities in the historical situation
and to act upon them. To understand the reasons for the Communist

successes of the Yenan years, and to appreciate the significance of the revolutionary legacy of the era, it is necessary to take into account the subjective as well as the objective forces of the time—and especially the particular intellectual and ideological orientations of Mao Tse-tung.

The Origins of Maoism

Although "Maoism" did not crystallize into an official ideological ortho-doxy until the early 1940s, its historical existence as a distinct (and distinctively Chinese) interpretation of Marxism began two decades earlier. To view Maoism as simply the ideological reflection of the "objective" conditions of the Yenan period is to ignore the truism that men are the producers as well as the products of history and that they make their history, at least in part, on the basis of what they think. Neither Yenan Communism nor Mao Tse-tung is an exception to this proposition; much of what went into the making of the former were molded by the now famous "thoughts" of the latter. And Mao did not arrive in Shensi in 1935 with an empty head.

When Mao became a convert to Marxism and Communism in 1919, many of the basic intellectual predispositions that were to mold his un-derstanding of Marxism and his concept of revolution were already pres-ent, and they were reinforced by his revolutionary experiences in the 1920s and early 1930s. By no means the least important of Mao's early (and persisting) intellectual orientations was a profoundly voluntarist belief that the decisive factor in history (and the making of revolution) is human consciousness—the ideas, the wills, and the actions of men. This faith in the ability of self-conscious men to mold objective social reality in accordance with their ideas and ideals survived the influence of the more deterministic tenets of Marxist theory, as Mao began to as-similate that theory in the course of his practical revolutionary activities.

To be sure, Mao derived from the objective laws of historical develop-ment proclaimed by Marx some degree of assurance in the historic inevi-tability of a socialist future. But, in the final analysis, Mao's faith in the future was not based upon any real Marxist confidence in the determin-ing, objective forces of sociohistorical development. For Mao, the essen-tial factor in determining the course of history was conscious human activity and the most important ingredients for revolution were how men thought and their willingness to engage in revolutionary action. This implied, among other things, that revolution in China need not be de-pendent upon any predetermined levels of social and economic develop-ment and that revolutionary action need not be restrained by inherited orthodox Marxist–Leninist formulas. It also implied a special concern for developing and maintaining a "correct ideological consciousness," the ultimately decisive factor in determining success or failure. Correct thought, in the Maoist view, is the first and essential prerequisite for effective revolutionary action, and it is this assumption that lies behind the enormous stress on the distinctively Maoist techniques of "thought reform" and "ideological remolding" developed and refined in the Yenan era. The *cheng-feng* campaign of 1942–1944 for the "rectification" of undesirable ideas and ideological tendencies was the most celebrated and intensive application of what has become a characteristic feature of Chinese Communist practice.

This whole emphasis on ideological solidarity was of central importance for the successful conduct of guerilla warfare in the Yenan decade. In a situation of guerilla war, where centralized organizational control is largely precluded, the forging of the strongest possible commitments to a common ideology and a common manner of thinking (and thus of acting) becomes a matter of supreme importance. That Mao and Maoists were already disposed to stress the role of "subjective factors" had a great deal to do with why the Communists adopted the strategy of "people's war" and the tactics of guerilla warfare—and why they were able to employ those strategic and tactical principles so successfully.

If Mao's voluntarism mitigated the more deterministic implications of Marxist theory, his particularly powerful nationalistic proclivities were equally important in making Marxism a more flexible ideological instrument for revolution in China. From the beginning of his Marxist intellectual life Mao's especially deeply rooted nationalistic impulses gave rise to the belief that the Chinese revolution was more or less synonymous with the world revolution, and indeed the belief that China had a very special role to play in the world revolutionary process. As early as 1930 Mao predicted that "the revolution will certainly move towards an upsurge more quickly in China than in Western Europe."[8] Implicit in this confidence was a faith that assigned to the Chinese nation an almost messianic mission in the restructuring of a future international revolutionary order. Internationalist aspirations and goals were no doubt inextricably intertwined with Chinese nationalist impulses. But it was in this treacherous area of what Trotsky once called "messianic revolutionary nationalism" that Mao departed from other Chinese Marxists whose nationalist feelings were more restrained by more orthodox Marxist considerations.

The nationalist component in Mao's Marxist world view was reflected not only in his long-standing hostility to the Comintern, but also, and more important, in his conception of the Chinese revolutionary process. Central to this conception was the conviction that the real enemies were not so much within Chinese society as without. The real enemy was foreign imperialism, and in the face of that continuing threat China stood as a potentially proletarian nation in a hostile capitalist-imperialist world order. In confronting the external foe, Chinese of all social classes could gather under the revolutionary nationalist umbrella held up by the CCP; and those who could not, or would not, were excluded from membership in the nation, or at least from "the people," excommunicated as representatives of foreign imperialism. Political circumstances permitting, class struggle thus could be subordinated to national struggle and, indeed, the two could be regarded as more or less synonymous. The notion that all Chinese were potentially revolutionary gave Mao a particularly keen appreciation of the revolutionary potentialities of Chinese nationalism and enabled him (as the Yenan period amply demonstrates) to harness nationalist sentiments for revolutionary Communist ends.

A populist-inspired notion of a "great union of the popular masses"[9] that Mao advocated at the beginning of his revolutionary career in 1919 also survived to influence the Maoist adaptation of Marxism–Leninism. Populist impulses grew to reinforce Mao's nationalist-inspired faith in the basic unity of the Chinese people in the face of external enemies and also led him to attribute to "the people" an almost inherent revolutionary socialist consciousness. "In the masses is embodied great socialist activism" is a recent Maoist slogan that derives from an early populist faith, expressed in 1919 in the affirmation that "our Chinese people possesses great intrinsic energy."[10]

Moreover, Mao's populist impulse, with its essentially rural orientation and its romantic celebration of the rural ideal of "the unity of living and working," served to define "the people" as the peasant masses (for the peasantry, after all, constituted the overwhelming majority of the Chinese population) and led him to prize the spontaneously revolutionary energies he believed they possessed. Thus, Mao's populism drew him to the countryside when the Communist revolution was still centered in the cities. In his famous (and heretical) "Hunan Report" of February 1927 he had found in the Chinese peasantry an elemental revolutionary force so great that it would sweep away everything before it, including, he predicted, those revolutionary intellectuals who proved unwilling or unable to unite and become one with the peasant masses. Then, as later, he expressed profound distrust for the "knowledge" brought by urban intellectuals and profound admiration for the innate "wisdom" of the peasantry.

Many other features of the Maoist mentality are typically populist, for example, Mao's hostility to occupational specialization, his acute distrust of intellectuals and specialists, his profoundly antibureaucratic orientation, his antiurban bias, and his romantic mood of heroic revolutionary self-sacrifice. Mao was not simply a populist in Marxist guise (any more than he was simply a Chinese nationalist in Communist dress), but populist ideas and impulses profoundly influenced the manner in which he adapted and employed Marxism.

Mao's populist faith in the peasant masses permitted, and indeed dictated, the much celebrated Maoist notion of the "mass line," the various principles and rules by which Communist cadres became intimately involved and identified with the peasant masses. The Maoist maxim that intellectuals and party cadres must become the pupils of the masses before they can become their teachers was in fact widely practiced in the Yenan days. Had it been otherwise, the Communists could never have acquired the mass support and cooperation among the peasantry that was so essential to the successful employment of the strategy of "people's war."

In attributing a latent socialist consciousness to the peasantry, Mao departed not only from Marx but also from Lenin. For Marx the bearer of socialist consciousness was of course the urban proletariat. And for Lenin, socialist consciousness was to be imposed on the "spontaneous" proletarian mass movement by an elite of revolutionary intellectuals organized into a highly centralized and disciplined communist party, with the peasantry playing an ambiguous auxiliary role in the revolutionary process. Mao departed from Leninism not only in his virtually total disinterest in the urban working class but also in his concept of the nature and role of the party. For Lenin the party was sacrosanct because it was the incarnation of "proletarian consciousness," and there was no question about who were to be the teachers and who the pupils. For Mao, on the other hand, this was precisely the question, and it remained unresolved; he proved unwilling to define fully the relationship between the organized consciousness of the party and the spontaneous consciousness of the masses in a purely Leninist fashion. His faith in the party as the bearer of revolutionary consciousness was never complete, for it was accompanied by a populist faith in the peasant masses, a belief that true revolutionary knowledge and creativity ultimately emanates from the people themselves. Although Mao proved a master in matters of organization and strategy, neither the methods of organization he devised nor the revolutionary strategy he pursued were derived from strictly Leninist principles. While Mao may have acquired absolute faith in his own revolutionary wisdom, his faith in the revolutionary wisdom of the party was a good deal less than absolutely Leninist.

The growth of massive popular support for the Communists during the Yenan decade no doubt served to reinforce Mao's populist faith in the spontaneous revolutionary energies and creativity of the peasant masses, but that pre-existing faith itself was of very considerable significance in determining the course of revolutionary events and the perception of the party's relationship to them. If Mao has proved to be something less than a pristine Leninist because of populist impulses, those egalitarian populist impulses proved to be salutary for bringing about the successful consummation of a Marxist-led revolution in the Chinese historical situation.

It is most unlikely that orthodox Marxist–Leninists could have appreciated fully the revolutionary opportunities offered by the wartime situation, much less acted upon them to build a Communist movement on a purely peasant base. It was precisely Mao's ideological unorthodoxies that allowed the Communists to seize upon these opportunities during the Yenan period. It was his voluntarist faith in the power of the human will and consciousness to shape historical reality that permitted him to ignore (or redefine) Marxian socioeconomic prerequisites and social class considerations that might otherwise have restricted the possibilities for revolutionary action. It was his nationalist–populist impulses which made him look to the broadest possible sources of national revolutionary support and which directed him from the cities to the countryside. And it was his populist trust in the spontaneous revolutionary energies of the peasant masses that allowed him to develop and pursue the unorthodox strategy of "people's war."

Yenan Marxism

The Yenan era was Mao's most productive period as a Marxist theoretician as well as a revolutionary strategist. The bulk of the writings, later canonized as the "thoughts of Mao Tse-tung," were composed during the Yenan period. While Mao's Yenan writings do more to obscure than to clarify the nature of the Maoist variant of Marxism–Leninism, they nonetheless are important for a number of reasons. First, they established Mao's place as an independent Marxist theoretician. Having achieved de facto political independence from Moscow, the Chinese Communists could now claim, at least implicitly, to have established their ideological independence as well—in the form of a body of Chinese Marxist doctrine that was hailed for having applied the "universal truths" of Marxism–Leninism to the specific conditions of the Chinese historical situation. Second, Mao's treatises on dialectics provided a rudimentary philosophical basis for some of the distinctive features of Chinese Communist theory and practice. Finally, the Marxist theoretical writings of the Yenan era (by Mao and others) were designed to reaffirm the Marxist–Leninist orthodoxy of the CCP, to convey some elemental knowledge of that doctrine to the many newly recruited members of the party, and more importantly, to rationalize Chinese Communist political practice in terms of Marxist–Leninist theory.

Yet if this latter task was accomplished to the satisfaction of Mao and other Chinese Communist leaders, it was done without dealing with the most crucial theoretical problem raised by the Chinese Communist Revolution. For Maoist writings say virtually nothing about the question of how a Communist party, almost totally separated from the cities and the urban proletariat, and based entirely on peasant support could carry out a revolution that aimed to bring about a socialist society, albeit preceded by a "bourgeois" phase of unspecified duration. The question posed not only a Marxist theoretical dilemma but also an enormous practical problem bearing directly on the goals and future of the revolution. For while the peasants were very much interested in socioeconomic reform and the redistribution of land, not even Mao, with all his faith in the inherent "socialist activism" of the peasant masses, really believed that the peasants, as a class, were inclined (spontaneously or otherwise) to socialism. At their radical best, the peasants were interested in the equal distribution of land on the basis of individual peasant proprietorship—an agrarian revolution to be sure, but one which precluded the socialist reorganization of society, by either Marxist or non-Marxist definitions. There is nothing in Maoism or in Chinese social reality to suggest that the peasantry, as such, is the bearer of the socialist future.

Who then were to be the agents of socialist revolution? In Maoist theoretical literature we find little more than repetitions of the Marxist orthodoxy that the socialist revolution is to be led by the proletariat and the Leninist orthodoxy that the Communist Party is the vanguard of the proletariat and the incarnation of "proletarian consciousness." Mao adds only the concept of "the people's democratic dictatorship," a notion born in the united-front strategy of the Yenan era and formally proclaimed in 1949, on the eve of the official establishment of the People's Republic. The formula for the bourgeois stage of the revolution provides for a government representing a coalition of four classes (proletariat, peasantry, petty bourgeoisie, and national bourgeoisie) but a coalition under "proletarian hegemony," which is to say, ultimate political power resides in the Communist Party.

Little is gained by dissecting these ideological formulae. The fact of the matter is that during the crucial Yenan years the CCP lacked the active support of the urban proletariat and made very little effort to acquire it. Indeed, such an effort was largely precluded by a revolutionary strategy which dictated that the crucial forces of revolution resided in the peasantry, and that their mobilization would lead to a situation in which the revolutionary rural areas would encircle and eventually occupy the nonrevolutionary cities.

What turned out to be crucial in determining that the revolution would move beyond the bourgeois-democratic phase are the "subjective factors" in history, upon which Maoism itself places such great emphasis, and most particularly the conscious determination of the Communist leadership to pursue socialist goals. However unorthodox their strategy of revolution, Maoists have remained firmly committed to orthodox Marxist goals. If they have not identified themselves with the actual proletariat, they have identified themselves with the political and social goals and the historic mission which Marx attributed to that class. And this "subjective factor" was to prove of enormous historical significance in determining the character and direction of the Chinese revolution.

What is thus implicit in Maoist theory, and demonstrated in Maoist practice, is the notion that the bearers of socialism are those who possess "proletarian consciousness" and that the latter exists independently of a specific social class, neither dependent on the actual presence of the proletariat nor attributed to the peasantry. A revolutionary elite (the party and its leaders) holds the socialist goal firmly in mind and directs the mass movement towards its realization. In a broader sense, "proletarian consciousness" is seen as a potential inherent in "the people" as a whole, for all are potentially capable of achieving (through revolutionary action) the spiritual and ideological transformation necessary to acquire a true proletarian spirit and a socialist world view.

This emphasis on the role of consciousness in the making of history and revolution reflects, of course, long-standing Maoist voluntarist and populist predispositions, and the uniquely Maoist treatment of the Marxist theory of class struggle. Mao, to be sure, was always intensely concerned with objective class conditions in Chinese society and was an ardent promoter of class struggle, both in theory and in practice. But he also tended to define "class position" less on the basis of objective social class criteria than by moral and ideological criteria. While for Marx the existence of a potentially revolutionary proletarian class was the prerequisite for the rise of revolutionary proletarian ideas, for Mao the existence of those deemed to possess "proletarian" ideas was sufficient to confirm the existence of a revolutionary class.

The Legacy of Yenan

The Yenan period not only proved decisive for the Communist victory of 1949 but bequeathed to the victors a heroic tradition of revolutionary struggle that was to be canonized as the "Yenan spirit" and the "Yenan style." Since those who fashioned the revolutionary victory were those who became the leaders of the new society born of that victory, it is hardly surprising that the policies they pursued and their responses to the new problems they were to encounter in the post-1949 years were to be significantly influenced by their experiences in those earlier and more heroic days. All Communists were to celebrate the "Yenan spirit" as the symbol of a heroic revolutionary past. But for many—and it is a natural enough phenomenon for revolutionaries who become rulers—it was a revolutionary past that could be buried safely in the past, an era to be commemorated on appropriate occasions, but not one deemed truly relevant to contemporary needs. For others, especially for Mao and those most inspired by him, the Yenan experience was not to become simply an object for commemoration but a living revolutionary tradition that provided a model for the future.

The Yenan heritage that Maoists praise and prize is in part an institutional legacy, and in part a legacy of sacred revolutionary values—and the two parts cannot easily be separated. Much of what was to be unique and distinctively Maoist in the political, economic, and educational life of the People's Republic was foreshadowed by the institutions and practices developed in embryonic form during the Yenan years. In the political realm, the development of bureaucratic forms of control from above was mitigated by the practice of the much celebrated principles of the mass line; campaigns for "simple administration"; the insistence on decentralized political structures that were responsive to local needs and conditions, and that provided for widespread popular participation; and various *hsia-fang* ("sending down") and *hsia-hsiang* ("to the village") campaigns which demanded that party cadres, government officials, and intellectuals periodically participate in productive labor together with the masses. Such measures tended to reduce (even if they by no means eliminated) the gap between leaders and led, and they reflected the long-standing Maoist hostility to all forms of bureaucracy. They were the harbingers of the massive anti-bureaucratic campaigns that were to mark much of the history of the People's Republic.

Moreover, the harsh conditions imposed by war and blockade created the need for economic self-sufficiency in the border regions and guerilla areas—and gave rise to a variety of experiments and innovations in economic policies and productive activities. To maintain and expand agricultural production during the war years, the Communists promoted cooperative forms of work organization in the villages, drawing, in part, on traditional methods of mutual aid. New industries were established in the Communist-ruled rural areas, partly to meet military needs and partly to provide the peasantry with essential nonagricultural products previously supplied by trade with the cities. In a wholly rural environment almost entirely lacking in capital resources, the new cooperative industrial undertakings were dependent upon labor-intensive methods, the employment of simple and indigenous technologies, and the use of local resources and raw materials. Self-sufficiency, self-reliance, and local initiative became the slogans and principles of Yenan economic policy—and from the experiences in employing those principles emerged the ideal of combining industrial and agricultural production in a rural setting. Combining education with production motivated and molded the educational policies adopted and pursued during the Yenan period. The emphasis was on popular education in the form of part-time schools, night schools, and various work–study programs. Designed not only to promote basic literacy and impart political consciousness, these policies also provided the practical technological knowledge directly relevant to the particular needs of local communities and production groups.

While the particular political, economic, and educational institutions and practices that emerged during the Yenan era were to prove enormously important in molding the uniquely Maoist approach to problems of postrevolutionary development, the system of values that lay behind those institutions and practices was a revolutionary legacy of equally great historical significance. What Chinese Communists today celebrate as the "Yenan spirit" is in fact largely concerned with spiritual and moral matters and, more specifically, with the kinds of social and ethical values and life orientations seen as essential to a continuing process of revolutionary transformation. The values which derive from the Yenan era, and which are attributed to that heroic revolutionary past, are essentially ascetic and egalitarian in nature. They are the values of selfless struggle and self-sacrifice on behalf of the people, the values of hard work, diligence, self-denial, frugality, altruism, and self-discipline. In the Yenan decade these values were, in fact, practiced by Chinese Communists, for they were imposed by the harsh imperatives of revolutionary struggle and the spartan and egalitarian way of life such struggle demanded. In the Maoist view, such values were not only responsible for the revolutionary successes of the past but remain essential to bring about the Communist society of the future.

It is paradoxical that, from a Chinese revolutionary process which was so incongruous with the Marxist conception of revolution, institutions and values emerged that (in many respects) were uniquely conducive to the pursuit of ultimate Marxist goals. Certainly neither Marx nor Lenin could have conceived of a socialist-oriented revolution in which the revolutionary forces of the countryside would organize to surround and overwhelm the nonrevolutionary cities, with the urban working class passively awaiting their liberation by revolutionary armies composed of peasants. Yet in the employment of that most unorthodox strategy of revolution in the Yenan years, there emerged social visions and practices that curiously harmonized with the utopian social goals prophesied in original Marxist theory. The Yenan practice of combining industrial with agricultural production, and combining education with productive labor, were eminently Marxist measures to achieve a socialist reordering of society.[11] From a Marxist perspective, they were the first and essential steps towards achieving the broader communist goals of abolishing the distinctions between town and countryside, between workers and peasants, and between mental and manual labor—and they were to be hailed as such in later Maoist celebrations of the Yenan legacy. The requirement of the Yenan years that officials and intellectuals participate regularly in productive activities struck an at least symbolic blow at the particularly sharp traditional Chinese separation between mental and manual labor, and was an affirmation of the Maoist commitment to strive to eliminate that separation. The campaigns for "simple administration," the demands for popular participation in government, and the generally antibureaucratic thrust of Maoist political policies, while hardly the prelude to the Marxist vision of the "withering away" of the state, nevertheless reflected a particularly strong concern to narrow the gap between state and society. And the Maoist ideal of the Yenan guerilla leader, the ideologically pure generalist capable of performing a variety of economic, political, and military tasks, bears strong affinities to the Marxist "all-round" man of the future communist society. In the Chinese Communist Revolution, more than in the case of any other twentieth century socialist revolution, the socialist forms and values of the new society were fashioned (in at least embryonic form) in the very course of the revolutionary struggle itself.

Yet the legacy of Yenan was not solely one of values and practices that pointed to liberation. The Yenan era was also the time when Mao and Maoists laid down rigid dogmas and orthodoxies in political and cultural life, conducted witch hunts against those who failed to conform to their orthodoxies, and relentlessly suppressed political and intellectual dissent in general. The incongruity between socioeconomic liberation, on the one hand, and political–intellectual repression on the other, is one that has characterized Maoism both before and after 1949.

The history and experiences of the Yenan decade, upon which the victory of 1949 was based, served to reinforce the Maoist belief in the primacy of moral over material forces, of men over machines, the conviction that the truly creative revolutionary forces reside more in the countryside than in the cities, and the view that ideological–moral solidarity is more important than the artificial unity that might be provided or imposed by any formal bureaucratic organization. More importantly, victory came on the basis of a massive popular social revolution that involved the active and meaningful support and participation of tens of millions of peasants.

At the end of World War II, when the uneasy Kuomintang–CCP truce inevitably collapsed into open civil war, Kuomintang armies enjoyed a four-to-one superiority in manpower over regular Communist military forces and an even greater advantage in modern military technology, largely supplied by the United States. Yet the Communist victory in the massive battles that marked the civil war of 1946–1949, however bloody and difficult, was surprisingly swift. It was, as Stuart Schram has so well characterized it, "one of the most striking examples in history of the victory of a smaller but dedicated and well-organized force enjoying popular support over a larger but unpopular force with poor morale and incompetent leadership."[12] On October 1, 1949, Mao Tse-tung was in Peking to proclaim the birth of the People's Republic of China, while Chiang Kai-shek with those who remained in his defeated army and bureaucracy had already fled to the island of Taiwan, there to impose their rule on a hostile population and to find a refuge granted by the grace of the United States Seventh Fleet.

The Communists rightly attribute their victory to the principles and practices of the Yenan era. Those principles were not to be forgotten, and in the postrevolutionary era they were to be recalled and revived to announce the opening of new revolutionary dramas.

Notes

1. Edgar Snow, *Red Star over China* (New York: Random House, 1938), p. 177.

2. Edgar Snow, "Interview with Mao," *New Republic*, February 27, 1965, pp. 17–23.

3. Snow, *Red Star over China*, p. 67.

4. Mao Tse-tung, "Strategic Problems of China's Revolutionary War," in *Selected Works of Mao Tse-tung* (London: Lawrence & Wishart, 1954), 1:193.

5. Cited in Jan Myrdal, *Report from a Chinese Village* (New York: Pantheon, 1965), p. xxvii.

6. Cited in Edgar Snow, *Random Notes on Red China, 1936–1945* (Cambridge, Mass.: Harvard University Press, 1957), pp. 60–61.

7. Anna Louise Strong, *Tomorrow's China* (New York: Committee for a Democratic Far Eastern Policy, 1948), p. 18.

8. Mao Tse-tung, "A Single Spark Can Start a Prairie Fire," in *Selected Works* (1954) 1:118.

9. This was the title of an article by Mao published in the summer of 1919. For a translation of extracts from the article, see Stuart R. Schram *The Political Thought of Mao Tse-tung* (New York: Praeger, 1963), pp. 105–106.

10. *Ibid.*, p. 106.

11. Among the "postrevolutionary" measures Marx suggests in the *Manifesto* for achieving a socialist society are the "combination of agriculture with manufacturing industries" and the "combination of education with industrial production." Karl Marx and Frederick Engels, *Selected Works* (Moscow: Foreign Languages Publishing House, 1950), 1:51.

12. Stuart R. Schram, *Mao Tse-tung* (New York: Simon & Schuster, 1967), p. 225.

Part Two

The New Order, 1949–1955

5

The Dilemmas of Victory

"THE SOCIALISTS MIGHT CONQUER, but not socialism, which would perish in the moment of its adherents' triumph," Robert Michels predicted at the turn of the century.[1] The history of modern revolutions, unhappily, offers no lack of evidence to support Michels' cynicism. Socialist parties have come to power in many countries in the twentieth century—both through revolutionary violence and peaceful parliamentary means—but the world has yet to see a land where the socialist promise of a "truly human society" has been realized. It is not the case that socialist movements have accomplished nothing except changes in the personnel of ruling elites, as contemporary disciples of Pareto might argue. On the contrary, they have changed much—often in fundamental ways and sometimes in dramatic fashion—and for the most part the interests of human and historical progress have been served well by such social transformations as they have brought. But one need not accept conventional biases against socialism in particular and against revolution in general to acknowledge the enormous gap between socialist promises and socialist performances, between revolutionary visions and the actual sociopolitical results of revolution. There is no need here to ponder the phenomenon of Social-Democratic movements which accommodate themselves to the existing political and economic order before they establish what are perhaps too easily called "socialist" governments, for they promise little more than the meager reforms of the contemporary "welfare state." One must take into consideration, however, the fate of the great social revolutions that have shaped much of the history of the modern world, the revolutions that inspired and were inspired by grand visions of a future perfect social order—and in that historical perspective consider the rather unique history of the Chinese Communist Revolution in the years since 1949.

What makes contemporary China unique and a matter of special historical interest is that the history of the People's Republic presents what seems to be a radical departure from the common pattern of the history of a "postrevolutionary" society. And that pattern, bluntly put, is that revolutions die when revolutionaries become rulers. The great humanitarian and egalitarian goals of the revolution typically are postponed to an increasingly indefinite and vague time in the future as the new rulers of society turn to deal with the harsh political and economic realities of the postrevolutionary situation; the new rulers compromise with the traditions and survivals of the past and, consciously or not, come to preside over historical processes that betray their own ideals and hopes for a radically new society. The familiar pattern in the history of revolutions is that revolutionary utopian goals soon become empty rituals to rationalize new forms of inequality and oppression that emerge in the postrevolutionary era.

This is not to suggest that revolutions necessarily are fruitless or undesirable. By destroying the political institutions and the ruling classes of old regimes, social revolutions open the way for societies to follow new directions and allow at least the possibility to create new and better social worlds. Moreover, the influences of great revolutions are never confined within the boundaries of the countries in which they take place. The impact and ideals of the French Revolution stimulated worldwide processes of revolutionary transformation and progressive social change that molded the course of much of the history of the nineteenth century. And just as the 1917 Russian Revolution had a profound impact on the nature of social and economic development in many lands during the first half of the twentieth century, the Chinese Communist Revolution appears to be having equally profound consequences in the second half of the century.

Yet however important their social and material accomplishments, and however great their international historical consequences, the French Revolution did not produce a society of liberty, fraternity, and equality; and the Russian Revolution no longer promises the Marxist vision of a classless society prepared to take that giant leap from the "realm of necessity" to the "realm of freedom." The ideals of the French Revolution were perverted by Napoleonic despotism and bureaucratic conservatism, and the promise of the Russian Revolution was corrupted by Stalinist despotism and the domination of another kind (albeit a different kind) of conservative bureaucracy. The societies that emerged from these vast revolutionary upheavals were far different from those they replaced, but also far different from the ideal social orders the revolutionaries originally envisioned. There is thus good reason that such terms as "Thermidor" and "Bonapartism" have become so widely used to describe the life cycles of revolutions, for the course of most postrevolutionary histories generally have been characterized by the institutionalization of new sociopolitical orders, which only faintly resemble the vision of the new society that the revolution promised to bring. The process of the ritualization of revolutionary ideals and the general decay of the revolutionary impulse is a phenomenon familiar to students of revolution, and there are familiar terms to describe it: the "universality of the Thermidorean reaction" is the term Crane Brinton long ago applied to the "law" that presumably governs the revolutionary life cycle,[2] while a process of inevitable "deradicalization" is a more recent notion currently popular in the literature on revolutions.[3] But one need not rely on observers who celebrate the retreat to "normalcy" to recognize the general phenomenon. Revolutionaries themselves have been painfully aware of the failures that came in the wake of their revolutionary successes. Less than five years after the Russian Revolution, for example, Lenin was moved to declare that "powerful forces [had] diverted the Soviet state from its 'proper road,'" and on his deathbed concluded that the forces of the past had overwhelmed the Bolsheviks, who "had given only a Soviet veneer" to the old czarist bureaucracy.[4] And in different historical circumstances and employing a different vocabulary, Mao Tse-tung was to be haunted by similar fears.

To appreciate the place and significance of the history of the Chinese People's Republic in the general history of modern revolution, it is well to keep in mind the generally unhappy fate of revolutions, to recognize that failure seems to be inherent in the very success of revolution. For what is perhaps the most remarkable feature of the generally remarkable history of China since 1949 has been an extraordinary effort to reverse the seemingly universal tendency for revolutions to die in the postrevolutionary era, to forestall the processes of "bureaucratic institutionalization" which spell the death of the revolutionary impulse, and to keep alive the utopian goals and ideals of the revolution as living sources for contemporary social action.

In 1949 there was nothing to suggest that the history of the new People's Republic would depart significantly from earlier patterns of postrevolutionary institutionalization. A new state and society was in the process of being born, but neither the theory nor the actions of the new Communist leaders of China reflected any special concern with the old problem of what happens to revolutions when revolutionaries become rulers. Indeed, in confronting immediate political and economic problems, and the future socioeconomic development of the new China, the Communists adopted ready-made Soviet methods of organization and control. It is ironic that the Chinese Communists, who had triumphed on their own and in their own way by rejecting Russian revolutionary advice, should have proved so eager to borrow the Soviet model of postrevolutionary development. Some of the consequences of this foreign borrowing will be discussed shortly. Here it need only be noted that the first half-decade of the history of the People's Republic was generally characterized by a quite familiar postrevolutionary pattern of the postponement of revolutionary social goals and the routinization and bureaucratic institutionalization of the new sociopolitical order.

Mao Tse-tung set the general pattern himself several months before the formal proclamation of the new People's Republic. In his major theoretical essay of the time, "On the People's Democratic Dictatorship," Mao began by reaffirming the classical Marxist goal of a classless society. With the revolution triumphant and the power of the Communists largely secured, Mao had no need to conceal his ultimate vision of an ultimately communist future to maintain the unity of a national "united front." Indeed, the petty bourgeoisie and the "national bourgeoisie" were invited to join the peasants and workers as part of "the people" who first would exercise a "democratic dictatorship" to eliminate the remnants of the landlord class and the "bureaucratic" bourgeoisie and then participate in a process in which all class distinctions eventually would be eliminated, thus preparing the way for the gradual "withering away" of all forms of political power and the realization of communism, "the realm of Great Harmony." But the importance of Mao's essay lies not in the familiar Marxian utopian social goals he proclaimed but rather in the manner in which he announced their postponement. While the achievement of a classless and stateless society was "only a question of time and conditions," Mao left no question that the time was far in the future and the required conditions would exist only after a long and indefinite period of preparation. As Mao put it, the description of the future communist utopia was merely "the long range perspective of human progress" which only had been "mentioned in passing . . . in order to explain clearly the problems we are about to discuss." Mao then proceeded to discuss two problems. One was "our present task . . . to strengthen the people's state apparatus—mainly the people's army, the people's police and the people's courts—in order to consolidate national defence and protect the people's interests." The second problem to which energies were to be devoted was "the serious task of economic construction [that] lies before us."[5]

Thus Mao set forth the two overriding objectives that were to mold the nature of state and society in China for the next five years: establishing a strong state power and a strong economy. The realization of these objectives demanded highly authoritarian means of social control and centralized bureaucratic forms of political and economic organization, measures which were to be introduced with extraordinary rapidity and efficiency during those early years. Also demanded was the postponement of Marxist socialist goals to a vaguely indefinite future, a process which Mao deftly had initiated in his essay of 1949.

It is hardly surprising that the new Communist leaders should have given priority to the need for a strong state and to economic development. The condition of the society they had inherited demanded no less and offered the possibility of little more. In a huge country where traditional forms of political authority had long ago disintegrated, where modern forms of government had existed only incompletely and superficially even in the best of times, where during most of modern times and in most places the Chinese people had been "governed" by marauding warlord armies, by foreign invaders and occupiers, and by corrupt and inefficient Kuomintang bureaucrats and militarists—in such a situation the establishment of a viable national political order and an effective administrative apparatus clearly was the first and most pressing task. Providing a reasonable degree of political order, security, and honest government for the first time in a century (even if not offering political freedom or democracy), was itself a momentous historical accomplishment. It was also a rather unique accomplishment. Whereas most revolutions are followed by long periods of political instability, disorder, violence, and often civil war, this was not the case in China after 1949. The triumph of the Chinese Communist Revolution did not create political chaos but rather resolved a century-long era of ever increasing chaos. The China which Sun Yat-sen had called "a loose sheet of sand" was rapidly cemented into a powerful modern nation-state with a strong sense of national purpose.

If political order was the essential prerequisite for economic rehabilitation and growth, a developing economy was essential for the consolidation and preservation of the newly emergent political entity. For China was not only the most populous country in the world, it was also one of the most backward and impoverished. The tiny and mostly foreign-dominated modern industrial sector of the economy—at the time even less developed than India's—had been ravaged by more than a decade of foreign invasion and civil war. China's woefully inadequate system of transportation and communication (mostly linking the areas of imperialist economic penetration in Manchuria and along the coastal treaty ports) lay in shambles. And, most crucially, agricultural production, long stagnating under a primitive technology and the persistence of traditional exploitative socioeconomic relations, deteriorated further during the long years of war and political misrule and instability. The population, provided with a minimum level of subsistence during the best of times, now faced massive starvation and famine characteristic of China's worst times. Compounding the economic crisis which the Communists inherited was the most ruinous inflation and monetary breakdown in world history—the last bequest of Kuomintang rule.

By 1952 the new state had consolidated its administrative control over all of the provinces and outlying dependencies and had extended it down to the village level. Agricultural and industrial production were restored to their highest prewar levels and the vestiges of imperialist influence were eliminated. China's long and frustrating search for "wealth and power" (*fu-chiang*) had not yet ended, but the Communists, it appeared, possessed the means and determination to successfully pursue that nationalist quest.

What the Communists accomplished in their first three years of rule were essentially the unfulfilled aims of the "national revolution" proclaimed in the ill-fated alliance with the Kuomintang in the mid-1920s. That alliance had rested on the common acceptance of the goals of national unification and national independence. Those goals had eluded the Kuomintang regime in the two decades following the breakdown of the alliance in 1927 and it fell to the new Communist government to carry out the long delayed "national revolution."

In one crucial area, however, the Communists went beyond purely nationalist aims in the early years of the People's Republic. In the land reform campaign of 1950–1952, the new regime presided over the abolition of traditional socioeconomic relationships in the countryside, the destruction of the landlord-gentry class, and the redistribution of land among the peasantry. It was, of course, largely on this question of agrarian revolution that the alliance of the 1920s had foundered and led to Chiang Kai-shek's bloody counterrevolution. Now, a quarter of a century later, no Kuomintang or warlord armies stood in the way of the radical demands of the masses of poor peasants. Yet while the land-reform campaign was socially radical, it was in no sense socialist. In Marxist–Leninist terms, the abolition of precapitalist agrarian relationships was no more than part of the necessary process of bourgeois-democratic revolution, an essential measure for the creation of a genuine national market and polity. In Maoist terms as well, land reform was an act in the "bourgeois" stage of the revolution. Like the creation of a centralized national government and the elimination of imperialist impingements, the antifeudal social revolution in the countryside was entirely consistent with the official ideology of "new democracy," the Maoist version of the Marxist concept of bourgeois-democratic revolution.

The novel Chinese version of the concept was originally formulated by Mao in 1939. He then had insisted that the Chinese revolution was not in its "proletarian-socialist" stage but rather in its "bourgeois-democratic" phase.[6] However, it was not a bourgeois-democratic revolution of the "old, now obsolete type" but rather a "new democratic revolution" suited to the particular needs of China and to the conditions of colonial and semicolonial countries in general. "The new democratic revolution," Mao argued, "is vastly different from the democratic revolutions of Europe and America in that it results not in a dictatorship of the bourgeoisie but in a dictatorship of the united front of all the revolutionary classes under the leadership of the proletariat." While the eventual aim was socialism, it was first necessary "to complete China's bourgeois-democratic revolution" and only later "to transform it into a socialist revolution when all the necessary conditions are ripe."[7]

The conditions for socialism had not yet ripened in 1949, for when the Communists assumed state power in that year they proclaimed not a dictatorship of the proletariat, not a socialist state, but rather a "people's democratic dictatorship," a term that was used to characterize the new political order until well into the 1950s. The term was semantically obscure and socially ambiguous, but it conveyed the Maoist view that the revolution remained within bourgeois limits. While the "people's democratic dictatorship" was presumably under the "hegemony of the proletariat," it was a state based, at least in theory, on a coalition of four social classes: the national bourgeoisie and the petty bourgeoisie as well as the proletariat and the peasantry.

The peculiar Maoist theory of bourgeois-democratic revolution was both a reflection and a distortion of Chinese historical reality. The elements of ideological distortion are patently obvious and need not be belabored here. Quite apart from the fact that neither the term "bourgeoisie" nor "democracy" bore any meaningful relationship to concrete Chinese social and political realities, we have the claim that the new state and the revolutionary process in general are under the leadership of the proletariat. In view of the totally rural character of the revolution and the absence of any organic link between the ruling Chinese Communist Party and the actual proletariat, it was (and was to remain) a hollow and purely ideological claim. There were, to be sure, Leninist precedents for Mao's radically redefined version of the Marxist concept of a bourgeois-democratic revolution. Responding to the Russian situation in which the bourgeoisie failed to play its "natural" historical role and compromised with the czarist autocracy, Lenin had advocated a "democratic dictatorship of the proletariat and the peasantry" in accordance with which the peasantry would serve as the surrogate for a politically inactive bourgeoisie—and, in alliance with the proletariat, carry out the unfinished "democratic" tasks of the revolutionary process. But whereas the Leninist formula (however irrelevant it became in the actual practice of the Bolshevik Revolution) presupposed an alliance between two political parties, each representing the interests of two distinct social classes, the novel Maoist formula completely obscured the Marxist demand for an organic relationship between political parties and social classes. In the Maoist version, the "bourgeois-democratic" phase of the revolution was to be presided over by a Communist Party that had no real tie with the proletariat it claimed to represent, the peasantry was without formal political representation, and the bourgeois classes (as we shall have occasion to observe) were politically represented only in the most formal (and in a mostly meaningless) sense. The Maoist notion thus served to disguise the social–political realities of the new order and marked a further deterioration of the relationship between political power and social classes, an ideological expression which reflected a characteristic feature of the modern Chinese historical situation in general.

While the Maoist notion of bourgeois democracy was an ideological distortion of actual sociopolitical relationships in one sense, it was an accurate reflection of Chinese historical reality in another sense. For the major measures that the new state undertook in the early years—political unification, the creation of a national economy and market, modern industrial development, and the abolition of traditional socioeconomic relationships in the countryside—were, in Marxist terms, not socialist measures but "capitalist" ones. They were the necessary bourgeois-democratic tasks, and the necessary prerequisites for socialism, which an underdeveloped modern Chinese capitalism and a weak Chinese bourgeoisie had failed to accomplish. That they now had to be performed under Marxist political auspices was dictated by objective historical conditions. In this sense, Mao's insistence that the Chinese historical process was in its "bourgeois-democratic" phase was fully in accord with Marxist–Leninist theoretical perspectives.

If the Chinese historical process was in its "bourgeois-democratic" stage in preparation for a future transition to socialism when, as Mao put it, "all the necessary conditions are ripe," then what were the "necessary conditions," who was to determine when they had "ripened," and on the basis of what criteria? What sociohistorical agency was to provide the impulse for China's passage from the "democratic" to the socialist stage? What was the nature of the new state and what was its actual relationship to the society and social classes it claimed to represent? While it is clear that the revolution destroyed the social classes and groups dominant under the old regime (i.e., the compradore bourgeoisie, the landlord-gentry class, and the Kuomintang bureaucratic caste), it is not at all clear which social classes became dominant under the new political order that emerged from the revolutionary upheaval. What, for example, is the concrete social meaning of a state presumably under "the hegemony of the proletariat" when the ruling party in that state structure had no tie to the actual proletariat for more than twenty years? On the question of the relationship between state power and social classes, the history of the People's Republic begins on a profoundly ambiguous note.

Notes

1. Robert Michels, *Political Parties* (Glencoe, Ill.: The Free Press, 1949), p. 391.
2. Crane Brinton, *The Anatomy of Revolution,* rev. ed. (New York: Vintage, 1965), pp. 205–236. Brinton defines Thermidor as "a convalescence from the fever of revolution."
3. See Robert C. Tucker, "The Deradicalization of Marxist Movements," in Tucker, *The Marxian Revolutionary Idea* (New York: Norton, 1969), pp. 172–214.
4. For an account of Lenin's last somber views on the results of the revolution he led, see Isaac Deutscher, "The Moral Dilemmas of Lenin," in Deutscher, *Ironies of History* (London: Oxford University Press, 1966), pp. 167–173.
5. Mao Tse-tung "On the People's Democratic Dictatorship," in *Selected Works of Mao Tse-tung* (Peking: Foreign Languages Press, 1961), 4:411–424.
6. Mao's conception of the relationship between the bourgeois and socialist stages of the revolution are set forth in his essays "The Chinese Revolution and the Chinese Communist Party" (1939) and "On New Democracy" (1940), in *Selected Works of Mao Tse-tung* (Peking, 1967), 2:305–334, 339–384.
7. Mao, "The Chinese Revolution and the Chinese Communist Party," pp. 326–331.

6

The New State

THE CHINESE COMMUNISTS did not come to power in 1949 with the messianic revolutionary expectations which the Russian Bolshevik leaders had held so fervently in 1917. For Lenin and his comrades, the promise of the Bolshevik Revolution was that it was the prelude to the realization of the Marxist prophecy of world revolution and international socialism. Utopian revolutionary hopes were soon dashed by the harsh realities of civil war, foreign intervention, and the isolation of the revolution to backward Russia. Instead of a workers' communal "semistate" which would soon "wither away," as Lenin had envisioned in *State and Revolution*, sheer political survival demanded an increasingly centralized and repressive state apparatus. Instead of the promised producers' control of economic life based on the "free and conscious discipline of the workers themselves," economic survival dictated a bureaucratically imposed discipline from above and the use of capitalist methods and incentives. Instead of the dream of world revolution, all considerations soon were subordinated to the interests of the survival of Soviet power in a single country. As the seeds of Stalinist despotism were being planted, it was not the state but utopian visions that began to wither away. On his deathbed, Lenin somberly questioned the moral and historical validity of the revolution he had led and the crushing of the revolutionary dream over which he had been forced to preside. Near the end, he was moved to confess that he stood "guilty before the workers of Russia."[1]

The Chinese victors of 1949, by contrast, appear as somber realists; not seized by the same chiliastic revolutionary visions as their Russian predecessors, they were not to suffer similar disillusionments. In the early postrevolutionary years, the minds of the Chinese Communist leaders were turned to the immediate political and economic problems of their nation, not to visionary thoughts of world revolution. For more than two decades the Chinese revolution had grown in an insular national mold; it had developed independently of international revolutionary currents and was both physically and spiritually isolated from them. The profoundly nationalistic character of the Chinese revolutionary experience and a vastly different world than that of 1917 had made "proletarian internationalism" a ritualized ideological phrase, no longer a genuine Marxist revolutionary belief. Unlike Lenin or Trotsky, Mao Tse-tung was an eminently national revolutionary leader, not an international revolutionary spokesman. Moreover, by 1949 the notion of socialism in one country—and even in a single backward country—was no longer a novelty; nor was it considered a Marxist heresy.

China in 1949 differed from Russia in 1917 in many other ways. In 1949 Mao had neither the political need nor the theoretical perspectives to write a Chinese equivalent of *State and Revolution*. It was sufficient to write "On People's Democratic Dictatorship." In that essay, Mao had reaffirmed the commitment to socialist and communist goals but relegated their realization to an unspecified future era, while presenting the creation of a strong state power and economic construction as the immediate tasks to be undertaken. In the Chinese case, unlike the Russian, the establishment of an authoritarian state (whatever its formal ideological description), which unified the nation and provided political order, was more the fulfillment of a popular hope than the betrayal of a revolutionary promise. Nor did the early socioeconomic policies of the new regime encounter significant popular opposition; what was done was largely in accord with what had been promised and what was expected. In the urban industrial sector, the large degree of managerial authority permitted in both new state-run enterprises and old capitalist ones did not arouse spontaneous workers' demands for direct control by the producers, as it had in Russia three decades earlier; a long politically dormant Chinese proletariat made few demands and could not serve as the social basis for a "Workers' Opposition" within the party or, for that matter, outside of it. And in the countryside, the new state was to prove capable of satisfying the demands for land of a long oppressed peasantry.

For the vast majority of the Chinese people and for their new Communist leaders 1949 was a time of great optimism and hope. But their hopes, for the most part, were tempered by a remarkably pragmatic recognition of what was possible. And what was deemed within the realm of the possible at the time was essentially the completion of the long-delayed "bourgeois" phase of Chinese historical development: national political unification, agrarian reform, and what promised to be a long and arduous process of modern economic development. In the early years these tasks were pursued on the basis of comparatively moderate policies and within a context of political and social stability unprecedented in postrevolutionary situations. In China, unlike Russia, political victory was neither accompanied by nor did it produce chiliastic expectations of the imminent emergence of a perfect order of justice and equality. As Mao put it at the time of the Communist triumph, "our past work is only the first step in a long march of ten thousand *li*."[2] And the new long march was to be undertaken in China to solve particularly Chinese problems of political and economic construction; there was no expectation that the *deus ex machina* of "world revolution" would make a timely arrival to hasten the process. "Three years of recovery and ten years of development" was the slogan of the time and it reflected the relatively sober temper of the times.

Political order and economic development was the order of the day. No one would have characterized Mao as a utopian visionary at the time, for he then accepted, along with all other leaders of the CCP, the fundamental Marxist view that a high level of the development of the material forces of production was an essential precondition for the socialist transformation of society. Revolutionary utopianism was not to appear on the historical scene until well after the new order had become consolidated, routinized, and seemingly institutionalized.

In many respects, the Chinese enjoyed more favorable conditions than had the Russians for consolidating the revolutionary victory in the short term and for establishing preconditions for an eventual socialist transformation. Whereas the Bolsheviks were forced to wage a materially and spiritually debilitating civil war after the October Revolution, in China the civil war had been fought and won during the revolutionary years; when the Communists established state power in 1949, they faced only scattered counterrevolutionary resistance. Moreover, the prolonged character of the Chinese revolution had permitted the Communists to develop their own organizational forms and administrative structures and had provided them with considerable governmental experience and many experienced administrators; they were thus much less dependent on the bureaucratic apparatus left over from the old regime than the Bolsheviks had been. And perhaps most significantly, the Chinese Communists came to power with far greater popular support than had their Russian predecessors, especially, of course, in the countryside where 80 percent of the Chinese people lived; unlike Lenin, Mao was not confronted with the problem of a hostile peasantry in a largely agrarian country. While the Communists had little organizational roots in the cities, they had at least the sympathetic cooperation of much of the democratic intelligentsia and the urban population in general, both on nationalist grounds and on the promise to bring order to a weary and long misgoverned people. Nationalism, which was not a significant factor in the Russian Revolution, was itself an important force that worked in favor of the new Chinese leaders. The CCP had emerged from the anti-Japanese war as the symbol of nationalist resistance to foreign intrusions and the Party's ability to continue to appeal to patriotic sentiments in the early postwar years served to fortify and expand the Communist base of popular support.

Moreover, unlike the early Soviet state, the People's Republic was neither completely isolated nor threatened to the same degree by foreign counterrevolutionary intervention. However ambiguous the relationship between Peking and Moscow, the mere existence of a powerful Communist country on its borders provided the new Chinese state with some measure of security in an otherwise hostile international arena. In addition, there was the prospect of Soviet economic and technical aid, which, while it was to prove far less than anticipated, was nevertheless significant.

But these relative advantages were overshadowed, and perhaps outweighed, by China's terrible backwardness, a backwardness that was cultural and social as well as economic—the historical legacy of a century of the failure of both reform and revolution. In 1949 the Chinese Communists inherited a war-ravaged economy far less developed than the Russian economy at the time of the October Revolution. It was this condition of massive backwardness and impoverishment that was the critical factor in the Chinese historical situation and subjective responses to the question of how to deal with it were to be crucial in determining the character of Chinese social development after 1949.

Three months before the formal proclamation of the Chinese People's Republic, Mao Tse-tung set forth the principles in accordance with which the new government was to be established—and established an ideological rationale for Communist political supremacy. Beginning with the premise that "bourgeois democracy" was bankrupt in a China so long oppressed by the imperialism of the bourgeois democracies of the West, Mao announced that the new state was to be not a bourgeois republic but a "people's republic." And more precisely, the new people's republic was to be "a state of the people's democratic dictatorship, a state under the leadership of the working class and based on the alliance of workers and peasants." Moreover, the new political order was to rest on an even broader social base, for the workers and peasants were to be part of a "national united front" which included the petty bourgeoisie and the national bourgeoisie. In accordance with this formula, indigenous Chinese capitalism (capitalist forces and classes not tied to the external imperialist order) was to be allowed to develop in order to meet the need for modern economic development. As Mao put it, "China must utilize all elements of urban and rural capitalism that are beneficial and not harmful to the national economy.... Our present policy is to control, not to eliminate, capitalism." Nevertheless, Mao repeatedly emphasized that the people's democratic dictatorship was to be firmly "under the leadership of the working class and the Communist Party," for its ultimate goal was to transform China from a "new democracy" into a socialist and communist society. Precisely when and how socialism and communism would come about was left ambiguous, although the implication was that it presupposed a lengthy process of economic development that would transform China from an agricultural to a predominantly industrial country.[3]

What is the relationship between these various Maoist propositions and Chinese sociopolitical reality in the early postrevolutionary years? One is first struck by the apparent contradiction in terms in the term "democratic dictatorship" which Mao chose to characterize the new state. Was the People's Republic to be a democracy or a dictatorship? Insofar as Mao was willing to address the question, his answer was that it was to be both; whereas democracy was to be extended to "the people," dictatorial methods were to be applied to those excluded from the ranks of "the people." The dictatorial function of the new state was made abundantly clear: the government was to exercise a "dictatorship over the running dogs of imperialism—the landlord class and bureaucratic bourgeoisie, as well as the representatives of those classes, the Kuomintang reactionaries and their accomplices." Such groups and classes were to be deprived of democratic rights and were to be suppressed—and all the forces of violence of the governmental apparatus were to be utilized to ensure that the suppression was complete.[4]

In attempting to understand what "democracy" means in Chinese Communist theory and practice, one enters a much more ambiguous realm. Democracy, Mao wrote, is something to be enjoyed by "the people" as distinct from the reactionaries. One area of ambiguity, of course, is precisely the question that Mao rhetorically posed: "Who are the people?" And, one might add, who is to determine who the people are, and on the basis of what criteria? Implicitly and sometimes explicitly, these questions were to be raised time and again throughout the history of the People's Republic and different answers were to be provided at different times.

In 1949 Mao's answer was deceptively simple; "the people" were the members of the four social classes which presumably had entered into a political united front: the working class, the peasantry, the petty bourgeoisie, and the national bourgeoisie. And "democracy," as the term was used in Maoist theory at the time, meant three things. First, it meant bourgeois democracy in the conventional sense. The people were, according to Mao, to "enjoy the freedoms of speech, assembly, association"; they were to have the right to vote and they were to "elect their own government," a government, in turn, which was to exercise a dictatorship

over the reactionaries who fell outside the ranks of the people.[5] Whether
the promise of these elementary democratic rights was to be honored is
a question to be taken up later—in light of the actual political practice
and history of the new state.

Secondly, democracy referred to a distinctive stage in China's socioeconomic development and governmental policies that correspond to that
stage. More precisely, in Marxist terms, it referred to fulfilling the tasks
of the "bourgeois-democratic" phase of historical development. The encouragement of capitalist economic enterprises in the cities and the redistribution of land to the peasants in the countryside were not socialist
but democratic measures. And democracy, in this sense, was descriptive
of an historical era during which the four popular classes cooperate in a
lengthy process of modern economic development in order to erect the
material foundations for a future socialist society. In the meantime, Chinese society was post-feudal and yet also "pre-socialist," and thus, ipso
facto, "democratic."

Thirdly, democracy was to mean the political representation of the
four classes defined as "the people." Here we encounter one of the most
murky areas of Maoist theory and practice, namely, the question of the
relationship between political power and social classes. That the role of
the dozen or so non-Communist "democratic" parties, formally represented in the creation and functioning of the People's Republic and its
various organs, would be no more than ceremonial—this, needless to say,
was inherent in the political situation and predetermined from the beginning. Even the best-known of these quasi-parties—such as the Democratic League and the Revolutionary Committee of the Kuomintang,
presumably the political representatives of portions of the petty bourgeoisie and national bourgeoisie—were political parties more in name
than in reality. None had any significant popular following or even much
in the way of a formal organizational structure. Having triumphed in the
civil war, there was no question (and no one questioned) that real political power in the new state (whatever its formal structure and official
ideological description) would be monopolized by the CCP and the Red
Army which stood behind it. Nor was much effort made to obscure this
elemental political fact in Chinese Communist ideology.

What is ambiguous is the relationship between the political power of
the Communist Party and the two major social classes of the postrevolutionary era, the proletariat and the peasantry. On the one hand, official
doctrine claims consistently and repeatedly that the CCP is the party of
the proletariat; yet the party's ties to the urban working class had been
severed in 1927 and the latter remained politically passive while the
Communist revolution developed and triumphed in the countryside. Indeed, even as late as 1957, when the size of the proletariat had grown
enormously and the Communists were well established in the cities, the

party could claim that no more than 14 percent of its membership were workers. On the other hand, no explicit claim is made that the CCP is the party of the peasantry; yet the peasantry proved to be the revolutionary class and provided the Maoist party its political victory. And it was from the peasantry that the overwhelming majority of the party's membership continued to be drawn.[6] Here is the paradoxical situation of a revolutionary party claiming to be the party of a politically inactive class but not claiming, at least not explicitly, to be the political representative of the revolutionary class that forms its actual social base.

The paradox was not unraveled when the body that officially established the People's Republic, the Chinese People's Political Consultative Conference, convened in Peking from September 21–30, 1949. The term, if not the institution, derived from the Communists' futile postwar proposals for a coalition government with the Kuomintang. With the Kuomintang crushed, there was no longer any need, or any political basis, for a coalition government in any meaningful sense. Nevertheless, the appearance of a genuinely national and other than purely Communist regime was politically useful. A wide variety of non-Communist political and social groups and individuals (or "democratic personalities" as they were called at the time) participated in the Political Consultative Conference,[7] which, having duly consulted, gave its formal approval to a new government organized in accordance with the proposals Mao Tsetung had set down three months earlier and appointed Mao head of state.

Many non-Communists were given high positions, or at least provided with high titles, in the administrative organs of the new state. Eleven of the original twenty-four ministries, for example, were headed by nonparty people, three of the six vice-chairmen of the Republic were non-Communists, the most illustrious of whom was Soong Ching-ling, the widow of Sun Yat-sen. While this aspect of the new state was largely decorative and ceremonial, it was not wholly meaningless. The political cooperation of many non-Communist luminaries reflected the widespread nationalist appeals of the revolution and the broad popular support the new regime enjoyed. And several concrete purposes were served as well: it assisted in enlisting the support of non-Communist Chinese for a national cause, reassured private entrepreneurs and the technical intelligentsia that capitalist enterprises would be allowed to exist for the time being, and gave some credence to the Maoist ideological claim that the new state rested on an alliance of the four classes who constituted "the people"—and the promise implicit in this claim that the new government would pursue relatively moderate policies.

There is no need to linger over the administrative structure of the new government, about which, in form, there was nothing exceptional. The major executive organ was under the premiership of Chou En-lai from the beginning; originally called the Government Administrative

Council and operating under the "Organic Law" enacted by the Political Consultative Conference of 1949, its name was changed to the State Council when a formal constitution was promulgated in 1954. Under this organ there emerged a centralized bureaucratic apparatus which extended downwards to the provincial, county (*hsien*) and administrative village (*hsiang*) levels. As chairman of the republic, it was Mao who originally appointed Chou as premier and, in different capacities, reappointed him. And it was Chou who provided much of the continuity and stability that the civilian state structure was to enjoy during its first, and often turbulent, twenty-five years.

During the first half-decade, the civilian administration was overshadowed by a military one. The revolution had been won and the new regime had come to power on the basis of a powerful and highly disciplined Red Army, and that army was utilized initially to establish order and a new administrative apparatus within the country as well as to protect it from without. In 1949 China was divided into six military regions and the country remained under what was essentially military control until 1954.

What cemented the civilian and military administrations into an extraordinarily efficient and powerful centralized state was the Chinese Communist Party. The political task that confronted the victorious Communists in 1949 was not to attempt to put the old pieces back together again—for there were few survivals from the past that could serve the needs of modern national unity and integration—but rather to forge an entirely new political structure. And this had to be undertaken in conditions of extreme economic backwardness, in a country which possessed only the most primitive system of communications and transportation, in a land where the persistence of strong traditional localistic and regional loyalties had retarded the development of a modern national consciousness and where the dominance of largely precapitalist forms of economic life provided only the most fragile material basis for national integration. To realize the goal of modern political unification under such conditions—and in the world's most populous country and territorially one of the largest —was a task of staggering proportions. That it was accomplished so effectively and so rapidly in the years between 1949 and 1952 can be attributed, in large measure, to the fact that the new rulers of China had on hand a uniquely effective organizational instrument in the Chinese Communist Party.

The Party had emerged from the revolutionary years as a highly disciplined and tightly knit organization with a membership of nearly 5,000,000. The imperatives of two decades of armed struggle had imparted a military-like discipline to its organization and to the behavioral habits and cast of mind of its members. Its leaders and cadres were not only experienced revolutionary organizers but also experienced governmental administrators—and they possessed a strong sense of national consciousness and purpose. Functioning as a quasi-government long before the formal establishment of the People's Republic, the party provided the main organizational base, leadership, and methods of mass organization as the new government took shape. The personal popularity of Mao Tse-tung and the administrative abilities of Chou En-lai, however great, were no substitute for the party's organizational apparatus and its dedicated and disciplined cadres.

There is, of course, a distinction to be made between the party organization and the formal administrative organs of the state, but the distinction is a thin one. For the most part, the leaders of the Party also held the key positions in the formal state administration, a phenomenon symbolized at the top by Mao Tse-tung who was both the party chairman and the Chairman of the People's Republic. The pattern was repeated down to the lowest levels of the state structure; party cadres either formally held official posts in the bureaucracy or were placed in positions to supervise the administrative work of nonparty functionaries. A similar situation had, of course, long prevailed in the Red Army, by virtue of the early adoption of the Soviet system of "political commissars" and in accordance with Mao's well-known dictum that "the Party commands the gun; we must never allow the gun to command the Party." In 1949 the generals of the People's Liberation Army and most of its officers stood high in the party hierarchy and an elaborate system of political controls was firmly installed throughout the military ranks. In addition, the network of party organization permeated all mass organizations and quasi-governmental institutions which were established (or reorganized) in 1949 or soon thereafter. In trade unions, peasant associations, the educational system, the "people's courts," and the popular militia, leadership positions were either held by party members or control was exercised through parallel organizational structures. Between 1949 and 1952 the organizational web of the CCP was extended throughout the fabric of Chinese society and this was to be the basis for the radical reweaving of that fabric.

Although the new political order was officially represented as based on an alliance of four social classes and appropriately decorated with a variety of "democratic personalities," the locus of state power resided in the CCP which officially represented itself as the party of the proletariat. Or more accurately, political power rested with the party's central committee (which had forty-four members in 1949) and more particularly with its fourteen-member Political Bureau (politburo); or more precisely still, the levers of state power were in the hands of the five men who made up the latter's standing committee in 1949: Mao Tse-tung, Liu Shao-ch'i, Chou En-lai, Chu Teh, and Ch'en Yün. The political history of the People's Republic is in large measure, although by no means exclusively, the internal political history of the CCP and its leading organs.

From the perspective of Marxist-Leninist theory, the chaotic political situation that the victorious Chinese Communists inherited offered a unique revolutionary advantage. It is a cardinal Marxist principle that any lasting revolutionary success demands the thorough destruction of the political institutions of the old regime. The working class, Marx wrote in his famous commentary on the Paris Commune of 1871, "cannot simply lay hold of the ready-made state machinery, and wield it for its own purposes;" rather what Marx called the "ubiquitous organs" of centralized state power—the bureaucracy, army, and police—had to be completely eliminated before genuinely revolutionary institutions could take their place.[8] This was a notion Lenin emphasized time and again, and most forcefully in *State and Revolution;* the existing state bureaucracy could not be "taken over" but had to be "smashed." And shortly before his death, Lenin partly attributed the failure of the October Revolution (or at least its failure to realize its promises) to the persistence of old czarist bureaucratic methods.

In this respect, the Chinese political situation of 1949 augured well for the future of the revolution. The Chinese Communists had little need to smash the old state bureaucracy, for little of its remained. Not encumbered by bureaucratic survivals of the old order, the Communists had an unparalleled opportunity to create afresh their own forms of political power and institutions. But this was not to resolve the perhaps unresolvable problem of bureaucracy. The persistence of traditional bureaucratic patterns of thought and behavior (if not the bureaucratic structures as such), and more importantly, the particular social conditions of the postrevolutionary situation, and indeed the very Leninist organizational structure of the CCP itself were some of the forces which were to foster the rapid growth of bureaucracy. If the Chinese Communists were not burdened by old bureaucratic structures, they soon were to be weighed down by new ones of their own making.

Territorial Unification: The Unfinished Task

When the People's Republic was formally proclaimed in October of 1949, vast areas of China had yet to come under the control of the new government. The military power of the Kuomintang had been broken many months before and Chiang Kai-shek had fled to Taiwan. But much

of South and Southwest China, as well as many of the provinces and outlying dependencies in the West and Northwest, were still occupied by
remnants of the Nationalist army or by various warlord armies which
had been allied with the Kuomintang during the civil war. Therefore
the first task of the new state was to extend its military control over these
territories.

The Red Army moved to the south with extraordinary rapidity, en-
countering only scattered resistance. "The battle of the feet," as it was
called, was not a serious military struggle but a question of whether
Kuomintang troops could retreat more rapidly than the Communists
advanced. The city of Canton, the last official "capital" of the Nationalist
regime on the mainland, was occupied by the Red Army on October 13,
having been abandoned by Kuomintang troops the day before. The
southwestern provinces were occupied over the next two months. The
province of Kweichow was under Communist control by mid-November
and Kwangsi fell to the Fourth Field Army (commanded by Lin Piao)
in early December; Hainan Island, where some of the Kwangsi Nationalist troops then retreated, was occupied by the Red Army in April of
1950. The governor of Yunnan surrendered in December of 1949 and
Communist control of this most remote area of the Southwest produced a
bizarre international by-product; remnant Nationalist forces fled to the
Shan region of Burma where they engaged in various mischief for almost
twenty years, supported by illicit opium trading and American supplies
air-dropped from Taiwan.

Military operations in the West and Northwest were somewhat more
difficult and prolonged. While Szechuan Province was under Red Army
control by end of December of 1949, Kuomintang resistance in Sinkiang
continued until March of the next year. That date marked the termina-
tion of organized Kuomintang military opposition on the mainland. The
reestablishment of Chinese control in Tibet posed not a military problem
(for the tiny Tibetan army was crushed in October, 1950) but rather a
cultural and political one. The relationship between China and Tibet was
marked by more than a thousand years of political ambiguities and cultural hostility. Tibet, incorporated within the Chinese empire by the
Ch'ing Dynasty in the eighteenth century, began to slip from Chinese
control as that empire began to disintegrate under the imperialist onslaught in the late nineteenth century and through British encroachments
from colonial India. When the Ch'ing Dynasty collapsed in 1911, Tibet
became formally independent. Nevertheless, all twentieth-century Chinese nationalists, Communists and non-Communists alike, considered Tibet
to be part of the modern Chinese nation-state, although the political
problem was complicated by the passing of the vague British suzerainty
over Tibet to an even more vague interest on the part of newly inde-

pendent India. While the leaders of the People's Republic were determined to reassert Chinese control over Tibet for both nationalist and strategic reasons, they were sensitive to the cultural and political problems involved. Negotiations with India and Tibetan leaders led to a 1951 agreement which recognized Chinese control while providing for a large measure of Tibetan cultural and sociopolitical autonomy; and Chinese troops occupied Lhasa in the autumn of that year. This did not resolve the matter, as the Tibetan revolt of 1959 was to demonstrate. Not only Tibet, but other areas populated by non-Han minorities, which, all told, account for 6 percent of the population of China, remain sources of internal tension. Although formally designated as "autonomous regions," the actual situation of the minority peoples remains obscure and few foreign visitors have been permitted to enter these areas.

A matter of far greater concern was the occupation of Taiwan by the defeated Kuomintang regime, for this not only left unfinished the task of territorial unification but also the civil war. Communist preparations to invade Taiwan, apparently planned for the summer of 1950, were frustrated by President Truman's administrative order of June 27 which sent the United States Seventh Fleet to "neutralize" the Taiwan strait. The pretext for intervention was the outbreak of the Korean War. The latter was no more than a pretext, for the Chinese were neither involved in the Korean conflict until General MacArthur's ill-fated "march to the Yalu" directly threatened Chinese borders, nor was there ever any satisfactory explanation of what the Taiwan situation had to do with the war in Korea. Indeed, when the truce ending the Korean hostilities was signed in July of 1953, the "neutralization" of the straits of Taiwan remained in effect. The de facto United States military protectorate over Taiwan allowed the Nationalist regime to linger on and represent itself in international councils as the government of China. And the United States established another base in the military cordon it was establishing around China, in a ring from Korea to Southeast Asia.

Even greater and potentially graver obstacles to territorial unification existed on China's long northern border with the Soviet Union. In addition to the vast territories which the old czarist empire had annexed from the old Ch'ing Dynasty in the late nineteenth century (principally the Maritime provinces in the East and parts of Sinkiang in the West), the Russians had reassumed their old predominance in Manchuria as a result of the Japanese defeat in World War II. They occupied Port Arthur, Dairen, and the Chinese Eastern Railway, and dismantled as much of the industry of Manchuria as they were able to carry away.

The birth of the People's Republic marked China's emergence as a unified, modern nation-state, but fulfillment of the modern Chinese nationalist demand for territorial unification remained incomplete. Foreign intervention prevented the recovery of Taiwan and long-standing Russian expansionism precluded recovery of the lost territories of the North. And both situations were fraught with danger.

Repression and Terror

The power of the new Chinese government rested ultimately on the forces of violence which all states wield over society: the army and the police. It would hardly be necessary to repeat this banal truism were it not for endless repetitions of the notion that the Chinese Communist state is uniquely characterized by rule through ideological education and "moral suasion." This piece of contemporary popular mythology has been propagated less by Chinese Communists than by various foreign observers, especially those inclined to find historical parallels between the Confucian past and the Communist present. From the Sinological disposition to accept (to greater or lesser degrees) the Confucian ideological rationalization for the traditional Chinese state—the myth that emperors and mandarins ruled the realm through "moral example"—it is but a short intellectual leap in the dark to cast Mao Tse-tung in the old imperial role, presiding over a revived "Middle Kingdom" in accordance with a perennial "mandate" to govern on the basis of virtuous example.

Mao Tse-tung, for one, has never been guilty of disseminating such nonsense. "Our present task is to strengthen the people's state apparatus," he wrote in 1949, and he went on to define the nature and function of the new government in Marxist terms, not in accordance with Confucian ideological precepts: "The state apparatus, including the army, the police and the courts, is the instrument by which one class oppresses another. It is an instrument for the oppression of antagonistic classes; it is violence and not 'benevolence.' "[9] Certainly the new state owed its existence and survival to the means of violence Mao enumerated, most notably the military and police forces; and the leaders of that state have made abundant use of these conventional means of state power to achieve their ends.

To be sure, Mao advocated a "benevolent policy" in governing "the people," employing "democratic" methods of "persuasion and not of compulsion," as distinguished from "the dictatorship over the reactionaries as a class." Even individual members of the reactionary classes were potentially amenable to educational "remolding," although, as classes, landlords and the bureaucratic bourgeoisie were, as Mao stated, to be "eliminated for good."[10] But behind Maoist processes of "persuasion"— educational methods, psychological techniques, "thought reform" campaigns, and a comparative de-emphasis on formal bureaucratic organs of control—there always stood the conventional institutions of "compulsion," the organized forces of violence upon which (as Mao well recognized) all states are ultimately dependent. And these forces were not to remain idle.

In addition to the Red Army, the new rulers had at their disposal powerful secret police organizations established during the revolutionary years. All units of the Red Army contained "public security headquarters" and since China was essentially under military rule until 1954, these organs performed police functions in civil society and their personnel supervised the functioning of local police agencies in both the cities and rural districts. Moreover, a secret police apparatus existed within the party headed by K'ang Sheng (in addition to the Control Commission which dealt with internal party discipline); in view of the network of party organization that permeated all levels of the formal state administration as well as mass organizations and large economic enterprises, it can be assumed that the party's own police units also exercised considerable control over the civilian population. Furthermore, the establishment of a formal state administration in 1949 was accompanied by the establishment of a formal state secret police organization, the "Public Security Forces," under the jurisdiction of the central government's Ministry of Public Security, headed by Lo Jui-ch'ing from 1949 to 1958, and it rapidly developed into a vast internal security apparatus which penetrated down to the very lowest levels of state administration and control. In addition to their independent police activities, the Public Security Forces were responsible for the supervision and control of all local civilian police agencies. In the cities, each urban residence committee (consisting of about one hundred households on the average) had a public security section as did each *hsiang* administrative unit in the countryside.

It is impossible to specify the political role of these various agencies; the activities of secret police (in China as elsewhere) are, after all, "secret" by definition—and in contemporary China the situation is further obscured by the overlapping functions of the party, the army and the formal state administration, each of which has separate police organizations whose activities ambiguously merge at various levels of control in civil society. Although never to acquire the gigantic political power of their Soviet counterparts, or to inflict upon society similar horrors or terror, China's secret police nevertheless constitute a formidable weapon of political control. They are very much part of the state machine, which, as Mao had written, "is an instrument for oppression."

The oppressive functions of the new state were particularly apparent from 1949 to 1953. These were years of great social and economic accomplishments, but also years marked by severe political repression and often political terror. Radical social and political transformations are almost always followed by reigns of terror, for classes and groups economically and politically dominant under the old regime are as reluctant to surrender their privileges as victorious revolutionaries are determined to guarantee the fruits of their victory. Successful revolutions always produce counterrevolutionary reactions and the latter, in turn, impel new rulers to employ all the means of violence they possess to preserve their newly won power.

The counterrevolutionary impulse was comparatively weak in China, for so much of the old order had disintegrated or had been destroyed in the years before 1949. The compradore bourgeoisie and the landlords were relatively weak and politically uncohesive social classes, and many of their members with either the money or opportunity to do so had fled to Hong Kong, Taiwan, or, more safely, to the United States. There were many who remained who opposed or feared the Communists (and often for good reasons), but there were no political banners for them to rally behind. The democratic "Third Force," despised by the Communists and suppressed by the Kuomintang, long had proven to be a figment of the political imagination of a small number of dissident intellectuals, its leaders now mostly in exile. And the Kuomintang, militarily defeated and so long politically bankrupt, inspired neither enthusiasm nor hope even among those who had actively supported it and perhaps still wished to do so. Even the once powerful Soong and Kung families, long the financial pillars of the Nationalist government, had not only fled China but abandoned the Kuomintang in Taiwan as well, retiring to New York and New Jersey with a substantial portion of the old regime's treasury. Other political parties and movements had long since passed from the historical scene. At the end of 1949 and during the early months of 1950, the Communists had little reason to fear any counterrevolution.

Of much greater and more immediate concern were the internal problems of governing the mainland. To establish administrative control over the country and revive a collapsed economy were formidable tasks which demanded authoritarian political measures and no doubt a degree of political repression as well. But internal political resistance of any organized fashion was relatively insignificant and the rulers of the new state harbored no counterrevolutionary fears during these early months.

What raised the spectre of counterrevolution and posed a threat to the survival of the new republic—and consequently precipitated an era of internal political terror—was an external event and, for China, an entirely fortuitous one: the outbreak of war in Korea in late June of 1950. We shall not pause here to inquire into the still murky question of the origins of that conflict except to note that the Chinese were in no way initially involved.[11] The Chinese leaders certainly could not have welcomed a war of potentially grave international consequences in a bordering land at a time when they were preoccupied with the internal consolidation of the new state, when they were beginning to demobilize much of the Red Army, at precisely the time their best military units were being deployed on the southern coast for the anticipated invasion of Taiwan, and when the opening of the land reform campaign just had been announced. It was not until advancing United States troops threatened the Manchurian border in November that Chinese troops crossed the Yalu and inflicted on the forces of General MacArthur the greatest defeat in American military history.

In what became a de facto Sino–American war China claimed that its troops were merely "volunteers" assisting a fraternal socialist country, and the United States claimed that its army was acting under the "command" of the United Nations. In their different ways, both claims were equally fictitious. For two and one-half years Chinese and American armies fought, most of the time in a bloody war of attrition roughly along the boundary line where the war first began and where it was to end. Although China received substantial quantities of Soviet military equipment (but perhaps less and more belatedly than might have been anticipated under the circumstances), the war placed a severe burden on a fragile Chinese economy just beginning to recover from the ravages of invasion and civil war. And Chinese losses in manpower were staggering; among the victims was one of the sons of Mao Tse-tung, Mao An-ying, killed in battle in 1951.

While the material and human losses were enormous, the war yielded unanticipated political benefits. The threat of yet another invasion by a foreign power solidified popular nationalist support for the government. The campaign to "Resist America and Aid Korea" appealed successfully to broad patriotic sentiments, but what was more important were the early Chinese military victories. For over a century China had been humiliated repeatedly by Western military forces, but now, for the first time, a Chinese army had defeated a Western army—and then fought the strongest military power in the world to a stalemate in a major conventional war. This event, perhaps more than any other in China's modern history, served to stimulate intense feelings of national pride and confidence among the Chinese people, feelings shared by many anti-Communist Chinese as well. The Chinese soldier, so long the object of scorn and ridicule, had proven himself in battle—and the lesson was not lost on the world. Just as the unexpected Japanese victory over Russia in 1905 had marked the emergence of Japan as a major power on the world scene (and stimulated nationalist sentiments throughout Asia), so the Chinese military accomplishment shocked Western military minds and dramatically announced that new China was a nation to be reckoned with in the international arena. It confirmed what Mao had proudly proclaimed in 1949: "Our nation will never again be an insulted nation. We have stood up ... no imperialist will be allowed to invade our territory again...."[12]

But this is the view in retrospect. At the time—in late 1950 and in 1951—the military clash with the United States had a different effect: the Chinese leaders then were more filled with fears over the survival of the new republic than they were with pride in a new China that finally had "stood up" in the world. The fears were by no means groundless. Not only did the encounter with the United States pose the threat of direct attack on China and a full-scale war (a course advocated by many American military and political leaders), it also raised the spectre of counter-revolution. At the outbreak of the Korean War, the United States had established a military protectorate over Taiwan, thus prolonging the life of the remnant Nationalist regime and tying an internal Chinese political conflict to a potentially explosive international one. The very real threat that confronted the Chinese Communists was that deadly combination which had crushed so many revolutions—the combination of civil war and foreign invasion. These twin forces of "restoration" had distorted the French Revolution, crushed the Paris Commune, and very nearly destroyed the Russian Bolshevik regime, and the long history of external and internal counterrevolution was very deeply etched in the Marxist historical memory. The Chinese leaders at the time certainly must have been as acutely conscious of the precedents of the past as they obviously were aware of the present danger. If the internal forces of counterrevolution were relatively weak, the threat of foreign invasion was very strong. And hardly a year after the founding of the People's Republic there loomed the possibility of a renewed civil war backed by a powerful foreign state.

On Taiwan the revived Nationalist regime did all it could to turn that possibility into a counterrevolutionary reality, assisted and encouraged by the influential "China Lobby" in the United States. Kuomintang political agents infiltrated the mainland through Hong Kong and Nationalist army units crossed the presumably "neutralized" Taiwan Strait to conduct commando attacks on the China coast. And in the United States, loud political cries were heard urging the Truman administration to carry the Korean War directly to China and to "unleash" Chiang Kai-shek.

The essentially external threat to the survival of the revolution turned the initially moderate policies and practices of the new state into increasingly repressive ones—and eventually to a reign of terror throughout most of the country in 1951. The employment of openly terroristic methods was officially sanctioned by Mao's decree of February 21, 1951 on "Regulations Regarding the Punishment of Counterrevolutionaries." Needless to say, there was nothing novel about punishing counterrevolutionaries; Kuomintang agents, supporters, and sympathizers always had been systematically suppressed in areas under Communist control both before and after 1949, and efforts to quell actual or potential political opposition intensified during the Korean War. But the purpose of the February decree was somewhat different; it not only extended the scope of politi-

cal repression by defining more broadly what were deemed to be counterrevolutionary activities, but was also designed to instill an atmosphere
of terror in society through public campaigns against all forms of political
dissidence. In addition to an intensification of secret-police repression in
general, the following months saw an endless series of mass meetings in
the major urban centers where the more prominent of accused counterrevolutionaries were publicly denounced and sentenced to death while
the less prominent were arrested and tried through the regular police
and judicial state agencies. Newspapers published daily and lengthy lists
of the names of those executed and prominently featured grisly accounts
of alleged political crimes and punishments. If the purpose of the campaign was to create a public climate of fear and terror as well as to
eliminate potential opposition to the state, it was successful on both
counts.

The People's Republic has never revealed comprehensive statistics on
the number of the victims of the terror (if indeed there are accurate
records) and the estimates of outside observers vary greatly, depending
of course on the political proclivities of the observer. However, such
fragmentary official reports as are available do suggest that the number
was substantial. In the province of Kwangtung alone, for example, local
authorities reported some 28,000 executions in the 10-month period from
October 1950 to August 1951.[13] In a speech delivered in 1957, Chou En-
lai stated that among an unspecified number of counterrevolutionary
cases officially handled by the government through 1952, 16.8 percent
were sentenced to death, 42.3 percent to "reform through labor," 32 percent placed under "surveillance," and 8.9 percent subject only to "reeducation."[14] Using the government's figure of 800,000 counterrevolutionary
trials during the first half of 1951, there were some 135,000 official executions during that 6-month period alone. The real figure is no doubt
greater, and taking into account the much longer period involved and
the considerable number of executions that took place outside of formal
judicial procedures, the estimate of many relatively impartial observers
that there were 2,000,000 people executed during the first three years
of the People's Republic is probably as accurate a guess as one can make
on the basis of scanty information. That figure includes the semi-sponta-
neous "executions" in the countryside when the long-repressed hatreds
of an oppressed peasantry were released during the land-reform campaigns of 1950–1952. And many more than 2,000,000 were imprisoned or
sent to forced labor camps during these years.

The human toll, whatever the actual number, is not lessened by noting that probably larger percentages of the population were killed in the
various reigns of terror which followed in the wake of the French and
Russian revolutions. Nor can the figure be reduced by remembering that
uncounted millions died annually from famine and malnutrition in pre-
1949 China, or by recalling the long lists of official executions and the

greater number taken in the wanton slaughters that marked Chiang Kai-shek's White Terror of the late 1920s and early 1930s. On these matters no one kept statistics and few bothered to make estimates.

These macabre comparisons are offered not as revolutionary apologetics but only to maintain some degree of historical perspective on a matter that does not easily lend itself to either moral complacency or moral outrage. In most revolutionary situations, the choice is not between terror or its absence but rather between revolutionary terror or counter-revolutionary terror; and since China had suffered so greatly from the latter over the decades, one should not be too quick to levy moral condemnations on the former. As Barrington Moore has observed, it has been the historical case that "revolutionary violence has been part of the break with a repressive past and of the effort to construct a less repressive future."[15] But it is also the historical case that the gap between the promises of revolution and the actual performances of revolutionaries has been far too great to a priori justify revolutionary violence on future promises alone. In the Chinese case, much more needs to be examined before beginning to attempt to weigh the social accomplishments of the revolution against its human costs.

If there is any cause for surprise in the political history of these early postrevolutionary years, it lies in the relative brevity of the period of overt political terror and the rapidity of the consolidation of the new state order. With the suppression of actual or potential sources of internal opposition, and as the war in Korea ground to a stalemate in 1951 and the fear of a direct United States military attack began to recede, the use of terror as a method of political control began to recede as well. By the end of 1951 the country began to return to more "normal" methods of administrative control and bureaucratic rule, although terror still reigned in parts of the countryside where the completion of the land reform program was to take another year. But if the return to "normalcy" signaled the end of an era of overt political terror, it did not mark the end of a continuing era of political repression. Three years after the establishment of the People's Republic the goal of a strong state had been realized—and it was a state (like all states) which rested on a powerful army and an extensive police apparatus as well as on a broad base of popular support. No doubt the experience of the terror of 1951, and the experience of the Korean War, lent a harsher and more authoritarian cast to the new order than might otherwise have been the case. But if there is any clear lesson to be derived from these political events it is Mao's simple truism that the state is an instrument of oppression and compulsion. And the history of China in those as well as subsequent years has more than amply demonstrated the truth of the Marxist proposition that, as Engels put it and Lenin once repeated, "while the state exists there is no freedom."

Notes

1. Cited in Isaac Deutscher, *Ironies of History* (London: Oxford University Press, 1966), p. 173.
2. Mao Tse-tung, "On the People's Democratic Dictatorship," in *Selected Works of Mao Tse-tung* (Peking, 1967), 4:422.
3. *Ibid.*, pp. 417–421.
4. *Ibid.*, pp. 417–418.
5. *Ibid.*
6. Of the 12,720,000 party members in 1957, according to official figures, 1,740,000 were classified as workers, 8,500,000 as peasants, 1,880,000 as intellectuals, and 600,000 as "others." See Franz Schurmann, *Ideology and Organization in Communist China* (Berkeley: University of California Press, 1966), p. 132.
7. Of the 662 delegates to the conference, only 16 were formally CCP members.
8. Karl Marx, "The Civil War in France," in Karl Marx and Frederick Engels, *Selected Works* (Moscow: Foreign Languages Publishing House, 1950), 1:468.
9. Mao, "On the People's Democratic Dictatorship," p. 418.
10. *Ibid.*, p. 419.
11. Interpretations of the origins of the Korean War range from the view that it was an independent North Korean decision; that North Korea was encouraged and manipulated by Moscow; that it was provoked by the Rhee government in South Korea; to the view that it was subtly instigated by the United States. Few diplomatic historians any longer give credence to the once popular theory that it was part of a Chinese design. Indeed, recent evidence indicates that while the Russians were aware that a war was in the making, they failed to communicate the information to Peking. For a study of the Chinese role, see Allen Whiting, *China Crosses the Yalu: The Decision to Enter the Korean War* (New York: Macmillan, 1960).
12. "Speech to the First Plenary Session of the Chinese People's Political Consultative Conference" (September 21, 1949), in *Selected Works of Mao Tse-tung* (London: Lawrence & Wishart, 1954), 4:411–424.
13. Cited in Ezra Vogel, *Canton under Communism* (Cambridge, Mass.: Harvard University Press, 1969), p. 64.
14. Chou En-lai, "Report on the Work of the Government," delivered to the Fourth Session of the First National People's Congress (June 26, 1957), in Robert R. Bowie and John K. Fairbank, *Communist China 1955–1959: Policy Documents with Analysis* (Cambridge, Mass.: Harvard University Press, 1962), p. 303.
15. Barrington Moore, *Social Origins of Dictatorship and Democracy* (Boston: Beacon Press, 1966), p. 506.

7

The Cities:

The Rise and Fall of National Capitalism

"IT IS VERY DIFFICULT to govern a country in the aftermath of a revolution and political talent is a scarce commodity."[1] This familiar postrevolutionary truism has proven less apt in the case of China than in any other of the great social revolutions of modern history. Three years after the Communist victory China was better governed than at any time in her long past and there was a relative abundance of political and administrative talent. It was the unique nature of the Chinese revolution, not any special Chinese genius for governing, that was responsible for this unique postrevolutionary situation. The Chinese Communists had not triumphed in the classic insurrectionary fashion whereby revolutionaries suddenly are catapulted into the unfamiliar position of rulers; their victory had come only after more than two decades of armed struggle during which they had been rulers as well as revolutionaries, governing significant territories and populations in accordance with their own organizational methods and structures.

But that experience had been confined to the countryside. In the cities, which fell to the Communists more rapidly than expected, political and administrative talents were very scarce commodities indeed. The problem was not wholly unanticipated. As early as 1939 Mao Tse-tung noted, "The capture of the cities now serving as the enemy's main bases is the final objective of the revolution, an objective which cannot be achieved without adequate work in the cities."[2] And when Communist armies were in fact capturing the cities, Mao announced that "the center of gravity of the party's work has shifted from the village to the city" and that "we must do our utmost to learn how to administer and build the cities."[3] The task was to prove a formidable one. Although the leaders of the Chinese Communist Party originally had emerged from an urban intelligentsia, most of those who survived the long revolutionary ordeal had lived and fought in the rural hinterlands for more than twenty years; and for the peasant cadres the cities were wholly unfamiliar and strange places. As a distinguished American scholar living in Peking at the time observed: "Some of these Communists had never seen a large city before; they did not even know how to turn off the electric lights. . . ."[4] Moreover, unfamiliarity was accompanied by distrust. A revolutionary strategy based on gathering the forces of rural revolution to surround and overwhelm the nonrevolutionary cities naturally bred and fortified powerful antiurban feelings. In the pre-1949 years, the revolutionaries viewed the cities as bastions of conservatism, the strongholds of the Kuomintang, the centers of foreign imperialist power, and the breeding grounds for social inequalities, ideological impurities, and moral corruptions. They entered the cities in 1949 no less as occupiers than as liberators, and for the urban inhabitants who had contributed so little to the revolutionary victory feelings of sympathy were intermingled with strong feelings of suspicion. The dichotomy between the revolutionary countryside and the conservative cities, which the whole revolutionary experience produced, had become a notion deeply ingrained in the Maoist mentality, and this ideological residue of the revolution was to play a role in the way in which the new rulers approached one of the crucial problems in the history of the People's Republic—the problem of the relationship between town and countryside.

While China was a largely agrarian country, and largely remains so, more than 60,000,000 Chinese lived in cities with populations of over 100,000 in 1949 and the urban population was to grow rapidly. Shanghai, now the world's largest city with a population of more than 11,000,000, had some 6,000,000 inhabitants in 1949; over 2,000,000 people lived in Peking and Tientsin; and more than 1,000,000 in Canton. The task of governing this unfamiliar terrain was compounded by the chaotic conditions which so tragically marked urban life during the last days of Kuomintang rule. In addition to chronic (and now exacerbated) problems of massive unemployment and underemployment, of corrupt and inefficient local administrations, of a population preyed upon by a vast underworld of gangster organizations and secret societies, widespread opium addiction, prostitution, and the lack of elemental standards of sanitation and municipal services, conditions of war and the misrule of a dying regime imposed more acute problems which destroyed the economic life of the cities and inflicted the most cruel burdens on their inhabitants. Severe shortages of food led to chronic malnutrition and often famine, to riots, looting, and to a wave of crime of all sorts in cities long notorious for crime. Factories and workshops closed due to lack of supplies and because workers often were too weakened by malnutrition to work. The wartime and postwar inflation reached staggering proportions. During the final 6 months of Kuomintang administration in the cities, it is estimated that the average increase in the cost of living was 25 percent per week. In Peking, for example, the price of flour rose 4,500 times the year prior to the Communist occupation of the city.[5] Under such conditions money became virtually useless; various "currency reforms" decreed by the government in Nanking merely brought new floods of worthless paper to an economy which had reverted largely to primitive barter for such goods and services as there were to be exchanged.

Not untypical was the situation in the Manchurian city of Mukden, the most industrialized city in China:

> Half a million people have left, either for Communist areas or as refugees to North China. Industrial production is down to almost nothing. A primary factor is lack of food, caused by the seige. Rationed food lasts a worker only ten days out of every month. Many people are forced to live on the large Manchurian soybean cakes, ordinarily used only for cattle and fertilizer. These, probably because of vitamin deficiency, eventually produce night blindness among adults and permanent blindness among children—in some cases even actual disintegration of the eyeballs. Lack of food results in lowered coal output, which cuts electric power, which in turn leads to flooding of coal mines. Production appears to be coming to a complete standstill. This coming winter there will surely be starvation.[6]

In Shanghai, rickshaw drivers, too weakened by malnutrition, declined to haul passengers. And from many Chinese cities came reports of starving people lying untended and dying in the streets.

Such was the final legacy of the Kuomintang era—the utter destitution of the cities. Not only were the new Communist rulers ill-prepared to govern cities, the cities they now had to govern were in a state of unprecedented chaos. The Communists lacked both organized political support among the urban population and the economic support of a viable urban industrial and commercial base. To the burdens of a primitive agricultural economy, there was added a new and unanticipated burden: the ruin of the whole modern sector of the economy. In this condition of total impoverishment the history of the People's Republic began.

The Communists possessed one political asset in the cities: an almost universal antipathy to the Kuomintang. The political discontent engendered by the economic miseries of the time was intensified by the increasingly corrupt practices of the dying regime and its resort to wholly terroristic methods of political control, arbitrary arrests and executions, the suppression of the liberal intelligentsia, and the crushing of an anti-Communist, but independent, trade-union movement which had emerged in the early post World War II years. The vast majority of the urban people, as unfamiliar with the Communists as the rural revolutionaries were with them, could not but welcome the triumph of the countryside over the cities, if for no other reason than that the Communist victory held the promise of peace and order.

While their general disgust with the old regime is well documented, it was rarely expressed in any open or organized political action, and there is little reliable evidence to gauge feelings about the new order. Sentiments varied according to place and certainly among different social groups and classes. From Peking it was reported that "the Communists come here with the bulk of the people on their side. As one walks the streets, the new feeling of relief and relaxation can definitely be sensed, even though it is hard to describe it in tangible terms."[7] The people of Canton, according to one account, awaited the arrival of the Red Army in a "cautious rather than exuberant" mood and "their main feeling was relief that the city had fallen peacefully."[8]

It was among middle-school and university students that the Communists found their most enthusiastic and active supporters in the urban areas, although genuine idealism often was mixed with opportunism and hypocrisy. Members of the politically uncommitted intelligentsia seemed, for the most part, willing to work within the new order. One liberal professor commented in September, 1948, four months before Peking fell to the Red Army:

> Most Chinese intellectuals would prefer not to bother about politics. But while they have heard the government repeatedly proclaim its intention of bringing democracy and honest administration to China, they have seen these protestations repeatedly flouted in actual fact. Indeed, far from improving, the government becomes steadily worse, so that today few thinking people hold much hope for its reform. . . . At first, most of us supported the [Nationalist] government, recognizing its many faults, but hoping it would reform. . . . We have become so completely convinced of the hopelessness of the existing government that we feel the sooner it is removed the better. Since the Chinese Communists are obviously the only force capable of making this change, we are now willing to support them as the lesser of two evils. We ourselves would prefer a middle course, but this is no longer possible.[9]

Many of the wealthier members of the bourgeoisie fled along with the Kuomintang, but most of those classified by the Communists as belonging to the "national bourgeoisie" remained—a varied assortment of commercial entrepreneurs, petty shopkeepers, owners of small factories and workshops, and managers of industrial and commercial establishments. Nearly ruined by the extralegal exactions of a corrupt bureaucracy and the economic chaos of the civil war, they had little left to lose. They hardly could have been enthusiastic about a government which proclaimed socialism and communism to be its aims, but they could hope

that the new rulers would honor the promise to control but not immediately eliminate capitalism. Their attitudes towards the new regime were
no doubt highly ambiguous, just as the Communists viewed them in an
ambiguous and suspicious fashion.

About the political attitudes and sentiments of the working class and
the masses of the urban poor—the downtrodden *lumpenproletariat* of
rickshaw drivers, casual "coolie" laborers, beggars, and petty thieves—
even less can be said with any degree of accuracy. They made up the
great majority of the population of the cities, but they were the least
articulate segment of that population. Among the people of the cities,
they were the ones who benefited most from the new regime, yet they
are the ones about whom the least is known. From their ranks came the
bulk of the participants in the victory celebrations of 1949 and the mass
demonstrations and meetings in the cities over the following years, but
they must have had the most ambiguous feelings about celebrating a
revolutionary victory to which they had contributed so little. One can
only surmise, on the basis of scanty information, that in 1949 the urban
workers greeted the Communist victory with hope and enthusiasm. The
members of a class so long victimized by the most extreme forms of socioeconomic oppression, largely unemployed and half-starved in the last
years of the old regime, could only have welcomed the triumph of the
new regime, even if they may have found it strange that the leading
party in that regime proclaimed itself to be *their* party.

Although the spectacle of an army composed mostly of peasants occupying the cities must have made for deeply ambiguous feelings among
the urban populace, the vast majority of the people of the cities probably
welcomed the new order, if only because of their deep revulsion with the
old one. Hope intermingled with apprehension, for the urban population
was as unfamiliar with the Communists as the Communists were with the
cities. But the dominant mood was a willingness to cooperate with the
new rulers of China to end the chaos in the cities that the discredited
Kuomintang regime had left behind. Mutual suspicions and distrusts remained, but at the beginning they were subordinated to a mutual desire
for peace, social order, an adequate supply of food, the restoration of a
shattered economy, and for elemental social reforms. What the Communists lacked in organized political support in the cities was compensated
for, at least in part, by a general and genuine public eagerness to participate in the work of reviving the social and economic life of the cities.
The Communists used this cooperative mood to good advantage and chan-
neled it into new organizational forms and programs which eventually
were to transform the physical appearance of the cities and the character
of urban social life.

The first task, however, was to establish public order and restore the
ordinary municipal services which had fallen into disarray. In striking

contrast to the situation in the countryside, where the Communists began with their own organizational forms and cadres, in the cities they had to rely on a good part of the bureaucratic apparatus left over from the old regime. Although most high Kuomintang officials had fled with the Nationalist Army, many lower level bureaucratic functionaries remained to reassume positions in the municipal administrations. To a lesser degree, the same was true for local police forces; old civil police organs and many of their personnel were retained for a time in the interests of restoring order. Over the years, most of the old functionaries were replaced by party cadres, many of whom were newly recruited from the urban youth.

The formal administrative and police structures of the cities were not far different from those which had existed under the Kuomintang, but they now were under the control of the public security agencies of both the army and the central government in Peking. While the formal organization of the old municipal administrations remained, as did many of the old officials and functionaries, party members occupied key positions to ensure that local city bureaucracies were responsive to the policies and directives of the new national government. Centralized control was further augmented by a variety of formally autonomous urban mass organizations which were in fact intimately tied to the state apparatus. Such nationwide organizations as the All-China Federation of Trade Unions, the All-China Federation of Women, the Students' Association, and various professional associations organized the key classes and groups in urban society. Established on the basis of pre-existing organizational structures, these organizations were in essence arms of the centralized state apparatus since they were dominated by the same party that controlled the national government. The associations organized and controlled much of the urban population on a national basis and served as centralized counterweights to the localistic tendencies of urban administrations and the independence of economic enterprises and educational institutions.

Beginning in 1952 "urban resident committees" (generally made up of about 100 to 500 households) added another layer of organizational control over the urban population. They were charged with a bewildering variety of purposes and functions. In addition to the general task of communicating (and popularizing) government policies and programs to their members, they were to communicate to the government the views and opinions of their members; they had the quasi-judicial function of arbitrating family and neighborhood disputes and the police function of controlling (and reporting) criminal activities and political dissidence; they were to carry out municipal services, such as public sanitation and fire prevention, as well as social welfare functions, such as providing relief to needy families and the organization of neighborhood cultural and recreational programs.

Although the welfare and other positive services provided by the resident committees were both needed and appreciated, they were basically coercive instruments of control. As Franz Schurmann has observed: "One of the basic tasks of the residents committees was to keep an eye on the population under their jurisdiction and to report regularly to the local police station, more or less in the fashion known from *paochia* days."[10] The quasi-police and judicial functions of the committees intruded into private lives and aroused deep popular resentments, just as had been the case with their pre-1949 counterparts. Yet, despite the reliance on many old bureaucratic forms and many old bureaucrats, Communist political power was quickly and firmly established in the cities. The revolutionaries in power were not overwhelmed by the remnants of the old bureaucracy; they simply used them.

If Communist political power was firm, there was little distinctively "communist" or "socialist" about the ends to which this power was put in the early years; the urban policies and programs were ones which any strong national government would have undertaken under the circumstances, and indeed, in large measure, ones which the old Kuomintang regime had attempted or promised to pursue, albeit futilely. The establishment of social order; registration of the population; collection of concealed weapons; control of inflation and introduction of a viable currency system; revival of industrial production and commerce; restoration of municipal services; improvement of sanitation facilities; and centralized control over viable local urban administrations were immediate tasks that any new Chinese government would have confronted. Nor should it have taken a Communist government to deal with the chronic social problems of the cities such as widespread opium addiction, prostitution, and the crime and corruption wrought by a vast underworld of secret societies and labor gangs.

The problem of opium addiction is a particularly striking (but not untypical) example of the failures of the old regime and the successes of the new one. The drug problem had plagued Chinese society since the late eighteenth century, and reached epidemic proportions after the Opium War of 1839. By the time the Nationalist regime inherited the massive problem, most of the trade was in the hands of Chinese criminal organizations. Kuomintang anti-opium laws and campaigns proved abortive not only because of the inefficiency of the regime but also for reasons of political and economic expediency; the Kuomintang had found politically useful the secret societies and gangster organizations which profited from the drug trade, while a corrupt bureaucracy and police force found it financially rewarding to protect it. Yet a problem that had persisted and grown under various Chinese governments for almost two centuries was resolved by the new government of the People's Republic in two years. The Communists employed a combination of drastic criminal penalties (including execution) for major suppliers and dealers, amnesty for petty traffickers, rehabilitation programs for addicts, and a massive nationwide campaign of education and public "ban opium" rallies, appealing to patriotic sentiments by stressing the nineteenth century imperialist origins of the affliction. By the end of 1951 opium addiction was no longer a major social problem, and before the end of the next year few drug addicts were to be found in China.

Other common urban vices were handled with the same efficiency and through similar measures of repression, reformation, mass mobilization, and education. In Canton, one of the most vice-ridden of old Chinese cities, Ezra Vogel summarizes one of the results of the first three years of Communist rule: "Prostitution, opium addiction, gambling, and alcoholism were virtually wiped out. For the first time in a century a public morality was restored so that people did not have to worry about robbery or about walking on the streets alone in the evening. A combination of assistance and tight supervision did not alter human nature but it did bring organized crime under control."[11]

Just as the internal social reforms in the cities fulfilled long-frustrated desires for the regeneration of China, so the departure of foreigners satisfied deep nationalist resentments against a century-long external impingement. The expulsion of foreigners from the cities was not an act of "Communist tyranny," as it was described and condemned in the Western press at the time, but a highly popular Chinese nationalist act, symbolizing the end of the era of imperialist domination. Although the expulsion was marked by occasional incidents of popular antiforeign violence, the process was carried out in a relatively orderly fashion. At first, foreign residents were required to register with the new authorities and their activities and travel were limited and supervised. Foreign businesses were regulated and eventually confiscated and nationalized. In late 1950, under tensions generated by the Korean War, government policy demanded the removal of virtually all Western nationals from Chinese soil. By then most Westerners already had left the country, but the few foreign businessmen, missionaries, and educators who had remained were forced to depart over the next year amidst a series of mass anti-imperialist rallies. The majority left peacefully despite the political terror that prevailed at the time and the nationalist passions aroused by the war in Korea. All foreign assets were frozen, foreign-owned property expropriated, and Chinese Christians were forced to terminate ties with foreign churches.

Among the expelled foreigners there were a good many who were favorable to the new order and who wished to remain and work in China. And the whole antiforeign campaign created problems in diplomatic relations and trade with Western nations. But these considerations were far outweighed at the time by internal political and psychological needs. As a non-Communist liberal Chinese intellectual explained the situation to an American friend, "Communist antiforeignism is the result of humiliation and oppression suffered by China for the past century. The Communists are out to show their people that they are masters of their own house and that no foreigner can lord it here any more."[12] No concrete political or economic gains or issues were involved; rather it was emotional compensation for a century of humiliation. The expulsion of the foreigners was the necessary psychological prerequisite for China to meet the Western nations on equal terms. Since 1842 Chinese politicians and governments, traditional and modern nationalist, had vowed to throw off the foreign yoke, but the People's Republic was the first government in modern Chinese history to demonstrate that it had the ability to do so.

The Urban Economy in the Early Years

The economic policies of the People's Republic were never purely "nationalistic," but in the early years they did largely conform with the Maoist conception of a revolutionary process still in its "national" or "bourgeois-democratic" phase. In the rural areas, the land-reform campaign of 1949–1952 produced not a socialist agricultural economy but a massive class of petty bourgeois individual peasant cultivators. In the cities socialist and capitalist forms intermingled for a time in what, for the lack of any better term, might be called a "mixed economy," but of a rather unique kind. The industries, commercial organizations, and banks owned by the "bureaucratic bourgeoisie" (those who had been politically allied with the Kuomintang or economically tied to foreign interests) were immediately confiscated and were nationalized without compensation. By 1949 most of the members of this class already had fled the country in any event. Through nationalization, the new state owned the crucial areas of the modern sector of the economy from the outset. If one defines socialism simply (and perhaps simplistically) in terms of state ownership or control of property, then most of the urban economy was "socialist" in nature from the beginning. However, large and significant portions of the economy remained on a capitalist or quasi-capitalist basis. In addition to more than a million petty shopkeepers and individual handicraftsmen who were largely untouched by the new order in the early years, the "national bourgeoisie," defined principally by the criterion of political loyalty, were permitted to continue to privately own their industrial and trading enterprises and operate them in a formally capitalist fashion. Indeed they were encouraged to expand their operations and establish new firms. By 1953 the number of privately owned industrial establishments increased from 123,000 to 150,000 and the number of workers in private firms increased from 1,644,000 to 2,231,000, accounting for approximately 37 percent of China's industrial output.[13]

The operation of the private sector, however, was tightly restricted. Prices, wages, and working conditions were determined by the state. In privately owned factories, trade unions and worker councils, both under party direction, enforced state policies and regulations, and also played a supervisory role in the management of the enterprises. Most importantly, private factories were dependent on the state for the allocation of raw materials to produce their goods and for outlets to sell them, and private commercial firms depended on the state trading organizations for both wholesale purchases and retail sales. This, in short, was a form of state capitalism, not a laissez faire economy. The "national bourgeoisie" in the People's Republic was now more dependent on the state bureaucracy than the old and condemned "bureaucratic bourgeoisie" ever had been. The difference was essentially political; it was a new state pursuing new social ends. Yet it was capitalism nonetheless. Owners of capital made profits on the commodities they produced and sold (in Marxist terms, they exacted "surplus labor"), and although profits were controlled, they were sufficient for some reinvestment and more than adequate to allow a class of capitalists to enjoy a bourgeois life style.

More than purely ideological considerations were involved in encouraging the revival of "national capitalism." The Communists were not simply attempting to give substance to the promises of "new democracy," nor were they motivated by any strong desire to historically document the Marxist proposition that history moves through progressive stages of development and that a "bourgeois-democratic" phase necessarily must precede a socialist one. The main consideration was a more mundane and pressing one. To reconstruct a wrecked economy and establish a foundation for future economic development, it was expedient to rebuild what had existed and then build upon that. Any program for total and immediate expropriation and nationalization would have inevitably resulted in organizational chaos. More importantly, the survival and revival of capitalism was necessary to utilize the managerial skills and technical expertise which the bourgeoisie alone possessed. Through a combination of economic and patriotic appeals, the new government enlisted the support and experience of the members of the bourgeoisie and technical specialists who had remained, and encouraged many who had left the country to return, to participate in the task of national economic reconstruction.

The era of "national capitalism" reached its peak in 1952–1953 and declined rapidly thereafter, as private industrial and commercial firms were nationalized outright, or more typically, reorganized as "joint private–state enterprises." In the latter case, the state assumed a controlling, and eventually complete, interest in the firms by government capital investments, with the former private owners usually staying on in managerial roles and receiving dividends of 5 percent on what the government calculated to be their remaining share of capital. In fact, if not in name, the firms became state-owned as well as state-managed. By 1956 the private sector of the urban economy had ceased to exist, and all industrial and commercial enterprises of any significant size had been effectively nationalized. What little remained of private enterprise was confined to a still numerically large, but an increasingly obsolete and economically insignificant, group of self-employed handicraftsmen and artisans, petty shopkeepers and peddlers. "National capitalism" survived only as a vestige—in the form of a tiny bourgeoisie receiving quarterly dividends on what the government determined to be their "capital investments" in the factories and commercial establishments they once owned, or receiving interest on nonredeemable government bonds they had received in compensation. Although they continued to enjoy a relatively high standard of living in the cities, the national bourgeoisie was a dying class since their dividends and bonds could not be passed on to their heirs. But if national capitalism had enjoyed only a brief life in the history of the People's Republic, it had fulfilled the economic role assigned to it; by 1952 the urban economy and industrial production were flourishing.

The new government had sought and had received the cooperation of three segments of the urban population who possessed specialized skills urgently needed for the immediate tasks of political unity and national reconstruction: liberal intellectuals and the technological intelligentsia; bureaucrats and urban administrators left over from the old regime; and the national bourgeoisie. Once political and economic stability had been achieved, the Communists moved quickly to end their reliance on what they regarded as the least politically reliable elements of the urban population. Beginning in late 1951, this took the form of three politically repressive campaigns: the thought-reform movement directed primarily against intellectuals; the *San-fan* ("three anti") campaign against bureaucratic corruption and inefficiency; and the *Wu-fan* ("five anti") campaign which was essentially an attack on the bourgeoisie. Unlike the preceding campaign against "counterrevolutionaries," which attempted to eliminate political dissent in society in general, the new movements had specific goals aimed against particular elite groups in the cities. And unlike the concurrent land reform campaign which served to destroy the rural gentry, a class which had nothing to offer to the new society, the urban campaigns aimed not to destroy social groups but rather to establish firmer political control over them. The thrust was to politicize people with expertise while preserving them and their talents to serve society. Unlike the gentry and the counter-revolutionaries, the people to be politicized were still regarded as members of "the people."

"Thought reform" (*ssu-hsiang kai-tsao*) is described by the Communists as a "democratic" method of education and ideological transformation through continuing processes of group criticism and self-criticism. Beginning with the "rectification" movements in Yenan in the early 1940s, it has since remained one of the central and distinctive means of social, political, and ideological control. It is not regarded primarily as a form of punishment—although it sometimes has been used for that purpose or led to that end—but principally as an "educational" tool to produce "correct thoughts," which in turn result in correct social and political behavior. Although it is seen as a particularly effective and appropriate method to reform intellectuals, it has not been confined to intellectuals; rather, it is regarded as a universally valid practice applicable to the least politically conscious peasants as well as to the highest leaders of the party.

The first of the major post-revolutionary thought reform campaigns began in the autumn of 1951 when Mao Tse-tung declared that the "thought reform of all categories of intellectuals" was essential for "the thoroughgoing democratic transformation and progressive industrialization of our country."[14] The campaign was thus tied to the completion of the bourgeois-democratic phase of the revolution and the building of the economic preconditions for the future transition to socialism. Beginning with a movement for the intensive study of the writings of Mao, with particular emphasis on the Yenan talks on art and literature which defined the social and political responsibilities of intellectuals, the campaign spread to all major urban areas employing familiar Maoist techniques of mass meetings, small group "struggle sessions" of criticism and self-criticism, public humiliations, and written and oral "confessions" from those deemed guilty of ideological deviations. Individualistic tendencies and "liberal" bourgeois thought were to be discarded in favor of ascetic Maoist values and the impartation of a collectivistic mentality of "serving the people." The campaign generally began with intellectuals in universities and spread to middle and elementary school teachers as well as to students and individual writers and artists. There was little overt political coercion (although some intellectuals were sent to the countryside for "reeducation through labor"), but the social and psychological pressures were intense. Contributing to the intensity of the campaign was the external threat posed by the war in Korea; a prominent feature of the movement was a patriotic appeal to defend the nation against imperialist aggression, coupled with condemnations of the bourgeois modes of thought prevalent in cities with a long heritage of foreign domination. The vague criterion for success was a subjective judgment, made by the "thought reformers," as to whether confessions and self-criticisms acknowledging past errors and accepting the new social morality were "sincere" or not. While it may be doubted that many intellectuals

achieved the desired Maoist inner spiritual transformation, the outer results were patently clear; the campaign ended in 1952 with tighter party
control over the educational system and the closing of the narrow realm
of freedom of expression that intellectuals had cautiously enjoyed during
the first two years of the People's Republic. Four years later, the "Hundred Flowers" period was to reveal how repression fostered deep intellectual and political resentments.

The *San-fan* movement against "corruption, waste, and the bureaucratic spirit" was launched early in 1952 and ran simultaneously with the
thought-reform campaign. Although not comparable to Stalin's bureaucratic purges of the 1930s (and after) either in scope or in the employment of secret police terror, the ("three anti") movement was designed to
remove politically unreliable government officials and party cadres as
well as to correct specific problems in the functioning of the administrative organs of the new state. The mass meetings of citizens to criticize
corrupt or oppressive officials, a distinctively Maoist political technique,
characterized this campaign as it did virtually all others. While this was
something far less than popular control over the bureaucracy, it was a
practice entirely foreign to Stalinism both in spirit and method.

San-fan fell hardest on three elements of the bureaucracy: old Kuomintang officials who had been retained in the urban administrations and
who now were dispensable; new party members hastily recruited during
the final years of the civil war who proved unsuited to the new tasks of
post-revolutionary administrative work; and older party cadres who were
deemed corrupted by revolutionary success and especially by urban
bourgeois influences. The latter was a distinctively Maoist theme, the
fear that city life fostered bureaucratic mentalities and the erosion of revolutionary values. In the end, however, the movement proved to be
something less than a massive attack on bureaucracy. Less than 5 percent
of administrative functionaries were subjected to formal punishment;
some were imprisoned, but most were simply dismissed or demoted.[15]

The *Wu-fan* campaign (against bribery, tax evasion, fraud, theft of
government property, and stealing of state economic secrets) was a
movement of greater scope and significance. Directed against corrupt
practices in the urban economy in general, its main weight fell on the
bourgeoisie and more than 450,000 enterprises were officially investigated
by state authorities in 1952 and early 1953. Although some businessmen
were imprisoned for illegal economic activities (and there were occasional reports of suicides), the penalties were mostly financial. Through
the collection of back taxes, heavy fines and other economic exactions,
the remaining assets of the bourgeoisie were further depleted and most
firms and factories were forced to become joint state–private enterprises,
in effect, well on the way to becoming nationalized.

The campaigns of 1951 and 1952 served to consolidate Communist
power in the cities and marked the beginning of the end of the era of

"new democracy." By early 1953 the civil administrations, the economy, and the educational institutions of urban China were firmly under the control of the party and the centralized state apparatus it directed. The new regime was authoritarian and often repressive, but the cities were governed honestly and efficiently for the first time in modern Chinese history.

In 1949 the Communists had announced their goal to be: "Three years of recovery, then ten years of development." By the end of 1952, with the restoration of the cities and the conclusion of the land reform campaign in the countryside, to be discussed in the next chapter, the new rulers had fulfilled the first half of that promise. The government was now to turn its attention to "ten years of development," the task of industrializing a still backward and impoverished land. But industrialization was to bring unforeseen and, for Mao, undesirable social, political, and ideological consequences. And the industrial development of the cities was to bring more sharply into focus the critical problem of the relationship between town and countryside in the new society, a question that was to dominate the entire history of the People's Republic, just as it had dominated the history of the revolution that produced that republic. A growing antagonism between town and countryside is perhaps inherent in the very process of modern industrialization. But in China the antagonism was to be accentuated by the rural origins and heritage of the revolution and by a curious imbalance between economic and political power in rural and urban areas. In the cities, the Communists had succeeded in reviving the economy and the strong state they had created exercised effective centralized control over the urban areas, but their sociopolitical ties to the growing urban working class remained weak and tenuous. Although strong efforts were made to acquire an urban proletarian base in the early postrevolutionary years, workers or people of working-class origin made up less than 10 percent of the 6,000,000 members of the Chinese Communist Party in 1953, and the percentage was not to increase significantly in the years that followed. In the countryside, on the other hand, the Communists had deep political roots among the peasantry, roots that the land reform campaign of 1950–1952 extended and reinforced. And the Communist party remained a "peasant party" in the sense that peasants constituted the overwhelming majority of its membership. But those political roots were in an agrarian economy low in productivity and still based on a system of individual peasant proprietorship. The industrialization of the People's Republic thus was to begin on the basis of a fragile petty bourgeois agricultural economy and in cities where the Communists had an ambiguous relationship with the working class.

Yet if the mass social base of the Chinese Communist Party remained with the peasantry, the higher organs of the Party were now based in the cities and the majority of its leaders rapidly became urbanized. They hardly became the "organic" intellectuals of the working class in the sense in which Antonio Gramsci had formulated that conception,[16] but they did identify their fortunes and the future of China with the growth of urban industry, and thus by implication, at least, with China's growing urban proletariat. Other Communist leaders, who might well be characterized as the organic intellectuals of the peasantry, did not so easily accept city life and the prospect of the domination of town over countryside. Foremost among the latter certainly was Mao Tse-tung, who, when he announced in 1949 the inauguration of the period of "the city leading the village," also warned of the danger that urbanization could corrupt the spirit and ideology of the victorious revolutionaries—that the rural style of "plain living and hard struggle" might give way to the "love of pleasure and distaste for continued hard living" that city life fostered.[17] The warning was to prove prophetic. The existing gap between town and countryside soon was to widen under the impact of rapid urban industrialization, and the gap was to find expression within the Chinese Communist Party itself—in the form of a split between urban- and rural-oriented Communist leaders, between those who placed their hopes for a socialist future in the development of modern urban industry and those who continued to identify themselves with the peasant masses and looked more to the socialist transformation of the countryside.

Notes

1. John Dunn, *Modern Revolutions* (London: Cambridge University Press, 1972), p. 17.
2. Mao Tse-tung, *The Chinese Revolution and the Chinese Communist Party* (1939) (Peking: Foreign Languages Press, 1954), p. 32.
3. Mao Tse-tung, "Report to the Second Plenary Session of the Seventh Central Committee of the Communist Party of China," *Selected Works of Mao Tse-tung* (Peking: Foreign Languages Press, 1961), 4:363–364.
4. Derk Bodde, *Peking Diary* (New York: Henry Schuman, 1950), p. 72. This book is a most perceptive and the most revealing account of the situation in the cities under the Kuomintang at the last and the early months of Communist rule.
5. *Ibid.*, p. 100.
6. Quoted in *ibid.*, p. 33.
7. *Ibid.*, p. 99. On the civilian participants in the Red Army's victory parade through the streets of Peking, Bodde observed that "the enthusiasm of most was too obvious to have been feigned.... The reaction of the spec-

tators, on the other hand, was, like that of most Chinese crowds, less out-spoken. Nevertheless, they seemed in general quite favorably disposed and obviously deeply impressed by the display of power [p. 104]."

8. Ezra Vogel, *Canton under Communism* (Cambridge, Mass.: Harvard University Press, 1969), pp. 45–46.

9. As related by Derk Bodde in *Peking Diary*, pp. 23–24.

10. Franz Schurmann, *Ideology and Organization in Communist China* (Berkeley: University of California Press, 1966), p. 376. *Paochia* was a traditional system of sociopolitical control imposed by the state; ideally, it was a grouping of a hundred households with each bearing responsibility for the actions and behavior of all other members.

11. Vogel, *Canton under Communism*, p. 67.

12. Bodde, *Peking Diary*, p. 158.

13. Figures calculated by Barry M. Richman, *Industrial Society in Communist China* (New York: Random House, 1969), p. 899.

14. *Jen-min jih-pao* (*People's Daily*), October, 24, 1951.

15. Schurmann, *Ideology and Organization*, p. 318.

16. For Gramsci's notion of the "organic" intellectual (organically belonging to a particular social class), and his distinction between urban and rural-type intellectuals, see his provocative essay "The Intellectuals" in Antonio Gramsci, *Selections from the Prison Notebooks* (New York: International Publishers, 1971), pp. 5–23.

17. Mao Tse-tung, "Report to the Second Plenary Session of the Seventh Central Committee of the Communist Party of China," *Selected Works* (1961), 4:363–364, 374.

8

Land Reform:

The Bourgeois Revolution in the Countryside

IN 1952, THREE YEARS after the establishment of the People's Republic, the gentry ceased to exist as a social class. The destruction of the elite that had dominated Chinese society for more than two millennia marked the consummation of a momentous social revolution, but not a socialist one. Although that process of class destruction was carried out under Communist political auspices, the demise of the gentry was socially and economically an eminently bourgeois revolutionary act. Just as the eighteenth century French Revolution had destroyed the power of the landed aristocracy and removed feudal institutions hindering the growth of bourgeois property, the Chinese Communist revolution in the countryside, by expropriating the landlords and redistributing land among the peasantry, created a massive class of capitalist-type individual peasant proprietors.

That the gentry and precapitalist agrarian socio-economic relationships had survived to the mid-twentieth century reflected the failure of bourgeois revolutionary movements in modern Chinese history. It fell to a Communist party that aimed to abolish private property to establish the conditions for the flourishing of bourgeois property in the countryside. This historical paradox was, of course, not without historical precedent. A similar failure on the part of bourgeois political parties in Russia had forced the Bolsheviks to preside over an agrarian bourgeois revolution, with the result that the first decade of Soviet history saw the emergence and growth of a capitalistic peasantry. In both China and Russia, however, the existence of a bourgeois economy in the countryside was short-lived, and in both countries the same political power that had allowed a bourgeois agrarian revolution to take place also was to prove the instrument to destroy bourgeois property.

One of the ironies of the history of Marxism in the modern world is to be noted here. The abortiveness of bourgeois revolutionary movements in Russia and China offered a socialist political advantage. Had bourgeois revolutions occurred earlier, before political conditions permitted Marxist revolutionaries to come to power, the peasantries of both countries likely would have become politically conservative forces intent on preserving their smallholdings and thus opposed to revolution. This was the case in most of Western Europe and especially in France. The radicalism of the French peasantry during the Revolution of 1789 was followed by more than a century of political conservatism; Marx often commented on the phenomenon, perhaps best summed up in his sarcastic comment that "the Bonapartes are the dynasty of the peasants."[1] Such was not the case where the agrarian revolution was retarded and took place in conjunction with, or as part of, a socialist revolutionary process. In Russia, the new peasant smallholders did not have the time to consolidate themselves as a class sufficiently strong to withstand the terror of Stalinist collectivization. In China the political advantage was much greater. The Chinese Communists, unlike the Russian Bolsheviks, came to power on the basis of massive peasant support and with deep organizational roots in the countryside. Peasant resistance to collectivization was to prove minimal, and peasant support for revolutionary social transformation substantial. The socialization of agriculture in China was to proceed in a way strikingly dissimilar to the way it had in the Soviet Union, and with vastly different social results and political implications.

The formal legal basis for the destruction of the gentry class and traditional socio-economic relationships in the villages was the Agrarian Reform Law of June 1950. The nationwide land reform campaign of the next two and one-half years was based on the experiences gained and the methods developed in the rural areas under Communist control in the 1930s and 1940s.

Land Reform, 1950–1952

When the People's Republic formally was proclaimed in 1949, land reform had been carried out in no more than one-fifth of the villages of China. The Communists were determined to extend the process from their old revolutionary base areas throughout the vast countryside that only recently had come under their control, and to do so quickly. More than an ideological demand to eliminate feudalistic socio-economic relations in the rural areas (and thus fulfill one of the major promises of "new democracy") lay behind this determination. Also involved were a variety of crucial political and economic considerations. For one thing, land reform was necessary to maintain and expand the new regime's base of popular support; "land to the tiller" had been promised to the poor peasants who made up 70 percent of China's rural population of 500,000,000 and from whom the Communists drew the bulk of their political support. The universalization of land reform was a necessity for two other reasons. First, it was the means to destroy the gentry-landlord class (and thus eliminate a potential counterrevolutionary threat), the means to establish Communist political power within the villages, and thus a prerequisite for building a state structure which exercised firm administrative control over the countryside. Second, land reform was seen as an economic necessity for the new society. It was anticipated that it would expand agricultural production, at least within the limits imposed by traditional technology; establish the political foundation for a technological revolution in agriculture upon which hopes for modern industrial development rested; and provide the base for the future socialist transformation of the countryside.

While the Communists were intent on completing the agrarian social revolution, they were determined to avoid the violence and excesses that had marred many of the land reform campaigns in northern provinces during the last years of the civil war. With military victory assured by the spring of 1949, the emphasis turned from the political mobilization of the peasantry for revolutionary victory to the establishment and consolidation of a new state order and to a concern for a stable agrarian economy. Party leaders called for an end to revolutionary terror in the villages and attempted to control the spontaneous forces of peasant radicalism, which now seemed politically and economically disruptive to revolutionaries turned rulers. Many of the younger village cadres, now accused of "leftist deviations" and "indiscriminate killings," were expelled from the party in early 1950. In the meantime, while new national guidelines were being formulated, land reform was slowed or halted and the actions of peasants and local cadres in the newly liberated areas of the southern and central provinces were restrained.

A strong reaction against the violence and disorder of the earlier land-reform campaigns figured prominently in party debates of late 1949 and early 1950 as to how the process should proceed. The debate was dominated by two considerations: a determination to destroy the landed gentry as a social class; and an equally strong determination to complete land reform in a manner consistent with maintaining agricultural production. The two aims were by no means inconsistent. The gentry traditionally had been a basically parasitic class, deriving wealth through rents from their landholdings but contributing little or nothing to production. Quite apart from social and political considerations, the simple economic fact of the matter was well put by the anthropologist Fei Hsiao-t'ung: "The landlord cannot find a way to eliminate the tenant and get income directly from the land, but the tenant can cultivate the land without the assistance of the landlord."[2] Unlike the bourgeoisie of the cities, whose economic and technical skills were needed and cultivated by the new regime, the gentry had nothing to offer to society. They were a class dispensable on economic grounds as well as socially and politically undesirable.

The results of party deliberations on land reform were summarized in a speech by Liu Shao-ch'i to the People's Political Consultative Conference on June 14, 1950, and formally adopted by the government two weeks later in the Agrarian Reform Law. Although Liu's speech—eighteen years later—was to be cited as evidence of his alleged "capitalist roadism," there is no reason to believe that Mao Tse-tung at the time disagreed with the moderate thrust of his report: that the old agrarian system was to be eliminated "step by step and with discrimination" while agricultural production was to be developed at the same time.[3] The need to maintain the productivity of the rural economy during the course of the social revolutionary transformation was recognized as essential to the political as well as the economic viability of the new state by all Communist leaders, including Mao. Indeed, a week before Liu had delivered his speech, Mao had presented a report to the party's central committee foreshadowing the relatively moderate agrarian program that was to be adopted. It was economically necessary, Mao argued, to pursue a policy of "preserving a rich peasant economy, in order to further the early restoration of production in the rural areas."[4] And what Liu proposed as the "general line" to be followed in the land reform campaign—"to rely on the poor peasants and farm laborers, to unite with the middle peasants, and to neutralize the rich peasants"—was a cardinal principle that Mao advocated and practiced before and after 1949. In practical socioeconomic terms this meant protecting the economically efficient farms of the rich as well as the middle peasants from radical egalitarian demands for complete and immediate social leveling.

This concern for maintaining productivity was reflected in the provisions governing the treatment of the estimated 30 percent of the rural population not classified as poor peasants or agricultural laborers under the Agrarian Reform Law and subsequent government directives over the summer of 1950. The lands and properties of landlords (the 4 percent of the rural population who owned about 30 percent of the cultivated land) were to be confiscated and distributed among landless and poor peasants, as were institutional lands (usually indirectly controlled by gentry families) such as property owned by village shrines and temples, monasteries, churches, and schools. But dispossessed landlords were to be given shares of land equal to those of poor peasants "so that they can make their living by their own labor and thus reform themselves through labor." After five years of demonstrated productive activity and political loyalty, the stigma of "landlord-class status" could be removed. More significant was the provision prohibiting the confiscation of "the land and other properties used by landlords directly for the operation of industrial and commercial enterprises," a provision in accord with Mao's 1949 injunction that "China must utilize all elements of urban and rural capitalism that are beneficial and not harmful to the national economy," and one which permitted some members of the gentry engaged in entrepreneurial enterprises in the cities and the towns to be reclassified as members of the "national bourgeoisie." Thus while the traditional economically parasitic role of the gentry was to be eliminated, their economically beneficial functions were to be preserved, even though the latter often involved the exploitation of labor.

More revealing of the Communist willingness to subordinate social considerations to immediate economic concerns was the relatively lenient policy adopted toward rich peasants. Although only 6 percent of the rural population, their farms accounted for almost half the total agricultural production. The Agrarian Law stipulated that the lands "cultivated by themselves *or by hired labor,* and their other properties, shall be protected from infringement" (emphasis added). Moreover, rich peasants were permitted to continue to rent land to tenant farmers; only leased land exceeding in size the amount cultivated by themselves and their hired laborers was subject to confiscation.[5] Thus rich peasants were permitted to engage in two traditional types of rural exploitation: they were able to hire agricultural laborers and to rent parts of their holdings to tenant farmers.

Special efforts were made to increase the economic productivity and win the political cooperation of middle peasants. Although they constituted 20 percent of the rural population, one-third of the leadership of the peasants' associations were to be drawn from the middle peasants. None of their lands or properties were subject to confiscation and the introduction of the new category of "well-to-do middle peasant" made it possible for them to draw as much as 25 percent of their income through exploitation, that is by hiring laborers or renting portions of their land.[6]

Although the Agrarian Law of 1950 was a relatively moderate document, preserving the economic position of middle and most rich peasants, it did retain the main social revolutionary thrust of land reform—the destruction of the landlord-gentry class. Nevertheless, it provided for less than what had been promised in the slogans around which the poor peasant masses had rallied to the Communist cause during the civil war: "the equal distribution of land" and "the land belongs to the man who plows it."

The promise was left unfulfilled because any attempt to achieve complete egalitarianism in the countryside would have created havoc in the rural economy, as the 1947–1949 land-reform campaigns in the North had demonstrated. The dilution of social radicalism in the new agrarian program reflected the lessons of that experience as well as new concerns for political and economic stability, concerns that befitted revolutionaries who now had become rulers. These political and economic considerations are evident in the official documents and pronouncements of the time. The destruction of the gentry as a social class was seen as a good and necessary end, but not an end in itself. As the opening paragraph of the new Agrarian Law made clear, the long-range goal was "to set free the rural productive forces, develop agricultural production, and thus pave the way for New China's industrialization."[7] And as Communist leaders emphasized time and again, land reform itself, however egalitarian, would not solve the problem of the poverty of the peasantry, a problem which could be resolved only by increasing total agricultural production and the development of modern industry and technology. Land reform, in any case, was viewed by the Communists, although perhaps not by their peasant supporters at the time, as only the first stage of a long-term social and economic revolution in the countryside, only a first step on the way to the eventual collectivization of agriculture and to industrialization. In the meantime, the interests of the nation would best be served by maintaining social order and economic productivity in the rural areas. Granting temporary concessions to the rich and middle peasants seemed a small price to pay to facilitate a long-term process of socioeconomic development.

From the perspectives held by most Communist leaders in mid-1950, the specific provisions of the law were less important than the means by which the process would be carried out. Unlike the earlier land revolution in North China, where matters were largely left to young and radical peasant cadres and to the spontaneous radicalism of the poor peasantry, the new campaign was to proceed in a more controlled fashion, with land-reform cadres acting in accordance with centralized party and state instructions. If political and economic needs demanded a more gradual approach, then that also was a price that would be paid. As Liu Shao-ch'i remarked in his June 1950 report, "If deviations occur in some areas after agrarian reform is started and give rise to certain chaotic conditions which cannot be corrected quickly, agrarian reform then should be held up in these areas until the next year."[8]

The campaign was not to follow the orderly course envisioned in the summer of 1950. Once the forces of class struggle within the villages were released, they were not to be easily controlled by official regulations or bureaucratic restraints. Both the resistance of the relatively privileged rural classes and the demands of poorer peasants for land (and for retribution against their former oppressors) were to prove stronger than the leaders in Peking anticipated.

The movement began peacefully enough in the summer of 1950 with the training of local party cadres for land-reform work, the organization and expansion of local peasant associations and congresses, surveys of landownership, the social classification of the population in the newly liberated areas of South and Central China, educational campaigns, and the popularization of model "pilot" projects. Since there were great regional variations in social and economic conditions, directives from Peking placed special emphasis on the need for provincial authorities to adapt the movement to local needs. There were, to be sure, serious problems at the outset. In the South, clan organizations (which cut across class lines) were stronger than in the North, and party organization was weaker. The social and economic power of landlords also was greater in most of the newly liberated areas than it had been in the northern provinces, and the gentry used kinship ties to protect themselves and as much as they could of their properties from the oncoming social revolution; many fled to the cities to hide among relatives, disguised some of their holdings and properties by "lending" them to poorer members of their clans in the villages. Sometimes they simply bribed peasants to resist the transformation of traditional relationships. Moreover, the dispatch of northern land reform workers to the South and West sometimes created political conflicts with local party officials and cadres. Northerners were intent on carrying out land reform as fully and as quickly as possible, local cadres were often restrained by kinship ties and personal friendships. On the whole, however, the campaign proceeded smoothly and with relatively little physical violence through the end of 1950.

The land-reform process usually began with the organization of the peasants' association and a people's militia, the former replacing the traditional system of village elders drawn from the wealthier families while the latter replaced what remained of the old *paochia* system of local military "self-defense"—and what remained were mostly "local bullies," armed criminal gangs engaged in terror and extortion against peasants and who were usually at the disposal of the gentry. Many of the local bullies were executed or imprisoned when Communist military forces first entered the villages. With Communist political power established through these new village organizations, the campaign turned to social and economic ends. First landlords had to refund rent deposits and then the complex process of defining the class status of the villagers and identifying landownership began. These were controversial matters and the decisions were often arbitrary since social class lines within the villages tended to be fluid and overlapping and ownership rights were sometimes uncertain. In general, however, the results conformed to socioeconomic realities, even though tempered by political judgments. The sociologist C. K. Yang, who conducted a study of a village in Kwangtung during the last year of Kuomintang rule and the first two years of the People's Republic, reported that "The general proportion of the classes [as determined by the land-reform surveys] corresponded roughly to what we had learned about the class composition of the village previous to the Communist rule."[9]

The determination of class status and landownership was the prelude to land confiscation and redistribution and it produced a most unusual social phenomenon: a general effort by villagers to represent themselves as low as possible in the social hierarchy. It also gave rise to a general atmosphere of fear among the less impoverished villagers:

> A great anxiety and tenseness pervaded the village, for now every family was assigned a status fraught with social, economic and political consequences. Those families listed as landlords waited for the axe to fall. Those listed as rich peasants were extremely uneasy, for they knew their fate was undecided, in spite of the temporary policy of "preservation of the rich peasants' economy.". . . The middle peasants experienced considerable suspense . . . they were uncertain how long their land property could be preserved. Furthermore, many of the relatively well-to-do were in juxtaposition to the rich peasants, and they did not know whether they would some day be "promoted" to that rank.[10]

The drawing of class lines inaugurated the period of open class struggle within the villages. The purpose of land reform was not only to economically dispossess the gentry but to humiliate them socially and discredit them politically in the eyes of the peasantry. Through the mass mobilization of the villagers at "struggle meetings," poor peasants were encouraged to express their long-suppressed angers, to publicly denounce the oppressions and oppressors of the past. The landlords who were the principal targets of these sessions could hope at best to receive a small plot of land to till in return for "bowing their heads" before the masses and sincerely admitting their guilt; at worst, they faced summary execution at mass public trials. A large potential for violence and terror was no doubt inherent in the internal dynamics of the rural social conflict which the land reform movement released, but it is unlikely that the terror that was soon to be unleashed against the gentry would have been so massive had it not been for the Korean War.

The war in Korea broke out the same month the Agrarian Reform Law was promulgated, although it was not until Chinese troops became directly involved at the end of the year—and the spectre of full-scale war with the United States was raised—that it had serious internal political repercussions. Many landlords, hoping that the Communist regime would prove short-lived and that the old regime would be restored, stiffened their resistance. For the new government, the war raised the fear of counterrevolution, and this fear centered on the gentry. Of the two social classes the Communists had vowed to eliminate, the bureaucratic bourgeoisie had largely eliminated itself by fleeing the country with the Kuomintang, but most members of the gentry remained, either in the countryside or in hiding in the cities. As the war in Korea intensified and as internal political tensions increased in late 1950, directives from Peking called for more radical agrarian policies, an intensification of the rural class struggle, and for a general speeding-up of the land-reform campaign to break the actual or potential threat posed by the continued existence of the gentry class. Political considerations began to outweigh economic concerns. Pressure from the central authorities combined with increasing resistance at the local level led to more frequent and more bitter struggle meetings in the villages and more mass public trials pronouncing harsher judgments. Land reform began to take on the terroristic features of the earlier agrarian revolution in North China, although less spontaneous in character. The campaign remained under central direction and control and became intertwined with the general secret-police terror against suspected counter-revolutionaries which continued through most of 1951. Many landlords were executed or sent to forced labor camps, but the great majority of the approximately 20,000,000 people classified as members of landlord families were provided with small plots of land and reduced to the unaccustomed role of cultivators of the soil, even though still socially designated as "landlords."

Except for regions populated by national minorities, the land reform campaign was substantially completed by the end of 1952, although it continued in certain areas of South China into mid-1953. Its great and historic accomplishment was precisely what had been announced when the movement was launched in 1950, the destruction of the gentry as a social class, although that process of class destruction involved more terror and physical violence than originally had been anticipated. Fears that the movement would undermine agricultural production proved unfounded. Between 1950 and 1952, total agricultural output increased at a rate of 15 percent per annum, the largest increase coming in 1952.[11] Although much of the increase can be attributed to the establishment of political order (and the restoration of trade and transport), after a decade of foreign invasion and civil war, agricultural production was still significantly higher in 1952 than in 1936, the best of the prewar years. The disruptive effects of land reform were more than compensated by the new irrigation and flood-control projects begun in 1949 and, to a lesser extent, by an increase in cultivated acreage, organized anti-pest campaigns, and a limited but significant increase in the use of insecticides and fertilizers. And farmers who now tilled their own land had a greater incentive to work more efficiently and adopt better methods of cultivation.

Land reform completed a momentous social revolution in rural China but it did not bring about an economic revolution in agriculture. Productive patterns in the villages were unaltered by land reform alone and technological improvements were slight. To be sure, the fruits of peasant labor were now more equitably distributed and no longer was it

possible for "gentlemen" wearing long gowns and cultivating long finger-
nails to live off the labor of others. The horrors of the old system disappeared, but general poverty did not. If total food grains production in
1952 was 9 percent higher than during the peak prewar years, as official
figures claimed, it hardly kept pace with population growth, much less
provide much of a surplus for capital investments in either agriculture or
industry. Traditional agricultural technology and productive patterns imposed stringent limits on increases in productivity—and even that was
dependent on the vagaries of the weather.

The economic limitations of land reform had been recognized from
the beginning. As Liu Shao-ch'i had warned on the eve of the campaign,
"the basic aim of agrarian reform is not purely to relieve the impoverished peasants. . . . The problem of poverty among the peasants can be
finally solved only if agricultural production can be greatly developed, if
the industrialization of New China can be realized. . . ."[12] Until that modern economic revolution, the burdens of backwardness would have to be
borne, although they now might be shared more equally.

Nonetheless, the poor and landless peasants benefited immediately
from the confiscation and redistribution of nearly half of China's cultivated land. Tenants and agricultural laborers now had their own plots
to till and the poorest owner-cultivators were given additional land, usually of better quality. Even though they now were socially and politically
favored under the new system, poor peasants were still relatively poor in
villages still suffering from conditions of general poverty. Land reform
was a vast process of social leveling, but it was by no means a complete
egalitarian leveling. Significant economic distinctions remained among
the rural population. Overall the farms of poor peasants were about 90
percent of the average landholding in their locality, middle peasant holdings were somewhat above the established *hsiang* norm, and the holdings
of rich peasants were generally about twice the average. In addition, the
exploitation of labor was not wholly abolished; rich and some middle
peasants still rented land to tenants and employed hired wage laborers.

Moreover, the economic benefits of land reform were offset to some
extent by new economic problems it created. Land redistribution created
a larger number of small farming units and greater fragmentation, thus
intensifying traditional barriers to productivity. Although usury had been
abolished, the old problem of adequate rural credit for small owner-cultivators was aggravated; rich and middle peasants who had money to lend
were reluctant to do so at the relatively low rates of interest imposed by
the new state. And the state had only the most limited means to establish
a new rural credit system. The general tax levy was now higher than it
had been under previous regimes; it is generally estimated that state
taxes after land reform took approximately 30 percent of the gross yield,
about twice the pre-1949 rate, although it was now the richer peasants

who bore the heavier burdens. And while most former tenant farmers benefited from land reform, it was not universally the case that land redistribution increased either their productivity or income; in some areas of South China where tenant farms were relatively large and tenant rights relatively secure, land reform sometimes actually resulted in smaller and less efficient farms and owner-cultivators less well off than they had been before as tenant farmers. On the whole, however, the economic position of the majority of the peasantry improved, even though the general problem of rural impoverishment remained.

The significance of the land reform campaign cannot be measured in purely economic terms in any case. No less important in the long run than the elimination of the worst forms of exploitation was the establishment of the social and political foundations for the future economic development and the social transformation of the countryside. A revolution from below, carried out from village to village by the political activation of the peasant masses, created the basis for a centralized state power to firmly establish itself in the villages. The gentry were replaced by a new rural leadership of young peasant activists drawn from the poor peasantry and intimately tied to a national political structure. Although the formal organs of state administration rested at the level of the *hsiang*, CCP political organization of the peasantry at lower levels extended the authority of the centralized state down into the "natural" village itself. With the breaking down of traditional regional, local, and kinship loyalties and the establishment of central state control, the local isolation of the villages was broken, peasants became part of a national polity and were increasingly drawn into a national market economy.

Another political result was a general transformation of the political consciousness of the peasantry. The land-reform campaign was not carried out by administrative decrees and bureaucratic means but through the stimulation of class conflict within each village, a conflict in which all villagers participated and one whose consequences no one could escape. The latent energies and hatreds of the peasantry were released at mass struggle meetings and public trials, where the formerly passive victims of oppression now denounced, judged, and punished their former oppressors. If the ends of land reform were determined from above, the process itself was carried out from below, providing peasants with a sense that they themselves were changing the conditions under which they lived and that they could be the masters of their own destiny. Especially for peasants who had not been involved in the pre-1949 revolutionary struggles, land reform was a profoundly traumatic psychological experience and a profoundly revealing political action which instilled a new sense of their own powers and gave them new hope for the future.

The completion of the campaign resulted in the establishment of a system of individual peasant proprietorship that reflected the bourgeois character of the Chinese revolutionary process. The government issued title deeds to the new landowners and the latter were legally free to buy, sell, and rent their lands. Although political power was in the hands of a party that proclaimed socialist goals, the rural socio-economic situation in 1953 was favorable to the development of bourgeois property and conducive to the growth of a rural capitalist class.

The Communists had made no secret that they viewed individual peasant proprietorship as a temporary phase in the socioeconomic development of the countryside, as but a transitional step on the way to collectivization. A year before the land-reform campaign was launched, Mao had announced that agricultural collectivization was only a matter of time, but he then suggested that it might take a long time:

> As the peasant economy is decentralized, the socialization of agriculture, according to the Soviet Union's experience, will require a long time and much painstaking work. Without the socialization of agriculture there can be no complete and consolidated socialism. And to socialize agriculture we must develop a powerful industry with the state-owned enterprises as its main component.[13]

When and how agricultural production would be collectivized, and the question of the relationship between the industrialization of the cities and the socialization of the countryside were questions that were to dominate the history of the next decade.

Notes

1. Karl Marx, "The Eighteenth Brumaire of Louis Bonaparte," in Karl Marx and Frederick Engels, *Selected Works* (Moscow: Foreign Languages Publishing House, 1950), 1:302.
2. Fei Hsiao-t'ung, *China's Gentry* (Chicago: University of Chicago Press, 1953), p. 119.
3. Liu Shao-ch'i, "Report on the Agrarian Reform Problem," June 14, 1950. For translated excerpts, see Chao Kuo-chün, *Agrarian Policies of Mainland China: A Documentary Study (1949–1956)* (Cambridge, Mass.: Harvard University Press, 1957), pp. 38–41.
4. *New China's Economic Achievements* (Peking: Foreign Languages Press, 1952), p. 6.
5. See article 6 of the Agrarian Reform Law, in Chao, *Agrarian Policies*, p. 48.
6. *Ibid.* The Agrarian Reform Law stipulated a limit of 15 percent. It was raised to 25 percent in a governmental directive of August 4, 1950.
7. *Ibid.*, p. 41.
8. *Ibid.*, p. 35.

9. C. K. Yang, *A Chinese Village in Early Communist Transition* (Cambridge, Mass.: MIT Press, 1959), p. 143.

10. *Ibid.*, pp. 143–144.

11. State Statistical Bureau, communiniqué, reproduced in *People's China* (Peking), July 16, 1956.

12. "Report on Agrarian Reform Problem," p. 38.

13. Mao Tse-tung, *On People's Democratic Dictatorship* (Peking: Foreign Languages Press, 1959), p. 14.

9

The Social and Political Consequences
of Industrialization

THE HISTORY OF THE PEOPLE'S REPUBLIC in the years after 1952 is historically incomprehensible if one does not take into account the fundamental commitment of its leaders to achieving the socialist and communist goals proclaimed in Marxist theory. It remains fashionable, of course, to view the Chinese Communists as simply a new political elite, to see their revolution as yet one more case historically documenting a presumably universal process of the "circulation of elites," and to dismiss their Marxism as little more than an ideological disguise for the ambitions of power-hungry men. It is more fashionable still to view the Communists as essentially "nationalists" and "modernizers" pursuing in their particular fashion the goals of national "wealth and power" inherited from their non-Marxian predecessors. Thus Chinese Marxism, it is said, is basically an "ideology of modernization" and its "real content" is modern Chinese nationalism, "objectively" serving to bring China into the modern world as a modern nation-state. Or, as some more deterministically minded theorists would have it, Marxist ideology plays a temporarily "dysfunctional" role in an otherwise historically impersonal "modernization process," which ultimately determines the actions of its Communist actors.

That the leaders of the Chinese Communist Party constitute a new political elite who fought to attain political power and seek to maintain their power goes without saying. Nor is there doubt that Chinese Communists are fervent nationalists, that they strive to modernize a backward country, and that they have always sought those eminently modern nationalist goals of "wealth and power" to enable China (as Mao once put it) to "stand up" in the world. But if the Chinese Communists are simply a "modern nationalist elite," then why do they pursue social policies and proclaim social aims so radically different from so many other modern nationalist elites who dominate the histories of modern

113

nations? Why, for example, did the Kuomintang elite, also modern and also nationalist, ally itself with the big bourgeoisie of the cities and the gentry of the countryside while the Communist elite championed the interests of the workers and peasants exploited by these classes? Why did the Kuomintang in power attempt to preserve the existing social structure whereas Communists in power were intent on radically transforming it? Why, in short, was one modern Chinese nationalistic elite socially conservative while the other socially revolutionary? Contemporary disciples of Pareto and contemporary theorists of "modernization" do not answer these questions; indeed, they do not even bother to pose them. Surely the differences between the two elites cannot be explained in terms of "nationalism" or "modernization," for both were nationalistic and both desired to modernize China. And references to a change in ruling elites explain nothing about social change; the notion of "the circulation of elites," after all, is based on the assumption that revolutions do not and cannot change anything except the personnel of the ruling class.

The Chinese Communist Party originated as an intellectual elite, to be sure, but one that was intellectually committed to Marxism and socialism. An intellectual commitment to Marxism not only demanded a political commitment to revolutionary action but also a social commitment to the liberation of the oppressed and the exploited. However far Chinese Communist revolutionary strategy departed from the premises of classical Marxism and indeed from orthodox Marxism-Leninism, and however ambiguous the relationship between Communist political power and Chinese social classes, the Communists emerged from a rural revolutionary environment without having abandoned their vision of a socialist future. It was this vision that was crucial in determining the social and economic policies that the victorious revolutionaries pursued. In the first three years of the People's Republic, the Communists wrought more fundamental changes in the social structure of China than had occurred in the previous 2,000 years. And at the end of 1952, having completed what were deemed to be the essential "bourgeois" tasks of the revolution, the Communists prepared to move the revolutionary process to a new stage—the transition to socialism. If the Communists shared with the Kuomintang the nationalist goal of "wealth and power," they differed from their vanquished predecessors in that they viewed wealth and power not as the ultimate end but as the means to attain Marxian socialist ends.

Marxist and Leninist Views on Economic Backwardness and Socialism

Yet if an intellectual commitment to Marxist theory provided the impetus to attempt a socialist transformation of society, that same body of theory taught that socialism was a historical impossibility under conditions of economic backwardness. Nothing is more central to Marxism than the proposition that socialism presupposes capitalism, that socialism becomes a real historical potentiality only on the basis of the material and social accomplishments that only the full development of modern capitalist forces of production bring about. For Marx (and for Lenin as well) the large-scale capitalist development and organization of modern industry, a high level of specialization in the division of labor based on the complexities of modern technology, and the collectivistic patterns of social labor thereby produced, are the essential prerequisites for socialism, for only these processes create the necessary conditions of economic abundance on which the future socialist society must inevitably rest. Moreover, there could be no retreat from the course that history presumably dictated. To those who advocated the socialist reorganization of society before capitalism had done its necessary historical work, to those "utopians" who wished to avoid the social evils that capitalist industrialization entailed, Marx once replied that "the country that is more developed industrially only shows, to the less developed, the image of its own future."[1] Indeed, the Marxist predecessors of Mao often warned that a "premature" socialist revolution—one attempted before the full development of capitalist industrialization made the abolition of private property possible—would be historically futile and possibly regressive. Under conditions of economic scarcity, socialism would be what Marx called a "primitive" and "crude" form of "social leveling" that would only lay the basis for the development of more extreme social inequalities and more oppressive kinds of political despotism.

The leaders of the Chinese Communist Party were not unaware of the Marxian-defined material preconditions for socialism, and they were painfully aware that a preindustrial and impoverished China lacked those preconditions. But they confronted a cruel historical paradox. For it was precisely the failure of modern capitalism to develop in China that had permitted socialist revolutionaries to come to power in China in the first place, while at the same time it was also precisely that failure that denied to revolutionaries in power the material means to realize their socialist goals. Had the state or bureaucratic capitalism of the Kuomintang (or of earlier regimes) been successful in establishing a modern industrial economy, as had been the case in Japan and Germany, then the road to revolution would have been closed in China, just as it was closed in other countries that were "latecomers" on the industrial scene and where conservative modernization had proved successful. As it was, the failure of industrialization under conservative regimes had created socioeconomic conditions favorable for revolution under socialist political auspices but left economic conditions that precluded, at least theoretically, the socialist reorganization of society. The Communists were thus both the beneficiaries and the victims of the retardation of modern capitalist development in

China and the consequent heritage of economic backwardness. Possessing
state power, they had no alternative but to use that power to pursue a
non-capitalist road to socialism.

The Chinese were not the first to face the dilemma. The nineteenth-
century Russian Populists had made a socialist virtue out of Russia's
economic backwardness by arguing that it was precisely the relative
absence of capitalist development that gave Russia special social and
moral advantages to allow her to become the pioneer socialist country.
Russia could "bypass" the capitalist phase of development and proceed
immediately to a socialist restructuring of society on the basis of the
precapitalist village commune (mir). By appropriating modern technologies of the advanced industrial nations of the West within a new socialist
framework, Russia could avoid the social evils of capitalist industrialization and the moral decadence of bourgeois society. Marx did not dismiss
the Populist argument out of hand. He recognized that some of the possible "advantages of backwardness," such as the role of cultural contact,
foreign borrowing, and the utilization of traditional communal forms of
social life might telescope the socioeconomic phases of modern historical
development.[2] But his ultimate conclusion was that such advantages
could be turned to socialist ends only if a revolution in preindustrial
Russia coincided with proletarian revolutions in the industrialized countries of Western Europe.[3] In the final analysis, the potentiality for socialism resided in the material and social products which only capitalism
had brought into being: modern industry and the modern proletariat.

Marx's conclusion formed the essential theoretical perspectives held
by Lenin on the eve of the Bolshevik Revolution of 1917. However much
he departed from original Marxism in the realm of revolutionary strategy,
for Lenin, the Russian Revolution was to serve as the "spark" that would
ignite the long delayed and necessary socialist revolutions in Western
Europe. Revolution in Russia was not seen as a non-capitalist road to
socialism but rather as a political event whose socialist promise was ultimately dependent on the timely intervention of the proletariat of the
advanced industrialized countries. But for Lenin, unlike Marx and unlike
the Populists, the possibility of bypassing capitalism soon came to be a
concrete political question and not merely a theoretical one. When the
anticipated socialist revolutions failed to materialize, the Bolsheviks were
confronted with the problem of what to do with a successful anti-capitalist
revolution in an economically backward and politically isolated country,
a problem anticipated neither in the theories of Marx nor of Lenin. While
Lenin harbored the most grave doubts about the historical viability and
moral validity of attempting to build a socialist society in conditions of
economic and cultural backwardness, his response to the problem generally foreshadowed the "revolution from above" over which Stalin was
to preside. Lenin's conclusion, briefly put, was that the survival of Bol-

shevik political power was dependent on using that power to complete what was in effect a bourgeois socioeconomic revolution, to carry out in the most rapid and rational fashion possible the yet unfulfilled tasks of capitalist economic development under socialist political auspices. Above all, this meant rapid urban industrialization, which in turn presupposed an authoritarian state which would impose its control over the country-side and extract from agricultural production the capital necessary for the industrial development of the cities. Lenin's preoccupation with the need for rapid economic development (which he stressed increasingly after mid-1918) was reinforced by what is often referred to as his "tech-nocratic bias" (epitomized by his striking shorthand formula that "elec-trification plus Soviets" equals socialism, his slogan "learn from the capitalists," his fascination with the work efficiency and managerial ra-tionality of "Taylorism," and his emphasis on the primacy of heavy in-dustry), as well as by his unqualified praise of the virtues of the central-ization of both political and economic life. While the brutalities and irrationalities of Stalinism were in no sense immanent in Leninism, Lenin provided the ideological and policy points of departure for the Stalinist strategy of rapid urban industrialization based on forced rural collectiv-ization, the nature and social consequences of which are now too well known to require discussion here. In view of his bitter anti-Populist polemics, it is one of the ironies of history that Lenin was forced to assume the historical role of the pioneer of a "non-capitalist road to socialism" or, more precisely, a road assumed to have a socialist end. The guiding theoretical premise of postrevolutionary Leninism (and more explicitly of Stalinism) was deceptively simple: the combination of rapid economic development with the existence of socialist state power and the nationalization of the key means of production would more or less auto-matically guarantee the arrival of a socialist society. And in 1952 the Chinese Communists uncritically accepted this assumption.

The First Five Year Plan: Industrialization and the Transition to Socialism

Unlike the Russian Bolsheviks three decades earlier, the Chinese Com-munists were not haunted by the Marxist theoretical dilemmas posed by economic underdevelopment, for the Soviet historical experience had dem-onstrated to their satisfaction that it was possible to employ the power of a socialist state to industrialize a backward country. Yet if the Chinese could derive psychological and ideological comfort from the Russian ex-perience, there was nothing comforting in the objective economic prob-lems they faced. Even at its peak pre-1949 levels, the modern industrial sector of the Chinese economy was less than half the size of its czarist Russian counterpart; and the population of China was fourfold that of Russia. Even this comparison tends to obscure the extent of China's backwardness. China's modern industrial base was not only tiny but one built largely under foreign imperialist auspices, and thus far more dependent on external economic relations than had been the case in Russia. Moreover, agricultural technology was even more primitive than it had been in prerevolutionary Russia. And China suffered from a higher rate of illiteracy and a generally lower level of education, especially in modern science and technology.

Despite the revival of a war-wrecked economy, at the end of 1952, when the government announced the First Five Year Plan, total industrial and agricultural production was still barely higher than the levels attained in the mid-1930s. At a comparable time in Russian postrevolutionary history, when Stalin launched the Soviet Union's First Five Year Plan in 1927, per capita industrial output in Russia was more than four times greater than China's in 1952. Per capita agricultural output in China in 1952 was only about 20 percent of what it had been in the Soviet Union twenty-five years earlier, thus offering a far smaller potential for extracting capital from the rural sector for urban industrialization. Moreover, modern transportation facilities were much less developed.

China thus began her drive for modern industrial development in economic circumstances far less favorable than those from which Soviet industrialization had proceeded. If Russia lacked the Marxian-defined material prerequisites for socialism, this was infinitely more the case in China. Yet the very absence of the objective conditions for socialism served to stimulate efforts to bring those very conditions into being; if China was even more backward than Russia, it was the very consciousness of that backwardness that gave the Chinese Communists an even greater determination to overcome it. Just as Chinese Marxist revolutionaries did not wait passively on the historical sidelines for capitalism to lay the material and social basis for revolution, Chinese Marxists in power were not disposed to rely on a "natural" process of economic development to bring about a socialist society or its material prerequisites. The socialist reordering of society and the building of the economic preconditions for it had to be accomplished by utilizing the political and human resources on hand—and both had to be done simultaneously, and in the here and now. The beginning of the First Five Year Plan for industrialization in January, 1953 was thus accompanied by announcements that the bourgeois-democratic phase of the revolution was passing and that its socialist phase was beginning. On October 1, 1953, the fourth anniversary of the founding of the People's Republic, the government formally proclaimed "the general line for the transition to socialism."

The Chinese Communists viewed the problem of building a socialist society in an economically backward land as an enormous practical task, but not as an agonizing Marxist theoretical question, perhaps partly because they had never been intellectually burdened by orthodox Marxist perspectives on the relationship between political and economic forces in history. Nevertheless they did not believe that socialism could be built amidst conditions of poverty. The proposition that socialism demanded (even if it did not necessarily presuppose) industrialization was a constantly emphasized theme in Chinese Marxist theoretical and popular writings and no one emphasized it more strongly than did Mao Tse-tung. The development of "a powerful industry with the state-owned enterprises as its main component" was the prerequisite to the collectivization of agriculture whereas the latter was the prerequisite for a "complete and consolidated socialism,"[4] as Mao insisted at the time.

In 1953 the order of the day was industrialization and the First Five Year Plan was essentially a plan for the development of heavy industry. To be sure, at the same time the Communists launched the Five Year Plan they also announced the beginning of China's transition to socialism. But the emphasis was less on the transformation of social relations than it was on modern economic development. "Socialism" at the time meant the more or less gradual abolition of private property. In the cities this resulted in the nationalization of most of the remaining private sector of the urban economy between 1953 and 1956. In the countryside, it was limited to the gradual introduction of cooperative forms of farming in a rural economy based on individual peasant proprietorship. It was not until late 1955, with the launching of a campaign for rapid collectivization, that rural social relationships were suddenly and dramatically transformed in a socialist direction. But the essence of the Five Year Plan, at least through 1955, was an intensive drive for rapid urban industrialization to establish the economic foundations for socialism. It was a drive characterized above all by the wholesale adoption of Stalinist methods, techniques, and ideological assumptions.

In retrospect it seems strange that the Chinese should have so uncritically accepted the Soviet model of development. Mao, after all, long had warned against the dangers of applying foreign techniques to Chinese conditions. "China has suffered a great deal from the mechanical absorption of foreign material," he wrote in 1940.[5] The Chinese revolution itself was massive historical proof of the Maoist determination to domesticate Western theories and adapt foreign-derived formulae to the concrete needs of the Chinese historical environment. The CCP, after all, had come to power by forging its own revolutionary strategy, by rejecting Russian domination, and Mao Tse-tung had come to power in that party in direct defiance of Stalin. Yet however much the Chinese distrusted Stalin's revolutionary advice, they apparently had no reservations about his strategy for postrevolutionary development. The Soviet Union provided the only historical model for industrializing an economically backward country under socialist political auspices. Nor were there any doubts at the time about whether Stalinist means of economic development had led to the desired social ends. The question of whether the Soviet Union was a socialist society or not was never debated; it was simply assumed to be the case. Although the Chinese knew little about the nature of Soviet society other than what they had read in official Soviet textbooks, it was an article of faith that Russia was "the land of socialism," as Mao had put it in 1940, and "a great and splendid socialist state," as he proclaimed in 1949.[6] And although Mao consistently had been critical of "the mechanical absorption of foreign material," he was remarkably uncritical in accepting the Soviet pattern of development as the appropriate model for China. If anyone harbored heretical doubts about these views, they did not, and dared not, express them.

Quite apart from the general faith in the Soviet Union as "the land of socialism," there were other more immediate and practical reasons why the Chinese looked to Russia. For one thing, the Chinese leaders saw Russian economic and technological aid as essential for their industrialization program. China hardly could expect such aid from the capitalist countries, especially not in the cold war years, and assistance provided by a presumably socialist country was seen as more desirable in any event. Russian economic aid and technicians began flowing into China with the signing of the Sino–Soviet Treaty of Friendship, Alliance, and Mutual Aid in February 1950, following the first of Mao's two pilgrimages to Moscow. Among other provisions, the Russians agreed to provide China with fifty model industrial units. Obviously, Russian factories manned by Russian economic specialists demanded the adoption of Soviet methods of economic and managerial organization. With the launching of the First Five Year Plan, the continuation and expansion of Russian economic aid, and perhaps more importantly, access to Russian technology and experience in centralized economic planning, became more essential than before. New Sino–Soviet agreements in 1953, 1954, and 1956 provided precisely for that. Although Soviet assistance was to prove much more limited than the Chinese had hoped for, and was to prove to have far greater political implications than anticipated, it nevertheless was a highly significant factor in the early industrial development of the People's Republic.

The adoption of the Soviet model of economic development was also closely related to Chinese national security concerns. Long before the victory of 1949, Mao had proclaimed the inevitability of China "leaning to one side" in international affairs. As he put the matter in 1940, "unless there is the policy of alliance with Russia, with the land of socialism, there will inevitably be a policy of alliance with imperialism. . . ."[7] However much the Maoists had come to politically distrust the Russians during the revolutionary years, there was never any question as to which side a Communist-governed China would lean. The need for a political alliance with the Soviet Union in a hostile international arena was powerfully reinforced by American support of Chiang Kai-shek during the civil war and even more by United States intervention in Korea and Taiwan. And the political tie served to reinforce an already strong predisposition to emulate the Soviet pattern of postrevolutionary socioeconomic development.

At the beginning it was Mao Tse-tung who took the lead in advocating the Russian way. "The Communist Party of the Soviet Union is our best teacher and we must learn from it," he proclaimed on the eve of the establishment of the People's Republic.[8] Just as Lenin had advocated "Learn from the capitalists," the Maoist slogan during the early years of the People's Republic was "Learn from the Soviet Union," although Maoists then believed that they were emulating a model of socialist development as well as learning the technology necessary for modern economic development. The popular rallying cry of the time was "Let's be modern and Soviet."

In the formative years of his intellectual development, during the New Culture era of 1915–1919, Mao had been a follower of the New Youth intellectuals who believed that the panacea for China was learning the principles of "science" and "democracy" from the advanced capitalist countries of the West. Now the Chinese Communists no less uncritically and no less enthusiastically looked to Russia to teach them modern science and modern socialism. Maoists soon were to become disillusioned with their Soviet model, just as the youthful Mao and his intellectual mentors had become disillusioned with their Western bourgeois models almost four decades earlier.

Nature and Economic Results of the First Five Year Plan (1953–1957)

The First Five Year Plan began in January 1953 on the orthodox Marxist assumption that socialism presupposed a high level of industrial development and with the orthodox Marxist–Leninist view that industrialization (and thus the necessary material foundations for a socialist society) could best and most rapidly be accomplished in an economically backward land under the centralized direction of a strong socialist state power. Further assumed, in good Leninist and Stalinist fashion, was that the socialist transformation of social relations, or what Maoists called "proletarianization," would follow more or less naturally in the wake of industrialization. Chinese leaders also accepted the Marxist, and the general Western, assumption that industrialization demanded urbanization. Much of the history of the People's Republic would later revolve around disputes over these issues. But in 1953 these were the universally accepted premises with which China began her search for "wealth and power"— and for socialism.

The details of the First Five Year Plan were not publicly revealed until mid-1955—precisely at the time, paradoxically, when Maoists began to question its theoretical premises—but its general outline was determined at a meeting of the party's central committee in the autumn of 1952.[9] The Chinese plan was closely patterned on the Soviet First Five Year Plan of 1928–1932 and it was anticipated that China could achieve similar rates of growth in both industrial output and industrial employment.[10] While it was expected that industrialization would proceed rapidly, the Chinese leaders at the time held long-term perspectives on the transition to socialism; Mao predicted it would require three five year plans to lay minimally necessary economic foundations for a socialist society, and the remainder of the century "to build a powerful country with a high degree of socialist industrialization."[11]

The State Planning Commission was established in 1952 to determine production targets and quotas and how they were to be accomplished. Over the following years it was supplemented by the creation of a variety of more specialized central-government economic ministries and organs of planning and control. The Chinese plan emphasized to an even greater degree than had been the case in the Soviet Union the development of such heavy industries as steel, machine building, fuel, electric power, metallurgy, and basic chemicals. Only 11.2 percent of state capital investment in industry was to go to light industry (consumer production) while 88.8 percent went to heavy industry.[12] The priority was justified both on grounds of national defense and because of the structural imbalance of the imperialist-dominated modern sector of the pre-1949 economy, where industrial backwardness in general was aggravated by the dominance of processing industries dependent on imported raw materials.[13] It was assumed that the establishment of a heavy industrial base was the prerequisite for both the development of consumer industries and the technological modernization of agriculture. The amount of state investment in the rural sector was negligible.[14]

While what remained of privately owned urban enterprises were effectively nationalized between 1953 and 1956, the socialization of agriculture was seen as a long-term process dependent on the prior socialist industrialization of the cities. According to Li Fu-ch'un: "For the laboring peasants . . . to give up finally the way of the individual small producer and step out on to the new highroad of socialist development calls for a step-by-step process, a fairly long period of hard work and certain necessary transitional forms of organization."[15]

While intensive efforts were made to develop the heavy industrial base established by the Japanese in Manchuria, the government emphasized the need "to build up new industrial bases [as opposed to the large treaty-port cities like Shanghai and Canton] in North, Northwest and Central China, and make a start with a part of our industrial construction in Southwest China." Of the 694 major industrial enterprises to be built during the 5-year period, 472 were to be located in the interior. The purpose was to correct the geographical imbalance left by the imperialist heritage, and to build new industries closer to sources of raw materials and to areas of consumption and distribution.[16]

The 156 industrial units that the Russians had agreed to supply (in accordance with the treaty of 1950 and the supplementary economic agreements of 1953 and 1954) were regarded by the Chinese planners as "the core of the industrial construction programme" and the economic models for the whole First Five Year Plan.[17] Mao and other Chinese Communist leaders were as effusive in their praise of Soviet generosity as they later were to be bitter in their condemnations of Russian perfidy. At the time, the "fraternal assistance of the Soviet Union" was typically described as "an expression of the noblest and loftiest spirit of internationalism."[18]

In actuality, Russian financial aid was very limited, accounting for only 3 percent of total Chinese state investment for economic development during the period of the First Five Year Plan. And the Russians paid for less than one-third of the cost of even the original 156 industrial units.[19] More significant than Soviet financial assistance was access to their technology and experience in centralized economic planning. The Russians supplied the equipment necessary for the rapid installation of model factories and the personnel (and training of Chinese personnel) necessary for their operation. In addition, the Soviets provided detailed blueprints and technological information for the establishment of a wide variety of other industrial plants and construction projects. Over 12,000 Russian and East European engineers and technicians were sent to China in the 1950s while over 6,000 Chinese students were trained in modern science and technology in Russian universities and some 7,000 Chinese workers were sent to the Soviet Union to acquire experience in modern factories. Thus the Chinese were not wholly dependent on their own meager technological resources. Nevertheless, during the First Five Year Plan "97 percent of the investment for basic development came from the Chinese people themselves."[20]

Between 1952 and 1957 Chinese industry grew at an even more rapid pace than the ambitious 14.7 percent yearly increase set in the Plan.[21] The actual per annum increase was 18 percent, according to official statistics, and 16 percent according to more conservative Western estimates.[22] Total Chinese industrial output more than doubled, and the growth in key heavy industries was even greater, despite a 1956 revision of the plan which placed a somewhat greater emphasis on light consumer industries. Rolled steel production, for example, increased from 1.31 million metric tons in 1952 to 4.48 million in 1957; cement from 2.86 million to 6.86 million; pig iron from 1.9 million to 5.9 million; coal from 66 million to 130 million; and electric power from 7.26 billion kilowatt hours to 19.34 billion.[23] In addition, China was now for the first time producing small but significant numbers of trucks, tractors, jet planes, and merchant ships. In all, the Chinese had proved to be excellent students of the Soviet model, for Chinese industrial production between 1952 and 1957 grew more rapidly than Russian industry during the first Soviet Five Year Plan of 1928–1932.[24]

At the same time, of course, urban industrial employment increased substantially, from approximately 6,000,000 workers (including construction workers) in 1952 to an industrial working class of about 10,000,000 in 1957.[25] And China's urban population increased from 70,000,000 to almost 100,000,000 in the 5-year period, with the most rapid growth taking place in the newly industrializing inland cities of the North and the Northwest. In 1957 there were 13 cities with populations of over 1,000,000 as opposed to only 5 in 1949.

The First Five Year Plan provided China with a significant and stable modern industrial base, even though it was still a tiny one compared with the advanced industrial countries. But this success was not achieved without social and economic costs, and the major costs were borne by China's 500,000,000 peasants—for the industrialization of the cities was based largely on the exploitation of the countryside. While the cities were rapidly industrializing, agricultural production was stagnating. According to probably inflated official statistics, the output of food grains between 1952 and 1957 increased at an annual rate of 3.7 percent; according to foreign estimates, the increase was more on the order of 2.7 percent, hardly keeping pace with the 2.2 percent average annual population growth. Nevertheless, the capital for urban industrialization was extracted primarily from the countryside by means of a relatively high state grain tax and high quotas of grain which peasants were forced to sell to government stores at low state-fixed prices. The industrialization of the 1950s was a remarkable economic accomplishment by any standard of judgment, but like all economic advances in history it was based on the exploitation of one part of society by the other. Nor did industrialization resolve the chronic problems of urban unemployment and underemployment, problems that were aggravated by the spontaneous migration of millions of peasants from the depressed rural areas to the developing cities.

As much as anyone, it was Mao Tse-tung who launched the program for rapid urban industrialization. But there was little distinctively

"Maoist" about the way in which the process took place. For "Maoism" as a distinctive strategy of socioeconomic development had not yet emerged on the historical scene—and it was to do so only in response to the social and political consequences of Soviet-style industrialization.

Political Results of the First Five Year Plan

The decision to adopt the Soviet model of industrialization necessitated the development of Soviet-type forms of political organization and state administration. Centralized economic planning demanded the rapid bureaucratization and routinization of state and society. The Maoist preference for administrative simplicity gave way to complex and increasingly specialized structures; the cadres of a revolutionary party were transformed into administrators and bureaucratic functionaries; workers in factories were subjected to increasing control by factory managers; the revolutionary ideal of the "guerilla" generalist was replaced by a new-found faith in the virtues of specialization and the technological specialist; old egalitarian ideals clashed with a new hierarchy of ranks and the emergence of new patterns of social inequality; the revolutionary faith in the initiative and spontaneity of the masses and mass movements faded as industrialization demanded authoritarian discipline, social stability, and economic rationality; socialist goals were postponed and partly ritualized in favor of the immediate and all-embracing goal of economic development. The tendency for revolutionaries to become bureaucratic rulers began in 1949, but it was now vastly accelerated. The whole character of political and social life was increasingly determined by the economic targets of the Plan. It was an eminently Stalinist development, albeit without the irrationalities and brutalities of a Stalin to preside over the process.

Bureaucratization was most immediately apparent in the expansion and centralization of the formal state apparatus, particularly in the proliferation of government agencies responsible for the development and control of the modern sector of the economy. The State Planning Commission, similar in organization and function to Stalin's Gosplan, was established in November 1952 to direct the industrialization process. It was originally headed by Kao Kang, the political and economic czar of Manchuria, where Soviet influence was strongest and Soviet political and economic methods most firmly entrenched. Bureaucratic centralization and complexity were further increased and formalized in 1954 with the creation of the State Council, the main organ of the central government and the successor to the Government Administrative Council; its power, and thus state power in general, lay in its standing committee, whose membership was almost identical with the politburo of the Party. The State Council generated and directed an enormous number of specialized organs dealing with economic life, a variety of temporary and permanent committees (such as those dealing with Capital Construction, State Economics, State Planning, and Science and Technology), and a multitude of centralized economic ministries. Among the latter, the largest number and the most powerful were concerned with the development of heavy industry; there were, for example, six separate ministries dealing with machine building alone.

Another political result of the Plan was the centralization and expansion in 1954 of control agencies in the Ministry of State Control, a vast and pervasive bureaucratic network to check inefficiencies and corruption in the industrial sector of the economy and to counter local and regional deviations from state economic directives and quotas. Modeled on its Soviet counterpart and the Soviet system of external economic control, it worked closely with secret-police agencies, and, as had been the case of the Soviet Union, the power of the secret police grew with the power of the Ministry of State Control. But the secret-police forces in China, now centralized under the Ministry of Public Security headed by Lo Jui-ch'ing, never were to acquire a fraction of the terrible power they had in Stalinist Russia. However, the general political structure that began to emerge in China in the mid-1950s increasingly resembled the Soviet state structure of centralized "vertical" forms of bureaucratic rule and control, just as the Chinese First Five Year Plan resembled the Russian one.

As the formal state bureaucracy grew in size and power, the political and ideological authority of the CCP was diluted and its functions underwent subtle changes. In industrial enterprises this tendency was most apparent in the Chinese adoption of the Soviet system of "one-man management," although (except in Manchuria) the system was introduced in a less extreme form with less enthusiasm. The rapid development and efficient operation of large-scale industry demanded a highly specialized system of the division of labor and responsibility based on the criterion of technological expertise. Crucial to meeting this need was the skilled factory manager who had clearly defined lines of responsibility and authority, a man who was responsible for carrying out directives of the central government from above and with the power to implement those directives below in the factory over which he had sole authority. Reflecting the Soviet temper of the times, the need for what was termed "the system of sole responsibility of management" was justified by Lenin's dictum: "Any large-scale industry—which is the material source and foundation of production in socialism—unconditionally must have a rigorous unified will to direct the collective work of hundreds, thousands, and even millions of men. But how can the rigorous unity of wills be assured?

Only by the wills of the thousands and millions submitting to the will of a single individual."[26] The introduction of a Soviet-type managerial system was a logical result of the First Five Year Plan and was well in tune with the general bureaucratization of state and society, for "one-man management" firmly established a chain of command from the central government in Peking down to the lowest levels of the individual plant or enterprise.

The system had grave implications for both the role of the party organizations in the factories and for the workers who labored in the factories. As Franz Schurmann observed:

> In the early 1950s the Chinese, emulating the Soviet experiences, sought to place great power in the hands of the managers. The Party's role was to be limited to that of moral leadership. The commands that counted came from high echelons in the administrative system. Management commanded and the worker had to obey. . . . The factory, under one-man management, was conceived of as a coldly rational arrangement of individual workers commanded by an authoritarian manager.[27]

The professional industrial managers were drawn largely from the pre-1949 technological intelligentsia, for few party members possessed the necessary technical and economic expertise. And those party members who had or acquired such expertise served as economic managers first and as political leaders second. The manager who controlled the factory was primarily responsible to the economic demands of the central government ministries, and increasingly less to the political demands of the factory party organization. Nor were local Party officials and cadres able to challenge the authority of the manager, for they themselves were responsible to the directives of higher-level Party organs and ultimately to the same Party leaders who controlled the State and determined its economic policies. Although it constantly was repeated that managers were to be under "the ideological leadership of the Party," the significance of this injunction was problematic; it was the Party, after all, which had given the managers their authority in the first place and the operational ideology of the Party at the time was centered on fulfilling the economic targets of the Five Year Plan.

For the workers, the industrialization drive meant subjection to increasingly strict codes of labor discipline set by state policy and implemented by factory management. It also meant increasing wage and status differentials within their ranks. The more skilled workers were put in charge of factory work teams or became foremen exercising authority over former fellow workers. In wage policy there was a growing emphasis on material incentives, with monetary rewards for skill, expertise, and productivity, a policy that culminated in the "wage reform" of 1956, formalizing wide wage differentials based on the criteria of skill and output. Before the First Five Year Plan trade unions had acquired some degree of independence as representatives of the interests of the workers, but by the mid-1950s the unions had become instruments to raise workers' productivity, in effect, instruments of management and of state and party economic policies.

The political role of the urban workers was of course ambiguous from the beginning, as was necessarily the case in a society born from a rural revolution in which workers had played little part. As industrialization proceeded and as the proletariat consequently grew in size and in socioeconomic importance in the mid-1950s, the question of the relationship of the proletariat to state and society became even more ambiguous. For while the workers benefited economically and materially from industrialization, the manner in which industrialization was carried out left Chinese workers with little more to say about the operation of the factories in which they worked than workers in capitalist countries. The authoritarian managerial system negated any hope of moving toward the socialist principle of workers' control of industry while the general bureaucratization of political life further removed the working class from the centers of political power—from a state which, in theory, they "led," and from a Communist party which was theoretically the party of the proletariat.

The social composition of the Party, and its patterns of recruitment, are revealing in this respect, even if such statistics do not reveal much about where the real levers of political power lay and who controlled them. In 1949 Communist leaders emphasized the need to build an urban proletarian base for a party then composed almost entirely of peasants, but the results of the effort to make the "party of the proletariat" a real proletarian party met with mixed success at best. In 1957, at the end of the First Five Year Plan, those officially classified as workers made up less than 13 percent of party membership. Workers were outnumbered by intellectuals and the latter were being recruited at a much more rapid rate. Since the beginning of 1949 party membership had increased fourfold, from a little over 3,000,000 to 12,700,000, but most of the new members came from the countryside.[28] Moreover, the emphasis in urban recruitment during the mid-1950s was on strengthening the upper levels of the Party by drawing in those who already occupied positions of socioeconomic importance; intellectuals and technicians were favored over workers, and skilled workers were given preference over the non-skilled.

More important than the social composition of the Chinese Communist Party was its transformation into a bureaucratic organization and the erosion of its revolutionary spirit, tendencies particularly reflected in the changing nature and function of Party cadres in the 1950s. The term "cadre" (kanpu), narrowly defined, means someone who occupies a leadership position in an organization; for all practical purposes, it refers to a Communist Party member who is a leader in a Party organ or in a Party-dominated institution or mass organization. During the revolutionary years, the concept of the cadre acquired a far broader meaning as a revolutionary leader. Ideally, the cadre is a selfless person imbued with the proper revolutionary values and committed to the achievement of revolutionary goals, a person of "all-round" ability able to perform a variety of tasks and capable of quickly adapting to changing situations and requirements, one who is both "red and expert" but first and foremost politically and ideologically "red" and potentially "expert," a person who faithfully carries out party policy yet does so with independence and initiative, a person who submits to the discipline of the party organization but at the same time is intimately tied to the masses; as Mao formulated it, the cadre is both "the teacher and the pupil of the masses," and indeed must be their pupil before he can become their teacher. The ideal cadre is the very antithesis of the bureaucrat who "dozes at his desk" or the official who commands from behind his desk. The Communist revolution owed its success in large measure to the fact that there were indeed many such Party cadres who more or less measured up to this Maoist ideal of revolutionary leadership. They were people committed to the goals and ideals of revolution, not to a vocation or a career.

It was inevitable that the reality, if not the ideal, of the cadre would change after 1949 when revolutionaries became rulers. Cadres filling posts in the new state apparatus had to undertake more specific functions in political and economic administration and were required to learn specialized skills. Once leaders of the masses in a revolutionary situation, party cadres were becoming state administrators governing the masses—and often doing so from office desks, which further separated a new governing elite from the governed masses. Before 1949 the party attracted and recruited revolutionaries; after 1949 it increasingly attracted people who saw Party membership as the avenue for a career in government. Moreover, increasing numbers of nonparty people with experience and expertise in administration and economic affairs became cadres after 1949 to run the expanding bureaucracy—and were later recruited into the party less because of their political and ideological commitments than because they now occupied leadership positions in the new postrevolutionary order.

During the First Five Year Plan "old revolutionaries," who clung to the simple values and heroic ideals of the revolutionary era, were increasingly overshadowed by the "new cadres," who were more motivated by vocational ethics and the values associated with industrialization. Conflicts and tensions between the "old" and "new" cadres intensified as industrialization proceeded and as the technician and engineer replaced the revolutionary as the new social model. From the "old revolutionaries"

there came complaints that the bureaucratization of political and economic life was a repudiation of the revolutionary heritage and a betrayal
of socialist ideals. From official quarters came criticisms of the "village
habits" and the "guerilla mentality" of old cadres unable to adapt to the
rational division of labor and responsibilities which the new industrial
order demanded. The "wage reform" of 1956 symbolized the victory, at
least temporarily, of the new cadres. The old cadres had come from a
revolutionary milieu and were the carriers of the values of a spartan and
egalitarian style of life and work. In the early years of the People's Republic they had been treated in a relatively equal fashion, the government providing housing, food, and a small monetary allowance for the
basic necessities of life. By 1955, however, cadres were divided into 26
distinct ranks with corresponding salaries ranging from 30 to 560 *yuan*
($12–$224) per month; and in the cities, at least, rank assignments
largely were determined by the importance of the cadre in the industrialization process. The new inequality was defended in official theory
by the argument that China was not a communist society but only in
transition to socialism, a situation which demanded that people be paid
according to their contribution and not according to their needs. Old
revolutionary cadres who had not reconciled themselves to the new order
of things were accused of the ideological heresies of "absolute egalitarianism" and "equality mongering."

The bureaucratization of the party and its cadres was a development that fitted well the general temper of the times, a temper molded
by the all-embracing drive for modern industrialization, and one characterized by a newly found faith in the powers of modern science and
technological specialization. "Rationalize," "systematize," and "regular-
ize" were the slogans of the day and they reflected, as Vogel has observed, "a radical departure from the 'guerrilla mentality,' "[29] in effect,
an implicit repudiation of the Maoist revolutionary heritage. In the process, the goals proclaimed in Marxist theory tended to become ritualized.
While socialist and communist goals were still ardently proclaimed, and
no doubt ardently believed, the really operative goal was rapid industrial
development, and the actual governing values were those most conducive
to industrialization—the values of economic rationality and administrative efficiency.

The Kao Kang Case

If the Chinese leaders saw Soviet economic methods as both necessary
and desirable, they were not about to allow the Russians to acquire political dominance over China in the process. They had fought too long and

hard to prevent Moscow from gaining control over their party during the revolutionary years to permit Moscow now to reap the political fruits of their revolutionary victory. And it was their bitter experiences with the Comintern during the revolutionary decades that made them acutely sensitive to the danger. It was precisely that fear which lay behind the first major political purge in the Chinese Communist Party in the history of the People's Republic—and one that was to be a prophetic pointer to the future history of Sino–Soviet relations. The principal victim of the 1953–1954 purge was Kao Kang, the head of the party and state apparatus in Manchuria, and the main issue involved, although unstated at the time, was Russian political influence in Manchuria.

During the revolutionary years, Kao Kang had acquired seemingly impeccable Maoist political credentials. A leader of peasant guerilla forces in Northwest China in the early 1930s, Kao was one of the founders of the Communist base area in Shensi where Mao brought the survivors of the Long March at the end of 1935. During the war years he worked closely with Mao in consolidating control over the party and was the head of its Northwest China Bureau in Yenan. After the defeat of the Japanese in 1945, and the subsequent renewal of civil war with the Kuomintang, Kao was dispatched with Lin Piao's army to Manchuria, where he came to head the party and state apparatus of the Northeast. He was also a member of the politburo, chief of its secretariat, and in 1952 was appointed chairman of the new State Planning Commission, and thus the man principally responsible for carrying out the First Five Year Plan.

The political downfall of Kao Kang, and the expulsion of his followers from the party, was determined at a December 1953 politburo meeting and formalized by the party's central committee in February of 1954. Kao was charged with having set up an "independent kingdom" in Manchuria (independent, that is, of the control of the central government in Peking) and having organized a conspiracy to seize state power. Allegedly, he conveniently responded to the accusations by committing suicide. It is a mark of the secretiveness that has generally enshrouded important political and economic decisions in the People's Republic that the purge was not revealed to the Chinese people until more than a year later, in March 1955.

What was not publicly mentioned at all was the fear of Soviet political penetration that Kao's "independent kingdom" in Manchuria symbolized. While there is little evidence to substantiate the vague charges of any nationwide conspiracy to seize power, there is much to suggest that Kao had close political ties with the Russians, who continued to exercise strong influence in Manchuria long after their postwar military occupation of the region had ended. Direct Soviet aid and participation restored the heavy industrial base of Manchuria after Soviet troops had carried

away much of Manchurian industry as "war booty" during the occupation period. The Russians controlled the joint Sino–Soviet stock com-
panies, established in 1950, and retained their hold on the Central Manchurian Railroad (and its economic subsidiaries) as well as Dairen and
Port Arthur. These were not returned to Chinese control until 1955, after
the death of Stalin and the removal of Kao Kang. While Kao Kang
reigned in Manchuria, however, Soviet economic and political influence
also was dominant and there is little to suggest that Kao objected to it.
Kao reportedly went on a mission to Moscow as early as 1945.[30] He did
so again in July of 1949, when in his capacity as head of the People's
Government of the Northeast (Manchuria), he negotiated an economic
agreement with the Soviet Union, several months before the formal establishment of the People's Republic in Peking and before Mao's negotiations with Stalin in February 1950. Moreover, Kao was the foremost
advocate of Soviet methods of industrial organization, both before and
after the inauguration of the First Five Year Plan, and nowhere were
these methods introduced and pursued more rigorously than in Manchuria, China's major center of heavy industry.

The Kao Kang affair was partly a case of what it was presented to be
—a case of a region acquiring an intolerable degree of autonomy from
the central government in Peking. But Kao's "independent kingdom" in
Manchuria was intimately tied to Soviet predominance in an area which
historically had been a key object of Russian expansionism in East Asia.
To bring Manchuria under the control of Peking meant throwing off Russian control. It is not entirely fortuitous that the fall of Kao Kang followed shortly after the death of Stalin; it was the apparent weakness and
instability of the post-Stalin Soviet leadership that made Peking sufficiently confident to remove Kao and move against Soviet influence in
Manchuria. The move resulted in a temporary improvement in Sino–
Soviet relations, and a more equal relationship between the two countries,
symbolized by Khrushchev's late 1954 visit to Peking and the Russian
agreement to relinquish their positions in Manchuria.

While the fall of Kao Kang is one of the more opaque episodes in the
political history of the People's Republic, there is no doubt that Mao regarded the former czar of Manchuria as Stalin's foremost representative
in China. Several years after the event, in a private talk highly critical of
Soviet influences in the Chinese party over the decades, Mao observed:
"Stalin was very fond of Kao Kang and made him a special present of a
motor car. Kao Kang sent Stalin a congratulatory telegram every 15
August." (August 15, 1945 was the date of the Japanese surrender to the
Soviet Union). And Mao referred to Manchuria and Sinkiang as two
former Soviet "colonies" in the People's Republic.[31]

The purge of Kao Kang was accompanied by the purge and disappearance of Jao Shu-shih, who controlled the party and state apparatus

in the Shanghai region (East China Central Bureau). Jao also was the head of the Organization Department (Orgburo) of the party cental committee and one of the original members of the State Planning Commission. Like Kao, he was accused of running an "independent kingdom," and was charged with being allied with Kao in a conspiracy to seize state power. There is nothing to indicate that Jao Shu-shih had any Soviet ties or any special pro-Soviet proclivities. What he and Kao had in common was that they controlled the two major industrial centers of China, Manchuria and Shanghai. Why the two were linked in what later became denounced as the "Kao–Jao anti-party conspiracy" remains obscure, as does the nature of the alleged conspiracy itself.

The SuFan Campaign

The March 1955 party conference also launched a more general and extensive bureaucratic purge, the *SuFan* movement, or the "Campaign to Wipe Out Hidden Counterrevolutionaries," which continued through the early months of 1956. In the wake of the Kao Kang incident, "hidden" acquired an ominous significance; if leaders so high and powerful as Kao Kang and Jao Shu-shih could turn out to be counterrevolutionary conspirators, then no one was above suspicion. Unlike the 1951 campaign against counterrevolutionaries, *SuFan* was primarily an internal party affair marked by constant references to reactionaries "cloaked as Marxist–Leninists." Any party cadre under suspicion was detained, interrogated, and in the manner of past "rectification" campaigns, required to make written or oral "confessions" detailing past and present political views and associations. An atmosphere of fear pervaded the bureaucracy during the latter half of 1955 as some 150,000 party and government cadres were investigated. Many tens of thousands who were deemed to hold "wrong attitudes" and labeled as "counterrevolutionaries," were sent to "labor reeducation" camps, usually by administrative decrees which bypassed regular criminal procedures. Most were released and reinstated by mid-1956, often with official apologies for having been falsely accused.

The *SuFan* campaign was undertaken, in part, to eliminate the suspected followers of Kao Kang and Jao Shu-shih. More significantly, it was an attempt to reestablish centralized party control over the economic and political bureaucracies which the First Five Year Plan had spawned. The power of the State Planning Commission, dominated by pro-Soviet professionals, was drastically reduced, as was the power of managers in industrial enterprises. Closer party supervision was established over the various economic control agencies and especially over the Ministry of State Control. The reassertion of party power over the latter was per-

haps the most important development over the long run. While *SuFan*
resembled a Stalinist bureaucratic purge in many respects, it differed
significantly in that it served to reduce rather than enhance the hitherto
growing power and independence of the secret police. As it later was
officially interpreted: "The first task of the (*SuFan*) movement was to
strengthen the leadership of the Party over public-security work, to put
public-security agencies under Party leadership."[32]

The *SuFan* campaign, however extensive, was a rather feeble response to the endemic problem of bureaucracy in a presumably socialist
society, for it contributed nothing to the only socialist remedy for the
problem—popular control over bureaucratic organs of rule. The evils of
bureaucracy, which Mao had so long denounced, remained and grew—
and nowhere more than within the party which Mao chaired.

The growing power of party bureaucrats was dramatically revealed
when the *SuFan* movement came down particularly hard on intellectuals
in 1955, a development foreshadowed by an extraordinary political-ideo-
logical campaign against the Marxist literary critic Hu Feng. A follower
of the celebrated Lu Hsun, Hu Feng long had been an outspoken critic
of official party literary policies and party dictates to writers and artists.
One of the most prominent nonconformists within the left-wing literary
movement, his debates with more orthodox Communist literary figures
extended back to the mid-1930s. After the establishment of the People's
Republic, Hu Feng, committed to Marxist socialist aims and generally
supporting party policies, nevertheless continued to oppose the political
stifling of artistic and intellectual creativity and warned of an approaching "cultural desert." He continued to be assailed, as he had been since
the late 1930s, for his "subjectivism" and his "bourgeois" deviations from
Maoist principles of art and literature. His main protagonist in the earlier
debates, Chou Yang, was now firmly entrenched as the party's czar on
literary and cultural matters.

Although Hu Feng found it difficult to get his writings published
after 1949, and while many of his followers were the victims of the
thought-reform movement of 1951 and the ensuing "literary remolding"
campaign, Hu was still treated as a revolutionary writer whose ideological errors were amenable to proper Maoist reform and therapy. Indeed,
in a brief era of relative freedom for intellectuals in 1953, Hu was appointed to the executive board of the Chinese Writers' Union. Optimistically seeing the promise of a new birth of freedom, he wrote a report
to the central committee of the party in July 1954 criticizing the restrictions imposed by party literary bureaucrats and appealing for the freedom
of writers and artists to express their creative talents. Open discussion of
the report soon gave way by the end of the year to a nationwide campaign of vilification against Hu Feng as an archetypal representative of
bourgeois ideology. The attack was first led by Hu's old adversary Chou

Yang, but the full weight of the party was thrown against him when Chou En-lai joined in the public denunciations. As the *SuFan* movement got under way in the spring of 1955, Hu Feng was portrayed not only as an ideological heretic but as a political subversive as well—an agent of the Kuomintang and of imperialism, it was said. In July he was arrested and imprisoned as a "counterrevolutionary."

The campaign against "Hu Fengism" continued after Hu was removed from the scene, for its real purpose was to establish strict ideological controls over the intelligentsia in general. The campaign served both to silence intellectual dissent and to create deep resentments against the Party among intellectuals.

Social Consequences

Since Chinese industrialization proceeded largely on the basis of Soviet methods, it is hardly surprising that it should have produced similar social tendencies. The most significant social result of the First Five Year Plan was the emergence of new patterns of inequality.

The imperatives of rapid industrial development, or at least the imperatives of the manner in which it was pursued, gave rise to two new bureaucratic elites (albeit still embryonic ones) exercising increasingly formal control on the basis of their respective spheres of expertise. One was a political elite of Communist leaders and cadres rapidly becoming administrators and functionaries in the growing state apparatus that presided over the industrialization process; the second was a technological elite of engineers, scientists, and managers necessary for the development and operation of the expanding modern economic sector. These newly emerging social groups tended to become increasingly motivated by professional and vocational ethics, rather than by Marxist goals and communist values, and increasingly separated from the masses of workers and peasants by virtue of status, power, and material benefits.[33]

For the workers, the First Five Year Plan brought increasingly repressive conditions of life and work. Whether factories were run by professional managers or by party officials who functioned as managers, the workers were forced to submit to the ever greater labor discipline that the drive for increased productivity demanded. They were subjected to increasingly repressive forms of control at the places they worked and, through the urban neighborhood resident committees, at the places they lived as well. Moreover, inequalities within the ranks of the working class itself grew as larger wage differentials and monetary rewards based on skill and productivity were introduced.

Inequality was most glaringly apparent in a sharpening distinction between town and countryside. The industrialization of the cities was based in good measure on the exploitation of the countryside. While material conditions in the cities improved, the rural economy was largely stagnant, thus widening the economic and cultural gap between the modernizing cities and the backward countryside.

The new educational system, heavily influenced by borrowed Soviet methods and curricula, tended to reinforce these tendencies toward social inequality and stratification. The growth in formal education was highly impressive. Between 1949 and 1957 the number of primary school students more than doubled (from approximately 26,000,000 to more than 64,000,000) and university enrollments increased fourfold, from 117,000 to 441,000. But the urban population benefited from the new educational opportunities far more than did people living in the rural areas. Although officially proclaimed policies gave preference to the children of workers and peasants, in practice the examination requirements for admission to middle-schools and universities strongly favored the sons and daughters of the already privileged strata: the old bourgeoisie, higher party and government officials, intellectuals, and technicians. And to meet the needs of industrialization, the educational system in general, and university education in particular, overwhelmingly emphasized science and technology. Much like its Soviet counterpart, Chinese higher education functioned to create and perpetuate a privileged technological intelligentsia.

When the First Five Year Plan was launched at the beginning of 1953, the government also had announced the inauguration of the era of "the transition to socialism." While the pursuit of modern economic and industrial development was clear enough, the meaning of socialism became increasingly ambiguous. Chinese society seemed to be moving further away from, rather than closer to, the socialist future that the revolution had promised. Industrialization served to further increase the division between town and countryside; the separation between mental and manual labor tended to grow sharper; new social elites emerged to take up the more complex tasks demanded by the newly emerging industrial order; and the state became stronger and more oppressive, presided over by an increasingly bureaucratized party. Modern industrial development was conceived as the means to achieve socialist ends, but as time went on industrialization itself became the primary goal while socialist goals tended to be postponed to an ever more distant future.

Mao and "Maoism" were soon to be forced to confront the dilemma of means and ends that the results of the First Five Year Plan posed. And just as the Maoist revolution itself was born and developed in the rural areas, Maoists again were to turn to the countryside to revive the socialist goals and spirit of a revolution that was dying.

Notes

1. Karl Marx, Preface to *Capital* (Chicago: Kerr, 1906), 1:13.

2. For a fascinating analysis of Marx's consideration of Russian Populist ideas, and their influence on him, see A. Walicki, *The Controversy over Capitalism* (Oxford: Clarendon Press, 1969), pp. 179–194. That Marx entertained the possibility that the traditional village commune might serve as the basis for Russia's modern socialist regeneration is suggested in his March 8, 1881, letter to Vera Zasulich. See Karl Marx and Frederick Engels, *Selected Correspondence* (Moscow: Foreign Languages Publishing House, n.d.), pp. 411–412.

3. In his preface to the 1882 Russian edition of *Capital,* Marx held out the possibility that the precapitalist village commune might serve as a "starting point" for socialist development—but only if a revolution in Russia served as the "signal" for proletarian revolutions in the Western European countries.

4. Mao Tse-tung, *On People's Democratic Dictatorship* (Peking: Foreign Languages Press, 1959), p. 14.

5. Mao Tse-tung, "On New Democracy," *Selected Works of Mao Tse-tung* (Peking: Foreign Languages Press, 1967), 2:380.

6. Mao, *Selected Works* (1967), 2:364 and 4:423.

7. Mao, *Selected Works* (1967), 2:364. With the achievement of state power, Mao put the matter in more forceful terms: "All Chinese without exception must lean either to the side of imperialism or to the side of socialism. Sitting on the fence will not do, nor is there a third road" (4:423). In the context of the time, "the side of socialism" was of course the Soviet Union.

8. Mao, *On People's Democratic Dictatorship,* p. 19.

9. The general principles of the plan were publicly outlined in a *People's Daily* editorial on September 16, 1953. The detailed plan, probably revised downward over the following two years, was presented to the Second Session of the First National People's Congress on July 5–6, 1955 by Li Fu-ch'un, then chairman of the State Planning Commission. See Li Fu-ch'un, "Report on the First Five Year Plan for Development of the National Economy of the People's Republic of China in 1953–1957," translated in Robert R. Bowie and John K. Fairbank, *Communist China 1955–1959: Policy Documents with Analysis* (Cambridge, Mass.: Harvard University Press, 1962), pp. 42–91.

10. According to official statistics, industrial output grew approximately 18 percent per annum in Russia during the first Soviet Five Year Plan while the industrial working class increased from 3,000,000 to 8,000,000. For an analysis of why the Chinese believed they could match the Russian performance, see Christopher Howe, *Employment, and Economic Growth in Urban China, 1949–1957* (London: Cambridge University Press, 1971), pp. 102–104.

11. Li Fu-ch'un, "Report on First Five Year Plan," p. 48.

12. *Ibid.*, p. 59. As calculated by Li Choh-ming, the actual ratio for the 1953–57 period was 87 percent for heavy industry and 13 percent for light industry. Li Choh-ming, "Economic Development," *China Quarterly,* January–March 1960, p. 40.

13. Li Fu-ch'un, "Report on First Five Year Plan," pp. 46–47.

14. Of total state investment for development during the First Five Year Plan, only 8 percent went to agriculture, forestry and water conservation. (Li Choh-ming, "Economic Development," p. 40; figures taken from 1959 State Statistical Bureau "Communiqué on the Results of the First Five Year Plan for National Development.")

15. Li Fu-ch'un, "Report on First Five Year Plan," pp. 48–49.

16. *Ibid.*, p. 60.

17. *Ibid.*, p. 51.

18. *Ibid.*, p. 44.

19. Li Choh-ming, "Economic Development," p. 38.

20. *Ibid.*, p. 39.

21. Li Fu-ch'un, "Report on First Five Year Plan," pp. 53, 61. A higher rate of growth was envisioned in the original draft of the plan in 1952, although how much higher cannot be determined since the original draft was never published. It was reported, however, that downward revisions were made in 1953 and 1955.

22. For Chinese government figures, see *Ten Great Years* (Peking: Foreign Languages Press (1960), p. 87. For the general consensus of Western economists, see Joint Economic Committee of the U.S. Congress, *An Economic Profile of Mainland China* (Washington, D.C.: Government Printing Office, 1967), 1:273.

23. See Table 7–12 in Barry M. Richman, *Industrial Society in Communist China* (New York: Random House, 1969), pp. 636–637.

24. Official Soviet statistics claim a 18.5 percent per annum growth rate, but most Western estimates give a figure of about 12 percent.

25. See Tables 8 and 9 in Howe, *Employment and Economic Growth,* p. 14.

26. Tientsin *Ta Kung pao,* December 31, 1953. Quoted in Franz Schurmann, *Ideology and Organization in Communist China* (Berkeley: University of California Press, 1966), p. 255. For a brilliant and lengthy analysis of this complex matter, see pp. 220–308.

27. *Ibid.*, p. 256.

28. Of the 12,720,000 members in 1957, 1,740,000 were officially classified as workers; 1,880,000 as intellectuals; 8,500,000 as peasants; and 600,000 as "others," presumably mostly soldiers. Total membership was approximately 2.5 percent of the population, the lowest party/population ratio of any Communist country at the time (*ibid.*, pp. 128–139).

29. Ezra Vogel, *Canton under Communism* (Cambridge, Mass.: Harvard University Press, 1969), pp. 127–128. For an analysis of the transforma-

tion of cadres into officials, see *idem*, "From Revolutionary to Semi-Bureaucrat: The 'Regularisation' of Cadres," *China Quarterly*, No. 29 (January–March, 1967), pp. 36–60.

30. According to a Soviet source, Kao and Liu Shao-ch'i went to the Soviet Union in 1945 to discuss issues arising out of the Soviet occupation of Manchuria and Kao's Northeast China Bureau maintained contacts with the Soviet Communist Party thereafter. See James Harrison, *The Long March to Power* (New York: Praeger, 1972), p. 376.

31. Mao Tse-tung, "Talks at the Chengtu Conference" (March 10, 1958), *Mao Tse-tung Unrehearsed: Talks and Letters, 1956–71*, ed. by Stuart R. Schram (Middlesex: Penguin, 1974), pp. 100–101.

32. Ho Kan-chih, *Chung-kuo Hsien-tai Ko-ming-shih* (1958), quoted in Schurmann, *Ideology and Organization*, p. 344.

33. In the mid-1950s, high-level industrial managers and engineers were paid as much as 280 yuan per month while the average workers' salary was 65 yuan. Moreover, the higher members of the technological and managerial elite were provided better housing, paid vacations, and often even servants. The "wage reform" act of early 1956 formalized and widened salary differentials.

10

Agricultural Collectivization, 1953–1957

IN 1953, WITH THE COMPLETION of the land-reform campaign, China was basically a land of individual peasant owner-cultivators. A modern Communist state, ironically, had recreated the traditional Chinese ideal of a system of more or less equal family-owned and -operated farms. And for a few years the traditional ideal was probably more fully realized than it ever had been in China's long history.

Although there remained socioeconomic differences between the majority of poor peasants, a substantial body of "middle peasants," and a small minority of "rich peasants," differences in land holdings and income were relatively small. Virtually every peasant now had a title deed to land unemcumbered by landlords, mortgages, usurers, extralegal bureaucratic exactions, or marauding warlord armies and bandit gangs. It was as close to a "peasants' utopia" as achieved by any society in modern times, the ideal of a relatively egalitarian society in which most families tilled their own farms in relative security. Socially and economically the People's Republic was for a time a "petty bourgeois" society par excellence.

The peasants, for the most part, were deeply attached to the individual family farm, an attachment strongly reinforced by the persistence of traditional habits of work, religious practices, and social values. And the majority who benefited from land reform looked forward to a relatively prosperous life that they anticipated work on their land would bring. Yet the post–land reform rural situation was conducive neither to prosperity in the countryside nor to the modern economic development of the nation. Small farm units and the fragmentation of plots inhibited the introduction of more efficient work patterns and the use of modern methods of agricultural technology, thus severely limiting the potential for increased productivity. In 1953 and 1954, the production of food grains barely kept pace with population growth. Moreover, the peasants bore the burden of a relatively high state grain tax and compulsory deliveries of grain to government stores at fixed low prices. While the state was taking a great deal out of the rural economy to finance urban industrialization, it was putting very little back; under the First Five Year Plan, less than 10 percent of state investment for development went to the agrarian sector.

Quite apart from the poor harvests of 1953 and 1954, there were many other indications of social and economic problems in the countryside. No sooner had land reform been completed, there reappeared the traditional practice of usury; better off and more economically efficient peasants began to lend money to poorer and less efficient ones, and in some cases the debtors were forced to sell their lands to their creditors.[1] It was inevitable that the rural economy, if left to govern itself, would generate traditional forms of exploitation and reproduce old patterns of socioeconomic differentiation.

Another indication of economic difficulties in the countryside was a flood of peasant migrants to the cities. While some went to take jobs in industry, most fled to the cities because of food shortages in the countryside. The result was to intensify already serious problems of urban unemployment and underemployment. During the First Five Year Plan the increase in the population of the cities far exceeded the rate of urban employment growth, partly because the planners gravely overestimated the capacity of the new industries to absorb a larger work force. And the problem was further aggravated by the demobilization of much of the army in 1954–1955, following the signing of the Korean War truce.

The Communists never assumed that land reform alone would result in either the necessary economic revolution in agricultural production or the desired social reorganization of the rural areas. From the beginning they saw land reform as a necessary but transient stage in a process that would lead to the collectivization of agriculture. But they viewed the transformation from individual peasant proprietorship to collective farming as a long-term process that would proceed gradually through three distinct phases of development. The first step would be the organization of mutual aid teams whereby the members of about six or more households would assist each other in the working of their still individual family farms, initially on a seasonal basis and later as a year-around organization, serving to enlarge the working unit and to forge patterns of cooperative work. Second, mutual aid teams would combine into "semi-socialist" or "lower" agricultural producer cooperatives where land would be pooled and farmed cooperatively, although each family would retain private ownership of land and families would divide the crop (or its proceeds) partly in accordance with the labor contributed and partly according to the amount of property pooled. Finally, "lower" cooperatives

eventually would be amalgamated into "higher" or "advanced" cooperative farms, i.e., collectives, which would abolish private land ownership
and remunerate its members in accordance with the socialist principle of
"to each according to his labor."

Both the formation of mutual aid teams and "lower" cooperatives were
to be entirely voluntary—and the peasants who joined were free, at least
according to official policy, to withdraw from them.[2] Party cadres in the
countryside were told to use only methods of persuasion, encouraged to
set up model examples of teams and cooperatives, and were continually
warned against "commandism." Since party leaders were well aware of
the deep attachment of peasants to the family farm, a matter noted repeatedly in party documents of the time, the process of socialist transformation presupposed a long period of popular education. Moreover,
the general assumption was that the socialization of agriculture demanded the modern means of mechanization and technology which only
industrialization could provide; and, since Mao, among others, had said
that the necessary level of industrialization would require at least three five-
year plans, collectivization was seen as a rather distant goal. Those who
called for a more rapid transition were denounced for the heresy of advocating "utopian agrarian socialism." As the party's central committee
summed up the matter in February 1953, "Under the present economic
conditons of our country, the peasants' individual economy will exist to
a very large extent and for a considerable length of time. . . ."[3]

This gradual and cautious approach to rural social change was fully
in accord with Mao Tse-tung's 1949 thesis that modern industrialization
was the prerequisite for the socialization of agriculture, and there is no
evidence to suggest that he dissented from the policies the Party adopted
in 1953. It was not until two years later that Mao was to emerge as the
foremost advocate of "utopian agrarian socialism."

The provisions for agricultural development in the First Five Year
Plan incorporated these gradualist perspectives. The modest target announced in the Plan was that only one-third of peasant households would
be organized into lower-stage agricultural producer cooperatives by the
end of 1957. Nothing was said about the establishment of fully socialist
collective farms. Agrarian social change was no more rapid than envisioned; by mid-1955, about 15 percent of the peasants had joined the
"lower" cooperatives. But the persistence of a small producer's agrarian
economy posed far greater economic problems than had been anticipated. The First Five Year Plan assumed a 23 percent increase in agricultural output and subsidiary rural production;[4] in 1953 and 1954,
however, agricultural production was falling far short of that goal. Since
industrialization was dependent on a developing agrarian economy or,
more precisely, on extracting from the countryside a sizable surplus for
capital investment in the cities, stagnation in the rural economy threat-

ened the industrialization program and created increasing economic hardships among the peasantry.[5] The plight of the peasants was aggravated by a mid-1954 decision prohibiting the sale of surplus grain on the private market; henceforth all grain beyond that consumed by the peasants themselves was to be sold (at the low controlled rate) to the government. While this measure slightly increased what the state was taking out of the countryside, it reduced the income of many peasants. Peasant income was further reduced (and the program of industrialization endangered) when peasants responded to the food shortages of early 1955 by planting more grain to the neglect of industrial crops. That the demands of the First Five Year Plan had imposed grave hardships on the peasantry was later gingerly conceded by Chou En-lai: "In 1954, because we did not completely grasp the situation of grain production in the whole country, and purchased a little more grain from the peasants than we should have, discontent arose among a section of the peasants."[6]

Party leaders, long sensitive to "peasant individualism," recognized that land reform would reinforce the peasants' attachment to their own private plots. This understanding of traditional peasant individualism, however "petty bourgeois" it was in Marxist terms, was reflected in the insistence that cooperative forms of agriculture be introduced only gradually and only by gaining the voluntary support of the peasants, primarily by demonstrating that cooperatives would raise both production and income. Above all, the Communists were determined not to alienate the class to which they so long had been intimately tied and to whose support they owed their revolutionary success. Yet by early 1955 the Communists saw peasant individualism as not only a barrier to social change in the countryside, but as a hindrance to the development of the national economy. A stagnant rural economy threatened industrialization and posed a threat to the internal political viability of the new state, its external security, and to the socialist goals of its Communist leadership.

Concerns over agricultural productivity were accompanied by a growing fear about socio-economic relationships in the countryside. As Mao put the matter in mid-1955: "During the past few years, the influence of forces tending to develop spontaneously toward capitalism has been developing daily in the rural areas; new rich peasants have emerged everywhere, and many prosperous middle peasants are exerting efforts to turn themselves into rich peasants. Many poor peasants, due to their lack of means of production, still remain in poverty, some of them having contracted debts; others are selling their land or renting out their land. . . . If this situation is allowed to develop further, there will become increasingly more serious [class] polarization in the rural areas."[7] Communist leaders expressed increasing anxiety about the rise of an exploiting "kulak" class and the recreation of traditional rural social class differentiations, as a result of the "four freedoms" retained by land reform: the freedom to purchase, sell, and rent land; to hire agricultural laborers; to lend money; and to engage in trade on the private market.

Another manifestation of the persistence of peasant individualism was the inclination of the Party's own rural cadres to succumb to petty bourgeois "peasant ideology." In the period after the land-reform campaign, many cadres who had been the leaders in that campaign withdrew from political activities to concern themselves with their own farms and the welfare of their families. Since rural cadres were themselves peasants, the phenomenon reflected their own latent desires and their own peasant vision of a good society. In some cases it reflected resentments that the rural areas, the wellspring of the revolution, were being neglected as the new state turned its energies to the industrialization of the cities; in other cases it reflected resentments over being forced to remain in the rural hinterlands when the political center of gravity had moved to the dynamic urban areas. Many rural cadres had only the most vague understanding of the socialist aims of the party and saw their political role as representing the general peasant desire to become "rich peasants" in a new era of peace and stability. As Party leaders began to complain, "the attitude of some of our comrades to the peasant question still remains at the old stage.... They are satisfied that the peasants have obtained land from the landlords, and want to keep things as they are in the villages.... They fail to understand that this means ... allowing capitalism to develop freely in the rural areas."[8]

The situation was largely of the party's own making. As the emphasis turned to urban industrialization, the Communists were content to rule the countryside through the formal state bureaucratic apparatus, the *hsiang* governments and the public security organs attached to them. This was sufficient to serve immediate state needs for political control of the rural areas and the collection of taxes and compulsory grain purchases from the peasantry. Little attention was paid to the development of party organization within the villages and cadres who remained in the villages, no longer at the forefront of any social movement, tended to retreat to private endeavors.

The New Agrarian Revolution

Communist leaders originally assumed that the organization of the peasantry into mutual aid teams and the gradual development of "lower" agricultural producer cooperatives would be sufficient to blunt spontaneous capitalist tendencies in the countryside and also increase productivity. By making more efficient use of land, labor, and farm implements through collective efforts, it was believed agricultural production would grow, peasants would be drawn to the virtues of cooperative organization, and the small-producer mentality gradually would be overcome.

There were traditional and earlier Communist precedents for cooperative work in agriculture. In traditional times it was a common practice among peasants, especially those who could not afford to hire agricultural laborers, to exchange labor during planting and harvest seasons, although such arrangements usually were limited to a few families and generally ones already tied together by kinship bonds. And in the war-time base areas, the Communists had organized peasants into mutual aid organizations and experimental cooperative-type farms as well.[9]

In quantitative terms, the post-1949 development of the cooperative movement was impressive, especially in view of the fact that it was, on the whole, organized on a largely voluntary basis. As soon as land redistribution had been completed in a particular area, campaigns were launched to organize individual peasant proprietors into mutual aid teams. Unlike traditional forms of work cooperation, the new teams were larger (consisting of six to twenty or more families), cut across kinship lines, and were quickly transformed from seasonal arrangements to permanent organizations. Moreover, the members of the permanent teams engaged in supplementary handicraft production on a collective basis. By the end of 1952, 40 percent of peasant households had joined mutual aid teams and the figure had grown to approximately 65 percent in early 1955. The percentages were, of course, higher in North China where land reform had come earlier, and lower in the central and southern regions. And while only 15 percent of the peasantry had been organized into semi-socialist cooperatives by early 1955, this was entirely in accord with the gradual and cautious policies that were being pursued.

However, the mutual aid teams and the producer cooperatives were beset with a variety of difficulties. The popular enthusiasm of the revolutionary years and the land-reform campaigns waned in an era dominated by a mood to return to normalcy after decades of turmoil and struggle. Press reports complained that the mutual-aid teams were often only *pro-forma* organizations. Better-off middle peasants, possessing more land and better techniques, often refused to join poor peasants in cooperative efforts. In other cases, middle and rich peasants came to control newly organized cooperatives, to the detriment of poor peasants. While the mutual aid teams and cooperatives facilitated state collections of taxes and grain, they failed to achieve what had been established as the main criterion for their success—a rapid increase in productivity. The harvests of 1953 and 1954 were poor, and there was little to indicate that the "lower" producer cooperatives would fulfill the expectation that they would increase productivity by 30 to 50 percent "within two or three years."[10]

Although the majority of peasants had been organized into various forms of cooperative labor and economic interdependence by the end of 1954, this did not halt the process of growing class differentiations in the rural areas. The problems were attributed to the continued existence of a system of individual peasant proprietorship and the petty producer mentality that accompanied it. Newspaper articles and party reports began to quote Lenin's well-known dictum that "small-scale production gives birth to capitalism and the bourgeoisie constantly, daily, hourly, with elemental force, and in vast proportions."

It was in response to the problem of a stagnating rural economy, a problem which threatened to undermine the whole Five Year Plan for industrial development, and, to a lesser extent, the phenomenon of what Mao later called "autonomous capitalistic forces (which) have been developing day after day in the villages," that Peking once again turned its attention to the countryside. A politburo meeting of October 1954 called for a more rapid timetable for the organization of cooperative farms. In preparation for the new campaign, a March 1955 party conference worked out a program to revitalize party organizations in the rural areas. The formal decision to speed up the pace of cooperativization was made by the party's central committee in May.

Between the October 1954 and May 1955 Party meetings there was much that happened both in the countryside and within the secret councils of the Communist leadership—and there is much that remains obscure. According to Mao Tse-tung's later account, the decision of October 1954 was to increase the number of lower-stage cooperatives sixfold, from 100,000 to 600,000. And again according to Mao, that target had been achieved and exceeded by June of 1955, when there were some 650,000 cooperative farms in operation comprising 16,900,000 of China's 110,000,000 peasant households.[11] However, political opposition to the more rapid pace of cooperativization emerged, apparently reflecting long-standing party differences, and in March 1955 the State Council had ordered a halt to further expansion. The May central committee meeting resumed the campaign, but at a much more gradual pace; 400,000 additional cooperatives were to be organized over the next year and one-half. It was not a decision that Mao found satisfactory, and two months later he was to override it in dramatic fashion.

The secretiveness that shrouds the internal history of the Chinese Communist Party, and the absence of public debate, makes it impossible to be at all precise in reconstructing the political events and the ideological considerations involved in the new agrarian policies that were embarked upon in 1955 and after. From such evidence as is available, it would appear that by early 1955 the top Party leadership had arrived at a loose consensus— and one that Mao did not share. The majority of the central committee believed that an accelerated program of building agricultural cooperatives was necessary if only to ensure meeting the economic requirements for industrialization, and, indeed, satisfying industrial needs was the primary consideration. But they also believed that the cooperatives should be established in an orderly manner and at a gradual pace so as not to endanger agricultural productivity. Moreover, the cooperatives were still to be the "lower" or semi-socialist producer cooperatives; it was generally assumed that a high level of technological development and the means to mechanize agricultural production were the essential prerequisites for fully socialist collective farms, a problem and a prospect that lay well in the future.

The Soviet experience in collectivization was very much on the minds of Chinese Communists in their debates over agrarian policies, and from that experience they derived two lessons. The first was that collectivization too long delayed could lead to rural class polarization and the solidification of a dominant rich peasant class opposed to the socialist state. But the lesson most deeply impressed was that rapid collectivization imposed from above could have catastrophic results. The Chinese were not unaware of the bloody cataclysm that Soviet collectivization had become under Stalin in the early 1930s: the murder or deportation to Siberia of 10,000,000 peasants; the total disruption of production as vast lands were left untilled and livestock slaughtered; and the famines that came in the wake of the holocaust. It was more out of ideological timidity than historical ignorance that Chinese Communists made only the most veiled references to those horrors; they could hardly denounce Stalin's methods of agricultural collectivization at the same time they were pursuing his path to industrialization, quite apart from the general ideological and political considerations that made it impossible to be openly critical of Stalin. Yet, however much they were attracted to the Soviet model of development in general, they were determined to avoid the economic and human costs of Stalinist-style collectivization.

The fear of the emergence of a kulak-type class was a matter of less concern. It was generally assumed that the expansion of party organizations in the rural areas, coupled with the slow and orderly growth of cooperative farming, would be sufficient to check whatever spontaneous capitalist forces that had appeared or would appear.

What had become the party consensus on agrarian policy was summarized in Li Fu-ch'un's report on the First Five Year Plan. The emphasis was on the need for a stable and productive agrarian economy to serve the needs of industrial development. The establishment of cooperative farms would continue, but in a gradual and systematic fashion and on a voluntary basis. The modest goal announced was to expand the existing 600,000 semi-socialist cooperatives to 1,000,000, encompassing about one-third of peasant households, by the end of 1957. The whole thrust of the report was to raise agricultural productivity for the purposes of urban industrialization. The peasants, to be sure, were to be led to socialism, but that would be a gradual transition of unspecified duration, dependent on the mechanization of agriculture and the development of a high level of technology. In the meantime, the state was to offer "vigorous assistance" to individual peasant proprietors who would make up the vast majority of peasant producers for the foreseeable future.[12]

Such, in brief, were the perspectives on the agrarian question generally held by the leaders of the Chinese Communist Party in early July. Before the month was out, Mao Tse-tung single-handedly and dramatically dissolved the consensus with his speech on "The Question of Agricultural Cooperation," thereby launching China on a distinctively Maoist road to "agrarian socialism." As a leading party official later caustically remarked, Mao's speech "settled the debate of the past three years."[13]

The debate was "settled" in a manner unprecedented in the history of the Chinese Communist Party. Mao delivered his speech not to the central committee, in which he was in a minority, but rather to a meeting of provincial and regional party secretaries who were in Peking at the time for a session of the National People's Congress. In effect, Mao overrode the central committee and appealed to the Party at large. It was not until October that the central committee convened to formally ratify the new Maoist policies.

At a time when other party leaders felt that rural cooperatives were being established too hastily, Mao declared the movement was proceeding too slowly.[14] In place of the goal of 1,000,000 cooperative farms to be established by the end of 1957, Mao demanded an additional 300,000 cooperatives and moved up the timetable to the autumn of 1956. By the spring of 1958 no less than half of China's peasant households were to be organized in semi-socialist cooperatives, he declared, and the remaining half were to be drawn in by 1960. However, the significance of Mao's speech lay not in the accelerated timetable he set forth, but rather in the revival of a voluntarist approach to sociohistorical change and a populist faith in the peasant masses to effect that change, the same voluntarist and populist impulses that had characterized Maoism during the revolutionary years. Mao's speech also was an implicit rejection of many of the crucial theoretical assumptions that had guided Communist policies since 1949, thus foreshadowing the Chinese abandonment of the Soviet model and announcing the appearance of "Maoism" on the postrevolutionary historical scene.

"Throughout the Chinese countryside a new upsurge in the socialist mass movement is in sight," were the words with which Mao began, and it was this belief that permeates the whole report. The peasants were demonstrating a spontaneous "socialist initiative" and there was "an active desire among most peasants to take the socialist road." The perceptions and the imagery were strikingly similiar to those of the famous "Hunan Report" nearly three decades earlier, when Mao began his career as an agrarian revolutionary. In 1927 Mao had found the peasant movement to be an elemental, "tornado"-like revolutionary force that would sweep away everything that stood in its way. Now he saw a "tide of social reform in the countryside" soon to "sweep the whole country. . . . This is a huge socialist revolutionary movement which involves a rural population of 500,000,000 strong, one which has very great world significance," he proclaimed, confidently predicting that "an upsurge in socialist transformation will soon come about all over the country's rural areas. That is inevitable." Just as in 1927 Mao had perceived the countryside to be the repository of true revolutionary political energies, now in 1955 he again turned to the countryside to find the forces and impetus for radical social change. Just as the "Hunan Report" announced the appearance of Maoism as an unorthodox strategy of revolution, the 1955 report marked the emergence of Mao as the advocate of a new and no less unorthodox strategy for the socialist development of a backward land.

Mao's 1955 speech harkened back to the "Hunan Report" in another respect: the manner in which he perceived the relationship between the mass movement and the Leninist party. In 1927 he had found the true sources of revolutionary creativity to reside not in the party but in the spontaneous movement of the peasantry acting on its own; it was not the party that was to judge the revolutionary capacities of the peasantry, but rather it was the actions of the peasants themselves that were to serve as the criterion to judge the revolutionary sufficiency of the party.[15] Now again in 1955 Mao counterposed a revolutionary peasantry to a party that was insufficiently revolutionary. While most of the peasants were striving to achieve radical social changes, many party members were "tottering along like a woman with bound feet, always complaining that others are going too fast." It was not the peasants who were backward, but rather it was the party that had become too timid and conservative. Mao gave the conventional warning to avoid both "leftist" and "rightist" errors, but it was clearly from the latter that the party now suffered. "As things stand today," he declared, "the mass movement is in advance of the leadership" and Party members who argued that the cooperative movement had "gone beyond the understanding of the masses" merely revealed their own lack of faith in the masses. And he was bitterly critical of party leaders who "cover up their dilatoriness by quoting the experience of the Soviet Union."[16]

For Mao, the experiences and lessons that really mattered were to be derived from the history of the Chinese Communist Revolution itself. And the most important lesson, the one revived in 1955, was the celebrated Yenan principle of the "mass line," which demanded that distinctively Maoist view of the intimate interrelationship between leaders and masses and which also demanded a process of self-education through revolutionary action. In the postrevolutionary present, just as in the revolutionary past, it was thus necessary to act boldly and act in the here and now:

"Both cadres and peasants will change of themselves as they learn from their own experience in the struggle. Get them into action themselves. They will learn while doing, becoming more capable, and large numbers of excellent people will come forward." Most leaders would emerge from below in the course of the campaign, for the socialist transformation of the countryside was not to be a revolution imposed from above by bureaucratic means. If it was necessary to "send down" cadres from the cities to the rural areas, their first task was "to learn how to work from the movement itself."[17] The "mainstay" of the leadership in organizing the peasants into cooperatives, Mao stressed, was to be "local cadres in the rural areas," the old veteran peasant cadres of the revolution and land reform years as well as newly-recruited peasant members of *hsiang* party and Youth League branches. The cadres sent from above were to be only "an auxiliary force" whose function was to "guide and help," rather than "take everything into their own hands."[18] The ideal leader was to be the Yenan ideal of the local guerilla leader, the cadre who sprung from the peasants of a particular locality and remained closely tied to them.

Mao's July 31 speech marked not only a departure from existing party policies on the pace of cooperativization and the methods to be employed, however important these matters were at the time, but also set forth new perspectives on the ends the movement was to serve and on the more general question of the relationship between economic development and social change. The policies that the Communists had pursued through mid-1955 had been governed by two hitherto unquestioned assumptions. One was that the major purpose of cooperative farming was to increase agricultural production in order to provide the capital necessary for the industrialization of the cities. As the building of a modern industrial order tended to become the overriding goal, rather than the means to achieve socialist ends, economic productivity and the ability of the state to extract an increasing surplus from the rural economy tended to become the criteria for determining the utility and value of agricultural cooperativization. Secondly, it was assumed that the socialization of the peasantry presupposed the industrialization of the cities, for only modern industry could provide the technology and the mechanization for large-scale collective farming. In 1949 Mao had accepted (and indeed had promoted) these views; by 1955 he had come to reject both assumptions. His July speech implicitly challenged the first and explicitly repudiated the second.

On the one hand, Mao now placed as much emphasis on the social and economic benefits that collectivization would bring to the peasants themselves as he did on its potential for financing industrial development. The majority of peasants remained impoverished, Mao noted, and the socialization of agriculture was the only means "to throw off poverty, improve their standard of living and withstand natural calamities." It was not simply the means to an urban industrial end. Industrialization and the socialist transformation of the countryside were two interlocking revolutionary tasks, Mao argued, warning against attempts to "over-estimate the one and underrate the other." Behind this warning there lay a deep resentment that the First Five Year Plan had led to the exploitation of the rural areas for the benefit of the cities—and a challenge to the whole strategy of urban industrialization and the Soviet model of socioeconomic development.

Secondly, Mao now rejected the proposition he himself had put forward in 1949: the view that the socialization of agriculture was dependent on the prior development of "a powerful industry."[19] Instead, he now argued that "the economic conditions of our country being what they are, technical reform will take longer than social reform."[20] And he estimated that the modern industrial base necessary to carry out a technological revolution in farming would "take roughly four or five five-year plans, that is, twenty to twenty-five years." In the meantime, the socialist transformation of the countryside was not to be delayed: "In agriculture, under the conditions prevailing in our country, cooperation must precede the use of big machinery."

In the summer of 1955 Mao still viewed the socialist transformation of rural China as a fairly lengthy process, even though a more rapid one than many party leaders thought practical or possible. The movement, he emphasized, was to proceed in accordance with the "principles of voluntariness and mutual benefit." He was no less insistent than others that coercive methods and disruptions in production be avoided. And he was more opposed than anyone to any sort of "revolution from above." But he was confident that the majority of the peasantry—the 70 percent classified as poor and lower-middle peasants—would move to socialism on their own accord and that the remainder would follow their example when they saw the economic benefits of cooperative farms. The immediate program still centered on the organization of lower-stage or semi-socialist cooperatives, and that would take four and one-half years to complete. The establishment of fully socialist collectives would proceed more slowly and also on a voluntary basis, and that would require another decade. The still relatively gradual process Mao envisioned in the summer of 1955 was to be overtaken by the extraordinary events of the winter of 1955–1956.

Formal Party approval of what was already *de facto* policy came in October in the form of a document entitled "Decisions on Agricultural Cooperation," apparently authored by Ch'en Po-ta, one of Mao's closest personal and ideological associates. The document essentially repeated the views Mao had set forth in July and added detailed guidelines for the organization and operation of cooperative farms.[21]

High-level party opposition to the Maoist program remained, and was to reemerge shortly, but the opponents were silenced and denounced as "right opportunists" as the program was put into action in October, just after the fall harvest was completed. The harvest had been a good one, and this no doubt facilitated the launching of the movement. During the intervening months, between Mao's July speech and the October central committee meeting, regional and local party leaders were engaged in frenzied efforts to revitalize and expand the rural party organizations to implement the campaign.

Cooperativization proceeded at an extraordinarily rapid pace in the last months of 1955 and the results far exceeded even Mao's most optimistic expectations. By the end of the year, 1,900,000 lower-stage cooperatives had been organized, almost 50 percent more than the goal of 1,300,000 Mao had proposed for the following October. The expansion of the size of the cooperative farms was as remarkable as the increase in their number. In July 1955 cooperatives had an average membership of 26 households; in December the average was 40 households. Sixty-three percent of the peasantry had now joined cooperatives, more than a fourfold increase since midyear. The movement from below had acquired a fantastic momentum of its own, and Mao responded from above in terms that anticipated the full-blown utopianism of the Great Leap Forward era. He described the cooperativization movement as "a raging tidal wave [that] had swept away all the demons and ghosts" and attributed its success to a belief that "the people are filled with an immense enthusiasm for socialism."[22] The peasants who were transforming the Chinese countryside, and who had made 1955 "the year of decision in the struggle between socialism and capitalism," were motivated not merely by economic self-interest but more importantly by an inherent spirit of "socialist activism." It was this long-held faith in the spontaneous "socialist" strivings and actions of the peasantry that was the most striking feature of Mao's views on what he called "the high tide of socialism" in the countryside. While the cooperative movement was bringing about fundamental social and economic changes, Mao's emphasis was on the "severe ideological and political struggle" that the movement involved and especially on the decisive role of ideas in transforming objective historical reality. "Before a brand-new social system can be built on the site of the old," he wrote, "the site must first be swept clean. Old ideas reflecting the old system unavoidably remain in people's heads for a long time. They do not easily give way."[23] The fact that old ideas and old institutions were being swept away by the actions of the peasants, that they had dispelled the "dark clouds" that hung over China in the first half of 1955, fortified Mao's faith in the revolutionary creativity of the peasantry and in the power of ideas and consciousness. Thus he confidently predicted that "by the end of this year [1955] the victory of socialism will be practically assured."[24] It was a prophetic pointer to the future evolution of Maoism that Mao saw events in the countryside and the conscious actions of the peasantry as the decisive factors in China's transition to socialism.

Since the goals Mao had set forth in the summer of 1955 were surpassed within a few months, new targets were announced at the end of December. Semi-socialist cooperativization was to be completed by the end of 1956, and the transition to fully socialist collectives would take place over the next three to four years.[25] In late January 1956 the politburo further accelerated the timetable, calling for full socialist collectivization to be completed in 1958.[26]

The revised targets, as well as the realities of the rapidly changing social situation in the countryside, demanded revisions in rural social class policies. At the beginning of the cooperativization drive, the policy was to organize the poor and lower-middle peasants as the spearhead of the movement. Upper, or "well-to-do" middle peasants were to be drawn in only gradually, through the forces of example and education. It was feared that middle peasants (who provided a good part of the surplus collected by the state) would reduce productivity to a subsistence level if they believed their economic interests were being jeopardized. Rich peasants and ex-landlords, on the other hand, were to be politically and economically isolated, and prohibited from joining cooperatives, for it was feared that rich peasants might gain control of the new organizations by virtue of their superior education and abilities and what remained of their traditional influence as village leaders. Moreover, there was a concern that rich peasants might establish "sham" cooperatives, composed largely of wealthier peasants, thus perpetuating old socioeconomic inequalities disguised in new forms.[27]

With full collectivization in sight sooner than anticipated, however, it became imperative to draw the entire rural population into the collectives. Rich peasants still owned a substantial share of the land in many areas, and often the most fertile land, as well as a good portion of the better agricultural implements and livestock. Since the socialist collectives that were emerging from an amalgamation of the lower-stage cooperatives were much larger organizations and generally coincided with the natural village (*ts'un*), the persistence of individual family farms was no longer organizationally feasible or economically desirable. Moreover, since the establishment of collectives meant the abolition of the private ownership of land and remuneration for peasants in accordance with the socialist principle of "to each according to his labor," the fear that rich peasants might maintain their economic dominance receded as collectivization proceeded. Thus, in January of 1956, the politburo attempted to resolve the problem of transforming rich peasants and ex-landlords into ordinary peasants. "Those who have behaved well and worked well," were "allowed to join cooperatives as members and change their status to that of peasants." Others deemed less well behaved were to be subject to various restrictions and means of supervision.[28] In June virtually all barriers to admission were removed,[29] and the vestiges of social-class differences in the countryside seemingly were eliminated.

The newly revised and radically ambitious collectivization goals announced by party leaders in January were quickly overtaken by the movement from below. Collectivization was nearly completed during the first half of 1956, and accomplished largely without violence. As the campaign gained increasing momentum in the early months of the year, virtually all remaining individual peasant proprietors were organized into lower-stage cooperatives and the latter were rapidly transformed into socialist collectives. By the end of the summer, some 100,000,000 peasant households (or 90 percent of the peasant population) had joined approximately 485,000 collective farms, or what were officially called "higher-stage agricultural producer cooperatives"; virtually all of the rest were drawn in before the spring planting of 1957. Except for tiny plots individual households were permitted to till for their own consumption or for sale on the private market, private land ownership was abolished, and all peasants, at least in theory, worked the land collectively in accordance with the principle of "equal pay for equal work."

The transition from semi-socialist cooperative farms to fully socialist collectives was a far less difficult task—and a less traumatic experience for the peasants involved—than the original establishment of the lower-stage cooperatives. Even though collectivization was a much more radical social change, involving as it did the complete socialization of property (including draft animals and major farming implements), organizationally it was a much less complex matter. The former "lower" cooperatives remained as production brigades within the new collectives. Moreover, the earlier cooperative organizations already had introduced the peasants to the principles and habits of collective work. The general policy of making collective farms correspond to *ts'un* boundaries simplified organizational problems and served to make peasants more receptive to the new system. Although collectivization was completed much sooner than even the most radical Communist leaders had anticipated, the transition was made in accordance with Mao's injunction that it should be brought about in a fashion that would "minimize any feeling [among the peasants] that their mode of life is being changed all of a sudden."[30]

Nevertheless, the rapid socialization of agriculture was not accomplished without creating serious organizational and economic problems. During the most intensive and decisive period, the first half of 1956, peasant resistance was minimal. While most upper-middle peasants, who constituted about 20 percent of the rural population, and the smaller number of rich peasants no doubt were less than enthusiastic about having their properties collectivized and being reduced to the status of ordinary peasants, they did not resort to overt resistance. There were scattered reports of the slaughter of farm animals and some vague references in the press and party documents to efforts of former landlords and rich peasants to sabotage the movement, but there was no violent peasant resistance and the state refrained from employing force. The compulsion generated by the movement itself was sufficient to sweep the wealthier peasants into the collectives. Serious manifestations of dissatisfaction among the peasantry did not appear until after the collective farms had come into being, and then it took mostly nonviolent forms— the withholding of labor efforts, withdrawals from collectives, sometimes spontaneous disbandments of collective farms entirely (especially in the southern provinces, where often they had been established in a particularly hasty manner), and a renewed exodus of peasants to the cities in the last months of 1956 and early 1957.

Despite these problems, collectivization in China was accomplished in a manner that stands in striking contrast to its brutal Soviet precedent. The manner in which Stalin brought "socialism" to the Russian peasants is well known. Armed forces were sent from the cities to carry out a rural "movement" that assumed the character of a military campaign and became a virtual civil war between town and countryside. Villages were literally surrounded by Red Army troops, forced to surrender, and reluctant peasants herded into collectives by machine guns. Those who openly resisted were shot on the spot. Stalin's policy of "liquidating the kulaks as a class" meant the liquidation of 10,000,000 peasants, since kulaks were not allowed to become members of collectives even if they wished to do so. Millions were killed outright and millions more deported to desolate lands in Siberia. Most of the remaining "collectivized" peasants were thrown into sullen opposition to the regime, a political result that came back to haunt Moscow during the Nazi invasion. The immediate economic results were catastrophic; half of Russia's livestock was destroyed, production ceased over wide areas of the countryside, and the ensuing famine came near to wrecking the very industrialization drive collectivization was designed to serve. By comparison, China's collectivization was an almost peaceful social revolution. Collective farms were established without the use of guns or soldiers, peasant resistance was confined to a minority of the rural population and took passive and nonviolent forms, and the country was not thrown into economic chaos.

Little light is shed on the reasons why the Russian and Chinese experiences were so different by references to differing historical traditions in prerevolutionary rural life. Chinese peasants were no less firmly attached to their land and to the ideal of the individual family farm than peasants in Russia or elsewhere; indeed, Chinese Communist leaders, as well as Western observers, believed that Chinese peasants had a particularly strong reverence for their land. Nor were old collectivistic village traditions as strong in traditional China as they had been in czarist Russia, even discounting Russian Populist idealizations of the allegedly "socialist" traditions of the village *mir*. In no premodern society had private property in land developed further, or existed longer, than it had in imperial China—and nowhere was the ideal of the individual peasant proprietor more firmly imbedded. If sociohistorical and cultural traditions were crucial factors, then the abolition of private property should have been much more difficult in the Chinese countryside than in Russia and should have encountered far more stubborn resistance.

Certainly one factor of enormous importance for understanding why this was not the case was the particular nature of socioeconomic conditions in rural China on the eve of collectivization. In China, the rich peasants who survived the land-reform campaigns were, proportionately, a much smaller class than the Russian kulaks and a much less powerful one. And, unlike the kulaks, the rich peasants in China were not permitted the time or conditions to consolidate themselves as a class of capitalist farmers dominant in the rural economy. Moreover, in China, unlike Russia, the great majority of peasants were impoverished; they had little to lose and could be convinced that they might have something to gain by collectivization. In Russia in the late 1920s, two-thirds of the peasantry were "middle class" peasants who aspired to kulak status and who were firmly resistant to socialist collectivization.[31] In China in the mid-1950s, two-thirds of the peasants were, as Mao described them, "still badly off." The Chinese countryside held a much greater mass of destitute peasants who were potentially amenable to radical social change.

Yet it is unlikely that that potential could have been tapped had it not been for the particular character of the Chinese revolution and the distinctive nature and methods of the Chinese Communists. While the Russian revolution had been based, in Leninist theory, on an alliance between the proletariat and the peasantry, in fact the Bolsheviks had no significant following among the peasantry and little in the way of an organizational structure in the rural areas. Lenin had taken the Socialist Revolutionary Party to be the political representative of the peasantry, and after its suppression in 1918, the countryside, insofar as it was not left to itself, was ruled by a wholly urban-based administrative apparatus. The Chinese revolution, on the other hand, had been led by a party composed mostly of peasants, which had mobilized tens of millions of rural inhabitants for revolutionary action. However much the party had urbanized itself in the 1950s, it retained deep organizational roots and strong ties to the peasantry, which were revitalized in 1955. The socialization of the Chinese countryside was accomplished by the local cadres and activists who came from among the poorer peasants and remained closely tied to them and who were thus able to bring into being a genuine mass movement from below. It is inconceivable that so massive a social transformation could have come about so rapidly and relatively peacefully without the active participation of a very substantial portion of the peasantry. And it is equally inconceivable that peasants could be mobilized to effect so radical a transformation in their social lives had it not been for the rural revolutionary heritage of the CCP. Mao had neither the need nor the inclination to organize a brutal "revolution from above."

In view of the vast differences in both the nature and results of collectivization in China and Russia, it is strange that Mao Tse-tung, when he launched the Chinese campaign in 1955, felt obliged to applaud the agrarian successes of Stalin during "the six years between 1929 and 1934" and to declare that "the Soviet Union's experience is our model."[32] One cannot attribute this homage to Stalin—and indeed to a now dead Stalin—to Mao's ignorance of Soviet history, for he was well aware of the terrible human and economic toll Stalin had exacted during those "six years," and he was not about to plunge China into a similar disaster. That he felt a need to claim he was following the Soviet "model" is an incongruity that bears on the larger question of the relationship between Maoism and Stalinism, a relationship filled with the most complex and puzzling ambiguities. For the moment, it need only be noted that, in the instance of collectivization, Mao invoked the ideological authority of Moscow and Stalin to launch a very non-Stalinist mass movement—just as in the pre-1949 years he had hailed Stalin in public pronouncements while defying him in revolutionary practice.

It was inevitable that collectivization, especially in view of the unanticipated rapidity with which the transition took place, would result in at least temporary economic dislocations and organizational confusion. If the establishment of collective farms had proved less difficult than the organization of the lower-stage cooperatives they replaced, their functions and operations were much more complicated and posed far more difficult tasks of economic and political management. The collectives were much larger organizations than the cooperatives, averaging 246 households (or about 1,200 people) as opposed to several dozen households—and in some cases the collectives included many individual peasant proprietors who had not joined, or who had been excluded from, the lower-stage cooperatives. Moreover, the collectives demanded much more complex fiscal procedures and methods of economic planning. With virtually all land, animals, and farm implements now transformed into collective property, peasants were to be remunerated in accordance with the amount of labor they contributed, mostly in the form of a share of the crop and partly in the form of small cash payments. Each collective was thus faced with the problem of establishing, on the basis of very general state regulations, an equitable system of work norms and wage standards and a fair way of calculating the number of "work days" or "workpoints" accumulated by its members. In addition, the collectives were confronted with the task of fairly long-term economic planning, determining how much of the crop was to be distributed to the peasants and how much was to be set aside for welfare needs and capital investment after meeting state tax and grain-delivery requirements. All of this demanded complex bookkeeping and accounting procedures that most collectives were ill-equipped to undertake. While the young cadres drawn from poor peasant families and demobilized soldiers had been effective leaders in organizing the peasantry for establishing collective farms, few possessed the managerial and fiscal skills to operate them in an effective manner. The dispatch of urban cadres and middle-school graduates to the countryside did little to alleviate the organizational problems that beset the collectives and served to aggravate other problems. Whatever technical and managerial talents they possessed were more than offset by their unfamiliarity with rural problems and their difficulties in adapting to the rigors of life in the countryside; the "sending down" of urbanites increased the burdens on the fragile rural economy; their "city ways" compounded the perennial problems of "commandism" and "bureaucratism," and their presence was generally resented by the peasantry. Because of the lack of a local rural leadership trained in the techniques of large-scale economic planning and management, the first year of collectivized farming was plagued by organizational confusion and uncertainties about how the system was to function.

Despite the early problems of collectivization, there were modest increases in the production of food grains in 1956 and 1957, averaging about 4 percent per annum. This itself could not have been disappointing to the advocates of rapid collectivization, since they had warned earlier that it would take several years for the collectives to demonstrate their economic superiority. However, such gains in productivity as were achieved did not necessarily benefit the producers. On hastily organized and poorly managed collectives there were sharp drops in production. Moreover, most peasants judged the new system by their own incomes and standards of living, not on the basis of general production statistics or future promises. On the matter of income levels in the early post-collectivization period, the picture is murky. On a national level, there was a general leveling of peasant income; in 1957 per capita income and expenditure differentials between those formerly classified as poor, middle, and rich peasants were slight. This meant that a substantial portion of the rural population—about 25 percent who were formerly upper-middle or rich peasants—were less well-off than they had been before. And it was not necessarily the case that there was any universal increase in income among the remaining 75 percent. Collectivization reduced subsidiary production on private plots and handicrafts, thus adversely effecting peasant income in general. The press reported administrative confusion in many collectives, resulting in inequities in the distribution of the harvest. Even where there were productive gains, uncertainty about how to meet the competing demands of the state, the collective, and the individual peasants often meant that the latter did not derive any immediate benefits from increased production. And where production seriously declined, all peasants experienced reductions in income and serious economic difficulties. Dissatisfactions in the immediate aftermath of collectivization led to desertions from collectives and often their dissolution, a movement led by former rich and middle peasants for the most part, but often joined by others as well.

Although party leaders often publicly attributed these economic and organizational problems to sabotage by former landlords and rich peasants who still harbored counterrevolutionary hopes, it was soon recognized that the newly collectivized peasants lacked sufficient incentives to increase their productive efforts. In the last months of 1956 and throughout most of 1957, the government moved to stabilize and liberalize the regulations governing the functioning of collectives. Mao, in a temporarily less optimistic mood, predicted that five or more years of work and consolidation would be required to establish collectivization on a sound foundation. In the meantime, policies were oriented to increasing agricultural production by providing greater material incentives for the peasantry. State agricultural taxes and compulsory grain purchases were reduced to 25 percent of the total output in 1956–1957 and the peasant producers guaranteed no less than 60 percent of the collective harvest. Greater freedom was given to peasants to work on private plots and sell what they produced on the private market. The First Five Year Plan was slightly revised to place more emphasis on the development of light industry to provide more consumer goods. The size of economically inefficient and organizationally unwieldly collectives was reduced. In 1956 the average collective numbered 246 households; in 1957 the number had been reduced to 169. Once the proper size had been determined in accordance with local conditions, it was proclaimed that there should be no further changes for at least 10 years. For the peasantry the new policies promised a moratorium on further social change and a period of economic stability.

The more "liberal" agrarian policies were designed to raise agricultural production, and in that they were eminently successful, as the excellent harvest of 1958 was to demonstrate. But they also gave rise to a seemingly unresolvable dilemma. The purpose of a higher agricultural output was not only to alleviate the economic difficulties of the peasantry but also to provide the state with a greater marketable surplus of grain and raw materials necessary for capital investment in urban industry. Yet the very measures taken to give the peasants the material means and incentives to raise productivity deprived the state of the surplus required to fulfill the industrial targets of the First Five Year Plan and the more ambitious goals announced for the Second Five Year Plan, due to begin in 1958. By taking a lesser share of the agricultural output and by devoting more capital to light consumer industries, the state assisted the rural economy and the peasantry but undermined, at least in the short run, its own plans for rapid industrialization.

The dilemma was to be resolved—and new dilemmas were to be created—at the end of 1957, when Mao led the Party to embark on that momentous and extraordinary campaign that came to be known as the Great Leap Forward. Just as he had personally intervened in the summer of 1955 to "settle" the debate on the pace of collectivization, he now was to intervene with a much more radical solution for the problem of the relationship between agricultural and industrial development.

The Maoist policies of the Great Leap Forward era, particularly the formation of the people's communes, were to bring to a head a long-simmering internal Party debate over the course of Chinese socioeconomic development, and they were to create divisions within the Communist leadership that were to prove irreparable. The debates and divisions were to remain hidden within the inner councils of the party for another decade, not to be publicly revealed until the party itself was burst asunder in the Cultural Revolution. But the origins of the conflict go back to mid-1955, when Mao delivered his speech on agricultural cooperativization. As rapid cooperativization was quickly succeeded by rapid collectivization, many Party leaders had come to believe that Mao and his followers had become reckless utopians, pushing radical social change much more rapidly than could be sustained by China's weak economic base. At the same time Mao was becoming convinced that an increasing bureaucratized party and state apparatus had become conservative obstacles along the new road to socialism he was mapping. The debate became particularly acute in 1957, the year after collectivization had been completed, as Maoists demanded ever more radical policies. By then the conflicts were no longer confined to the question of agricultural policy. A variety of other political and ideological issues, both international and domestic, had become intertwined with differences over economic questions to widen the scope and dimensions of the debate. To understand what was being debated on the eve of the Great Leap Forward campaign and the manner in which the debate was resolved, it is necessary to return to the year 1956 to consider that brief but crucial episode in the history of the People's Republic known as the "Hundred Flowers."

Notes

1. Although it is impossible to ascertain the extent of this particular practice, it appears to have been fairly widespread. Vogel, for example, has noted that a survey taken in one area of the Kwangtung countryside in 1953 revealed that 10 percent of the households of the area were engaged in money lending. Ezra Vogel, *Canton under Communism* (Cambridge, Mass.: Harvard University Press, 1969), p. 142.

2. Official party policy on this question stipulated that "members withdrawing from a mutual aid team or from a cooperative are entitled to withdraw their investments in capital and reserve funds. But if a member of an APC who bought his shares with land wants to withdraw, it is better if he does so only after the year's crops have been harvested." Cited in Chao Kuo-chun, *Agrarian Policies of Mainland China: A Documentary Study (1949–1956)* (Cambridge, Mass.: Harvard University Press, 1957), pp. 63–64.

3. *Ibid.*, p. 61.

4. The plan called for a 17.6 percent in food grain production and much greater increases in the production of industrial crops. It was emphasized that, "We cannot industrialize our country without an adequate development of agriculture." Li Fu-ch'un, "Report on First Five-Year Plan" in Robert Bowie and John K. Fairbank, *Communist China 1955–1959: Policy Documents with Analysis* (Cambridge, Mass.: Harvard University Press, 1962), p. 62.

5. The report of a central committee meeting of October 1955 on cooperativization put the problem in the following fashion: "China's industry is growing rapidly. Facts show that if the development of agricultural cooperation fails to keep pace with it, if the increase in grain and industrial crops lags behind, China's socialist industrialization will run into great difficulties." Cited in Bowie and Fairbank, *Communist China*, pp. 106–107.

6. Chou En-lai, "Report on the Proposals for the Second Five-Year Plan for Development of the National Economy," September 16, 1956, in Bowie and Fairbank, *Communist China*, p. 62.

7. Mao Tse-tung, "On the Cooperativization of Agriculture," July 31, 1955, in Chao, *Agrarian Policies*, pp. 85–86.

8. Central Committee of CCP, "Decisions on Agricultural Cooperation," October 11, 1955, Bowie and Fairbank, *Communist China*, p. 107.

9. The impetus for the cooperative movement came from Mao's report on economic problems at a central committee meeting in December 1942. For perceptive descriptions and analyses of the Yenan cooperative movement, see Franz Schurmann, *Ideology and Organization in Communist China* (Berkeley: University of California Press, 1966), pp. 416–427, and Mark Selden, *The Yenan Way in Revolutionary China* (Cambridge, Mass.: Harvard University Press, 1971), pp. 237–254.

10. Teng Tzu-hui, "Report to the Rural Work Conference of the Central Committee, New Democratic Youth League," July 15, 1954, in Chao, *Agrarian Politics*, p. 73.

11. Mao Tse-tung, "The Question of Agricultural Cooperation," July 31, 1955, in Bowie and Fairbank, *Communist China*, p. 95.

12. Li Fu-ch'un, "Report of the First Five-Year Plan," in Bowie and Fairbank, *Communist China*, pp. 65–66.

13. The remark is attributed to Ch'en Yi, Foreign Minister of the People's Republic and a member of the politburo, and reportedly made in November 1955. See James P. Harrison, *The Long March to Power* (New York: Praeger, 1972), p. 470.

14. Mao's report on "The Question of Agricultural Cooperation" was not published until October 1955, although the new policies it set forth were communicated to party organizations during the preceding months. The English edition, from which the following discussion and quotations are drawn, was published in Peking in 1956 and is reprinted in Bowie and Fairbank, *Communist China*, pp. 94–105.

15. "All revolutionary parties and all revolutionary comrades," Mao had declared in the Hunan Report, "will stand before them [the peasants] to be tested, and to be accepted or rejected as they decide," *Selected Works of Mao Tse-tung* (London: Lawrence & Wishart, 1954), 1:22.

16. Mao Tse-tung, "The Question of Agricultural Cooperation," in Bowie and Fairbank, *Communist China*, pp. 94, 101.

17. *Ibid.*, p. 94.

18. *Ibid.*, p. 98.

19. Mao Tse-tung, *On People's Democratic Dictatorship* (Peking: Foreign Languages Press, 1959), p. 14.

20. "Question of Agricultural Cooperation," in Bowie and Fairbank, *Communist China*, p. 104.

21. The document was adopted by the party central committee on October 11, 1955. An English translation was published in Peking in 1956, along with "explanatory notes" by Ch'en Po-ta. The new program received formal governmental approval in November 1955, when the State Council promulgated "Draft Model Regulations for the Agricultural Producers' Cooperatives."

22. Mao's views appear in the comments he made on various local reports on the collectivization campaign, compiled in three volumes in January 1956. For the English translation, from which the references here are taken, see Mao Tse-tung, *Socialist Upsurge in China's Countryside* (Peking: Foreign Languages Press, 1957), pp. 44, 160.

23. *Ibid.*, p. 302.

24. *Ibid*, p. 160.

25. *Ibid.*, "Preface," p. 8.

26. "The Draft Program for Agricultural Development in the People's Republic of China, 1956–1967," January 23, 1956, in Bowie and Fairbank, *Communist China*, p. 120.

27. The central-committee document of October 1955 made note of "landlords, rich peasants and counterrevolutionaries [who] have already wormed

their way in various guises in cooperatives" and were attempting to turn them to their own ends. However, former landlords and rich peasants were to be permitted to join cooperatives "in those places where the great majority of peasants have joined" and where the cooperatives were "on a sound basis." Cited in *Communist China,* p. 114.

28. "Draft Program for Agricultural Development" Jan. 23, 1956, in Bowie and Fairbank, *Communist China,* p. 121.

29. First National People's Congress, "Model Regulations for Higher Stage Agricultural Producer Cooperatives," June 30, 1956, in Chao, *Agrarian Policies,* p. 106.

30. Mao, "Question of Agricultural Cooperation," in Bowie and Fairbank, *Communist China,* p. 102.

31. It is generally estimated that of Russia's 25 million peasant households, only about 5 million were poor peasants, 18 million "middle peasants," and 2 million *kulaks* or "rich peasants." In China the 60–70 percent of peasants classified as "poor" or "lower-middle" were destitute, whereas in Russia only about 20 percent could be so described.

32. Mao, "Question of Agricultural Cooperation," in Bowie and Fairbank, *Communist China,* p. 102.

Part Three

Revolutionary Revivalism, 1956–1960

The Hundred Flowers:
Socialism, Bureaucracy, and Freedom

AT THE BEGINNING OF 1956 China, in the eyes of its Communist leaders, was on the verge of completing "the transition to socialism." The events of the latter half of 1955, Mao proclaimed in January of the new year, had proved decisive in determining the outcome of "the struggle between socialism and capitalism" and he predicted that "by the end of this year [1956] the victory of socialism will be practically assured."[1] In the same month, Chou En-lai and others were celebrating "the high tide of socialist transformation."[2] A year later, in February 1957, Mao was to turn his attention to the problem of "contradictions in a socialist society"; that Chinese society was now socialist was taken for granted, even though it was acknowledged that the new social system had yet to be "fully consolidated."[3]

Whether Chinese society in 1956–1957 was truly socialist by any Marxist definition of that term—or indeed whether it is truly socialist today—is a matter to which we shall return. For the moment it is sufficient to note that seven years after the founding of the People's Republic the leaders of the Chinese Communist Party believed that they had succeeded in transforming China into a basically socialist country. And on the basis of how socialism was defined in what was then known as "the Communist camp," they had good and sufficient reasons to believe as they did. If socialism is taken to mean the abolition of private property and the control of the means of production by a state in the hands of a socialist party, then China was no less socialist than the Soviet Union, the land still hailed as the "homeland of socialism." By mid-1956 agricultural collectivization largely had been completed and such industrial and commercial enterprises as still remained in private hands were national-

ized by the end of the year. Even individual entrepreneurship in handicraft production had been largely reorganized into socialist cooperatives.
Just as the Soviet Union, China by the end of 1956 was essentially a
country with a dual system of property; in the urban economy state
property predominated, while collective property prevailed in the rural
areas. In both town and countryside, private ownership of property had
been abolished, and by the prevailing Marxist-Leninist criteria of the
time China was a socialist society.

With the assumption that the transition to socialism was completed,
or soon would be, the Communists began in early 1956 to chart the future course of socioeconomic development and turned their attention to
the problems that the rapid socialization of society had created and the
problems yet to be solved. One problem that the arrival of a presumably
socialist society had not solved—and it dominated the concerns of the
Communist leaders—was China's continued economic backwardness. If
the Communists could hail the successes of the First Five Year Plan, they
could not but recognize that China's modern industrial sector was still
tiny and fragile. If the collectivization of agriculture was being accomplished without plunging the country into economic chaos and without
driving the peasantry into political opposition, it nevertheless was taking
place without any technological revolution in agricultural production.
China remained a poor country and its people impoverished. No one, not
even Mao, believed that a socialist society could long maintain itself,
much less flourish, amidst conditions of general economic scarcity. The
question was how to create a modern economic base that could sustain a
presumably socialist superstructure. Modern economic development was
clearly the order of the day, but it was by no means clear who would
issue the order and how it would be carried out. To the order of a Second Five Year Plan, which was already on the drawing boards at the
beginning of 1956, there emerged a radically different Maoist alternative
that demanded the wholesale abandonment of the "Soviet model" of development and one that had radically different social implications.

For Mao and Maoists, the question of how to achieve a modern
economy was inseparable from the question of how to avoid the bureaucratization of state and society that modern economic development
fostered. China's "transition to socialism" had been accompanied by a
transition from revolutionary forms of organization to bureaucratic forms
of rule and control. The general institutionalization of the post-revolutionary order, and especially the Soviet-borrowed methods of the First
Five Year Plan, had given rise to the emergence of new political and
economic elites. These developments were perhaps inherent in the process of industrialization, but they clashed with the socialist goals which
industrialization presumably was to serve—and clashed more directly
with the emerging Maoist vision of the proper course of socioeconomic

development. What came to be known as the "Hundred Flowers" campaign was partly intended to serve, at least on the part of Maoists, an antibureaucratic purpose.

The problem of bureaucracy was a reflection of a larger and more general phenomenon, the growing cleavage between state and society. Socialism, according to Marxist theory, is a historical process whereby the social powers usurped by the state in man's "prehistory" are restored to society. But in the People's Republic, as in the Soviet Union, "the transition to socialism" had produced precisely the opposite historical tendency: the growth of a vast bureaucratic state apparatus that was increasingly alienated from society and increasingly stood above it. The problem did not go wholly unrecognized. The new party constitution adopted at the Eighth Congress in September 1956, called for a "maximum effort in every Party organization, state organ and economic unit to combat any bureaucratic practice which estranges the masses or leads to isolation from the realities of life."[4] And in February 1957, Mao spoke of "certain contradictions" which existed "between the government and the masses."[5]

The relationship between state and society was not treated as an abstract theoretical question. In 1956 and 1957 the Communist rulers began to reassess the role of the people over whom they exercised political domination, and confronted the demands of the people themselves. The most dramatic and politically explosive demands came from the urban classes, the industrial working class and the intelligentsia, and posed the most fundamental questions about the nature of a socialist society in general and about the nature of socialism in China in particular. For China's rapidly growing proletariat, "socialist transformation" brought increasingly repressive social and political controls over their lives and an increasingly harsh labor discipline in the factories. Growing unrest among the workers was expressed in 1956 in strikes, which were motivated by political as well as socioeconomic discontents. The strikes were scattered and quickly suppressed by the regime, but they raised a question that could not be so easily suppressed, the question of the role of the proletariat in a presumably socialist society that, according to official ideology, is presided over by a state "led by the working class."

For China's intellectuals, the transition to socialism resulted in less freedom, not more. For a time, it seemed that the Communists were willing to grant the Marxist promise that socialism and freedom went hand in hand. The events of 1956–1957 were to reveal the limitations of the Maoist conception of freedom as well as the limits that an entrenched bureaucracy placed on freedom of thought.

What came to be called the "blooming and contending" of 1956–1957 was a time when the most critical questions about the present and future of socialism in China were raised and debated. Questions about the relationship between state and society, between leaders and led, and questions involving human and intellectual freedom were discussed more openly and candidly than ever before in the People's Republic. In part, the questions were posed by the Communist leaders themselves as they reflected on the achievements of socialization and industrialization—and the problems which seven years of rapid socioeconomic change had created. In part, the Communists were forced to confront issues which were raised from below by those whom they ruled.

The manner in which the problems or "contradictions" of the time were perceived, the way in which they were resolved or left unresolved, and the outcome of the public debates and the secret party debates of 1956–1957 are crucial for understanding the nature of socialism in China and the distinctively Maoist theory of socioeconomic development which crystallized during these years.

Like most modern constitutional documents, the constitution of the People's Republic, promulgated in 1954, formally guaranteed the citizens of China freedom of speech, freedom of assembly, and freedom of the press. That the actual practice and policies of the government were not constrained by such legal formalities long had been obvious, particularly to China's intellectuals. From the founding of the regime in 1949, they had been subjected to continuous processes of thought reform and ideological remolding; if their thoughts had not been "reformed," they had become painfully aware that unreformed thoughts were best left unsaid. The constitution did nothing to lift the burdens of intellectual conformity and political discipline that the state demanded. Indeed, the *Sufan* campaign and the imprisonment of Hu Feng in 1955 intensified intellectual repression and made a mockery of the legal right of "freedom of speech" that had been proclaimed the year before. In 1949 the Communists had come to power with the support of the vast majority of the intelligentsia; now, much of that support had dissipated and the hopes of 1949 had degenerated into passive compliance with the ideological and political dictates of an increasingly repressive state power.

In the latter months of 1955 party leaders began to formulate new policies to regain the active support of a disaffected intelligentsia. It was not the case that the Communists suddenly had come to appreciate the virtues of intellectual freedom. The purpose was largely economic, although Mao Tse-tung's own motives were rather more complex. As industrialization proceeded, it became clear that a more rapid development of scientific and technological research—and the creation of a larger and better trained technological intelligentsia—would be required to sustain modern economic development. Instructions were thus issued to draw up a twelve-year plan for scientific development. At the same time, Mao pro-

posed a twelve-year program for agriculture which called for a vast technological revolution in agricultural production. An intelligentsia terrified
into silence and driven into political hostility was not likely to provide the
cooperation that was required or display the intellectual creativity that
was needed. Intellectual repression was becoming an economic liability.

In the fall of 1955 nonparty representatives to the National People's
Congress and the People's Consultative Conference were asked to prepare reports on the conditions under which intellectuals lived and
worked. Over the next months the advice of non-Communist parties and
groups were solicited on the question of how best intellectuals might be
"unified" and how they might be reunified with the CCP. When Mao
presented his new agricultural program to the politburo in December
1955, he took special pains to urge that intellectuals be brought into
fuller participation in the economic and political life of the country. It
was the first call in the campaign that soon was to proceed under the
slogan "Let a hundred flowers bloom, let a hundred schools of thought
contend."

In January 1956 the party's central committee convened a special conference to deal with the matter. Nonparty representatives of academic
institutions and organizations were invited to participate and to hear
speeches by both Mao Tse-tung and Chou En-lai. Chou's speech is of
particular interest, for it reflected the consensus of the party leadership
at the time "On the Question of Intellectuals." The social classification of
intellectuals posed difficult ideological problems, for unlike workers,
peasants, or the bourgeoisie, their class status could not be defined by the
usual Marxist criterion of their relationship to the means of production.
However important intellectuals were in the economic, political, and cultural life of the country, they remained only a social "stratum" or "element" and occupied a most ambiguous place in the four-class alliance
upon which the People's Republic presumably rested. But if intellectuals
did not constitute a social class as such, they were the carriers of class
ideologies, and especially bourgeois class ideology, and thus were politically and ideologically suspect. Chou attempted to remove the suspicion
by assigning intellectuals a class status they never had been accorded before. "The overwhelming majority of intellectuals," he announced, "have
become government workers in the cause of Socialism and are already
part of the working class." Thus the "question of intellectuals" was no
longer mainly a question of their political and ideological reliability, but
rather a technical problem of the scarcity of experts and expertise. "The
fundamental question now," Chou stated, "is that the forces of our intelligentsia are insufficient in number, professional skills and political
consciousness to meet the requirements of our rapid Socialist construction." The problem could be resolved through largely technical means.
Chou suggested that through more rational organization and work as-

signments intellectuals might be better able to "develop their specialized skills to the benefit of the state." And for that same purpose they should be provided with better equipment and more books, better housing and higher wages, more rewards and rapid promotions, and not be burdened unduly with administrative tasks and political study sessions to the neglect of their professional work. Enrollments in universities were to be increased and long-term programs for the development of scientific and technological knowledge were to be undertaken.

The political problem, Chou suggested, resided more in the Party than among the intellectuals. He complained of "certain unreasonable features in our present employment and treatment of intellectuals, and, in particular, certain sectarian attitudes among some of our comrades towards intellectuals outside the Party," of "unnecessary suspicion" to which intellectuals had been subjected, and a proclivity to label loyal intellectuals as counterrevolutionaries. This did not mean that the intelligentsia was to be freed from political controls and responsibilities. Intellectuals would still be subjected to established processes of political "reeducation" and "ideological reform;" the small number who remained counterrevolutionaries or who were otherwise "bad elements" were to be "weeded out" by the party; bourgeois ideological tendencies were to be combatted, and all intellectuals were to study Marxism–Leninism and eventually become "red experts." As all this would take time, the party would be tolerant: "If they do not turn against the people in speech and action and, even more, if they are prepared to devote their knowledge and energies to serving the people, we must be able to wait for the gradual awakening of their consciousness and help them patiently, while at the same time criticizing their wrong ideology." In the meantime, intellectuals were to be granted a wide realm of professional autonomy within their particular areas of expertise in order to master the scientific knowledge that was essential for China's modern economic development.[6]

While the party was to retain its political and ideological mastery, the intellectuals were recognized as the masters of science and technology, and indeed, encouraged to master a universal body of modern scientific knowledge. The Party was taking the initiative to end what Chou called "a certain state of estrangement" that existed between the intellectuals and the state. One manifestation of this new confidence in the intelligentsia was Chou's call for removing barriers for the recruitment of intellectuals into the party. The result was a 50 percent increase in the number of intellectuals in the party over the next year. In 1957 there were more intellectuals in China's "party of the proletariat" than there were members of the working class.[7]

It is hardly likely that Mao Tse-tung could have found Chou En-lai's speech to his liking, for the new policy implied the creation of a technological intelligentsia that could effectively separate its professional activities from politics and ideology, at least so long as it was not openly hostile to the state and to Marxism. It was a policy that would have accelerated the stratification of professional elites separated from the masses by virtue of their specialized knowledge and privileged social and economic positions. It was precisely this social result of the Soviet-modeled Five-Year Plan that Mao was already attempting to reverse and against which he was soon openly to rebel. Mao, to be sure, shared Chou's desire for modern economic development and the need to master modern science. And Mao was demanding, more strongly than Chou, that the weight of Party bureaucrats be lifted from the backs of intellectuals. But he was advocating a very different course of economic development than the Party was pursuing at the time and one that had radically different social implications, particularly for intellectuals.

If Mao found uncongenial the social implications of Chou's speech, there was one political point with which he must have heartily agreed. Among the reasons Chou advanced for the party's new policy toward intellectuals was a need for China to end its dependence on the Soviet Union. "We cannot indefinitely rely on the Soviet experts," he stressed, and he was critical of the "sectarian" tendency of the "undue haste, arbitrary learning, and mechanical application" of Soviet methods. It was a reflection of a lack of national self-confidence, he suggested, and emphasized the need for China to achieve "self-sufficiency" in modern science and technology. This distinctively Maoist theme was to prove a prophetic pointer to the future, and probably neither Chou nor Mao fully appreciated its significance at the time.

When Chou En-lai delivered his speech "On the Question of Intellectuals" in January 1956, Mao Tse-tung was pressing the party to adopt more radical social and economic policies; economic development was to proceed in a manner that was "greater, faster, better and more economical" than it was under the Five Year Plan, while the socialist reorganization of society was to be accelerated as well.[8] At issue in the emerging internal Party dispute was not only the pace of socioeconomic change but its nature. Whereas most Communists were still wedded to the Soviet model of development and thinking in terms of a Second Five-Year Plan that was to be basically an extension of the first, Mao was proposing policies that presupposed the wholesale abandonment of the Soviet model. Instead of proceeding in accordance with the dictates of bureaucratic rationality, urban industrialization, and centralized state control, the new Maoist conception flowed from a generalization of the Yenan model of the "mass line" and, more immediately, was inspired by the populist-type upsurge in the countryside that Mao had launched with his July 1955 speech on agricultural collectivization. The rapid socialist reorganization of society was to be combined with rapid economic development, and industry was to develop simultaneously with agriculture in decentralized fashion and through a populist reliance on the initiative of the masses. The emerging Maoist conception posed a threat to existing state and party bureaucracies and was bitterly resisted. The debate on the proper course of socioeconomic development raged throughout 1956–1957 and was only resolved (and then only temporarily) in late 1957, when the Maoist conception began to be implemented in the Great Leap Forward campaign.

While the "question of intellectuals" was openly debated, the Party debate on socioeconomic policy remained secret. But the two were intimately related. Chou En-lai's January 1956 speech flowed quite logically from the premises of the Five Year Plan, for it implied the creation of a Soviet-type technological intelligentsia essential to modern industrial development under bureaucratic auspices. But while Chou, and most party leaders, wanted to use intellectuals for economic ends, Mao wanted to use them for political ends as well, as part of a mass socioeconomic movement that would bypass established bureaucratic channels and controls to effect the radical social and economic changes he envisioned. Mao already had come under considerable Party criticism for having forced a too rapid transition to agricultural collectivization. Although his twelve-year plan for agriculture was formally approved by the central committee in January 1956, Mao later was to charge that most party leaders greeted his proposals with indifference. The plan itself was put on the shelf over the next 18 months as the party pursued policies of moderation and retrenchment.

It seems likely that Mao was preparing to begin his antibureaucratic drive by announcing a much more dramatic lifting of political restraints on intellectuals than Chou En-lai proposed. But the launching of what was to become known as the "Hundred Flowers" campaign was delayed by the traumatic impact of Nikita Khrushchev's "secret" speech denouncing Stalin at the Twentieth Soviet Party Congress in February 1956.

Khrushchev's condemnation of the crimes of Stalin surprised the Chinese as much as it did the rest of the world, and they later complained of the Russian "failure to consult with fraternal parties in advance." If the Chinese resented having not been forewarned, it was a resentment they shared with all other Communist parties. Khrushchev delivered the speech at the closing session of the congress and the decision to do so was apparently made at the last minute; the speech bears the marks of hasty composition, and much of it was of an impromptu nature. But it was the internal Chinese political implications of the indictment of Stalin, not the surprise of the occasion, that made for problems.

The leaders of the Chinese Communist Party were not so ignorant of Soviet history as to have found Khrushchev's "revelations" about Stalin very revealing, even though they may have been shocked by some of the more bizarre aspects of Stalin's personality and methods of rule that the speech detailed. Of the greater and general crimes of Stalin they were already well aware. The immediate problem was how to explain the matter to the rank-and-file membership of the Chinese Communist Party and the Chinese people generally. How were the Chinese leaders to explain why they had for decades extolled as a great revolutionary leader a man who now stood condemned as a bloodthirsty tyrant? Whatever Mao and other Communist leaders privately thought of Stalin, the public record was one of unmitigated and lavish praise. And it was a long record. In 1939 Mao had celebrated Stalin's sixtieth birthday by hailing "Comrade Stalin [as] the saviour of all the oppressed." "Comrade Stalin is the teacher and friend of mankind and of the Chinese people," Mao wrote on the Soviet dictator's seventieth birthday. And on Stalin's death in 1953, Mao lamented the passing of "the greatest genius of the present age." Similar panegyrics had come from other Communist leaders and had filled the Chinese press over the years.

The embarrassing problem could be alleviated, but hardly resolved, by simply not publishing the text of Khrushchev's speech. Just as Khrushchev had concluded his remarks with an admonition not to "wash our dirty linen" in public and had left the matter of publication to the American State Department, so the Chinese refrained from publication, and what details of the speech became publicly known in China appeared only in 1957, in the form of translated excerpts from the English text, which appeared on wall posters written by unknown hands. The general thrust of the speech, even if not its specifics, did of course filter down through party circles and among the intelligentsia shortly after it was delivered.

The Soviet condemnation of Stalin posed more serious political and ideological issues for the Chinese Communists than such personal embarrassments they may have felt because of the idolatrous public praise they had bestowed on the Russian dictator for over a quarter of a century or any annoyance about not having been forewarned about his de-idolization. It raised grave questions about the social and moral validity of the socialist system which the Chinese were then emulating. If socialism was a higher stage of sociohistorical development, and Soviet socialism its most advanced model, then how could it have produced and been presided over for so long by a leader whose crimes and brutalities Khrushchev had so vividly, if selectively, described? And it raised the more specific, and for the Chinese, the more immediate problem of the relationship between leader and party in a presumably socialist society. The major theme of Khrushchev's speech, after all, and his "explanation" for the evils he recounted, was that Stalin was a usurper who had "placed himself above the party," and placed himself beyond criticism by fostering a "cult of the personality." Had not Mao also placed himself above the party with his July 1955 speech and the collectivization campaign? And was not Mao also becoming the object of a similar form of hero worship?

The Chinese pondered these questions for more than a month before commenting on Khrushchev's speech. The commentary came on April 5 in the form of an editorial in the *People's Daily* entitled "On the Historical Experience of the Dictatorship of the Proletariat," a treatise probably written by Mao himself. The editorial referred to Stalin's "mistakes" and "errors" only in the most general terms and disclosed little of the contents of Khrushchev's denunciation. The new Russian leaders were praised for their "courageous self-criticism of . . . past errors" while Stalin was portrayed as a great socialist leader who "creatively applied and developed Marxism–Leninism" and carried out Lenin's policies of industrialization and collectivization. Acknowledging that Stalin "made some serious mistakes" in his later years, the Chinese commentary was implicitly more critical of Khrushchev for his failure to explain how those mistakes came about. For the most part the document was a defense of the socialist system Stalin built in Russia—and, by implication, the socialist system that was being built in China—and an attempt to explain (and to explain away) the problem of "the cult of the individual."[9]

The Chinese commentary was hardly more satisfactory than Khrushchev's speech in explaining how the evils of Stalin could have been perpetrated in a presumably socialist society, but Mao, unlike Khrushchev, was unwilling to separate Stalin from the Stalinist era. Khrushchev disposed of the problem by simply attributing all the socialist achievements of the Soviet Union to the party, the masses, and Leninism, and blaming all the failures and horrors of the era on Stalin alone; the evils, he repeated time and again, were due to "the willfulness of one man." Mao, on the other hand, insisted: "We should view Stalin from an historical standpoint, make a proper and all-round analysis to see where he was right and where he was wrong, and draw useful lessons therefrom. Both the things he did right and the things he did wrong were phenomena of the international communist movement and bore the imprint of the times." Thus Stalin was to be credited with the socialist achievements of the Soviet Union as well as to be held responsible for its defects. And since the achievements exceeded the defects, the historical picture of Stalin that emerged was a generally favorable one. Therefore, it was emphasized that "Stalin's works should, as before, still be seriously studied and that we should accept, as an important historical legacy, all that is of value in them, especially those many works in which he defended Leninism and correctly summarized the experience of building up the Soviet Union." To be sure, they were to be studied more critically than before, with care being taken to distinguish between correct and incorrect ideas. But for Maoists, Stalin remained a "great Marxist–Leninist revolutionary," albeit an imperfect one—at least on the public record.[10]

Mao also offered an historical explanation for the problem of "personality cults," but the intent was more to bury the question historically than to confront it politically. "The cult of the individual," it was explained, "is a foul carryover from the long history of mankind. The cult of the individual is rooted not only in the exploiting classes but also in the small producers. As is well known, patriarchism is a product of small-producer economy." The appearance of such cults in a socialist society was attributed to the "poisonous ideological survivals of the old society" which "still remain in people's minds for a very long time." While it was "quite natural for the name of Stalin to be greatly honoured throughout the world" for his contributions to socialism, it was to be deplored that he exaggerated his role and succumbed to backward ideological influences. The problem was not likely to appear in China, it was implied, for the Chinese party "has incessantly fought against elevation of oneself and against individualist heroism." In any event, the necessary measures to prevent the appearance of the problem were on hand: an appropriate balance between "democracy" and "centralism;" modesty and prudence on the part of leaders; and reliance on "the mass line."[11]

Having thus temporarily disposed of the question of Stalin, Mao turned to deal with a party leadership and apparatus increasingly resistant to the radical social and economic policies he was proposing. One way to revive the revolutionary spirit of a party that was seen to be degenerating into a conservative and routinized bureaucracy was to challenge it from without. The task was first assigned to the nonparty intelligentsia. It was more to revitalize the party than because of any desire to liberate intellectuals from ideological and political discipline—although Mao saw some limited virtues to be derived from a limited degree of intellectual ferment and opposition—that Mao revived the slogan "let a hundred flowers blossom, let a hundred schools of thought contend," in a speech delivered to the Supreme State Conference on May 2, 1956. It was left to Lu Ting-yi, the head of the central committee's Propaganda Department, to announce the new Maoist policy when he addressed a meeting of artists, writers and scientists in Peking on May 26.[12]

The phrase "let a hundred schools of thought contend" applied to scientists, whereas "let a hundred flowers blossom" was directed to writers and artists. The distinction was significant. The natural sciences were declared to have "no class character" and thus scientists were free to advocate and debate different scientific theories without fear of political intrusion or ideological dictate; the goal was scientific progress, a politically neutral matter. For writers, artists, and scholars, on the other hand, the realm of freedom was more ambiguously defined. There was, to be sure, the promise of intellectual freedom for all. "History shows," Lu Ting-yi observed, "that unless independent thinking and free discussion are encouraged, academic life stagnates." And he proclaimed that the new policy "means that we stand for freedom of independent thinking, of debate, of creative work; freedom to criticize and freedom to express, maintain and reserve one's opinions on questions of art, literature or scientific research."[13] But the promise of freedom was subject to numerous qualifications. While artists and writers were free to "blossom" in the realm of style and subject matter—"socialist realism" was the preferred but no longer the only method permitted—they were offered no license to freely decide the social and political content of their works. Unlike the natural sciences, work in art, literature, history, and philosophy retained a class character and therefore were still to be under political supervision in a country where "the class struggle is still going on." Moreover, the freedom granted was "freedom among the people" and the artistic and literary works produced under the new dispensation were "to serve the people." Lu left hanging the questions of who constituted "the people" and what served them—and who was to make the determination. Furthermore, the ends of the campaign for "blooming and contending" were largely predetermined. "Only through open debate," Lu noted, "can materialism conquer idealism."[14] There could be a free "battle of ideas," but the possibility that non-Marxist ideas might triumph was precluded from the beginning.

But what Mao launched through the vehicle of Lu Ting-yi's speech was not, or at least was not intended to be, another movement to rectify the thoughts of the intellectuals. Mao now was attempting to turn the tables: it was the Party that was to be rectified, and the non-Party intelligentsia was the instrument to be used for that purpose. Lu Ting-yi's speech was filled with bitter and sarcastic comments on the arrogance and ignorance of party members:

> They claim to be always right and fail to see the merits of others. . . . They take offence at the critical opinion of others. They always see themselves as the erudite teachers and others as their puny pupils. . . . These comrades had better stop this self-glorification right away . . . they had better be modest, listen more often to others' criticism, work harder at their studies, make a point of learning what they can from people outside the Party, and really cooperate with them. . . .
>
> The point I want to make is that it is time for Party members to take note of their own inadequacies and remedy them. There is only one way to do so: to seek advice and learn honestly and modestly from those who know. The great majority of those intellectuals who are not

Communist Party members study very hard. Members of the Communist Party must not be behind-hand in learning from them.[15]

Since the natural sciences now had been declared free of class character, scientists began to protest the interference and the scientific incompetence of party cadres. Soviet-adopted ideological orthodoxies were ignored or criticized, and a remarkably free debate developed on the still politically sensitive subject of genetics and heredity. The intelligentsia as a whole, however, were wary of "blooming" and "contending" in the fashion they were now presumably free to do. One speech was hardly sufficient to remove the fears that resulted from six years of repression. Lu Ting-yi's speech itself was by no means wholly reassuring; his repeated references to the "reactionary" and "counterrevolutionary" ideas of Hu Feng must have had a chilling effect, as did his warning that "the work of ferreting out hidden counterrevolutionaries has not been completed."[16] Moreover, Lu had been careful to draw distinctions between "friends" and "enemies," between "the people" and "counterrevolutionaries"—and the distinctions were vague. What guarantee did the intellectuals have that openly discussed views might not be used as evidence to condemn them as "enemies" or "counterrevolutionaries" rather than members of "the people?"

Perhaps even more inhibiting was the open hostility of most party officials and cadres. While Mao encouraged intellectuals to voice their criticisms, the party officials they confronted in their day-to-day work were not nearly so encouraging. As Lo Lung-ch'i, the head of the Democratic League and a minister in the Peking government, later explained the problem:

> During the past year, not many flowers bloomed and few schools of thought contended in the academic and ideological fields . . . the basic cause lies in the fact that the higher intellectuals are still suspicious . . . this phenomenon is primarily due to the lack of a correct appreciation and comprehension of these two slogans on the part of some Party member cadres. . . . They feel that since the advancement of these slogans, the society has swarmed with heresies. They are therefore over-eager with the work of defending the faith.[17]

Nevertheless, by the summer of 1956, a significant number of intellectuals, especially writers, encouraged by special forums sponsored by the Writers' Union and by literary journals, began to express their views on matters of more than purely literary significance. Criticism of the evils of bureaucracy and the heavy hands of party bureaucrats was an especially prominent theme and one very much in the desired Maoist spirit of the time. Socialist realism was attacked as "cheap optimism" and calls were heard for the revival of nineteenth-century Western realism to expose rather than hide real social conditions and the economic hardships of the masses. The party itself was criticized for having disregarded the humanitarian ideals of Marxism. Many of the ideas for which Hu Feng had been condemned and imprisoned the year before were now heard and unpublished works written in the early 1950s appeared in print. At Peking University, courses on Keynesian economics and the philosophy of Bertrand Russell were offered in the 1956–1957 academic year. Birth control, hitherto considered a Malthusian heresy as far as intellectuals were concerned (although it quietly had been discussed and promoted in official circles since 1954), was now being strongly and publicly advocated.

Although the Hundred Flowers campaign received formal endorsement at the Eighth Party Congress in September 1956, approval was little more than formal. The party apparatus, for the most part, and many of its highest leaders were opposed to the campaign from the beginning —and the antibureaucratic thrust of much of what intellectuals were now writing confirmed suspicions that Mao's policy posed a threat to their positions and power. The anti-Stalinist revolt in Hungary in November served to solidify Party hostility to the movement. Although the situations in the two countries were hardly analogous, the analogy was drawn nevertheless. Freedom for Hungarian intellectuals had led to a workers' uprising against the Communist state. Did not critical intellectual ferment among the Chinese intelligentsia portend the same result, especially since unrest among the Chinese working class had resulted in an unprecedented wave of strikes earlier in the year? Whether party leaders really feared a "Hungarian situation" is dubious, but the revolution in Hungary served as the pretext to launch a counterattack. By the end of the year, party organs were warning of "poisonous weeds" that had sprung up among the blooming flowers. Criticism of dogmatism and bureaucratism in the party suddenly turned to party criticism of "rightism" among the intelligentsia. In the early months of 1957 the campaign was suppressed and intellectuals awaited the retribution of the party bureaucrats they had been invited to criticize.

The time of retribution was to be delayed, and the Hundred Flowers campaign was to be revived, and in much more radical form, as a result of Mao's now famous speech "On the Correct Handling of Contradictions Among the People," delivered at the end of February 1957. Mao's lengthy speech is undoubtedly one of the most significant theoretical expressions of "Maoism" in the postrevolutionary era. To understand its significance it is necessary to return to the debate on socioeconomic policy that was raging in late 1956, inexorably dividing the party into "Maoist" and "non-Maoist" factions.

In 1956 China's leaders were celebrating the industrial successes of the First Five-Year Plan and preparing the Second Five-Year Plan, scheduled to begin in 1958. At the time, China's economic planners were still committed to following the Soviet model of development, albeit in somewhat modified form. The modifications were not insignificant and some were introduced in the last phase of the first plan. The rigidities of the one-man management system already had largely been eliminated; more emphasis was to be given to the development of light industry to meet consumer needs and mitigate economic discontent among workers and peasants; economic organization was to be partly decentralized by reducing the power of the ministries in Peking and increasing the autonomy of provinces and large-scale industrial enterprises, measures not dissimilar to those then being undertaken in the Soviet Union; and finally, the new plan was to proceed at a somewhat slower and more gradual pace. Nevertheless, the general thrust of the proposed Second Five-Year Plan, and the fundamental assumptions on which it rested, basically were in accord with the Soviet model which had guided the first. Priority was still to be given to the development of heavy industry, and accordingly, special emphasis was placed on the rapid training of a modern scientific and technological intelligentsia.[18] It was taken for granted that industrialization meant urban industrialization and urbanization; as Chou En-lai enthusiastically proclaimed in his report on the proposed plan, "we shall build up many new cities and enlarge many existing ones."[19] Moreover, it was assumed that the building of a modern industrial base was the essential prerequisite for the further socialist transformation of society, and thus Mao was under heavy criticism for having forced agricultural collectivization prematurely, because conditions of industrial backwardness precluded the mechanization and technology that a fully socialist agriculture presumably required.

Mao, in turn, was increasingly critical of the Second Five Year Plan, which he felt would only compound the undesirable social, political and ideological consequences that four years of urban industrialization already had produced. It implied a further expansion and proliferation of bureaucracy and the solidification of professional and bureaucratic elites, an increasing gap between the modernizing cities and the backward countryside, a postponement of radical social change, and a further decay of ideology. In April 1956 Mao had offered an alternative proposal to the politbu ro; his speech on "The Ten Great Relationships" (the text of which was only revealed a decade later), was cryptically worded but clearly called for an abandonment of Soviet-type five-year plans and outlined a radically different strategy. Although heavy industry was to grow no less rapidly than before, investment was to be concentrated on the development of light industry and agriculture; in place of the further growth of the advanced coastal sectors, the backward inland and interior areas were to be developed; instead of large-scale urban industrialization, the emphasis would shift to medium- and small-scale industries in the countryside; instead of centralized bureaucratic direction (or decentralized regional bureaucratic controls), relatively autonomous local communities were to become the main socioeconomic units; labor-intensive projects were to be favored over capital-intensive ones, and moral incentives were to replace material incentives. Rapid social change was to proceed simultaneously with rapid economic development, and the decisive factor for both was the initiative and consciousness of the masses. Modern economic development was not to proceed more slowly; indeed, it was to proceed more rapidly and efficiently, but from different starting points, in a far different fashion, and with vastly different social and political implications.[20]

Mao's unorthodox ideas on economic development were largely ignored in the documents on the Second Five Year Plan approved by the party's Eighth Congress in September. It was now politically possible to ignore Mao's ideas because he no longer exercised the supreme authority over the party he once held. A vast and routinized bureaucratic apparatus is not easily bent to the will of one man, no matter how much personal prestige he may enjoy. In 1955 Mao had overridden the party's central committee—and had appealed directly to the rural cadres and the peasantry—in order to implement his program for rapid collectivization, an event that was a source of continuing resentment among party leaders. Conditions in 1956 were less conducive for another such *tour de force*. Khrushchev's denunciation of Stalin and the evils of "one-man" rule in February had served to weaken Mao's position. The Eighth Party Congress in September, the first held since 1945, was presided over by Liu Shao-ch'i and Teng Hsiao-p'ing. It was Liu and Teng, not Mao, who presented the main reports to the congress—and to reinforce the new principle of collective leadership, the phrase "guided by the thought of Mao Tse-tung" was deleted from the new party constitution. The Eighth Congress further reduced Mao's power in the party by reestablishing the post of General Secretary, which had been abolished in 1937. Appointed to the revived office was Teng Hsiao-p'ing, who came to exercise considerable control over the organizational apparatus of the Party. It was with good reason that Mao later complained that in 1956 his views were met with "indifference" by most party leaders. While Mao's personal prestige remained enormous, the control of the party organization had fallen into other hands; he remained the master of Marxist–Leninist theory but no longer the master of policy.

Mao's February 1957 speech "On the Correct Handling of Contradictions Among the People," must be seen in the light of his relative political powerlessness in the party and his conviction that conservative state and party organs were pursuing policies that precluded radical social change. The debate over questions of economic policy thus became inseparable from the question of political power. The breaking down of bureaucratic resistance to the alternative policies of socioeconomic development Mao was proposing became the immediate task, and the February speech was designed to do precisely that. It established an ideological justification and set off a train of political events whereby Mao could set himself above the party (or, at least, above the established party leadership) and emerge as a supreme leader speaking directly to "the people."

"On the Correct Handling of Contradictions Among the People" served to revive the Hundred Flowers campaign, which the party bureaucracy had been busily suppressing during the preceding two months. The speech was presented not at a party meeting but rather to an enlarged session of the Supreme State Conference, an organ of the People's Government. Just as Mao had used a nonparty forum to deliver his July 1955 speech on agricultural collectivization, he now again went outside regular party channels to announce policy initiatives and theoretical innovations; in both instances the Maoist position had failed to receive the support the majority of the politburo, and in both cases the Party was presented with a *fait accompli*. Although the text of the February speech was not published until June (and then only in revised form), the content of the original was quickly circulated among the party and the nonparty intelligentsia.

The political significance of Mao's speech was not only that he extended a new invitation to the intellectuals to speak their minds at the very time the party apparatus had silenced dissenters and was eliminating the "poisonous weeds" produced by the limited "blossoming" of the latter half of 1956, but that he did so on the basis of an argument that suggested the Communist Party did not necessarily possess a monopoly on correct ideas and therefore was subject to criticism from outside its ranks. The renewal of the Hundred Flowers movement was justified not only because of the desirability of stimulating intellectual creativity for purposes of economic development, but also because of the continued existence of "contradictions" in a socialist society. The latter thesis by itself was neither novel nor radical. That contradictions are the motivating force of social development—and that they are inevitable, desirable, and eternal—long had been a principal tenet of Maoist theory. Nor was there anything novel in Mao's distinctions between "antagonistic" and "nonantagonistic" contradictions, and between "the people" and their "enemies." There are Leninist and Stalinist as well as Maoist precedents for the view that contradictions between productive forces and relations of production exist in the socialist era, that they are reflected in contradictions between state and society, and that such nonantagonistic contradictions are amenable to peaceful resolution. Had Mao confined himself to restating these familiar views, his speech would hardly have raised any political or ideological eyebrows. What made the speech politically significant—and politically threatening—was the introduction of two new propositions, both of which were to prove to be prophetic pointers to the

Cultural Revolution. While Mao enumerated many contradictions, the one that he emphasized was that between the "leadership and the led." Not only were there contradictions between the government and the masses in general, but also among "leaders" and "people" in particular. And "leaders" were not simply low-level bureaucratic functionaries. Nowhere did Mao exclude the possibility that the leaders who stood in contradiction to the people might be the very highest officials of the party, nor the possibility that on certain questions such leaders might be wrong and "the people" right: "Correct and good things have often at first been looked upon not as fragrant flowers but as poisonous weeds," and this might well be the case even in a socialist society.[21] Only a period of trial through ideological struggle could distinguish correct from incorrect ideas. Since it was possible for the party and even its leaders to fall into error, the party should be exposed to criticism from the people. "For a party as much as for an individual," Mao declared, "there is a great need to hear opinions different from its own." Since the people were broadly defined as all those supporting socialism, the range and scope of critical opinion that the party could hear was potentially very great. Intellectuals, assumed to be basically united in their support of socialism, were thus theoretically free to criticize the party. And the "democratic parties" who "enjoy the confidence of the people" were enjoined to "exercise supervision over the Communist Party" under a policy of "mutual supervision."[22]

This questioning of the infallibility of the Leninist party had far greater political implications than offering the largely fictious "democratic parties" entrée into the political arena. If the people in general were now free to criticize the party, then who was to speak for "the people" if not Mao himself? Mao, after all, was not only the chairman of the party but also the head of the People's Government. Moreover, as the leader of the people's revolution, Mao had special bonds to the masses which no one else could claim; if the people were free to speak, then Mao was their preeminent spokesman. What Mao's argument on "contradictions among the people" did was to free Mao himself from the Leninist discipline of the party and enable him to criticize the party from without in his unique role as the representative of the people. It was a role he soon was to assume.

If the suggestion that the party was not infallible (and thus subject to criticism from the people—and from Mao) was an implicit threat to party authorities, especially those who opposed Mao's policies and programs, that threat was reinforced by another proposition, the view that class struggle continues under socialism and that it takes a primarily ideological form. Much of Mao's treatise proceeded on the premise that socialism had been established in China and that class exploitation was abolished; therefore such social divisions and contradictions that still existed among a basically united people were nonantagonistic in nature.

But Mao then qualified the argument by proclaiming that "class struggle is not yet over." Remnants of the old exploiting classes still remain, he observed, although it was not the remnants of social classes but rather the continued influences of their ideologies that was at the source of the struggle: "the class struggle *in the ideological field* between the proletariat and the bourgeoisie will still be long and devious and at times may even become very acute . . . the question whether socialism or capitalism will win is still not really settled."[23] While the proletariat and the bourgeoisie as such may not have been engaged in combat, the conflict between what was deemed to be their respective ideologies was sufficient to proclaim the continued existence of a grave class struggle. The proposition was a logical culmination of a long-held Maoist tendency to define classes and class struggles in terms of conscious attitudes rather than on the basis of objective social criteria—and it marked the appearance of a rigid ideological determinism that since has governed the history of Maoism. It also directly contradicted the official view expounded only a few months earlier at the Eighth Party Congress to the effect that the struggle between capitalism and socialism had been decided in favor of the latter and that class differences had been reduced to "only a matter of division of labor within the same class."[24]

That Mao chose to proclaim the continued existence of class struggle at the very time he sought to revive the Hundred Flowers campaign had ominous implications for the course and fate of the movement. Since "class struggle" was now a matter of a struggle between class ideologies and not between actual social classes, the way was open to condemn as "class enemies" those who expressed incorrect ideas. Nonantagonistic contradictions among the people quickly could be converted into antagonistic class contradictions between the people and their enemies, thus sanctioning the use of "coercive methods" in place of "painstaking reasoning." It was precisely under this rationale that the second phase of "blooming and contending" was to be brought to an end.

The new doctrine had no less threatening political implications for Mao's opponents in the party. If the Communist Party and its highest leaders were no longer ideologically infallible, as was now suggested, then presumably they were not immune to bourgeois ideological influences. And if class struggle now expressed itself in "the ideological field," then ideological and policy conflicts within the party could be interpreted as class conflicts, and the party itself could become the political arena for a "class struggle" between the "proletariat" and the "bourgeoisie." These views were to become fully politically explicit only in the Cultural Revolution, but in 1957 Mao established the theoretical basis to arrive at such conclusions, and he was increasingly drawn to them over the following years.

The first political result of Mao's February speech was the revival of the Hundred Flowers movement. But the revival was not immediate. The party apparatus was opposed, and the intellectuals were suspicious. Party officials hardly could have been enthusiastic about promoting a campaign to resolve the contradiction between "leaders" and the "led," especially since Mao had identified the bureaucratic practices of the former as the source of the contradiction and had called on the masses to criticize and supervise their leaders as the method to resolve it. And Party resistance reinforced fears among intellectuals that Mao's call was a trap or could prove to be one. The intellectuals, the historian Chien Po-tsan explained,

> have to speculate for example whether the call for flowers to bloom forth is sincere or just a gesture. They have to guess to what extent, if the call is sincere, flowers will be allowed to blossom forth and whether the call will be recalled after the flowers are in bloom. . . . They have to guess which are the problems that can be brought up for discussion and which are the problems which cannot be discussed. . . . When the leadership cadres of some establishments limit themselves to the giving of lip service to the call without taking action to make flowers blossom forth . . . the intellectuals also refrain from airing their views.[25]

Mao persisted nevertheless. Although the text of his February speech remained unpublished, the major points were revealed and elaborated upon in the *People's Daily* and other newspapers. Forums were held in major cities during March and April where intellectuals and leaders of non–Communist groups and parties were assured that the party was sincere in inviting criticism. Mao again spoke to a gathering of intellectuals and emphasized that the Communists welcomed and required criticism. He prodded the central committee to officially sanction "blooming and contending;" at the end of April a party rectification campaign was launched to eliminate the evils of "bureaucratism, subjectivism, and sectarianism." The campaign was to proceed in a manner as gentle as "a breeze" and "as mild as rain," but it was made clear that it was the party that was to be rectified and that it was the nonparty masses in general, and the intellectuals in particular, who were to do the rectifying. And criticism was to focus on the eminently political question of the relationship between "leaders and led."

Once party officials and cadres were ordered not to interfere with free expression, the trickle of dissatisfactions timidly voiced at officially-organized meetings in March and April turned into a torrent of social and political criticism in May and early June. The critics became increasingly bold and their accusations increasingly bitter as the virtual absence of official rebuttals seemed to confirm the solemn promises of party leaders that criticism was genuinely desired. The movement spread and acquired a more and more spontaneous character. Forums sponsored by the "democratic parties" and the United Front Work Department of the Communist Party were supplemented by less formal meetings called by *ad hoc* organizations. Established newspapers were filled with reports of the speeches and comments of the critics, but harsher criticisms were expressed on *ta-tzu-paos* (big character posters) that appeared on the walls of schools and public buildings. Emotions ran high as long-suppressed views and pent-up feelings were expressed in increasingly strident terms.

The atmosphere, for a time, was not unlike that of the early phase of the May Fourth Movement of 1919 when the country was swept by a similar sense of liberation from the oppressions of the past and a similar feeling of freedom and power to strike out against established orthodoxies and institutions. Indeed, many of the student participants compared themselves to their May Fourth predecessors and saw themselves in that hallowed tradition. But, unlike the May Fourth Movement, the Hundred Flowers campaign did not spread, or was not allowed to spread, from urban intellectual circles to the urban masses. No forums of criticism were set up for workers and peasants. The movement remained largely confined to intellectuals and students, although some members of the intelligentsia spoke about the condition of the masses and spoke in their behalf.

The criticisms of the intellectuals which emerged during the brief time they were permitted to express their views ranged from everyday petty grievances to wholesale indictments of the sociopolitical order. Many confined themselves to pleas for a realm of professional autonomy, but others addressed themselves to fundamental social and political questions, such as the monopoly on political power exercised by the Communist Party, a matter brought up for public discussion for the first time in the history of the People's Republic. The Constitution of 1954 provided a "leading role" for the party, but both the constitution and Maoist theory provided freedom and a meaningful political role for the democratic parties. Yet in political reality, no such role existed. The democratic parties' only "freedom" was to formally ratify decisions already made in secret by the CCP. They were neither consulted in advance nor allowed to debate matters of significance, and the condition prevailed from the National People's Congress down to the *hsien* people's councils. What then, it was asked, was the meaning of the heralded "united front," the "democratic dictatorship" of four classes, and the Constitution of the Republic? While the critics detailed specific abuses of power perpetrated by party organs and members, they also raised the larger question of the validity of one-party rule and the absence of any meaningful distinction between the People's Government and the CCP. Although most of those who raised this politically sensitive issue were careful to point out that they accepted the general leadership of the party, they nonetheless made known their objections to a "party-monopo-lized country."

Calls for "socialist legality" were heard, just as they were then being heard in the Soviet Union and the Eastern European countries. What, it was asked, had become of such constitutional rights as freedom of speech, press, and residence, and especially the "inviolable" guarantee of the "freedom of the person of citizens"? The violations of these freedoms were set forth in great detail. The case of Hu Feng was raised time and again. Why, it was asked, had the arrested Hu Feng not been brought to trial in accordance with the law? And why was he still under arrest since most of what he had advocated now had been sanctioned by Mao Tse-tung's February 27 speech? It was proposed that a commission of inquiry investigate illegal arrests and imprisonments that had taken place during the *San–fan* and *SuFan* campaigns. Demands were made that those who had accepted the current invitation to "bloom and contend" would not suffer similar fates.

Aspects of social as well as political life were attacked. There were complaints, for example, that neither the letter nor the spirit of the Marriage Law of 1950 were being observed; old feudal attitudes toward ᵥ ᵣomen persisted even among many party members, it was charged, and the All-China Federation of Democratic Women demonstrated little concern for the continued oppression of women.

Perhaps the most significant—and certainly the most striking—critiques that appeared were those that judged the Communist order on the basis of its own socialist standards. Although the critics of the Hundred Flowers era were soon to be silenced because, it was alleged, they attacked and threatened the socialist system, what was being attacked, in large measure, was not socialism but the failure of the Communists to practice their own socialist principles. For the Communist rulers, nothing that emerged from the Hundred Flowers movement was more dangerous and threatening than the charge that the Communists had betrayed their socialist promises and their revolutionary ideals. The critiques took different forms but they all pointed to the conclusion that the Communists had abandoned their revolutionary traditions, were becoming a "new class," and were promoting socioeconomic inequalities rather than eliminating them. As a leader of the Peasants' and Workers' Democratic Party typically put the matter:

> In leading the masses to carry through the revolution in the past, the Party stood among the masses; after the liberation, it felt the position had changed and, instead of standing among the masses, it stood on the back of the masses and ruled the masses. . . . [leaders] should differ in duties, not in status. Some are deeply conscious of being officials; they occupy special positions even when taking meals and seeing operas.[26]

Party officials and cadres, it was charged, had come to adopt the attitudes of traditional mandarins and Kuomintang bureaucrats and enjoyed similar privileges; they lived in special residences, hired servants, sent their children to "aristocratic schools," and enjoyed special access to vacation resorts, recreational facilities, and medical care—all denied to the masses and all enjoyed at the expense of the masses. "Who are the people who enjoy a higher standard of living?" one critic asked. "They are the Party members and cadres who wore worn-out shoes in the past, but travel in saloon cars and put on woolen uniforms now."[27] The conclusion was drawn by a veteran Communist revolutionary in a lengthy letter to Mao and the central committee: "There is a privileged class in existence. Even if a national united class has not yet been formed, the embryo of this class is forming and developing."[28] The estrangement of the party from the masses, particularly from the peasantry, and its power to appropriate an increasingly disproportionate share of the products of the laboring masses, threatened to create a new division between exploiters and exploited.

For the Marxist critics of the regime, intellectual and political freedom were not abstract principles that could be separated from the nature and content of social development. Nor was freedom a right to be enjoyed by intellectuals alone. Freedom was not only one of the essential ends of socialism, it also was an essential means to achieve socialist goals. Intellectual and political freedom for all the people was necessary to check the growth of bureaucracy, necessary to prevent the formation and solidification of a new bureaucratic ruling class, and necessary for the realization of genuine social equality. A privileged ruling party attracted careerists and bureaucrats who separated themselves from the masses and stood above them. Only when special privileges were eliminated would genuine revolutionaries join the party and the party play its true revolutionary role as the socialist vanguard of the masses. They thus called for a reduction in the number of full-time officials, the abolition of their special privileges, popular supervision over state and party organs, popular control over political and economic life, and the introduction of "socialist democracy," both within and without the party.

The critics did not confine themselves to condemning the inequities between leaders and led; they also pointed to undesirable social inequalities that had emerged among the masses. The party was criticized for ignoring the oppressive burdens under which the peasants labored and for sanctioning, if not promoting, the growing gap between the cities and the countryside. Marxist critics deplored the lack of workers' control in the factories, the absence of free trade unions, and the new system of wage differentials which was creating divisions among the urban proletariat.

It is striking how much of this critique repeated and anticipated the

Maoist critique of Chinese state and society. At the very time of the Hundred Flowers movement, Mao too was lashing out against the privileges and power of a party bureaucracy that had separated itself from the masses and abandoned its revolutionary traditions of "plain living and hard work." In his February speech he had identified "bureaucratic practices" among the leaders as the principal cause of the "contradictions among the people" and declared that "we must stamp out bureaucracy." His attacks on bureaucracy were to become increasingly radical, and he soon was not only to condemn "bureaucratic practices" but to demand the elimination of what he termed "the bureaucratic class"—and, like the critics of 1957, he was to find that class imbedded in the Communist Party. Already in 1957 Mao complained that, "A dangerous tendency has shown itself of late among many of our personnel—an unwillingness to share the joys and hardships of the masses, a concern for personal position and gain."[29] And he long had been concerned with the growth of inequality in Chinese society, and especially the differences between town and countryside. He had referred to the matter briefly in his February speech, noting that "the wages of a small number of workers and some government personnel are rather too high" and that therefore "the peasants have reason to be dissatisfied. . . ."[30] An egalitarian drive to narrow the gap between town and countryside and to strike down urban elites was to be a major purpose of Maoist policies during both the Great Leap Forward campaign and the Cultural Revolution. Even before the year 1957 was out, Mao was to lower wage differentials among urban workers, reversing the "wage reforms" of 1956.

Yet the socialist critics of the spring of 1957 were to be branded as "enemies of socialism" in the summer and fall and condemned as "counterrevolutionaries" in the antirightist campaign that tragically brought the Hundred Flowers movement to an end. And Mao was to place himself at the head of the heresy-hunting campaign of the latter half of 1957 whose victims included many of those who apparently shared his view of the condition of Chinese society and its deficiencies as a socialist society. It is both ironic and tragic that Mao should have participated, or at least acquiesced, in the persecution of intellectuals whom he had invited to "bloom and contend" and whose social and political criticisms were similar to his own. There is an explanation for this seeming paradox, and it lies in differing conceptions of the relationship between freedom and socialism. While Mao shared the egalitarian and anti-bureaucratic aims of the socialist critics, he did not fully share their commitment to freedom and democracy. Mao's inability, or unwillingness, to recognize that the building of institutions of political democracy and institutional guarantees of intellectual freedom are integral parts in the building of socialism was to prove to be one of the fatal flaws in the "Maoist vision."

Beyond the attacks on bureaucracy and inequality, the Hundred

Flowers campaign raised other issues that Mao was soon to take up and champion. Particularly prominent were criticisms of the Soviet Union and the uncritical adoption of Soviet methods. Some attacked the Russians for having dismantled the industrial base of Manchuria at the end of World War II, for having forced China to bear the costs of the Korean War, and for economic aid that entailed political strings and heavy interest payments. In 1957 they were to be denounced as "anti-Soviet and anti-socialist nationalists," but Mao and others were to denounce the Soviet Union in more virulent fashion three years later. Others criticized the "mechanical copying" of Soviet curricula and textbooks in schools and the "blind imitation" of Soviet theories and techniques in science and industry. And they did so on the very eve of the wholesale Maoist abandonment of "the Soviet model." Teachers and students criticized hierarchical distinctions and formalistic methods in schools and universities, anticipating the Maoist attack on the educational system during the Cultural Revolution. Complaints were heard about the neglect of preventive medicine for the masses, that doctors were spending much of their time attending to Party officials, and that traditional medicine was being ignored—complaints soon to be heard from Mao. And the government was reproached for "paying too much attention to the cities." In the summer of 1957, at the height of the anti-rightist campaign, the literary critic Ch'en Ch'i-hsia was accused of having engaged in a conspiracy against the Party; the "evidence" brought to support the charge included a reported statement that peasants might rise in revolt because "living standards are so unequal in town and country." Six months later Mao was to launch the Great Leap Forward campaign, which had as one of its central goals the elimination of the inequalities between urban and rural areas.

University students were the most radical and least inhibited of the Hundred Flowers critics. What became known as "the storm in the universities" began on May 19 at Peking University. Classrooms were emptied as students expressed their criticisms in the form of *ta-tzu-paos* pasted on university buildings and in classrooms; the main arena in "the battle of posters" became known as the Democratic Wall and it was there that the first Chinese translation of Khrushchev's speech denouncing Stalin appeared, an abridged version translated from the New York *Daily Worker*. The movement expanded into rallies, demonstrations and outdoor meetings, centering at an area of the campus renamed the Democratic Plaza. Like the May Fourth Movement, the example set by the students in Peking was emulated at universities throughout the country. The criticisms of the students were much the same as those of older intellectuals, although they put particular emphasis on reducing the power of party committees in the universities and eliminating Soviet influences in education. The main difference was that "blooming and contending" among students took a more explicitly political character. Quasi-political organizations (such as the Hundred Flowers Society) sprang up, distributing leaflets, organizing rallies and publishing mimeographed newspapers. Discussion meetings often turned into "struggle sessions," with party cadres and university administrators the targets of the struggles. Some student leaders quickly acquired national reputations; among the most prominent and outspoken was Lin Hsi-ling, a woman student at a party-cadre training school in Peking, the Chinese People's University, who attacked the "new class" system from a Marxist perspective and argued that China could not achieve a genuine socialist society until China became genuinely democratic. By early June, the growing student movement (which by then had spread from universities to middle-schools) was becoming increasingly militant and sometimes violent; there were reports of students occupying university offices, attacking government and party buildings, and holding school and party officials hostage. And in emulation of their May Fourth predecessors, there was an abortive attempt to "go to the people," as some students attempted to organize workers and peasants.

Although the budding student movement was cut short in mid-June, the rapidity with which students could spontaneously organize for political action against established authority proved a prophetic pointer to the future. In different political circumstances and for different political ends, the phenomenon was to be repeated in the Cultural Revolution on a much vaster scale. The "storm in the universities" of 1957 was not nearly so stormy as the one Mao was to unleash nine years later.

An editorial in the *People's Daily* on June 8 signaled the end of the Hundred Flowers campaign. The authoritative organ of the Party hitherto had remained editorially silent, largely confining itself to reporting the criticisms of the critics. Now it announced that "right-wingers" had abused their freedom in order to attack the socialist system and the leadership of the party. Subsequent editorials gave specific rebuttals of the views which had emerged from the era of "blooming and contending," warned of the danger of anarchy that unrestrained criticisms might produce, and emphasized the need for class struggle against the enemies who had revealed themselves during the campaign. By the middle of the month, the forums where intellectuals had been criticizing the party had turned into sessions where Party officials denounced the critics. The anti-rightist campaign had begun and it was to continue for a year as a heresy hunt for dissidents both within and outside the party. The slogan "let a hundred flowers bloom" remained official policy, but the policy was no longer to cultivate new flowers but to root out "poisonous weeds."

Lest Mao's unpublished February 27 speech be used to justify continued criticism of the party, a revised version was published on June 18 to justify the suppression of the critics. The published version noted that the author had made "certain additions" to the original verbatim record. Among the additions were a list of six criteria to distinguish permissible from unpermissible ideas. The *ex post facto* criteria were sufficiently vague to banish virtually every critic from the ranks of "the people"— and it was solely for the party to determine whether a particular idea tended to strengthen or weaken "the leadership of the Communist Party" or whether it was beneficial or harmful to "socialist transformation." There were other significant additions and deletions, judging from a tape recording of the original, extracts from which were then being circulated in Poland. In the February speech, for example, Mao argued that "Stalin made the mistake of substituting internal differences for external antagonism, which resulted in a rule of terror and the liquidation of thousands of Communists." This was deleted from the published version of June, for at the time the Chinese Communists were preparing to convert a variety of hitherto "nonantagonistic contradictions among the people" into antagonistic class differences. Also deleted was Mao's warning that the use of terroristic methods in dealing with internal antagonisms might result in their transformation into "antagonisms of the nation-enemy type, as happened in Hungary." The June version referred to "certain people in our country [who] were delighted when the Hungarian events took place. They hoped that something similar would happen in China. . . ." During the antirightist drive, some Chinese intellectuals were accused of emulating the Hungarian Petofi Club with the hope of stimulating a revolt to overthrow Communist rule. In the February speech, Mao had been critical of party officials who opposed the Hundred Flowers policy and attributed their opposition to "a fear of criticism"; there was, he said, no need to fear "that the policy of a hundred flowers will yield poisoned fruit," and added that even some of the latter might prove beneficial. In the June publication, by contrast, he emphasized the need to distinguish between "fragrant flowers and poisonous weeds." The officially published version was markedly harsher in tone than the original speech and the revisions were designed to justify repression on the grounds that the intellectuals had gone beyond the bounds of acceptable criticism.

The weight of the antirightist campaign first fell hardest on the leaders of the "democratic parties." Lo Lung-ch'i and Chang Po-chün (both heads of central government ministries) were the most publicized targets, although they had been among the most cautious critics. Subjected to endless denunciation in the press and at rectification meetings, they were forced to confess that they had formed a nationwide "antiparty clique" and organized an "invisible conspiracy" against the socialist system. When original confessions were deemed inadequate, other and more abject ones were demanded. Although the period of "blooming and contending" lasted little more than a month, the era of repentance dragged on into the spring of 1959. The public confessions were similar to those exacted during the heresy hunts in Stalinist Russia. For example, after "confessing" to a bewildering variety of political and ideological sins, Lo Lung-ch'i concluded his self-denunciation: "With contrition, I own that I have failed to live up to the expectations of Chairman Mao, the leadership of the Party, and the scores of thousands of [Democratic] League members. . . . I want to transform myself radically. And I want to work honestly for the socialist cause and the Chinese people."[31] Chang Po-chün concluded his detailed recantation of "my reactionary political program" with the following prostration:

> The whole nation is demanding stern punishment for me, a rightist. This is what should be done and I am prepared to accept it. I hate my wickedness. I want to kill the old and reactionary self so that he will not return to life. I will join the whole nation in the stern struggle against the rightists, including myself. The great Chinese Communist Party once saved me, it saved me once more today. I hope to gain a new life under the leadership and teaching of the Party and Chairman Mao and to return to the stand of loving the Party and socialism.[32]

And Ch'u An-p'ing, chief editor of the *Kwang-ming Daily* until the "anti-rightist" onslaught, was first publicly denounced by his son and then denounced himself: "I sincerely admit my mistakes, ask punishment from the people, and surrender to the people."[33]

But unlike Stalinist Russia, where flagellant "confessions" normally were presented as evidence to pronounce death sentences, in China punishment usually ended after a psychologically torturous ordeal. Lo Lung-ch'i and Chang Po-chün, removed from their ministerial posts in 1957, were reinstated as leaders of the democratic parties and in 1959 resumed their places as delegates to the People's Political Consultative Conference.

Students, who had been the most vehement and determined critics in May and June, were treated relatively leniently and with little public fanfare. The official party line was that the young students, who had grown to maturity in the new society, had been misled by the older bourgeois intellectuals, who were hangovers from the prerevolutionary order. Some student leaders were sent to the countryside for "reform through labor," but most students who were branded as rightists in party-sponsored struggle meetings held during the summer were permitted to remain in school under party supervision. There was at least one notable exception. Three middle-school students accused of leading a riot in Wuhan were publicly executed.

The harshest treatment was reserved for left-wing writers and artists who had advocated freedom to depict actual social conditions. Their earlier experiences with party bureaucrats had made them more suspicious than most intellectuals, and they mostly had confined themselves to oblique criticisms of Maoist orthodoxies on matters of art and literature. But this did not spare them the retribution of Chou Yang, who was reestablished as China's literary dictator by the antirightist campaign. The Hundred Flowers slogan, he declared, was not meant to be a policy of "liberalization as certain bourgeois writers and newspaper reporters imagine, but a militant slogan for the development of socialist culture." The militant development of "socialist culture" meant militancy in the political repression of socialist writers. Chou Yang had scores to settle with old opponents. His principal victim was the Marxist Ting Ling, perhaps the most creative of China's living writers. A Communist Party member since the early days of the revolution, she had spent three years in a Kuomintang prison in the 1930s for other political and ideological heresies. Ting Ling now was accused of fomenting anti-party activities, having been involved in the nonexistent "Lo-Chang" conspiracy, and denounced as a rightist bent on subverting the thoughts of younger writers. She was expelled from the party, removed from her position in the Writers Union, and dispatched to northern Manchuria for "labor reform." Her writings were removed from library shelves and declared prohibited. Similar fates befell other literary intellectuals who were reluctant to confess political sins and the Writers Union was turned into a police organ to punish heretical writers.

The suppression of the Hundred Flowers movement thus destroyed the hope that China's "transition to socialism" might proceed on the basis of some form of popular democracy and with some real measure of intellectual freedom. It reinforced (if, indeed, the political fact needed restatement) that the exercise of state power was a monopoly of the Communist Party, tearing away the last shreds of the facade that the "democratic parties" could play a meaningful role in the political life of the nation. It silenced the intellectuals, Marxists and non-Marxists alike; and if the intelligentsia was not driven into hostile opposition to the regime, the Communists subjected intellectuals to even harsher forms of political and intellectual repression that subsequent events have done little to mitigate. And it restored to absolute primacy Maoist orthodoxies on art and literature which continued to stifle Chinese intellectual and artistic life.

Why did the party—and Mao—betray the promise of a more democratic and free society and break their solemn pledges not to retaliate against the intellectuals they had invited to freely "bloom and contend" and openly criticize the party? Motivations are difficult to read and the passage of time has not made the task any easier. The Hundred Flowers still defies an entirely satisfactory interpretation. One view, widely held at the time both inside and outside China, was that the whole movement was a trap laid by the Communist leadership, a Machiavellian plot to "smoke out" dissenters and then punish them once they exposed themselves. With the "antirightist" campaign, the Hundred Flowers did in effect become that, and some Communist leaders later claimed that this had been the purpose all along. A July 12 *People's Daily* editorial suggested that the party deliberately had permitted "poisonous weeds" to emerge in order to destroy their cultivators. And Liu Shao-ch'i put the same interpretation on the Hundred Flowers policy in May 1958: "we allow the anti-socialist poisonous weeds to grow and confront the people with contrasts, so that by way of comparison, the people can see clearly what they really are, and roused to indignation, rally together to uproot them."[34]

This *ex post facto* explanation serves well the self-image of an infallible and unified Leninist party consistently pursuing a well-charted course. But the party was hardly a monolithic entity in 1956–1957, and all the evidence of the time points to the Hundred Flowers policy as a distinctively Maoist initiative taken in face of the reservations of most party leaders and the opposition of the party apparatus. The question of why the party as such broke its pledge does not really arise since the party as such never really made a pledge in the first place. The question is why Mao made the pledge and then broke it, and neither of the two parts of the question lends itself to easy explanation. There is perhaps some truth in the view that Mao was responding to the upheavals in Eastern Europe, and particularly in Hungary, by loosening the political reins to prevent a similar explosion in China; and then tightening the reins again when the Hundred Flowers seemed to threaten a political explosion in China. A deep concern with the Hungarian Revolution is certainly evident in Mao's February 1957 speech, or at least in the revised version of June. But while events in other Communist countries perhaps influenced the timing and outcome of the second phase of the campaign —the February speech and the resultant "blooming and contending" of May and June—the fact remains that Mao was advocating the Hundred Flowers policy well before the fall 1956 upheavals in Poland (which the Chinese supported against the Soviet Union) and Hungary, and indeed even before Khrushchev's February 1956 speech on Stalin. Maoist motives seem more complex, and more contradictory, than the "letting off steam" theory allows.

The optimistic premise upon which the Hundred Flowers policy was based was that the people were basically united in support of the established socialist system. Certainly one of the most striking features of Mao's speeches and writings from 1955 on is a populist conception of "the people" as a more or less single and organic entity, 600,000,000 "united as one" in the task of building socialism. The conviction that "the interests of the people are basically the same" and that they were conscious of their identity of interests is a notion Mao repeated time and again. And despite his long-standing distrust of intellectuals, or at least "intellectualism," Mao was also convinced that even if most intellectuals were not socialists or Marxists, the overwhelming majority were "patriotic;" and therefore were willing "to serve their flourishing socialist motherland."[35] The problem of "contradictions" lay not so much with the intellectuals, who were conceived to be part of an organically conceived "people," as with party officials who "are not good at getting along with intellectuals."[36] The vision that Mao presented in February 1957 (although there were contradictory strains) was of a relatively peaceful transition to socialism and communism based on "the united front of all patriotic forces."[37] The Hundred Flowers policy of criticism from below and "supervision" from outside the party would serve to prevent leaders from becoming alienated from the people, and peacefully resolve still nonantagonistic contradictions between leaders and led. Popular criticism, it was assumed, would lead to ever higher levels of unity as the nation progressed through ever higher stages of socialist transformation. And it was assumed that a basically united people understood that "freedom" should not go beyond the bounds of socialist "discipline," and that "democracy" should be combined with "centralism."

Another assumption of the Hundred Flowers policy was the long-standing Maoist belief in the value of struggle, partly as an end in itself, and partly as an essential therapeutic device for the development of the correct ideas necessary for the proper transformation of social reality. Marxism itself, Mao emphasized,

> can only develop through struggle—this is true not only in the past and present, it is necessarily true in the future also. What is correct always develops in the course of struggle with what is wrong. The true, the good and the beautiful always exist in comparison with the false, the evil and the ugly, and grow in struggle with the latter. As mankind in general rejects an untruth and accepts a truth, a new truth will begin struggling with new erroneous ideas. Such struggles will never end. This is the law of development of truth and it is certainly the law of development of Marxism.[38]

Thus the development and flourishing of correct Marxist ideas was dependent on Marxists being confronted with the challenge of incorrect ideas. For, as Mao put it, "correct ideas, if pampered in hothouses without being exposed to the elements or immunized from disease, will not win out against wrong ones."[39] Without the challenge of wrong ideas, Marxism would stagnate and the revolutionary spirit would die. Thus the class struggle "in the ideological field" was both inevitable and beneficial, and it was necessary to wage it; indeed, if it did not exist, it would be necessary to create it.

On the one hand, this tremendous emphasis on the necessity of struggle—and a never ending struggle at that—seems in conflict with the Maoist vision of a united people pursuing a peaceful path to socialism and peacefully resolving whatever nonantagonistic contradictions appear along the way. Yet it is precisely through struggle that "the people" attain the proper consciousness to keep them unified, achieve ever higher levels of unity through ever higher levels of ideological transformation, and remain on the proper course of social development. The Maoist notion of a united people peacefully building socialism presupposed constant processes of struggle and ideological transformation. Nor was it only "the people" and the nonparty intelligentsia who stood in need of ideological transformation; the party itself was badly in need in remolding and rectification. Struggle stimulated by criticism from below and outside the party, even (and perhaps especially) if such criticism demonstrated incorrect thoughts, would, it was assumed, serve to revitalize a leadership grown conservative and a party apparatus showing signs of bureaucratic degeneration.

The nature of the criticisms that burst forth in May and June, and the vehemence with which they were expressed, confirmed the worst fears of many party leaders and cadres. And Mao's faith in a basically unified people and a basically pro-socialist intelligentsia was shaken. For he took socialist critiques of the inadequacies of socialism in China as anti-socialist attacks, even though Mao himself was later to repeat many of the critiques he then condemned as "bourgeois rightism." Particularly disturbing was that the most outspoken critics were young students who had grown to maturity after 1949 and whose ideological errors could not be easily attributed to the influences of the old society.

It would be tempting to attribute the end of the Hundred Flowers campaign to conservative Party bureaucrats who opposed Mao's policy from the outset, who had the most to fear from freedom of criticism, and who thirsted for a pretext to suppress the movement and take retribution against their critics—and thus spare Mao the historical responsibility for having purged the critics he had called into being. But the weight of evidence suggests that Mao was little more prepared than other Communist leaders to tolerate criticism that went beyond the vague boundaries of "socialist discipline." As early as May 25 he expressed concern over the direction the campaign was taking: "Any speech or action which deviates from socialism is entirely wrong," he warned in an address to the Communist Youth League. And in June, when the campaign seemed to threaten social and political disorder, he was not reluctant to call on the full power of party and state to launch the antirightist witch hunt. He castigated newspapers for having printed "seditious reports showing the bourgeois point of view" and his statements over the summer months increasingly emphasized the continued existence of class struggle and stressed the need for "discipline" (rather than "freedom") and for "centralism" (rather than "democracy").[40] Although most of China's leaders would not have allowed the Hundred Flowers campaign in the first place, Mao clearly does not emerge from the episode as any champion of the free expression of ideas.

If the suppression of the Hundred Flowers movement and the subsequent antirightist campaign marked a defeat for what some observers have seen as Mao's "liberalizing" vision of a new united front of the whole people and a victory for Mao's conservative party opponents, that defeat was in large measure inherent in the very premises of Mao's Hundred Flowers policy. Both the assumption that "the people" were a basically united entity and the goal of unity lent themselves to a heresy-hunting outcome. For if the people were basically united in their aims and interests, then the implicit assumption was that they would express more or less similar ideas; ideas that diverged from what were deemed to be the socialist interests of the people put their exponents outside the ranks of "the people" and sanctioned depriving them of the right of freedom of speech, a right reserved only for the people and not their "enemies." For the latter, as Mao cavalierly put it in the revised version of his speech, "the matter is easy; we simply deprive them of their freedom of speech."[41] Since the ultimate criterion for determining one's membership in the ranks of "the people" was one's conscious attitudes, the right of "freedom of speech" was a most limited and tenuous one from the outset. Moreover, the stated goal of the campaign was not the free expression of ideas as an end in itself but rather the achievement of higher levels of sociopolitical unity. The Maoist formula in accordance with which the movement was to proceed was "unity–criticism–unity." If criticism threatened to produce disunity, the logical and inevitable Maoist response was to bring it to an end.

If the ending of the Hundred Flowers movement seemingly marked a defeat for Mao and a victory for the established party apparatus, Maoists soon were to turn the ensuing antirightist campaign into an instrument to serve their own political ends. The antirightist campaign began as a party witch hunt to silence and punish its critics. But at a central committee meeting held in Tsingtao in late July, Mao announced that it was to be extended from the cities to the countryside in the form of a "socialist education" campaign. The purpose was to consolidate the collectives, combat "spontaneous tendencies toward capitalism" in the rural areas, and oppose rightist policies which had permitted the expansion of private plots and free markets. By early fall, the sale of agricultural products on the private market was virtually eliminated, peasants who had drifted away from the collectives were persuaded or forced to rejoin, and generally stricter political controls were established over the countryside.

The final Maoist twist of the screw was to turn the Party's antirightist campaign into a massive purge of "rightists" in the Party itself, a campaign officially sanctioned by the central committee in September. Invoking the principle of the mass line, Mao launched attacks against bureaucratism and conservative resistance to socialist transformation. The *hsia-fang* movement, underway since early 1957, was intensified, and urban administrative offices were emptied as state and party officials and cadres were "sent down" to engage in physical labor, mostly in the countryside. By the time the purge had run its course in 1958, over a million party members had been expelled, put on probation, or officially reprimanded. In the process, Maoists regained control of the party apparatus. At the same time, Maoist socioeconomic policies gained the upper hand in the higher councils of the Party, for in the political atmosphere created by the growing antirightist drive it had become politically dangerous to advocate policies that might be considered conservative. Early in October the central committee formally approved Mao's radical twelve-year program for agriculture, thus settling the debate over economic policy that had raged over the previous two years. In effect, it meant the scrapping of the Second Five Year Plan and it led directly to the Great Leap Forward campaign of 1958. One immediate result of the Maoist ascendancy was the reversal of the wage-reform measures of early 1956. Material incentives now were denounced as a rightist deviation. The new and more egalitarian wage policy adopted in November 1957 emphasized social mobilization and moral incentives.

The period of the Hundred Flowers was the time that the Chinese abandoned the Soviet model of development and embarked on a distinctively Chinese road to socialism. It was the time that China announced her ideological and social autonomy from the Soviet Union and its Stalinist heritage. It is a cruel and tragic historical irony that the break with the Stalinist pattern of socioeconomic development was not accompanied by a break with Stalinist methods in political and intellectual life. The latter was precluded by the suppression of the critics who had briefly "bloomed and contended" in May and June of 1957. China thereafter was to follow a new path to socialism, but not one that was to lead to the goals of political democracy and intellectual freedom that the era of the Hundred Flowers seemingly had promised.

Notes

1. Mao Tse-tung, *Socialist Upsurge in China's Countryside* (Peking: Foreign Languages Press, 1957), pp. 159-160.

2. Chou En-lai, "On the Question of Intellectuals," January 14, 1956, in Robert R. Bowie and John K. Fairbank, *Communist China 1955–1959: Policy Documents with Analysis* (Cambridge, Mass.: Harvard University Press, 1962), p. 133.

3. Mao Tse-tung, *On the Correct Handling of Contradictions Among the People* (Peking: Foreign Languages Press, 1957), p. 24.

4. *The Eighth National Congress of the Communist Party of China: Documents* (Peking: Foreign Languages Press, 1956), 1:142.

5. Mao, *On Correct Handling*, p. 9.

6. Chou, "On the Question of Intellectuals," pp. 128–144.

7. The number of party members officially classified as intellectuals jumped dramatically from 1,255,923 in 1956 to 1,880,000 in 1957, out of a total of 12,720,000. Workers numbered 1,740,000 in 1957. See Franz Schurmann, *Ideology and Organization in Communist China* (Berkeley: University of California Press, 1966), p. 132.

8. Mao presented his new views on economic development on April 25, 1956 in the speech "On the Ten Great Relationships." For an English translation of the text, which became available only during the course of the Cultural Revolution, see Stuart R. Schram, ed., *Mao Tse-tung Unrehearsed: Talks and Letters, 1956–71* (Middlesex, England: Penguin, 1974), pp. 61–83. The document is discussed in greater detail in Chapter XIII below.

9. "On the Historical Experience of the Dictatorship of the Proletariat" was followed by a sequel in December 1956, another and more lengthy editorial in the *People's Daily* entitled "More on the Historical Experience of the Dictatorship of the Proletariat," which also dealt with "the question of Stalin" and in a more favorable light. The second installment was written largely in response to later events, and especially the Hungarian revolution.

10. Mao Tse-tung, *The Historical Experience of the Dictatorship of the Proletariat* (Peking: Foreign Languages Press, 1961), pp. 14–18. Mao's "private" views about Stalin were far less flattering. In a talk of 1958, for example; "The Chinese revolution won victory by acting contrary to Stalin's will. . . . If we had followed . . . Stalin's methods the Chinese revolution couldn't have succeeded. When our revolution succeeded, Stalin said it was a fake." Mao Tse-tung "Talks at Chengtu," in Schram, ed., *Mao Tse-tung Unrehearsed*, pp. 102–103.

11. Mao, *Historical Experience*, pp. 7–13.

12. "Let a Hundred Flowers Blossom, a Hundred Schools of Thought Contend!" appeared in the *People's Daily* on June 13, 1956. An English translation was published in Peking in 1958 and is reprinted in Bowie and Fairbank, *Communist China*, 151–163.

13. *Ibid.*, pp. 152–153.

14. *Ibid.*, pp. 152–157.

15. *Ibid.*, pp. 157–162.

16. *Ibid.*, p. 155.

17. Lo's speech to the Chinese People's Political Consultative Conference was delivered on March 18, 1957 and published in the *People's Daily* on March 23. For a partial translation, see Roderick MacFarquhar, *The Hundred Flowers Campaign and the Chinese Intellectuals* (New York: Praeger, 1960), pp. 20–21.

18. "Proposals of the Eighth National Congress of the Communist Party of China for the Second Five-Year Plan for Development of the National Economy," September 27, 1956, in Bowie and Fairbank. *Communist China*, pp. 204–216.

19. Chou En-lai, "Report on the Proposals for the Second Five-Year Plan for Development of the National Economy," September 16, 1956, Bowie and Fairbank, *Communist China*, p. 228.

20. For the most accurate English translation of "On the Ten Great Relationships," see Schram, ed., *Mao Tse-tung Unrehearsed*, pp. 61–83.

21. Mao, *On Correct Handling*, p. 49.

22. *Ibid.*, p. 58.

23. *Ibid.*, p. 50 (italics added).

24. Teng Hsiao-p'ing, "Report on the Revision of the Constitution of the Communist Party of China," *Eighth National Congress of the Communist Party of China*, 1:213.

25. Cited in MacFarquhar, *The Hundred Flowers Campaign*, p. 28.

26. *Ibid.*, p. 49.

27. *Ibid.*, p. 87.

28. *Ibid.*, p. 75.

29. Mao, *On Correct Handling*, p. 66.

30. *Ibid.*, p. 38.

31. Lo Lung-chi, "My Preliminary Examination," Statement presented to the National People's Congress on July 15, 1957. Translated in Bowie and Fairbank, *Communist China*, pp. 331–337.

32. Chang Po-chün, "I Bow My Head and Admit My Guilt Before the People," statement presented to the National People's Congress on July 15, 1957. Translated in Bowie and Fairbank, *Communist China*, pp. 337–341.

33. From a speech delivered to the National People's Congress on July 13, 1957. *Jen-min jih-pao*, July 15, 1957. Translated in MacFarquhar, *Hundred Flowers Campaign*, pp. 285–286.

34. Liu Shao-ch'i, "The Present Situation, the Party's General Line for Socialist Construction and Its Future Tasks," report to the second session of the Eighth National Congress delivered on May 5, 1958. Translated in Bowie and Fairbank, *Communist China*, p. 434.

35. Mao, *On Correct Handling*, p. 52.

36. *Ibid.*, p. 42.

37. *Ibid.*, p. 47.

38. *Ibid.*, p. 51.

39. *Ibid.*, p. 53.

40. See, for example, Mao's comments on "The Bourgeois Orientation of the *Wen-hui Pao*" and "The Situation in the Summer of 1957" in Jerome Ch'en, ed., *Mao Papers* (London: Oxford University Press, 1970), pp. 55–56.

41. Mao, *On Correct Handling*, p. 53.

12

Permanent Revolution:
The Ideological Origins of the Great Leap

NOTHING DOES MORE to obscure the history of the Great Leap Forward campaign of 1958–1960 than the conventional view that it was conceived as a crash program for "modernization." To be sure, the expectation of a "leap" in both agricultural and industrial production was very much a part of the campaign, but by no means the only part. Another part— and it was an inseparable and essential one—was the expectation that rapid economic growth would be accompanied by (and, indeed, propelled by) equally rapid processes of radical social and ideological change. In the Maoist mentality, as it reveals itself in the theory and practice of the Great Leap, the goal of developing China's material productive forces was inextricably intertwined with pursuit of communist social goals and the development of a popular communist consciousness. What distinguished Maoism at the time, and imparted to it a distinctively "utopian" character, was the belief that the building of communist forms of social organization was as much a precondition for modern economic development as its product. What Maoists rejected was the Marxist assumption that socialism and communism are dependent on the prior development of a high level of modern productive forces.

The Great Leap was the Maoist response to the consequences of early industrialization. In the early years of the People's Republic, all Chinese Communists believed that the road to socialism in an economically backward land began with urban industrialization in order to create the necessary material prerequisites for the new society, prerequisites that an abortive capitalism had failed to provide. By 1956 Maoists began to believe that the social costs exacted by that road was too heavy a price for socialists to pay. China's First Five Year Plan had led to the growth and routinization of bureaucracy, the emergence of new patterns of social inequality and privileged elites, a growing gulf between the modernizing cities and the backward countryside and the exploitation of the latter by the former, and processes of ideological decay and ritualization. The social, political, and ideological results seemed to be moving China further away from, rather than toward, a socialist and communist future. The Maoist conclusion was that socialist ends could be attained only by socialist means. And the Maoist remedy for the evils of urban industrialization was to industrialize the countryside. In the new rural communes Maoists would find what appeared to be the ideal agency to reconcile the means and ends of socialism, agencies that would serve the needs of modern economic development at the same time they served as the basic social units for China's "leap" to a communist utopia. In the communization movement of the summer of 1958 Maoists rejected in social practice what they already had come to reject in their socialist theory: the Soviet assumption that the combination of nationalized means of production and rapid industrial development automatically guaranteed the arrival of a communist society. The Second Five Year Plan, scheduled to begin in 1958, was never formally revoked, but it was left to gather dust on the drawing boards of the economic planners.

There were no detailed blueprints for the Great Leap. It was more the product of a social vision than an economic plan on the order of a five-year plan. When the "Great Leap Forward" slogan was set forth in January 1958, Mao outlined general guidelines for China's socioeconomic development, but it is unlikely that communization was firmly in mind. Yet underlying the Maoist vision of the Great Leap were a set of theoretical assumptions and a distinctive theory of economic development from which the communes logically were to emerge.

The ideological impetus for the Great Leap had deep roots in the Maoism of the revolutionary years. Many of the intellectual predispositions that originally had molded the Maoist interpretation and practice of Marxism—and had been reinforced by the whole Chinese Communist revolutionary experience—again came to the fore a decade after the revolutionary victory. A voluntaristic belief that human consciousness and the moral qualities of men are the decisive factors in determining the course of history, a populist belief that true revolutionary creativity resides among the peasant masses, and a particular faith in the revolutionary advantages of backwardness—such are some of the elements of the revolutionary heritage that were revived and given a more radical interpretation. These beliefs, combined with lessons derived from the experiences of a decade of postrevolutionary history, received their most general theoretical expression in what was announced on the eve of the Great Leap as "the theory of permanent revolution."

Mao Tse-tung emerged as an advocate of "permanent revolution" in an unpublished speech delivered to the Supreme State Conference on January 28, 1958 and elaborated on his interpretation of the concept in a report on "work methods" prepared for party circulation three days later.[1] Liu Shao-ch'i brought the term into the public realm in a speech to the second session of the party's Eighth Congress in May when he declared that the Chinese Communist Party always had been guided by "the Marxist–Leninist theory of permanent revolution."[2] The concept appeared prominently in the theoretical literature of the Great Leap period, and eventually was to be formally canonized as part of "Mao Tsetung Thought."

The term "permanent revolution" is identified primarily with Trotsky, but it was also employed by Marx. A brief review of its earlier history might be useful for understanding how the particular Maoist usage reflects the place that Mao Tse-tung occupies in the Marxist theoretical tradition.

Marxism and the Idea of Permanent Revolution

Although there are hints of the notion in the *Communist Manifesto* and earlier writings, the term "permanent revolution" or, more precisely, "The Revolution in Permanence" (*die Revolution in Permanenz*), was explicitly set forth by Marx in his 1850 "Address of the Central Committee to the Communist League." The original theory, was formulated with specific reference to Germany and its comparative socioeconomic backwardness, and took shape in response to the general weakness and political conservatism that the German bourgeoisie had demonstrated in the defeated revolution of 1848; and in anticipation that another European-wide revolutionary upheaval was imminent. The question Marx posed was what should be the role of an embryonic proletariat in a country where the bourgeoisie could not be counted on to carry out its democratic tasks when it was believed that an international revolutionary situation was emerging. Marx's answer was that once the proletariat appeared on the political scene it could not allow a timid bourgeoisie to halt the revolutionary process in midstream; the proletariat would be compelled to achieve political supremacy, establish a "proletarian dictatorship," and more or less immediately transform the bourgeois-democratic revolution into a socialist one. As Marx put the matter:

> While the democratic petty bourgeois wish to bring the revolution to a conclusion as quickly as possible ... it is our interest and our task to make the revolution permanent, until all more or less possessing classes have been forced out of their position of dominance, until the proletariat has conquered state power, and the association of prole-

tarians, not only in one country but in all the dominant countries of the world, has advanced so far that competition among the proletarians of these countries has ceased and that at least the decisive productive forces are concentrated in the hands of the proletarians.[3]

Thus, if the German workers were to pursue their own class interests and not be seduced by the bourgeoisie, their battle cry was to be: "The Revolution in Permanence!"[4]

There is no need here to enter into the old controversy over whether the concept of "permanent revolution" was no more than a temporary "Jacobin–Blanquist aberration" on the part of Marx or whether it was an integral part of his general theory of revolution. It need only be noted that the notion serves to modify the Marxist proposition that there are well-defined political stages of historical development that necessarily correspond to stages of socioeconomic development. For later Marxists in economically backward countries, it provided doctrinal authority to entertain the possibility that even a weak and small proletariat could seize the political opportunity to turn a bourgeois-democratic revolution into a socialist one, at least in the context of an international revolutionary situation.

The notion of permanent revolution does not appear explicitly in the writings of Marx and Engels after 1850, in the decades when the revolutionary situation did not develop according to their earlier expectations, although aspects of the concept reemerge in Marx's interpretation of the Paris Commune of 1871. After 1905, in different political and historical circumstances, it was revived and more elaborately formulated by Trotsky, with whom the theory is primarily identified.

In brief, Trotsky maintained that in the era of international socialist revolution the working classes of the backward countries (Russia, in particular, and the colonial and semicolonial countries of Asia and the Middle East by extension) were potentially more revolutionary than their counterparts in the mature nations of the West. Since the Russian bourgeoisie had proven too weak and too politically timid to perform its appointed bourgeois-democratic historical tasks, those tasks would fall to the proletariat with the assistance of the peasantry. The numerical weakness of the proletariat, it was assumed, was outweighed by its relative political strength and political militancy in economically backward lands, and thus the workers would assume the leadership of the bourgeois-democratic phase of the revolutionary process. Once having gained political hegemony, the proletariat would find it impossible to confine the revolution to bourgeois limits; the necessary outcome would be the establishment of a proletarian dictatorship and the more or less immediate transformation of the revolution into a socialist one. That outcome, in turn, would provide the stimulus for socialist revolutions in the advanced nations of Western Europe—while the materialization of the latter was necessary for the survival of proletarian power in its backward homeland. As Trotsky declared in 1906, in his classic inversion of orthodox Marxism, it was likely that "in a backward country with a lesser degree of capitalistic development, the proletariat should sooner reach political supremacy than in a highly developed capitalist state."[5]

Thus for Trotsky the revolution would be "permanent" in two respects. First, a revolution in an economically backward land could not be confined to any distinct "bourgeois-democratic" phase, but would proceed "uninterrupted" to socialism. Second, a revolution could not be confined to a single nation; the survival of a revolution in a backward country was dependent on the timely outbreak of socialist revolutions in the advanced countries, for only in an international revolutionary context could the permanence of the revolutionary process be maintained.

These perspectives guided Lenin as well as Trotsky in the Russian October Revolution. The events of 1917–1918 dissolved all but terminological and semantic distinctions between Lenin's theory of "the democratic dictatorship of the proletariat and peasantry" and Trotsky's theory of "permanent revolution." It was not until the advent of Stalin that the notion of permanent revolution became an ideological heresy in a newly canonized Marxist-Leninist orthodoxy. Stalin's doctrine of "socialism in one country" replaced the internationalist revolutionary perspective while the notion of an "uninterrupted" revolutionary process was replaced by the dogma that all revolutions (save perhaps the Russian) must proceed through distinct and well-defined stages of sociopolitical development. Thus when Mao proclaimed in January 1958 that "I advocate the theory of permanent revolution,"[6] he invited the charge of "Trotskyism," and he soon was to hear the accusation, despite the fact that such Trotskyists as could be found in the People's Republic languished in Chinese jails. It is hardly surprising that Mao hastened to add that the theory he was expounding should not be confused with Trotsky's, although between the two there are significant similarities as well as vast differences.

Maoism and the Concept of Permanent Revolution

The Maoist version of the theory begins with the view that the whole process to and through the realization of communism is characterized by an endless series of social contradictions and struggles which can be resolved only by radical revolutionary breaks with existing reality. Progress from one phase to another "must necessarily be a relationship between quantitative and qualitative changes. All mutations, all leaps forward are revolutions which must pass through struggles. The theory of [the] cessation of struggles [in a socialist society] is sheer metaphysics." Moreover, the resolution of contradictions can only be transient, for "disequilibrium is normal and absolute whereas equilibrium is temporary and relative."[7]

Mao's emphasis on "disequilibrium" as an absolute and universal law of historical development was the very antithesis of the rational planning and calculating mentality that went into the making of five year plans of economic development—a notion profoundly unsettling to Chinese economic planners and most party leaders. For Mao, on the other hand, the combination of rapid economic development and a continuous process of increasingly radical social and ideological transformations were necessary to fully release the latent productive energies of the masses and to prevent the ever-present danger of backsliding into capitalism. As he declared in his January 28 speech, "In making revolution, one must strike while the iron is hot, one revolution following another; the revolution must advance without interruption."[8] And the revolutionary advance was to be social as well as economic, for the central Maoist assumption was that the socialist transformation of the "superstructure" was more the precondition for modern economic development than the product of it. In setting forth the concept of "permanent revolution" in early 1958, Mao called for a "great technical revolution," but the call presupposed an already completed—or an about-to-be-completed—socialist revolution "on the political and ideological fronts."[9] And the Maoist practice of permanent revolution, as it was revealed in the policies of the Great Leap, stressed the cultivation of a popular "communist consciousness" and the creation of embryonic forms of communist social organization as much as it did the "technical revolution." In the Maoist view, the process of modern economic development begins with the seizure of state power, is followed by the transformation of productive relationships, and the latter in turn opens the way for the development of productive forces.[10]

What is rejected in the Maoist version of permanent revolution is not rapid economic development but rather the Marxist–Leninist view that there are well-defined and more or less prolonged stages of sociopolitical development that correspond to stages in the development of material productive forces. What is affirmed is that changes in the "superstructure"—in social relationships, political forms, and ideological consciousness—must be accomplished as quickly as possible, "one after the other," if the goals of the revolution are to be achieved. Thus in summarizing Chinese sociohistorical development since 1949, Mao emphasized the uninterrupted character of the revolutionary process. No sooner had the bourgeois phase of the revolution been completed (with the completion of the land-reform campaign), than China embarked upon the transition to socialism, a revolution "basically completed" in 1956 according to Mao. And now (in 1958) the Great Leap Forward campaign was not only to bring about a technological revolution but also was to mark China's passage from socialism to communism. For Mao these were fundamental revolutionary "leaps" in social, political, and ideological life—and the process of social change obviously was proceeding much more rapidly than the rate of economic development. Within a decade after the revolutionary victory, China had passed through the bourgeois-democratic and socialist revolutions and, according to the Maoist perspective of the time, was prepared for a leap to a communist society. But China, as Maoists acknowledged, remained a poor and economically backward country. This, of course, invited accusations of the Trotskyist heresy of "leaping over stages." To ward off the accusations Maoists countered with a purely verbal orthodoxy: "We are advocates of permanent revolution but also believe in revolution by stages." But the "stages" of social development, at least in theory, are passed through so rapidly that in this respect Mao emerges as a super-Trotskyist.

At the same time, he also emerges as an anti-Stalinist. It is, after all, a principal Stalinist (and post-Stalinist Soviet) orthodoxy that such contradictions as exist in a presumably socialist society can be resolved by a gradual process of evolutionary change. The Maoist view that the struggle to achieve socialism and communism demands qualitative "leaps," radical breaks with the past, and a continuous series of revolutions appears as an explicit theoretical rejection of Stalinism—just as the Maoist practice of the Great Leap marks a wholesale rejection of the entire Soviet pattern of socioeconomic development.

The whole vision of a continuous process of revolutionary change that would rapidly transform China into a country both economically modern and socially communist was based on a profound faith in the powers of the human consciousness and the human will to bring about that transformation. Just as Maoist revolutionary strategy had rested on a faith that determined men motivated by the proper ideas and moral values could triumph over the most formidable material obstacles, so now a similar faith was brought to bear to deal with postrevolutionary problems of social and economic development. If China lacked the Marxian-defined economic prerequisites for a communist society, those objective economic conditions could be brought into existence in the very process of striving to realize ultimate communist goals, a process that the notion of permanent revolution demanded be undertaken in the here and now. The key to success was a mobilized people armed with the proper revolutionary spirit, will, and leaders. In launching the Great Leap and setting forth the utopian social and economic goals it was to achieve, Mao looked to the "subjective" factors in history, to what he called "the boundless creative powers" of the masses and their "inexhaustible enthusiasm for socialism."

If modern economic development itself did not guarantee the arrival of a communist future, a modern economy and the abundant life it promised was nevertheless very much a part of the vision of that future.

Maoists did not envision a primitive communist utopia existing in per-
petual conditions of economic scarcity. From the very beginning of the
Great Leap, Mao emphasized the necessity for a "great technical revolution." Chinese industrial production, Mao declared in January 1958,
would overtake that of England in fifteen years, and this became one of
the great popular rallying cries of the time. The manner in which Mao
conceived the problem of carrying out the technical revolution, which he
discussed in outlining his theory of permanent revolution, reflects the
decisive role of human consciousness implicit in that theory. In analyz-
ing the relationship between economic and psychological factors, Mao
described a vicious cycle in which economic stagnation and mental stagnation tend to reinforce each other. Because of China's economic backwardness, her people were still "spiritually restricted" and "unable to
take much initiative." The way to break the cycle was to stimulate the
consciousness of the masses, release their latent energies, and turn them
to the task of economic development. The task was like fighting a never
ending war: "After a victory, we must at once put forward a new task.
In this way, cadres and masses will forever be filled with revolutionary
fervour. . . ."[11]

Once the process started, there would be a progressive and dynamic
cyclical development of ever higher levels of consciousness and economic
progress, each stimulating the progressive movement of the other. As applied to economic development, "permanent revolution" meant a constant
process of ideologically inspired mass activism: "Ideological work and
political work is the guarantee for the completion of economic technological work and it serves the economic basis. Ideology and politics are the
commanders, the soul."[12]

In the Maoist worldview, the emergence of the new society presupposes the emergence a spiritually transformed people. The slogans that
guided the Great Leap Forward campaign—"man is the decisive factor"
and "men are more important than machines"—logically flowed from
these views and assumptions, as did Maoist theoretical treatises that concluded with the striking proposition that "the subjective can create the
objective." The notion of permanent revolution is therefore above all a
formula for the continuous revolutionization of consciousness and the
activation of human energies as the key to the achievement of the social
and economic goals proclaimed in Marxist theory and promised by the
Chinese Revolution.

Another prominent aspect of the Maoist version of "permanent revolution," even though it is not explicitly formulated in the theory itself,
is a populist belief that the true sources of revolutionary creativity reside
in the countryside. Just as the Maoist revolutionary strategy of "people's
war" was based on a profound faith in the spontaneous revolutionary
strivings of the peasantry, so the emergent Maoist strategy for postrevo-

lutionary socioeconomic development took on an equally strong agrarian orientation. In 1958, as in 1927, "the people" were defined essentially as the vast peasant masses and Maoists again looked primarily to the countryside for the sources of progress and regeneration. The potential to achieve the appropriate transformation of morality and consciousness was attributed essentially to "the pioneering peasants," not to the urban populace. The functions of proletarian dictatorship and the tasks of the transition to communism were assigned not to the urban proletariat but rather to the rural people's communes. During the Great Leap Forward, the rural people's commune was seen as the agency to eliminate the differences between town and countryside, between peasants and workers, and between mental and manual labor; and, indeed, even to eventually abolish the domestic functions of the state. The policies of the Great Leap Forward campaign emphasized "the industrialization of the countryside" and one of the prominent slogans of the time was "the urbanization of the countryside and the ruralization of the cities." Permanent revolution meant the permanence of agrarian revolution.

Closely associated with the voluntarist emphasis on the decisive role of human consciousness in history and the populist faith in the revolutionary capacities of the peasantry was another long-held Maoist belief revived on the eve of the Great Leap Forward campaign, which underlies the whole conception of "permanent revolution"—namely, a particular perception of the "advantages of backwardness." What is involved here is not simply the now familiar idea that economically backward nations in the modern world are offered the advantage of speeding up their development by borrowing the technologies of the industrially advanced countries. Rather, it is a more general and pervasive faith in the moral–social virtues and revolutionary political advantages of backwardness as such, a faith not dissimilar to that which was held by the nineteenth-century Russian Narodniks. As early as 1919, before his conversion to Marxism, Mao deplored China's impotence and wretched backwardness but nevertheless saw in that very condition a huge reservoir of youthful creativity and revolutionary energy, which augured well for the future. "Our Chinese people possess great intrinsic energy. . . . The more profound the oppression, the greater the resistance; that which has accumulated for a long time will surely burst forth quickly."[13] And from the beginning of his career as a Marxist revolutionary, Mao was disposed to find the sources of modern revolution in those areas of society least influenced by modern economic forces—in a peasantry relatively uninvolved in capitalist relationships and in a deurbanized intelligentsia relatively uncorrupted by the bourgeois ideas which pervaded the cities. It was this conversion of China's backwardness into a revolutionary virtue that led Mao to predict in 1930 that "the revolution will certainly move towards an upsurge more quickly in China than in Western Europe,"[14] and to draw a dichotomy between the revolutionary countryside and the conservative cities in the making of the Chinese revolution.

This tendency to celebrate the revolutionary advantages of backwardness received its most radical formulation in the "poor and blank" thesis, the special revolutionary virtues that Mao attributed to the Chinese people in April of 1958:

> Apart from their other characteristics, China's 600 million people have two remarkable peculiarities; they are, first of all, poor, and secondly blank. That may seem like a bad thing, but it is really a good thing. Poor people want change, want to do things, want revolution. A clean sheet of paper has no blotches, and so the newest and most beautiful words can be written on it, the newest and most beautiful pictures can be painted on it.[15]

The condition of being "poor" and "blank" not only demanded a process of "permanent revolution" to overcome that condition rapidly but made possible an uninterrupted development leading to communism, for it was precisely because of China's backwardness that her people possessed special revolutionary capacities and were uniquely amenable to the appropriate spiritual transformation; they could write, or could have written on them, "the newest and most beautiful words." For, as Mao later declared: "In history it is always people with a low level of culture who triumph over people with a high level of culture."[16]

Implicit in the "poor and blank"' thesis is a notion strikingly similar to a central theme in nineteenth-century Russian Populist thought—the assumption that an economically backward country does not suffer from the historical "overmaturity" and the moral decadence that had stifled the revolutionary spirit in the advanced Western nations and is therefore potentially more revolutionary than other countries. Just as the Russian Populists proclaimed preindustrial Russia to be closer to socialism than the industrialized nations of the West precisely because of the relative absence of modern capitalist economic development, so Mao proclaimed the special Chinese revolutionary virtues of being poor and blank and saw preindustrial China pioneering the way to a universal socialist and communist future. Just as Herzen had declared that "we possess nothing" to declare his faith in Russia's socialist future,[17] Mao found China "a clean sheet of paper," and in this condition the promise of its future socialist greatness.

If the Chinese people in general were characterized by being "poor and blank," those virtues were especially characteristic of two special sections of the people. For the poorest of the people were the peasants and the most "blank" the youth. While poor peasants most wanted revolution, Mao believed, he also believed that the youth of China were the most receptive to the appropriate transformation of ideology and spirit.

If the "poor and blank" thesis served to reinforce Mao's belief that the peasantry was the truly revolutionary class in Chinese society, it also marked the revival of the special faith in youth that characterized the formative stages of his intellectual development, the New Youth era of 1915–1919. "From ancient times," Mao remarked in a speech in 1958, "The people who have created new schools of thought have always been young people without great learning."[18]

What relationship does the Maoist conception of permanent revolution bear to the conceptions of Marx and Trotsky? That Mao choose to adopt the Marxist term, and especially in view of its heretical standing in Soviet Marxist–Leninist orthodoxy, is itself a matter of some significance. The choice dramatized Chinese political and ideological autonomy from Moscow and the Maoist determination to pursue a distinctively Chinese road to communism, and at the same time it reflected the desire of Maoists to tie themselves to the Marxist tradition and draw upon its most voluntaristic strains. But apart from the use of the term itself, the Maoist theory has rather little in common with the conceptions of either Marx or Trotsky. While the Chinese version retains (and, indeed, magnifies) the general notion that a backward country might telescope stages of revolutionary development, it does so in an historical context, on the basis of ideological assumptions, and through proposed means that together constitute a wholesale rejection of many of the most fundamental premises of Marxist theory. While Marx and Trotsky raised the possibility of permanent revolution with reference to a bourgeois revolution passing over into a socialist one in an international revolutionary situation, the Maoist theory addresses itself to what was assumed to be the period of the transition from socialism to communism in China alone, without reference to any international revolutionary process. Whereas Marx and Trotsky assumed that the success of a socialist revolution in an economically backward country was ultimately dependent on successful socialist revolutions in the advanced industrialized nations, for only the latter could provide the material conditions for any genuinely socialist society, the Maoist assumption is that economic backwardness is not a barrier to either the socialist or the communist reorganization of society. Indeed, backwardness is converted into a revolutionary virtue which yields the human energies and moral purity for the process of permanent revolution, and thus China can advance to a communist utopia on the basis of her own meager material resources. And while Trotsky as well as Marx believed that only the urban proletariat could transform a bourgeois revolution into a socialist one, the Maoist belief is that the true sources for revolutionary social transformation reside in the peasantry and that the countryside is the main arena where the struggle to achieve socialism and communism will be determined.

The Maoist version of permanent revolution rests on a literal interpretation of the Marxist premise that "men make history," an extreme voluntarist belief that human consciousness (and the consequent political activity of men) is the decisive factor in determining the course of social development. Marx, to be sure, believed that "men make their own history," but he also insisted, as did Trotsky, that "they do not make it just as they please; they do not make it under circumstances chosen by themselves, but under circumstances directly encountered, given and transmitted from the past."[19] For Mao, such Marxian historical restraints on the emergence and activation of the human consciousness are largely absent, and thus dedicated men with the proper ideas and will are free to mold objective reality in accordance with their consciousness, "just as they please," in large measure, regardless of both the particular national socioeconomic conditions and the general international revolutionary conditions in which they may find themselves.

These Maoist departures from the premises of Marxism find their most radical expression in the "poor and blank" thesis with which the Maoist notion of permanent revolution is so intimately connected. Men, Marx once warned (and even Trotsky's conception of permanent revolution retained the warning), "do not build themselves a new world out of the fruits of the earth, as vulgar superstition believes, but out of the historical accomplishments of their declining civilization. They must, in the course of their development, begin by themselves producing the material conditions of a new society, and no effort of mind or will can free them from this destiny."[20] For Maoists, by contrast, it is not the accomplishments of the past that are important but rather the belief that the present is unburdened by the historical weight of the past. It is the condition of being "poor and blank" that gives rise to the confidence in the emergence of the new society. Reflected in this celebration of the "advantages of backwardness" is the absence of any real Marxist faith in the objective forces of history, the lack of the Marxist conviction that socialism and communism are immanent in the progressive movement of history itself. Rather, what is decisive in determining the historical outcome are the "subjective factors," the consciousness, the moral values and the actions of dedicated people. On the basis of this conviction the policies of the Great Leap Forward were formulated and implemented.

Notes

1. "Sixty Points on Working Methods," in Jerome Ch'en, ed., *Mao Papers* (London: Oxford University Press, 1970), pp. 57–76.
2. Liu Shao-ch'i, "The Present Situation, the Party's General Line for Socialist Construction and Its Future Tasks," May 5, 1958, Bowie and Fairbank, *Communist China 1955–1959: Policy Documents with Analysis* (Cambridge, Mass.: Harvard University Press, 1962), p. 425.

3. "Address of the Central Committee to the Communist League," March, 1850, in Karl Marx and Frederick Engels, *Selected Works* (Moscow: 1950), 1:102.

4. *Ibid.*, 1:108.

5. Leon Trotsky, *Our Revolution* (New York, 1918), p. 84. Trotsky originally set fourth the theory in his *Results and Prospects* of 1906. For a recent English edition of the work, see Leon Trotsky, *The Permanent Revolution and Results and Prospects* (New York: Pathfinder Press, 1974), pp. 29–122.

6. Mao Tse-tung, "Speech to the Supreme State Conference." For an English translation, see *Chinese Law and Government*, 1, No. 4:10–14.

7. Sixty Points on Working Methods," pp. 65–66.

8. Mao, "Speech to the Supreme State Conference."

9. Mao, "Sixty Points on Working Methods."

10. As Mao later formulated the matter in a 1961 critique of Stalinism entitled "Reading Notes on the Soviet Union's 'Political Economy,'" *Mao Tse-tung Ssu-hsiang Wan-sui* (Taipei, n.p., 1969), pp. 319–399.

11. Mao, "Sixty Points on Working Methods," p. 63.

12. *Ibid.*, p. 64.

13. "The Great Union of the Popular Masses," *Hsiang-chiang p'ing-lun*, July–August, 1919. For a partial English translation, see Stuart Schram, *The Political Thought of Mao Tse-tung* (New York: Praeger, 1969), p. 163.

14. Mao Tse-tung, "A Single Spark Can Start a Prairie Fire," in *Selected Works of Mao Tse-tung* (Peking: Foreign Languages Press, 1961), 1:118.

15. *Hung-ch'i* (Red Flag), June 1, 1958, pp. 3–4. For an English translation, see *Peking Review*, June 10, 1958.

16. Mao Tse-tung, "Reading Notes on the Soviet Union's 'Political Economy,'" *Mao Tse-tung Ssu-hsiang Wan-sui* (JPRS translation, p. 307.)

17. Alexander Herzen, "The Russian People and Socialism" (1851), in Herzen, *From the Other Shore* (London: Weidenfeld & Nicolson, 1956), p. 199.

18. "Talk at Chengtu," March 22, 1958, in Stuart R. Schram, ed., *Mao Tse-tung Unrehearsed: Talks and Letters 1956–71* (Middlesex, England: Penguin 1974), p. 118.

19. Karl Marx, "The Eighteenth Brumaire of Louis Bonaparte," in Marx and Engels, *Selected Works* (1950), 1:225.

20. Karl Marx, "Die moralisierende Kritik und die kritisierende Moral," in Karl Marx, *Selected Writings in Sociology and Social Philosophy* (London: Watts, 1956), p. 240.

13

Economics of the Great Leap Forward

THE "GREAT LEAP" STRATEGY of socioeconomic development relied ultimately on what Maoists perceived to be the "revolutionary enthusiasm" of the masses, especially the peasant masses, but it did not assume that moral zeal alone would bring about modern economic development. The utopian fervors and expectations of 1958 were accompanied by (and not wholly unrelated to) a distinctive Maoist theory of economic development, which even on strictly economic grounds emerges as neither illogical nor irrational when viewed in light of concrete Chinese socioeconomic realities.

To understand the economic rationale of the Great Leap Forward, it is useful to distinguish between the Maoist theory of economic development and the manner in which it was implemented during the course of the campaign. The distinction is partly artificial because Maoist theory only fully reveals itself in practice, but in this case a largely abstract exposition seems justified because of the vast gap between what was intended and what was actually done. In the final analysis, of course, Maoists, like all other historical actors, must be judged on the basis of what they have done rather than on the basis of what they intended to do.

A distinctively Maoist economic theory took shape in response to three major problems that confronted Chinese society as the First Five Year Plan was drawing to a close. First, there was the immediate and pressing problem of growing unemployment in the cities and underemployment in the countryside, chronic problems which the First Five Year Plan had failed to resolve and the proposed Second Five Year Plan offered little promise of alleviating. Second, there was the more general question of how to speed up the process of "primitive socialist accumulation." With little prospect of any significant foreign capital investment, the question turned on how to make most efficient use of China's major resource, human labor. And that, in turn, called into question the efficacy of concentrating on the development of capital-intensive heavy industries. Quite apart from the social consequences of urban industrialization, Maoists raised the question of whether China's long-range needs of national economic development could be met by a continued reliance on the Soviet model of development. Third, the general recognition that China required a "technical revolution" raised the problem of how modern technology and science could be rapidly mastered and how that mastery could be attained without fostering bureaucratism and social inequality—without, in short, permitting the development of a privileged technological intelligentsia.

Problems of Population, Unemployment, and Underemployment

One of the characteristic features of economically backward countries in the modern world is that urbanization has proceeded much more rapidly than industrialization. Among the results and contemporary legacies of imperialism and colonialism is not only the phenomenon of "lopsided development" between modern cities and backward rural areas, but the development of cities themselves in an economically distorted and socially disfigured form. In cities built on weak and structurally deficient industrial bases, huge populations conglomerate, the great majority living in destitution and squalor on the fringes of modern economic life. The horrendous social consequences are painfully apparent today in most of the urban centers of Asia, Africa, and Latin America, as they were in pre-1949 China. While the Chinese Communists succeeded in alleviating the worst social abuses in the cities during the first years of their rule, they were not successful in dealing with the more fundamental problem of "overpopulated" cities. Although urban industry and the urban proletariat grew rapidly in the 1950s, the increase in the urban population from 57,000,000 in 1949 to about 100,000,000 in 1957 cannot be accounted for in terms of the growth of the urban economy alone. Many of the new urban dwellers were peasant migrants unable to find work in urban enterprises and who subsisted on the fringes of the modern sector of the economy. The result was persistent widespread unemployment and underemployment in the cities.

The government was reluctant to recognize the problem. When the First Five Year Plan began in 1953, most economic planners assumed that a rapidly growing industry would create sufficient employment opportunities for a rapidly growing urban population. On the basis of that assumption they rejected birth and population control (denounced as anti-Marxist Malthusian heresies) and did little to control rural migration to the cities.

Only in the new intellectual atmosphere of the Hundred Flowers era was the issue of population control seriously debated and the proponents of birth control permitted to openly advocate it. Even Mao, in the original version of "On the Correct Handling of Contradictions Among the People," briefly emerged as an advocate of population control.[1] The new official interest in the matter reflected an increasing concern with the employment problem and a growing recognition that industrialization would not resolve the problem. Various *hsia-fang* campaigns to send urbanites to the countryside served only to compound the problem of underemployment in the rural areas, which already contained a larger population than the existing socioeconomic organization of agriculture could absorb.

Urban unemployment reached crisis proportions in early 1957, when the poor harvest of the previous autumn and dislocations resulting from collectivization greatly increased the flow of peasants moving to the cities; the problem was aggravated by a campaign to reduce the size of the bureaucracy, a greater than normal number of demobilized soldiers, and a reduction in the number of middle-school graduates permitted to enter universities. The intensified *hsia-fang* campaign in late 1957, partly an attempt to alleviate growing unemployment in the cities, did not address itself to the basic reasons for unemployment and underemployment in either town or countryside. By then, Chinese leaders were aware that urban unemployment was a fundamental socioeconomic problem that was inherent in the economic policies of the time, one that would not soon disappear. Even Mao's optimistic Twelve Year Plan for Agricultural Development (first proposed in early 1956 and officially adopted only late in 1957) assumed that it would take from five to seven years to achieve full employment in the cities, and even that hope rested on the assumption that a rapidly expanding rural economy would absorb the surplus urban population. And China's more orthodox economic planners, in drawing up the Second Five Year Plan, acknowledged that increasingly high levels of unemployment could be anticipated, on the order of 5,000,000 additional unemployed a year.[2] Given China's huge and rapidly growing population, a continued emphasis on large-scale, capital-intensive modern industries meant, at least in the short run, rising levels of unemployment and chronic underemployment.

The dramatic change announced by the new Maoist economic strategy in 1958 essentially involved a wholesale shift of emphasis from capital-intensive to labor-intensive projects—a shift from heavy industry to agriculture, light industry, and small- and medium-scale industries which required relatively little capital investment but rather demanded the maximum utilization of labor. In this sense, it was a policy designed to solve the problem of unemployment in both town and countryside— and to do so at one stroke. At the same time, it was a policy that announced itself as an immediate solution to China's population problem, for in the perspective of an economic strategy based on the maximal use of labor a large and growing population was seen not as a barrier to modern development but rather as an economic asset. Whereas in early 1957 Mao favored population control, in early 1958 he declared that "the more people there are the greater ferment of ideas, the greater the enthusiasm and the energy."[3] The debate on population control was thus "resolved" and advocates of birth control once again were accused of Malthusian heresies.

Labor Power and "Primitive Socialist Accumulation"

The task of "primitive socialist accumulation" (the raising of capital to build the modern industrial base on which a future socialist society presumably would rest) was accomplished in the Soviet Union largely through the exploitation of the peasantry. As the Soviet industrialization debates of the 1920s reveal, the economic strategy which Stalin adopted involved a conscious decision to extract from a "collectivized" peasantry the capital necessary to pursue a crash program of industrial development and to totally subordinate the development of agriculture and consumer goods industries to the overriding goal of creating a vast heavy industrial sector as rapidly as possible. It was accompanied by the belief that an established modern industrial base would have a "spread" effect, eventually leading to the modernization of the economy as a whole.

As in the Soviet case, the capital for China's industrialization in the 1950s had been extracted largely from the countryside. Whether the continuance of the Stalinist strategy, as proposed in the draft of the Second Five Year Plan, would have modernized China as it did Russia is highly problematic in view of the fact that China had begun her "primitive socialist accumulation" on a far lower economic level and with a vast peasantry existing on the barest margins of subsistence. At the very minimum, the continued pursuit of the Soviet model would have demanded the introduction of increasingly repressive and far more exploitive agrarian policies. A determination to avoid exploiting the countryside for the benefit of the cities was one crucial factor that motivated the new Maoist strategy of economic development. Another was the belief that capital could be accumulated more rapidly and invested more equitably through the intensive mobilization and utilization of the untapped labor power of the masses, particularly the peasant masses.

The policies introduced in 1958 did not reject the development of heavy industry, much less were they a Luddite repudiation of modern economic life in general. Indeed, it was envisioned that such capital-intensive and strategic industries as steel and iron, chemicals, and machine-building would develop even more rapidly than before—but not at the expense of the development of agriculture and light industries. Rather, all sectors of the economy were to develop together and develop rapidly through the formula of "simultaneous development," the principal economic notion of the Great Leap. Heavy capital investments in the advanced industrial sector would continue, but at the same time there would be increased investments in light industry and agriculture, and the three would grow together in dynamic fashion, with each stimulating the development of the others. The Maoist argument, simply put, was that the promotion of light industries producing inexpensive consumer goods for peasant consumption was essential to motivate peasants to increase agricultural production, while greater agricultural output, in turn, would further stimulate the development of light industry and was the essential prerequisite for the state to accumulate sufficient capital for heavy industrial development. On the basis of this concept of dynamic interaction among the three economic sectors Mao had declared as early as 1956 that, "if you have a strong desire to develop heavy industry, then you will pay attention to the development of light industry and agriculture."[4] From this statement flowed the policy of "simultaneous development" as the most rapid road to the building of a modern economy.

While a process of "simultaneous development" clearly would be the best of all possible economic worlds, it was by no means universally clear that the Maoist policy was within the realm of the possible. No one questioned the desirability of developing all sectors of the economy in a manner that was "faster, better, and cheaper," as the slogan of the time went, but questions were raised as to how it could be done. It had been assumed that the modern industrial sector could be developed rapidly only at the expense of other sectors—and most Chinese Communist leaders had been willing to accept the social and economic consequences of that assumption. If capital investments in heavy urban industry were not to be reduced, then how was a "great leap forward" in light industries and agriculture to be financed? The Maoist answer was that the key to simultaneous development was the labor power of the Chinese masses; through the establishment of new forms of social organization and through the proper ideological guidance, the hitherto unutilized or underutilized labor potential of the people could be released and mobilized in a vast crusade to conquer nature. It was a principal Maoist assumption that the new labor-intensive projects in industry as well as agriculture would not require new capital but rather would generate it.

Since most of China's labor power, and an even greater proportion of its underutilized labor, resided in the peasantry, the new strategy of rapid economic development focused on the countryside rather than on the cities. The labor potential of the peasants, which could be utilized only partially in agricultural production even under the best of circumstances, was now to be fully realized by promoting the industrial development of the rural areas. The huge reservoir of surplus labor left over by the "slack" seasons in agriculture was to be turned to the development of small- and medium-scale industries that required little capital investment. Labor-intensive industries such as crop processing, tool manufacturing, simple consumer-goods production, shale-oil production, and small chemical and fertilizer plants could grow in conjunction with agricultural production in rural areas. Such locally-based industrial projects not only would make more efficient use of the labor power of the peasant masses, but also would bring industry closer to sources of raw materials (and thus reduce strains on the fragile transportation system), exploit poorer quality raw materials not suitable for use in urban-based heavy industrial enterprises, encourage technological innovations based on local needs and conditions, and generally result in rapid capital accumulations to support large-scale construction and industrial projects.

This combination of industrial and agricultural production was seen as desirable on social as well as economic grounds. The growth of local industries would promote the economic development of the more backward regions of the country and reduce regional socioeconomic inequities; and rural industrialization, even initially in the form of small-scale labor-intensive projects, was viewed as a step in abolishing the distinctions between workers and peasants, and between town and countryside.

The new Maoist economic strategy presupposed a radical decentralization of socioeconomic life—and indeed, of political organization as well. In contrast to the form of decentralization that had been inaugurated in the autumn of 1957, whereby a large degree of administrative authority had been passed down from the central government and the economic ministries in Peking to provincial and municipal administrative units and to large-scale economic enterprises (a form similar to post-Stalinist changes in the Soviet Union and many East European countries), the Maoist policies of 1958 implied a wholesale dismantling of centralized bureaucratic structures and economic planning organs, and the transfer of economic decision-making to basic production units. The Maoist argument was that the full utilization of local resources and labor power demanded that economic decentralization be carried down to the localities, that the initiative and creativity of the masses in production could be brought forth fully only if the people themselves participated in economic planning in their own communities.

Decentralization and the emphasis on local development did not mean, or at least was not intended to mean, the abandonment of national economic planning, especially not insofar as the modern industrial sector was concerned. Even more ambitious plans were drawn up for the development of heavy industry. The new industrial policy of "walking on two legs" envisioned the rapid development of both the large-scale modern sector and small- and medium-scale industries in the interior based on indigenous technologies and local resources. Since the latter were labor-intensive operations, it was assumed that there would be no lessening of the rate of capital investment in heavy industry.

The Technological Revolution

What is often taken as Mao's "anti-technocratic bias" was not a bias against modern technology and science as such, but rather a profound concern with the social consequences and political implications of modern technological development. Indeed, the grandiose economic achievements that the Great Leap strategy promised presupposed an extraordinarily rapid introduction and application of both advanced and intermediate technologies as well as the general development of scientific knowledge and education. And no one more strongly emphasized the need for modern science and technology than did Mao. In launching the Great Leap Forward campaign, he hailed the successes of China's socialist transformation but lamented the country's continued economic backwardness. "We must now start a technological revolution," he declared in January 1958, "so that we many overtake England in 15 or more years.... The technological revolution is designed to make everyone learn science and technology."[5]

For Mao and Maoists, however, economic goals could not be separated from social and political ones. While no one questioned the necessity and desirability of mastering modern science and technology, Maoists were concerned with the question of how they were to be mastered and by whom. Part of the Maoist concern was a widely shared anxiety that China had become far too dependent on Soviet technology. In 1956 Mao had warned that "we should not become one-sided and copy everything which comes from abroad, and introduce it mechanistically."[6] That "abroad" meant the Soviet Union was unmistakable, and the point was made more explicitly early in 1958. "Learning should be combined with creativity," he then said, and "to import Soviet codes and conventions inflexibly is to lack the creative spirit." He proceeded to level a wholesale attack on the Soviet-modeled First Five Year Plan, complaining that,

> ... [A]ll we could do in our ignorance was to import foreign methods. Our statistical work was practically a copy of Soviet work; in the educational field copying was also pretty bad.... We did not even study our own experience of education in the Liberated Areas. The same applied to our public health work, with the result that I couldn't have eggs or chicken soup for three years because an article appeared in the Soviet Union which said that one shouldn't eat them.

.... We lacked understanding of the whole economic situation and understood still less the differences between the Soviet Union and China. So all we could do was follow blindly.[7]

Having embarked upon a radically new and distinctively Chinese strategy of development, it is hardly surprising that Mao was determined to break down China's reliance on Soviet technological assistance as well. It was not only a matter of the unsuitability of much of Soviet technology to the new economic policies the Chinese then had begun to pursue, especially to the new Maoist emphasis on small-scale rural industrialization. Also very much involved was the fear, reflecting long-standing nationalist resentments, that Chinese economic and technological dependence on Russia implied a degree of political dependence as well.[8] Moreover, economic and political dependence fostered psychological dependence, which, in turn, inhibited the initiative and activism of the masses; in the Maoist view, foreign borrowing had left the Chinese people "mentally fettered" and "passive," and their full liberation (and the liberation of their productive potential) required complete national independence and a spirit of "self-reliance." Thus the Maoist call for China to develop an independent and indigenous technology reflected a combination of old considerations of national pride and new economic considerations. It was a call that foreshadowed one of the principal themes that emerged in the Great Leap Forward era—the principle of "self-reliance," which was to survive the Great Leap and which since has become a cornerstone of the policies and practices of the People's Republic.

While Mao's desire to end mechanical copying of Soviet methods was generally shared by most party leaders and the nonparty intelligentsia— indeed, it had been among the more prominent criticisms heard during the Hundred Flowers campaign—it is unlikely that many were receptive to the alternative program for technological development that he proposed. Mao's program, simply put, envisioned the development and application of modern science and technology without professional scientists and technocrats. To Party economic planners, this seemed an economically irrational notion, and to the technological intelligentsia a professionally threatening one.

But for Mao science and technology were not politically neutral matters. If left to itself, modern scientific and technological development generated technological elites and fostered bureaucracy and social inequality. Whereas in 1956 party leaders had freed the natural sciences from any "class character," in January 1958 Mao restored the political and social links. "With the focus on technology," he warned, "[we are] apt to neglect politics. . . . Ideological and political work is the guarantee for the completion of economic technological work. . . . A slight relaxation in our ideological and political work will lead our economic and technological work astray."[9] In Mao's "technical revolution," politics, not technicians, were to be in command to guarantee that the means of modern science and technology were used in a fashion consistent with socialist ends.

Whereas two years earlier Chou En-lai had posed the problem in terms of a technological intelligentsia that was insufficient in numbers and lacking in professional skills, Mao now saw the problem in terms of how China could acquire modern scientific and technological knowledge without creating a privileged technocratic elite. The Maoist solution was deceptively simple and perhaps simplistically utopian: the masses of peasants and workers themselves were to master modern technology. Moreover, they were to do so in the course of everyday productive work, learning the necessary skills and expertise in the course of doing, studying while working, and applying their newly-acquired knowledge to immediate productive needs, and in ways appropriate to suit local conditions. There were to be no "experts," but only "reds and experts," a new generation of politically conscious "jacks-of-all-trades" who were to combine mental with manual labor and who were to be capable of engaging in "scientific and cultural undertakings as well as physical labor." The result would be the creation of a whole nation of what Mao called "socialist-conscious, cultured laborers." The "red and expert" formula was thus interpreted to mean neither simply "red" cadres acquiring technical expertise nor technical experts acquiring a "red" political consciousness (although it meant that too), but rather became a universal ideal to be universally realized. Just as the Chinese nation was to become technologically self-reliant and not dependent on other nations, so too were the Chinese people to become self-reliant and not dependent on a technological elite. Technological development was conceived as a mass movement, and one of the great rallying cries of the Great Leap Forward years was the slogan "the masses must make themselves masters of culture and science."

Notes

1. See Roderick MacFarquhar, ed., *The Hundred Flowers Campaign and the Chinese Intellectuals* (New York: Praeger, 1960), p. 273.
2. Christopher Howe, *Employment and Economic Growth in Urban China, 1949–57* (Cambridge, England: Cambridge University Press, 1971), p. 125.
3. *Hung-ch'i* (Red Flag), June 1, 1958, p. 3.
4. Mao Tse-tung, "On the Ten Great Relationships," in Stuart R. Schram, ed., *Mao Tse-tung Unrehearsed: Talks and Letters 1956–71* (Middlesex, England: Penguin, 1974), p. 63.

5. Mao Tse-tung, "Sixty Points on Working Methods," in Jerome Ch'en, ed., *Mao Papers* (London: Oxford University Press, 1970), p. 63.

6. Mao, "On the Ten Great Relationships," p. 81.

7. "Talks at the Chengtu Conference," March 1958, in Schram, ed., *Mao Unrehearsed*, pp. 96–99.

8. Mao's attacks on uncritical Chinese borrowing of Soviet methods were soon to be followed by wide-ranging criticisms of the Soviet Union in general and of Stalin in particular. These appear in their most comprehensive and forceful form in Mao's 1961 "Reading Notes on the Soviet Union's 'Political Economy,'" *Mao Tse-tung Ssu-hsiang Wan-sui* (Taipei, 1969). An English translation appears in *JPRS* document No. 61269, pp. 247–313. For a perceptive analysis, see Richard Levy, "New Light on Mao," *China Quarterly*, No. 61 (March 1975), pp. 95–117.

9. Mao, "Sixty Points on Working Methods," p. 64.

14

The People's Communes and the
"Transition to Communism" (1958–1960)

AT THE BEGINNING OF 1958, hardly more than eight years after the birth of the People's Republic, Mao Tse-tung was convinced that the transition to socialism had been carried out. To be sure, the "ideological" class struggle between "the proletariat" and "the bourgeoisie" had yet to be concluded (indeed he hinted that it might have to be waged indefinitely), and there remained the ever present danger of a regression back to capitalism, or at least to some "presocialist" state of affairs. But the fundamental tasks involved in the socialist reorganization of Chinese society had been achieved, or so Mao believed. Thus, the time was ripe for China to move to a higher stage of social development, a course dictated by the theory of permanent revolution whereby "revolutions come one after another." "Our revolutions are like battles," Mao had argued. "After a victory, we must at once put forward a new task."[1] The new task was "the transition from socialism to communism."

To most Chinese Communist leaders, the call to proceed to a communist reorganization of society must have seemed a wildly utopian notion. For one thing, the processes of socialist transformation had been under way for only a few years, and China's socialist system had yet to be consolidated. Moreover, industrialization was still in its infancy, and economically China remained a woefully backward country. Mao agreed with both of these assessments, but from them he drew strikingly different and novel theoretical and practical conclusions.

If China's socialist system was relatively new and unconsolidated, then this seemed to Mao more an opportunity to move to a higher social stage than an imperative to refine and institutionalize the existing system. For Mao had come to believe that it was precisely the relative immaturity and instability of a given social order that offered the greatest potential for radical social change. And, conversely, he believed that the more consolidated and stabilized a social system became, the more resistant it would be to change. Even more than ever before, Mao emphasized the decisive role of "consciousness" in sociohistorical development. As he put it in detailed (but unpublished) critiques of Stalin and Soviet theory he then was undertaking: "We cannot go on consolidating [a social system] for all time, otherwise we will make inflexible the ideology reflecting this system and render people incapable of adjusting their thoughts to new changes."[2] In bringing about the revolutionary transformation of social relations, the guiding Maoist principle was "to strike while the iron is hot."[3] To stabilize the existing order—and thus to delay moving to a higher stage of development—was a prescription for stagnation and regression.

Nor did Mao regard economic backwardness as a barrier to undertaking "the transition to communism." Indeed, in some respects he regarded it as an asset, for it was in 1958 that he set forth publicly his remarkable thesis on the revolutionary advantages of being "poor and blank," and he soon was to put forward the proposition that the more backward the economy was the easier would be the socialist and communist reorganization of society.[4] To be sure, economic backwardness also was deplored—and indeed was to be overcome—but it was to be overcome simultaneously with processes of social revolutionary change leading to communism. In launching the Great Leap Forward campaign, Mao promised both a "technical revolution" and a social revolution, both an economic miracle and a social miracle—but the latter was not dependent on the prior accomplishment of the former. Indeed, it was the revolutionary transformation of social relations and consciousness that would release the latent productive powers of the masses and provide the impetus for the "technical revolution"—and at the same time guarantee that modern economic and technological development would be carried out in a fashion consistent with the realization of communist social goals. Just as during the collectivization campaign of 1955 Mao had proceeded on the assumption that "the economic conditions of our country being what they are, technical reform will take longer than social reform," he now was even more firmly convinced that a social revolution was the necessary prerequisite for an economic revolution, that "proletarianization" must precede "mechanization."

In attempting to understand the rather extraordinary events of 1958–1960, it is important to keep in mind these Maoist assumptions on the relationship between social and economic change. For Mao and Maoists, the term "great leap"—which had been used several years before, but only with reference to rapid increases in productivity—now had acquired a social as well as an economic meaning. It conveyed the expectation of a qualitative transformation of social relationships as well as the expectation of a "leap" in economic development. In the Maoist mentality, as it reveals itself in both the theory and the practice of the Great Leap, the pursuit of communist social and ideological goals are inextricably intertwined with the goal of rapidly developing the material forces of production—and the former are seen as the precondition for the proper development of the latter. From the perspectives of Marxist–Leninist theory, the Great Leap is the time when Maoism emerges as an explicit rejection of the Stalinist orthodoxy that the combination of state ownership of the key means of production with rapid economic development automatically guarantees the eventual arrival of a communist society. In the Maoist view, by contrast, the promise of a communist future demands the introduction of communist forms of social organization and the cultivation of a communist consciousness in the here and now, in conditions of economic scarcity, and as the prerequisites for transcending those conditions. It is the time when Maoism announces itself as a doctrine that divorces communism from its Marxist-defined economic preconditions.

The Great Leap Forward campaign began at the end of 1957 and during the early months of 1958 as an intensive drive for increased productivity in both industry and agriculture. The campaign to produce "more, faster, better, and cheaper" (as the popular slogan of the time exhorted) proceeded in accordance with the new Maoist economic strategy formally adopted by the party in October 1957. A new emphasis on the importance of agriculture and the development of small industries accompanied the raising of production targets in the heavy industrial sector. The centralized bureaucratic economic apparatus was partially dismantled in favor of relative autonomy and decision-making authority for localities and basic production units. Administrative offices were emptied as officials were "sent down" (*hsia-fang*) to engage in manual labor on farms and in factories, in a renewed attack on bureaucracy, and to realize the Maoist (and Marxist) ideal of "simple administration." Ideological exhortations and moral appeals replaced material rewards as the incentive for workers and peasants to work harder and longer, accompanied by the promise that "three years of struggle" would be followed by "a thousand years of communist happiness." The social mobilization of the masses for labor rather than the bureaucratic direction of laborers became the central organizational feature of a campaign that acquired an increasingly militaristic character—and indeed was described as one which involved "fighting battles against the natural world" analogous to the battles that had been fought during the revolutionary years, demanding the same qualities of heroism and self-sacrifice.

In industry the Great Leap was marked by the implementation of the policy of "walking on two legs" (a policy announced three years before but hitherto largely dormant), in accordance with which medium and

small-scale, labor-intensive industries operating on the basis of indigenous technologies were to be developed simultaneously with the modern
industrial sector. For workers in modern factories it was a policy that
meant harder and longer working hours (and for some, lower wages as
well) to meet ever higher and increasingly unrealistic production quotas.
The "second leg" of the new industrial policy was most spectacularly
symbolized by the mobilization of tens of millions of people in urban and
rural areas in the abortive "backyard" iron and steel campaign; it was
the most publicized and least effective of the new labor-intensive local
industrial projects. Other small-scale undertakings, especially local chemical and fertilizer factories and coal mines in the rural areas, were less
publicized but often highly effective in meeting immediate needs and
yielding long-term technological innovations.

In the countryside, the size of private family plots was reduced; the
scale and intensity of collective labor expanded; millions of urban cadres
and technicians arrived to assist in the organization of new local industries; and armies of peasants were mobilized for large-scale irrigation and
water conservation projects. The "campaign to build water works," begun
in the autumn of 1957, was expanded enormously in the early months of
1958.

If Maoists were "utopian" in their economic expectations, they were
even more so in their belief that the Chinese people were prepared to
carry out "the transition from socialism to communism." As the campaigns for increased productivity grew in scope and intensity, Maoists
were searching for a new form of social organization to accomplish both
the economic revolution and the social one. The form that was discovered
was the people's commune, and by the summer of 1958 Maoists were
hailing the commune as the agency for China's transition to a communist
society.

The Emergence of the Rural People's Communes

The vast communization movement, which radically transformed the
Chinese countryside and the lives of its 500,000,000 inhabitants in the
summer and fall months of 1958, was not the product of any detailed
socioeconomic blueprint. Much of what happened during the period was
largely spontaneous, and many of the most crucial policy decisions seem
to have been improvised during the frenetic course of the movement or
made by local leaders on the spot. The spontaneous character of the campaign was partly responsible for the remarkable dynamism that communization generated—and it contributed a good deal to the organizational
and economic chaos that eventually resulted.

Although the communes can be seen as a logical outgrowth of the new socioeconomic strategy, especially when that strategy became connected with utopian visions of the imminent advent of communism, there is no evidence that Mao (or Maoists) had communization in mind when the Great Leap Forward began. Only a few months before the campaign Mao anticipated that it would take five years or more to consolidate the existing collective farms.[5] Through the early months of 1958 Mao never used the term "commune" in either his public pronouncements or his internal party speeches and writings. Nor did he explicitly advocate the wholesale "communist" reorganization of society. Although the December 1957 politburo meeting, which formally launched the Great Leap, called for amalgamating collectives into larger units, this policy seems to have been motivated more by the organizational needs of the massive irrigation and water-conservation movement (begun several months earlier) than by utopian visions of communism. It was not until the Great Leap Forward was well underway that the commune was discovered and in the late summer of 1958 seized upon by Maoists as the ideal form for China's "transition from socialism to communism."

The communization movement involved the complex interplay of the spontaneous radicalism of rural cadres and poor peasants from below with the radical utopianism of Mao and Maoists from above. And, just as in the collectivization campaign of 1955, the two proved mutually reinforcing, with the result that the movement acquired a fantastic momentum of its own and proceeded at a frantic tempo that far exceeded the hopes and expectations of even its most radical exponents. The first of the communes appeared on an experimental basis in Honan province in April 1958. While it is unlikely that the experiment could have been undertaken without at least the tacit approval of Maoist leaders of the party in Peking as well as the regional party organization, the initiative apparently came from radical local activists. Spontaneity and local initiatives were certainly predominant in July when (after an excellent summer harvest) the amalgamation of collectives into communes spread rapidly in Honan and Hopei provinces and certain areas of Manchuria. The movement grew without official party sanction and without central direction from Peking, but it received powerful ideological encouragement from Maoist party leaders. In the July 1, 1958 issue of the newly established party theoretical periodical *Red Flag*, Ch'en Po-ta, a leading Maoist theoretician and Mao's personal secretary, first used the term "people's commune" to describe an expanded and reorganized collective in Hupei. The Hupei commune, according to Ch'en, had succeeded in combining agricultural and industrial production, and it had produced new "all-round men" who were acquiring scientific and technological knowledge in the course of working, integrating "technological revolution" with "cultural revolution," and learning to perform essential administrative functions as well as advanced productive methods. The commune was thus in the process of realizing the Marxist goals of eliminating the distinctions between mental and manual labor, between industry and agriculture, and between town and countryside—and thereby opening the road "on which our country can smoothly pass over from socialism to communism." Ch'en attributed these present and future accomplishments to the heroic spirit and creativity of the working masses.[6]

In a lengthy speech delivered in early July at Peking University to commemorate the thirty-seventh anniversary of the founding of the Chinese Communist Party, Ch'en Po-ta elaborated on these themes in an even more utopian fashion and with the support of copious quotations drawn from the writings of Marx, Lenin, and Mao. He described the movement toward communism in the countryside in almost chiliastic terms and attributed the revolutionary upsurge not only to the creativity of "the pioneering peasants" but also (and especially) to the inspiration of the thought of Mao Tse-tung. And he attributed the idea and the ideal of the commune to Mao as well:

> Comrade Mao Tse-tung said that we should steadily and systematically organize "industry, agriculture, commerce, education and soldiers into a big commune, thereby to form the basic units of society." . . . This conception of the commune is a conclusion drawn by Comrade Mao Tse-tung from real life.[7]

In view of the exceptionally close personal and ideological relationship between Ch'en and Mao, Ch'en's *Red Flag* articles marked Maoist approval (if not necessarily official party approval) of the growing communization movement—and, in turn, served to stimulate the development and tempo of the movement. By the time Liu Shao-ch'i and other party leaders set out on tours to inspect communization in the northern provinces in late July, the movement already was widespread. Mao personally added to the momentum by undertaking an inspection tour of his own early in August; his glowing praise of the commune system was prominently reported in the press, as was his call for the extension of the system throughout the country. Thus when the members of the politburo met in "enlarged session" (a meeting which included provincial and regional party secretaries as well as the entire central committee) at the seaside resort of Peitaiho August 17–30, they were faced with another Maoist *fait accompli*. Many communes already had been established, the campaign to establish new ones was proceeding at an accelerating pace, and Mao's enthusiastic approval of communization had been widely publicized and celebrated in newspapers and periodicals. Despite the grave reservations of many (and probably most) of the highest party leaders, they had no alternative but to formally ratify what was already taking place, although the length of the meeting suggests that they did so only after considerable debate.

Formal ratification came in the form of a resolution issued on August 29 from Peitaiho in the name of the central committee. Observing that "the people's communes are the logical result of the march of events," that "they are already widespread," and that "it is highly probable that there will soon be an upsurge in setting up people's communes throughout the country and the development is irresistible," the resolution sanctioned rural communization on a nationwide basis and recognized the commune as the appropriate organizational form "to guide the peasants to accelerate socialist construction, complete the building of socialism ahead of time, and carry out the gradual transition to communism." The resolution recommended that wherever possible the commune should be coextensive with the *hsiang* and ideally should comprise about 2,000 peasant households. While the document accepted the Maoist demand that the commune system be universalized, at least in the rural areas, it also reflected the reservations and doubts of non-Maoist party leaders. The resolution was replete with warnings against "compulsory or rash steps" in the organization of communes and any measures which might have an adverse effect on agricultural production. Moreover, it insisted on the socialist rather than the communist character of the new organizations. The commune system of ownership was to be "collective" rather than characterized by "ownership by the people as a whole," while the system of distribution was to be in accord with the socialist principle of "to each according to his work" and not the communist ideal "to each according to his needs." While the communes were to prepare the way for "the gradual transition to communism," the resolution was vague on when that transition might come about. Indeed, it implied that it might take many decades, for it was suggested that the conditions for the transition to communism required not only an "advance in the people's consciousness" but also an unspecified level of "the development of production" and an "increase of income."[8] The August 29 resolution was a rather moderate document in contrast to the more radical utopian Maoist writings of the time, which advocated the immediate introduction of communist forms of work and organization and promised the more or less immediate advent of a communist utopia.

Communization proceeded more rapidly and moved in a far more radical direction than most party leaders anticipated or wanted. By the end of September, over 90 percent of peasant households were at least formally included in the new organizational structures. Before the year was out, virtually all of the rural population were organized in some 24,000 people's communes which had emerged from the hasty amalgamation of 750,000 collective farms. Much larger than officially proposed, the average commune comprised 5,000 households (approximately 30,000 people); but the populations varied greatly, ranging from less than 5,000 members to over 100,000. And in defiance of the injunctions set forth in the August resolution, many communes moved immediately to introduce communist forms of social life, work organization, and distribution.

The summer and fall months of 1958 were the most radical phase in the history of the Great Leap Forward. It was a time when hopes for a future of economic abundance and a future communist utopia were highest, and popular enthusiasm to work to bring that future into being was the greatest. It was a time when postponed Marxist utopian goals became immediate ones and Maoist leaders proclaimed them to be more or less immediately realizable. The ultimate goals of classical Marxism—not excluding the most utopian of all visions, the "withering away" of the state—were popularized not as distant ends but as the immediate tasks of the day. The achievement of these historically unprecedented tasks was assigned to the people's communes, which were conceived not merely as productive organizations but also (as typically described at the time) new social organizations that "combined economic, cultural, political and military affairs" and thus merged "workers, peasants, merchants, students, and militiamen into a single entity." By combining industry with agriculture, education with productive activity, and by merging economic with political power, the communes were to perform all the social revolutionary transformations that Marxists traditionally assigned to the period of "the dictatorship of the proletariat," the transition from socialism to communism. In the Maoist literature of the Great Leap, the commune was seen to be "the organizer of living" as well as the organizer of production; it was conceived not only as the means to realize ultimate communist ends but also as an embryonic communist society that was taking shape in the here and now, an embryo that would grow to become the basic social unit of the future communist utopia.

The commune was also conceived and popularized by Maoists as both the product and the producer of "new communist men," the ideal "reds and experts" who perform a vast variety of social functions and who were the carriers of that all-important "communist consciousness" upon which the emergence of the new society ultimately was dependent. Very soon, it typically was proclaimed, "everyone will be a mental laborer and at the same time a physical laborer; everyone can be a philosopher, scientist, writer, and artist." The more utopian themes and passages in classical Marxist writings were widely drawn upon to support this vision. Indicative of the utopian expectations that marked the early days of communization is that nothing was more frequently quoted than the famous passage in *The German Ideology* where Marx took one of his rare glimpses into the future and saw a communist society:

> [where] nobody has one exclusive sphere of activity but each can become accomplished in any branch he wishes, [a society that] regulates the general production and thus makes it possible for me to do one thing today and another tomorrow, to hunt in the morning, fish in the afternoon, rear cattle in the evening, criticize after dinner, just as I have a mind, without ever becoming hunter, fisherman, shepherd or critic.

These utopian visions of a future classless and stateless society evoked positive responses among the peasant masses during the early phase of the Great Leap and undoubtedly contributed to their willingness to work and sacrifice in order to bring about that future. Through these promises and appeals to the masses in the chiliastic atmosphere that marked those early days of communization Mao Tse-tung was able to partly bypass the regular bureaucratic channels and procedures of the party and state apparatus and establish, for a time, a direct bond between himself and the people, a bond between his utopian visions of communism and popular aspirations for social change and economic prosperity.

Even before the communes were established, a radical change in rural work organization had been wrought by the vast irrigation and water-conservation campaigns begun in autumn 1957. Peasants from different villages and localities were brought together in production brigades and work teams that functioned with militaristic discipline to perform specialized labor tasks, with labor organized (and remunerated) as in a modern factory. With the establishment of the communes, the large production brigades (generally consisting of several thousand peasants) became more formalized and extended their functions to agricultural production as well as to the operation of newly established commune industries and large-scale construction works. Within the large brigades there was established a dozen or more smaller brigades (later called work teams) whose members were recruited from a single village. Coordinating the work of the brigades was the commune which in theory functioned as a more or less autonomous and self-sufficient economic, social, and political unit.

The mobilization of peasants into production brigades demanded immediate and far-reaching changes in rural social life, changes which were celebrated as progress towards communism. The transfer of manpower to irrigation work, large-scale construction projects, and to the new industrial undertakings created widespread labor shortages in agriculture. The obvious solution was to draw women into full-time productive labor in the fields as well as in light industries. Although instituted to relieve an acute labor shortage, the result was hailed as a giant step toward sexual equality and proclaimed to be one of the communist aims the communes were designed to achieve. The measures necessary to free women from traditional domestic chores and thus to free them for agricultural labor, the establishment of communal mess halls and nurseries usually staffed by older peasant women, were celebrated as "the socialization of household work." Although the intensive mobilization of both male and female labor, coupled with the introduction of new communal forms of living, temporarily changed the pattern of family life and perhaps effected long-term changes in peasant consciousness about the family, the family as such remained intact. Disruptions occurred, primarily because some male workers were assigned to projects distant from their villages and temporarily separated from their wives and children, but contrary to widespread reports in the Western press at the time, the existing family structure was not abolished. Nor was there any attempt or inclination to do so. Even the most radical Maoists remained firmly committed to the maintenance of the nuclear family, just as they remained tied to highly puritanical sexual mores.

While the family remained secure, its private property did not. As visions of communism grew, so did demands for total abolition of personal possessions and for a general social leveling. The ideological demand was reinforced by the economic logic of the universal mobilization of labor. With most able-bodied men and women organized in production brigades and working from sunrise to sunset on collective projects, little time or energy was left to tend family plots and animals. Private holdings, which accounted for about 7 percent of the cultivated land at the beginning of 1958, were virtually eliminated by the end of the year and became communal property, as did hitherto family-owned pigs and fowl. In the areas where communization was most radically pursued, everything from homes to cooking utensils, furniture, and watches were collectivized and turned over to the commune—at least in theory.

The next logical step was to distribute the surplus product, that which remained after state taxes and what was set aside for investment and welfare, in accordance with the communist principle of to each according to one's need. While official regulations governing the operation of the communes specified that the new organizations were to be socialist in nature and that remuneration was to be based on one's labor, the problems in determining individual labor contributions for work performed in collective fashion proved formidable—and, in the hectic circumstances of the time, impossible to resolve. It was much easier to simply distribute the surplus equally, or according to real or perceived individual needs, than calculate the quantity and quality of labor. The national formula arrived at near the end of the year recommended that 30 percent of the surplus be distributed according to labor and 70 percent according to need, although the extent to which the general formula was applied remains obscure. Indeed, the evidence is too scanty to determine how much of the widely celebrated social radicalism of early communization was actually practiced, for it was the most radical and "model" communes that were the most widely publicized, both within and outside China. In reality, the communes differed enormously, not only in size and wealth but in nature. Some involved little more than formal administrative reorganizations of existing collective farms, whereas others moved rapidly to achieve what was perceived to be a new communist order. The only universal feature was the intensive mobilization of labor and the lengthening of the working day.

Of far greater and longer lasting significance than the more spectacular social radicalism of the time (much of which vanished as rapidly as it had appeared) was the implementation of new policies in industry and education. One was the policy of promoting "the industrialization of the countryside" and the other was the introduction of a new rural educational system based on the principle of "work and study." Maoists found theoretical support for these policies in the writings of Karl Marx. Despite Marx's aversion to drawing "utopian" blueprints of the future communist society and even his reluctance to discuss in any detail the course of social development in the postrevolutionary era, he did (on rare occasions) outline in general terms his conception of the "dictatorship of the proletariat" and the corresponding period of the transition from socialism to communism. In the Manifesto of 1848 he set forth ten "generally applicable" measures to be implemented by workers' parties following the overthrow of the bourgeois state. Among them was the "combination of agriculture with manufacturing industries" and the "gradual abolition of the distinction between town and country, by a more equitable distribution of population over the country." In educational policy, he urged the general principle of the "combination of education with industrial production."[9] If Maoist policies were not necessarily directly inspired by the writings of Marx, they nonetheless were consistent with the measures Marx had proposed and theoretically justified by repeated references to the classic texts, albeit pursued under vastly different historical conditions from those Marx had envisioned.

The positive accomplishments of the program for establishing commune-operated industries should not be obscured by the fanfare (given by the Chinese) to the spectacle of the "backyard" steel and iron production campiagn of 1958 and the widespread publicity and ridicule provided by foreign critics that accompanied its spectacular failure. The backyard furnaces resulted in an enormous waste of labor at a time when there was an acute labor shortage and soon were abandoned. But other rural industries, established at the same time with less fanfare, proved viable and often innovative. Relying on local human and material resources, and generally using primitive technologies, they served well the immediate goals they were intended to achieve by assisting agricultural productivity and development, providing peasants with small consumer goods which otherwise would not have been produced, and utilizing surplus rural labor which otherwise would have gone to waste. If there were waste, inefficiency, and false starts in the beginning, in the long run Chinese agriculture has benefited greatly by the commune-operated shops manufacturing and repairing agricultural implements, small chemical plants producing fertilizers and insecticides, small-scale power generators, and local crop-processing industries. And both rural society and the national economy have profited from local coal-mining operations, small oil refineries, and locally produced consumer goods.

The new education policies were closely related to the new emphasis on the industrialization of the countryside. Communization was accompanied by an ambitious effort to establish locally operated part-time educational facilities: "red and expert" universities, evening schools, spare-time educational programs, and a variety of "half-work and half-study" programs. The guiding principle was the "combination of education and production" and the main purpose was to provide the peasant masses with the minimal technological knowledge (in addition to basic literacy) necessary for the operation of local rural industries as well as to facilitate the future introduction of modern techniques in agricultural production. The program drew on a long modern Chinese tradition of radical educational concepts and experiences, which included the "half-work, half-study" ideal of young intellectuals in the May Fourth era (a program in which Mao personally had taken part) as well as the *min-pan* (popular-managed) schools and other educational experiments of the Yenan years.[10]

In addition to serving immediate productive needs, the new rural-oriented school system was seen as a means to realize the Maoist ideal for "the masses to make themselves masters of technology," reduce the need for specialized urban universities and schools, forestall the growth of a technological intelligentsia, and thus contribute to the realization of the Marxist goals of abolishing the distinctions between town and countryside and between mental and manual labor. In the utopian spirit of the times, the various programs based on the combination of education with productive labor were typically described as ones "designed to foster students who are socialist-minded and cultured laborers and ensure their moral, intellectual and physical development to produce new men of communism."[11] "The red and expert and spare-time universities are not intended to meet temporary needs alone," it was proclaimed. "Coordination between education and productive labor is one of the fundamental principles underlying our socialist education," and the new institutions were not only the ideal form to achieve this combination but they also "open our eyes to the germs of the educational system in a communist society."[12] Theoretical support for the new educational program was found in Marx's statement that "an early combination of productive labor with education is one of the most potent means for the transformation of present-day society" and Engels' vision of a future communist society which would educate "well-rounded human beings" who would "pass from one branch of production to another in response to the needs of society or their own inclinations."[13]

The radical utopianism that characterized communization was not confined to the socioeconomic sphere but extended to the political sphere as well. The Maoist choice of the term "commune" to characterize the new forms of social organization they had created was by no means fortuitous. The term was derived from Karl Marx's analysis of the Paris Commune of 1871 and the subsequent Marxist identification of the Paris Commune as the historical model of the dictatorship of the proletariat.

As such, the term "commune," in the Marxist tradition, conveyed the notion of an entirely new form of the organization of political power— the armed community of the laboring masses who smash the existing centralized bureaucratic-military state apparatus (what Marx referred to as "the ubiquitous organs of standing army, police, and bureaucracy") and replace it with popular "working bodies," which restore to society as a whole the social powers that had been usurped by the state. In Marx's description of the Commune, standing army and police are replaced by the armed populace; the state bureaucracy is destroyed in favor of popular organs, which combine executive and legislative functions; such socially necessary administrative functions as remain are performed not by appointed officials but by popularly selected members of the working people who carry out their duties at ordinary workingmen's wages, without special status or privileges, and are under the constant supervision and control of the masses; and national political organization as a whole is decentralized into a "free federation" of self-governed local communes in place of "those agencies of oppression in a centralized government."[14] It was with this conception of political power reorganized as the dictatorship of the proletariat that Marx envisioned the transition period that would lead to a classless communist society and, in the process, result in the disappearance of political power itself. It was a conception held by Maoists as they undertook to reorganize Chinese society into people's communes.

One way in which the Marxian model of the Paris Commune reflected itself (although in distorted form) in Maoist practice was in the general militarization of work and life. "Our revolutions are like battles," Mao had declared in January 1958, and by July peasants on communes were organized in battalions marching off to labor in the fields in step, with martial music blaring from loudspeakers. The slogans of the time called upon the masses not only to collectivize but also to "militarize," "combatize," and "disciplinize." Although the militarization of work was ideologically rationalized by Marxist references to the Commune as a community dominated by the armed masses, the purpose was increased labor efficiency and productivity. But the result was to be the physical exhaustion of the peasants, who were subjected to intolerable physical demands and an increasingly unrealistic extension of the working day.

More in harmony with the Marxist concept of the Commune was the revival of the people's militia and the arming of the peasantry, measures which accompanied communization and coincided with the Taiwan Straits crisis of August 1958.[15] In the literature of the time, the internal "war against nature" was closely linked to the threat of external aggression. As an August 1958 *Red Flag* editorial put it:

> Though militarization in agricultural work is not for the purpose of repulsing the enemies of mankind, but for the purpose of carrying on

the struggle with nature, it makes it easy to transform one of these two kinds of struggle into the other. . . . if an external enemy should dare to attack us, all people can be mobilized and armed, and made into an army decisively, resolutely, thoroughly, and completely to destroy the enemy.[16]

Although the immediate danger of war over Quemoy and Matsu soon passed, the militia campaign continued. By the end of 1959, it was reported that 220,000,000 people had been recruited into the militia and 30,000,000 had been armed with primitive rifles.[17] The revival of the popular militia (an act presented in terms of the Commune ideal of abolishing the standing army) was soon to become an issue in a bitter political struggle over the nature and role of the regular People's Liberation Army.

Perhaps the most radically utopian aspect of communization—and where for a brief time the people's communes approached most closely the Marxist model of the Paris Commune—was the role assigned to the communes in the reorganization and exercise of political power. The Maoist theoretical literature of 1958 strongly suggests that the communes originally were conceived as organs of "proletarian dictatorship," albeit without an urban proletariat.[18] The commune's appropriation of the administrative functions of the *hsiang* was widely interpreted as making the commune a political unit "performing the functions of state power" and "the most desirable organizational form" for the period of the transition from socialism to communism.[19] It was stressed that the communes were not merely productive organizations but ones which "combined economic, cultural, political and military affairs," and which combined "workers, peasants, merchants, students and militiamen into a single entity." Special emphasis was placed on the role of the commune in "merging" the basic economic units of society with the basic "organs of state power," a step that was hailed as the beginning of a process in which the internal functions of the state (now assigned to the commune, at least in theory) gradually would disappear.[20] The vision of the "withering away" of the state was the most utopian of all the utopian goals proclaimed and popularized during the early period of communization and it probably struck deeply responsive chords among the peasantry, for it meshed with traditional peasant anarchist dreams of freedom from the tyranny of officials and bureaucrats.

There is a striking similarity between the Maoist scheme for the decentralization of political power through communization and the federalist strains in Marx's writings on the Paris Commune. Marx noted with approval that the Paris Commune was not to exercise a Jacobin dictatorship over all of France but rather was to serve as the model for more or less autonomous communal units in the rural provinces and the secondary industrial centers where the old centralized bureaucracy would "have to give way to the self-government of the producers" in the local areas. "In a rough sketch of national organization which the Commune had no time to develop," Marx wrote, "it states clearly that the Commune was to be the political form of even the smallest country hamlet" and "the rural communes of each district were to administer their common affairs by an assembly of delegates in the central town."[21] And in his critique of the 1891 Erfurt program, Engels praised the earlier Parisian revolutionaries for envisioning "complete self-administration" for "every French department [and] every parish."[22]

References to the Marxian model appear frequently in the Maoist literature of the time. A Chinese Marxist theoretician writing in September 1958 typically observed that "the integration of the *hsiang* with the commune will make the commune not very different from the Paris Commune, integrating economic organization with the organization of state power."[23] More important than the possible influence of Marxist precedents is that the political functions which Maoists assigned to the communes in theory, and the realities of communization, posed a grave challenge to the functioning of existing party and state bureaucracies. Had the people's communes actually developed in the manner Maoists originally envisioned, centralized political power in China would have been fundamentally undermined—much in the way in which Marx had attributed to the Paris Commune the potential to restore to the producers those social powers which had been usurped by the state. The antibureaucratic implications of communization were unmistakable, and bureaucrats with vested interests in the pre–Great Leap order soon began to respond to the threat. Their first opportunity to blunt the radical thrust of communization came in early December, when the party central committee convened at Wuhan to deal with the economic and organizational difficulties that resulted from the hasty manner in which Maoist-inspired rural cadres implemented Mao's policies.

The First Retreat

Communization had begun in the summer of 1958 on the basis of an unusually bountiful harvest and with widespread popular enthusiasm. By late autumn, the movement was being undermined by food shortages and a marked decline in peasant morale. The haste with which communes were established resulted in organizational chaos. General uncertainties about how the new organizations were to operate were compounded by the lack of skilled personnel to properly manage complex fiscal affairs of the communes as a whole and the new forms of communal life and work within them. Peasants from richer collectives resented the economic leveling that came through their amalgamation with peasants from poorer or less efficient collectives, a practice carried out in defiance of official regulations stipulating that lower standards of living were to be raised rather than higher ones lowered; they expressed their dissatisfaction by slaughtering and consuming farm animals instead of turning them over to the commune. And peasants in general came to resent arbitrary work assignments, inequities in remuneration, inefficient management of mess halls and other communal facilities. The mobilization of peasant labor for industrial, irrigation and construction projects often resulted in the neglect of agricultural production and, consequently, food shortages. A general breakdown of national economic planning and coordination led to gross inefficiencies in the production and distribution of goods and materials, bottlenecks in an overtaxed transportation system, fiscal policies based on the acceptance of inflated production reports, and shortages of raw materials for industry. The "commandism" practiced by local cadres produced regimentation of labor rather than communal labor, and the lengthening of the working day to meet unrealistic production quotas resulted in the general physical exhaustion of the working population. The realities of communization bore little resemblance to the principles of the rational utilization of labor upon which the Great Leap Forward originally was based, much less to the ideal of communal life and labor voluntarily undertaken.

As economic difficulties multiplied and popular dissatisfaction grew, party leaders met at Wuhan on November 28 to attempt to restore economic stability. They emerged on December 10 with a resolution that retained much of the utopian rhetoric of the summer and fall and reaffirmed that the rural communes would be the agency for China's eventual transition to communism,[24] but one which set forth policies designed to blunt the social and political radicalism of communization. The policies were approved and implemented over the opposition of Mao, marking the beginning of a bitter political struggle that was to come to a dramatic climax the following summer.

Among the more important measures promulgated was the reestablishment of the "production brigade" as the basic unit of labor organization and production, or the "unit of account," in effect, a reversion to the pre-commune collective based on the natural village, although the commune retained ownership of local industrial enterprises. The resolution discussed at great length (and in orthodox Marxist–Leninist terms) the distinction between the socialist and communist stages of development, firmly identified the commune with the former, and thus insisted that the social product be distributed solely on the basis of work rather than need. It was emphasized that the road to communism involved "a long and complicated process," that a communist reorganization of society presupposed an advanced level of the development of the productive forces, and that it could be achieved "only after the lapse of considerable time." In the meantime, the resolution warned against "impetuous attempts" to introduce communist measures and "utopian dreams" of skipping over historically necessary stages of social development. Accordingly, it called for a restoration of individual ownership of personal property such as houses, furniture, consumer goods, small farm tools, and the restoration of small family plots for supplementary food production and individual family ownership of small domestic animals and poultry. And to undermine the influence of local rural cadres who had spearheaded radical communization, the central committee demanded the reestablishment of the authority of the regular party and state apparatus over the countryside.

A series of other party meetings in the early months of 1959 further moderated the operation of the communes and established stricter centralized controls over them. These meetings, as the Wuhan plenum of December, were dominated by Liu Shao-ch'i. It was reflective of the political trends of the time that Mao's presumably voluntary decision to step down as head of state was accepted and announced by the central committee during the Wuhan meeting and that the position of Chairman of the People's Republic formally was conferred on Liu in April 1959. Mao retained the more important post of chairman of the party, but he was no longer fully in command of the party apparatus. He later was to complain that, after the Wuhan plenum, he was treated like "a dead ancestor."[25]

While Mao may have been treated like a dead man, he did not behave like one. The first half of 1959 was marked by increasingly bitter party debates over socioeconomic policy, centering on the communes, with Mao and Maoists unsuccessfully attempting to revive the radicalism of the Great Leap. In April Mao sent a personal directive to local party committees condemning the decisions of the Wuhan meeting. But the retreat ordered in December continued. By the summer of 1959 most of the communes were little more than formal administrative structures. Communal mess halls were abandoned, peasants were devoting more and more of their labor to private family plots, and private rural markets (abolished in late 1957) reappeared and grew. Despite attempts by leaders in Peking to restore centralized planning and political controls, economic conditions continued to deteriorate. Shortages of raw materials and transportation difficulties gravely hampered industrial production. And unusually severe floods and drought in the spring and summer (affecting nearly half of the cultivated land) held ominous implications for agricultural production and the national economy in general.

As the economic situation became more critical, the political struggle between Maoists and the party hierarchy intensified. The struggle revolved about what Maoists later called "the two roads"—one presumably leading back to capitalism and the other forward to socialism and communism—although the political lines had yet to be fully drawn. Matters reached a head (the first of many) in early August, when the party central committee convened its eighth plenum at the mountain resort of Lushan in Kiangsi province.

The Lushan Plenum

Three issues of momentous import confronted the leaders of the Chinese Communist Party at the Lushan meeting: the future of the communes and the fate of the Great Leap Forward campaign in general; Mao's role and political future as chairman of the party; and the nature and control of the People's Liberation Army. The three issues came together (although they were to be resolved only temporarily) in the dramatic confrontation between Mao and P'eng Te-huai, a veteran revolutionary who had played a major role in the formation and history of the Red Army since joining Mao at Chingkangshan in 1928.

The prelude to the drama to be enacted at Lushan began when P'eng, in his capacity as Minister of Defense, led a Chinese military delegation on a visit to the Soviet Union and the Warsaw Pact countries of Eastern Europe in the spring of 1959. During the course of his travels, P'eng expressed to Khrushchev and other foreign Communist leaders his displeasure (which coincided with Soviet displeasure) over the policies of the Great Leap and the leadership of Mao. In P'eng's view, a view shared by other military leaders, China's domestic socioeconomic policies were intimately related to her military policies and to her relations with the Soviet Union. China's military security required a rational plan of modern economic development (to modernize the professional army that P'eng headed) as well as the sophisticated weapons and the nuclear shield provided by the Soviet Union. The Great Leap Forward campaign threatened both, for it was undermining modern industrial and technological development within China and undermining the Sino–Soviet alliance. And even more directly threatening to the professional army was the Maoist revival of the popular militia.

When P'eng returned to China in mid-June, he launched a wholesale attack on the policies of the Great Leap, culminating a month later in a "Letter of Opinion" addressed directly to Mao. With a striking lack of subtlety, he condemned communization, the collapse of national planning, the alienation of the party from the masses, and oppressive economic conditions and political practices—all of which he attributed to the "petty bourgeois fanaticism" of Maoists.[26]

Although it is doubtful that P'eng was involved with the Russians in any anti-Mao conspiracy, this must have seemed to Mao and others to be the case. For it was precisely at the time when P'eng returned from his military mission to the Soviet Union in June that Khrushchev unilaterally abrogated the 1957 agreement according to which the Soviet Union was to provide China with modern military technology, including, it was reported, a sample atomic bomb. And it was at the very time that P'eng was circulating his "Letter of Opinion" that Khrushchev, in a speech delivered in Poland on July 18, first publicly denounced the Chinese communes, attributing them to the ideas of people who "do not properly understand what communism is or how it is to be built."[27] Mao, at any rate, was firmly convinced that P'eng (among others) had gone "behind the back of our fatherland to collude with a foreign country."[28]

Mao, it might be noted, was by no means wholly uncritical of his own role in the Great Leap. On July 23, in one of the conferences preceding the formal opening of the Lushan plenum, Mao criticized himself for promoting the backyard steel campaign (which he described as "a great catastrophe") and for pushing communization with undue haste. "The chaos caused was on a grand scale and I take responsibility."[29] The speech, however, was a curious combination of confessions, a defense of the Great Leap policies in general and the communes in particular, a call for the revival of communization, and political threats. Mao still found mass "enthusiasm for communism" among the peasantry, reaffirmed his own enthusiasm for the communes and their future (while acknowledging the mistakes of the past), denied that he and the party had become isolated from the masses, and was harshly critical of comrades who "waver in times of crisis and show a lack of resolution in the great storms of history." And he put the most threatening of his political threats in the most dramatic fashion. Should the Great Leap and the communes be allowed to perish, he vowed to "go to the countryside to lead the peasants to overthrow the government. If those of you in the Liberation Army won't follow me, then I will go and find a Red Army, and organize another Liberation Army. But I think the Liberation Army would follow me."[30]

Mao hardly could have drawn the political lines more sharply. Nor could he have more narrowly limited the range of policy choices that the politburo and central committee could make. Not only did he challenge the Party to choose between himself and P'eng Te-huai, but he tied the question of his personal leadership of the party to his policy on the communes and to Maoist leadership of the army. Since most party leaders were not about to risk a major political upheaval (and perhaps even a civil war) by attempting to remove Mao, they had little choice but to reaffirm Mao's political supremacy, and in the bargain support, at least formally, his policies as well. While Mao sought dramatic and decisive confrontations, most of his opponents were, above all, men of order who were not about to compound a chaotic economic situation with political chaos. They did not share the boldness of a P'eng Te-huai, and, however much Liu Shao-ch'i and others may have shared P'eng's criticisms of the Great Leap, they shrank from following him into a battle that held such potentially explosive and unpredictable consequences.

Thus when the eighth plenum of the central committee formally convened on August 2, P'eng found himself politically isolated; and his criticism of the Great Leap was, for the time being, in political discredit as well. And Mao insisted that P'eng was also to be politically disgraced, a demand that party leaders hardly could refuse in view of the widespread suspicions that P'eng was involved in Khrushchev's heavy-handed attempts to interfere in internal Chinese affairs. For however great their differences on matters of domestic policy, most Chinese Communists were committed no less ardently than Mao to the principle of Chinese national independence. The Lushan plenum, accordingly, adopted a resolution denouncing "the antiparty clique headed by P'eng Te-huai," which subsequent statements likened to the antiparty conspiracy of Kao Kang in the early 1950s, and condemned him for having slandered the Great Leap. P'eng was dismissed as minister of defense and his supporters were removed from key positions in the army. In September he was succeeded by the then eminently Maoist Lin Piao.

The official communique that emerged on August 26 from the Lushan meeting was quite candid in acknowledging the failures of the Great Leap. The communique was particularly critical of the now abandoned backyard steel production campaign and the absence of central planning and direction. Also admitted was that due to inadequate accounting procedures, the celebrated increases in production for 1958 had been grossly overestimated. The officially announced figure of 375,000,000 tons for grain production was revised downward to 250,000,000 tons. The actual figure was probably about 215 million tons.[31] Nevertheless, the Lushan resolution called for the revival of the Great Leap Forward and reaffirmed the validity and viability of the system of people's communes. The difficulties experienced by the communes now were attributed to "right opportunists" who underestimated achievements and overestimated defects. Communal mess halls were to be restored and private peasant plots were to be reduced. But the Lushan plenum formalized the Wuhan decision that the production brigade not the commune was to be the primary "unit of account." For the time being, the concept of communal ownership of property was rejected.

The revival of the Great Leap in the fall of 1959 and the winter of 1960 was a pale reflection of the original movement and Mao's political victory at Lushan soon proved to be a hollow one. Maoist appeals and ideological exhortations fell on deaf ears as floods and drought ravaged much of the countryside and food shortages spread in the wake of a poor harvest. Facing the threat of a bitter winter, peasants resisted the reintroduction of mess halls and the abolition of their private plots—and demoralized rural Party cadres were little inclined to press the issues. The statements of party leaders were prefaced with the radical slogans of the Great Leap, but the substance of policy was to continue the cautious retreat from communization, implicitly sanctioning material incentives, the reemergence of private markets, and the return to the small intra-village team (in effect, the old mutual aid team) as the basic unit of production. Immediate economic needs rather than radical social visions also guided policy in the urban areas as food shortages spread to the cities and industrial production was increasingly hampered by problems of supply and distribution. The previous year's utopian fervor and popular enthusiasm withered as the struggle to achieve communism turned into an elemental struggle for basic subsistence and sheer survival.

By the end of 1959 Mao had come to recognize the gravity of the economic situation and had come to accept (however reluctantly) the inevitability of dismantling the Great Leap Forward. In a letter written in late November and circulated through the rural party organizations, he invoked not the principle of "permanent revolution," with which the Great Leap had begun, but rather uncharacteristically advised paying attention "only to real possibilities," the somber note on which the campaign came to an end. Over the following months Mao quietly withdrew from day-to-day party affairs and political life, although without relinquishing his formal position as chairman of the Chinese Communist Party, and seemingly acquiesced in the reassertion of the power of regular party and state organizations, personified in the growing dominance of Liu Shao-ch'i. Indeed, there is much to suggest that Mao no longer regarded the party as a reliable instrument of revolutionary social change. In September of 1959 he had complained that "bourgeois elements have infiltrated our Communist Party,"[32] and by the end of the year he perhaps concluded that the "bourgeoisie" (as Mao loosely used the term) had come to dominate the party. In 1960, at any event, Mao no longer commanded either the party or the state and no longer determined the policies they pursued. What remained of his victory at Lushan was tenuous control of the army through his protégé Lin Piao.

The last act in the Great Leap, although it was enacted neither in the spirit nor for the purpose of the original movement, was an attempt to establish "communes" in the cities during the first half of 1960. A number of urban communes had been organized in the summer and fall of 1958, but the urban movement was halted in December 1958, ostensibly because the complexities of urban life and the persistence of bourgeois ideology in the cities made urban communization a more difficult task than the communization of the countryside.[33] When the movement was revived in 1960, it was still accompanied by a good deal of the utopian rhetoric of the Great Leap, but the purpose was no longer social revolution but economic survival. It was a temporary expedient to cope with the shortages of food and other basic necessities by reorganizing the system of supply and distribution and organizing the unemployed, youth, and women into hastily established workshops to produce household goods and food in vegetable gardens on the outskirts of the cities. Unlike the rural communes, which remained, even though in attenuated form, the urban communes soon disappeared entirely as economic conditions improved in 1961.

Before that improvement came about, however, the people of China, in cities and countryside alike, were to endure the most difficult and calamitous year in the history of the People's Republic. In 1960 the forces of nature inflicted even crueler blows than they had the previous year. Typhoons caused unprecedented floods in South China and Liaoning, drought afflicted the middle and lower reaches of the Yellow River (whose flow was reduced by two-thirds), and pests afflicted wide areas of the countryside. More than 60 percent of the cultivated area suffered from flood or drought and agricultural production plummeted. As famine threatened the land, industrial production was further disrupted by the damage to industrial crops; disruptions in the transportation system; the transfer of labor to officially designated disaster areas; and finally by laborers physically exhausted and weakened by increasingly critical food shortages.

The economic crisis was gravely compounded in the summer of 1960, when Khrushchev abruptly recalled the 1,400 Soviet scientists and industrial specialists working in some 250 Chinese enterprises. The official Soviet explanation, which came only several years later, charged that the Russian specialists had been ill-treated by their Chinese hosts. The real reasons, of course, lay in the rapid deterioration of Sino–Soviet relations. A long series of events preceded the act which, perhaps more than anything else, precipitated the final rupture between the two countries. Russian anger over the Great Leap Forward and the Chinese abandonment of "the Soviet model" coincided with Chinese resentment over the absence of Soviet support in the Quemoy–Matsu crisis of 1958 and border disputes with India in 1959. Khrushchev's visit to Peking in late September of 1959, coming directly after his "summit" meeting with Eisenhower at Camp David, his public ridicule of the communes, and the P'eng Te-huai affair, served only to exacerbate the mounting hostility between the two countries and between Mao and Khrushchev personally. Not even the usual *pro forma* communique issued from the Peking talks. But in April 1960 the Chinese issued what was in effect a public declaration of independence from the Soviet Union in the realm of international affairs as well as domestic policy—in the form of the treatise *Long Live Leninism,* written in commemoration of the 90th anniversary of Lenin's birth and probably written by Mao himself. And in June, at the congress of the Rumanian party in Bucharest, Sino–Soviet hostilities came into the open —or at least openly before an international Communist audience—when Khrushchev made a scathing attack on China and the Chinese delegate P'eng Chen replied in kind. Several weeks later, upon his return to Moscow, Khrushchev ordered the Russian specialists to return home, and apparently ordered them to take their blueprints with them.

The move surprised and shocked the Russian specialists as much as it did the Chinese. In the words of Mikhail Klochko, a Soviet chemist (and Stalin Prize winner) who was a member of two Soviet scientific missions to China:

> As one of those who was suddenly and surprisingly ordered home in 1960, I can testify that all of the anger at the move was not limited to the Chinese. Without exception my fellow scientists and the other Soviet specialists whom I knew in China were extremely upset at being recalled before the end of our contracts. Like myself, others must have had difficulty hiding their amazement when told by Soviet representatives in Peking that dissatisfaction with our living and working conditions was an important reason for our recall. In fact few of us had ever lived better in our lives than we did in China. Our Chinese hosts were even more mystified; again and again they asked why we were leaving and whether anything could be done to prevent our going.
>
> The suddenness with which events developed indicated that the decision was irreversible. The first telegrams giving us the news arrived in mid-July 1960. By late August the hundreds of scientists, engineers, and technicians who had been scattered throughout China had departed with their families. At the beginning of September not a single Soviet citizen remained in China, apart from diplomats and a few trade officials.[34]

Klochko has provided a vivid summary of the immediate economic impact of the Soviet attempt to punish the Chinese for their insubordination:

> The abruptness of the withdrawal meant that construction stopped at the sites of scores of new plants and factories while work at many existing ones was thrown into confusion. Spare parts were no longer available for plants built according to Russian design and mines and electric power stations developed with Russian help were closed down. Planning on new undertakings was abandoned because the Russians simultaneously canceled contracts for the delivery of plans and equipment. A planned power and irrigation project for the Yellow River, which frequently overflows its banks, was one of those which had to be abandoned.[35]

Coming on top of two successive years of natural calamities, disastrous harvests, and the general economic and organizational dislocations produced by the Great Leap, the sudden cancellation of Russian technological assistance dealt a particularly crippling blow to the Chinese economy. It was thus that China's "fraternal socialist" ally made its contribution to the bitter winter of 1960–1961. Massive famine was avoided (but only barely) through the institution of a highly efficient system of rationing and distribution and by huge wheat purchases from Australia and Canada, but widespread malnutrition resulted in diseases which took a heavy toll of lives in 1961. And China's industrialization was hampered for the next half-decade.

Thus the Great Leap Forward campaign, which began with such great expectations in 1958, ended in 1960 in an economic disaster for China and a political disaster for Mao Tse-tung. It also contributed to the breakdown of the Sino–Soviet alliance. To a grave internal economic crisis, there was added the threat of an increasingly precarious external situation. Half-surrounded by the military bases of a hostile United States along her eastern and southern borders (reaching from Korea, Japan, Okinawa, and Taiwan to Southeast Asia), China was now also confronted by a Soviet threat from the north. Both the internal situation and the external threat, and particularly the combination of the two, called for acts of extraordinary statesmanship, but as China entered the new decade the statesmen of the People's Republic were in hostile confrontation with each other.

For most Western observers, the question why the Great Leap Forward failed has not appeared as a matter requiring extended discussion or investigation. The usual explanation is that the campaign was utopian in conception from the outset—"utopian" in the usual sense of the term, i.e., in principle unrealizable—and therefore failure was inherent in the very premises on which the movement was based. During the Great Leap, we are told, Maoists set out "in pursuit of the impossible," and thus were doomed to fail from the beginning. Nothing further in the way of explanation, therefore, is needed, although it is often conceded that such fortuitous factors as natural disasters and the sudden cancellation of Soviet aid made the ensuing economic crisis more severe than it otherwise might have been. But since the Great Leap was "utopian" in nature from the beginning, it is generally assumed that failure in the end was inevitable.

But a fair historical evaluation of the Great Leap in general and communization in particular does demand that one take into consideration the vast incongruities between what was intended and what was done, the striking differences between what originally were basically rational (and perhaps "possible") Maoist policies of socioeconomic change and the largely irrational fashion in which Maoists attempted to implement those policies.

While standard Maoist accounts now generally and simply attribute the failure of the Great Leap (insofar as the failure is acknowledged) to a combination of natural disasters and Soviet treachery, Mao himself early was aware of the discrepancy between the policies he advocated and the manner in which they were being practiced. At the Lushan conference of 1959 he was critical (and partly self-critical) of the hasty and disorderly manner in which communization and labor mobilization policies were being carried out, critical of the "commandism" of party cadres, and critical of the lack of national planning. "The planning organs do not concern themselves with planning," he then complained; "the Planning Commission and the central ministries have been in existence for ten years, and suddenly at Peitaiho they decided not to concern themselves with it. They called it a directive on planning, but it was tantamount to doing away with planning altogether."[36]

This censure of "the central ministries" for having abdicated their responsibilities is of particular interest, for it points to one of the principal conclusions that Mao soon was to arrive at in his analysis of why the Great Leap had failed: his conviction that existing state and party bureaucracies had become conservative obstacles to radical social change and had sabotaged the movement. In view of the threat that the communes, in their original radical form and conception, posed to bureaucratic positions and privileges, it should hardly be surprising that many party leaders and government officials were something less than wildly enthusiastic about the Great Leap from the beginning. Opposition to the Great Leap and the communes on grounds of economic rationality may well have been reinforced by fears over their political implications. Mao, in any event, was convinced that a large share of the responsibility for the failure was attributable to the opposition of what he began to call "the bureaucratic class." He also came to the conclusion that the Great Leap had been undertaken without sufficient ideological preparation on the part of the masses.

In the winter of 1960–1961, the failure of the Great Leap seemed as spectacular as the attempt itself. But the failure was by no means complete. Most importantly, the rural communes, the heart of the campaign, survived the demise of the movement itself. Although they existed and functioned in a form far different from which they originally were conceived, the new rural organizational structures remained and in the years that followed served to facilitate the introduction of new technologies and organizational patterns in rural life. The massive water-conservation projects, the dams and canals designed to alleviate the perennial problems of floods and drought, proved to be an important factor in the steady growth in agricultural production and productivity which the People's Republic has enjoyed since 1962. The break with the Soviet model of development, with its exclusive emphasis on heavy industry, proved to be irreversible. Maoists and non-Maoists were to clash on many issues of economic policy, but there was a general recognition that a viable agrarian economy was the first and essential prerequisite for China's modern economic development. Finally, the Great Leap and communization had long-term effects on the psychology and values of the Chinese peasantry, particularly in breaking down traditionally conservative attitudes and patterns of behavior. It was an era of experimentation and innovation and one which promoted a spirit of change—and many of the experiments in social life, in new rural industries, and in education, hastily undertaken and often hastily abandoned, were later to be revived and developed in more careful and rational ways.

Notes

1. Mao Tse-tung, "Sixty Points on Working Methods," in Jerome Ch'en, ed., *Mao Papers* (London: Oxford University Press, 1970), pp. 62–63.

2. Mao Tse-tung, "Reading Notes on the Soviet Union's 'Political Economy,'" *Mao Tse-tung Ssu-hsiang Wan-Sui* (Taipei: n.p., 1967, 1969), JPRS, p. 272.

3. Mao Tse-tung "Speech to the Supreme State Conference," *Chinese Law and Government*, 1, No. 4:10–14.

4. Mao, "Reading Notes," pp. 333–334.

5. Mao Tse-tung, *On the Correct Handling of Contradictions Among the People* (Peking: Foreign Languages Press, 1957), p. 35.

6. Ch'en Po-ta, "New Society, New People," *Hung-ch'i*, No. 3, July 1, 1958.

7. Ch'en Po-ta, "Under the Banner of Comrade Mao Tse-tung," *Hung-ch'i*, No. 4, July 16, 1958.

8. "Resolution of the Central Committee of the Chinese Communist Party on the Establishment of People's Communes in the Rural Areas," August 29, 1958, in Robert R. Bowie and John K. Fairbank, *Communist China 1955–59: Policy Documents with Analysis* (Cambridge, Mass.: Harvard University Press, 1962), pp. 454–456.

9. Karl Marx and Frederick Engels, *Selected Works* (Moscow: Foreign Languages Publishing House, 1950), 1:50–51.

10. For a discussion of the *min-pan* precedents, see Mark Seldon, *The Yenan Way in Revolutionary China* (Cambridge, Mass.: Harvard University Press, 1971), esp. pp. 270–274.

11. Chang Kuang-chun, "Will Half-Work and Half-Study Lower the Educational Quality?" *Shih-shih Shou-ts'e* (Current Events), No. 20, October 27, 1958. (SCMM 151; revised translation from original).

12. Chin Hao, "Repudiate Criticisms of the Red and Expert Universities," *Chung-kuo Ching-nien* (Chinese Youth), No. 13, July 1, 1958. (SCMM 143; revised transl.).

13. Karl Marx, "Critique of the Gotha Program," in Marx and Engels, *Selected Works,* 2:36.

14. Karl Marx, "The Civil War in France," in Marx and Engels, *Selected Works,* esp. 1:468–475.

15. The Chinese began intensive bombardments of the Kuomintang-occupied offshore islands of Quemoy and Matsu in late August 1958, following the breakdown of Sino–American talks in Geneva. The United States countered with threats of air and naval action against China itself while the Chinese spoke with increased determination of the need to liberate Taiwan. The bombardments ceased a month later and the talks were resumed in Warsaw.

16. *Hung-ch'i,* No. 7, August 1958, quoted in Franz Schurmann, *Ideology and Organization, in Communist China* (Berkeley: University of California Press, 1966), p. 479.

17. Schurmann, *Ideology and Organization,* p. 478.

18. The term "dictatorship of the proletariat," it might be noted, now had replaced the formula of a "people's dictatorship" as the official designation of the nature of state power in the People's Republic.

19. As typically put by the Maoist theoretician Kuan Feng, "A Brief Discussion of the Great Historical Significance of People's Communes," *Che-hsueh Yen-chiu* (Philosophic Research), 1958, No. 5.

20. *Jen-min jih-pao* editorial, September 3, 1958; Wu Chih-pu, "From APCs to People's Communes," *Hung-ch'i* (Red Flag), 1958, No. 8. For a translation of the latter, see SCMM No. 147, pp. 1–10.

21. Karl Marx, "*Civil War in France,*" in Marx and Engels, *Selected Works,* 1:471–472.

22. Karl Marx and Friedrich Engels, *Werke* (Berlin: Dietz, 1963), 22:236.

23. Wu Chih-pu, "On People's Communes," *Chung-kuo ch'ing-nien* (Chinese Youth), September 6, 1958 (SCMM, No. 524, p. 5).

24. The opening paragraphs of the resolution reiterated the Maoist definition of the nature and function of the communes:

> In 1958 a new social organization appeared fresh as the morning sun above the broad horizon of East Asia. This was the large-scale people's commune in the rural areas of our country which combines industry, agriculture, trade, education and military affairs and in which government administration and commune management are integrated. . . . The development of the system of rural people's communes . . . has shown the people of our country the way to the gradual transition from collective ownership to ownership by the whole people in agriculture, the way to the gradual transition from the socialist principle of "each according to his work" to the communist principle of "to each according to his needs," the way to the gradual diminution and final elimination of the differences between rural and urban areas, between worker and peasant and between mental and manual labor, and the way to the gradual diminution and final elimination of the domestic functions of the state. . . . It can also be foreseen that in the future

communist society, the people's communes will remain the basic unit of the social structure. ["Resolution on Questions Concerning People's Communes," sixth plenary session of the eighth central committee of the CCP (December 10, 1958). New China News Agency, Peking, Dec. 18, 1958].

25. Mao Tse-tung, "Talk at the Report Meeting," October 24, 1966, in Stuart R. Schram, ed., *Mao Tse-tung Unrehearsed: Talks and Letters, 1956–71* (Middlesex, England: Penguin, 1974), pp. 266–267.

26. P'eng Te-huai, "Letter of Opinion," *The Case of Peng Teh-huai, 1959–68* (Hong Kong: Union Research Institute, 1968), pp. 7–13.

27. Prior to this time, public Soviet commentaries largely were confined to veiled criticisms of the Great Leap and Mao, often in the form of attacks on the "Blanquist" heresy of Communists who failed to recognize the necessary stages of historical development. There was one notable exception. On December 1, 1958, in a private conversation with Senator Hubert Humphrey, Khrushchev voiced his disapproval of the communes. Humphrey proved incapable of keeping the news to himself and Khrushchev's comments appeared in the European edition of the New York *Herald Tribune* in late December and in the January 12, 1959 edition of *Life*, much to the embarrassment of the Soviet leader.

28. Mao Tse-tung, "Speech at the Enlarged Session of the Military Affairs Committee and the External Affairs Conference," September 11, 1959, in Schram, ed., *Mao Tse-tung Unrehearsed*, p. 151.

29. Mao Tse-tung, "Speech at the Lushan Conference," July 23, 1959, in Schram, ed., *Mao Tse-tung Unrehearsed*, esp. pp. 143–46.

30. *Ibid.*, p. 139 and pp. 131–43, passim. While Mao cataloged in some detail and with candor the errors and mistakes of both himself and others, he implicitly excused the former by noting that even Confucius and Marx had made mistakes.

31. Production fell perilously in 1959 to a generally estimated 192,000,000 tons and to 161,000,000 in 1960.

32. Mao Tse-tung "Speech at the Enlarged Session of the Military Affairs Committee and the External Affairs Conference," September 11, 1959, in Schram, ed., *Mao Tse-tung Unrehearsed*, p. 148.

33. "Resolution on Questions Concerning People's Communes," December 10, 1958, *Current Background*, No. 542, p. 6. The resolution still called for the transformation of "old cities" into "new cities" but the transformation was postponed, for the reasons noted.

34. "The Sino-Soviet Split—the Withdrawal of the Specialists," *International Journal* (Toronto), Vol. XXVI, No. 3 (Summer, 1971), p. 556. Klochko, needless to say, did not write his recollections of the event in the Soviet Union. He was granted political asylum in Canada in 1961.

35. *Ibid.*, p. 559.

36. Mao, "Speech at the Lushan Conference," p. 142.

Part Four

The Thermidorean Reaction, 1960–1965

15

The Bureaucratic Restoration

FROM TIME IMMEMORIAL, or at least from the time of the appearance of the social division of labor, bureaucracies and the perfection of bureaucratic organization universally have grown and developed together with the development of civilization. In modern times, the growth of bureaucracy and "bureaucratic rationality" has been propelled by the development of capitalist forces of production and the increasing complexities of modern socioeconomic life in general. And nowhere has the growth and power of bureaucracy been greater and more apparent than in the "postcapitalist" societies produced by ostensibly socialist revolutions; the gigantic Soviet bureaucracy is, of course, only the most obvious example.

China has not been an exception to the general phenomenon. In a land where bureaucracy took root in the most ancient times and where the bureaucratic state received its fullest and most sophisticated development in pre-modern world history, it is hardly to be expected that its modern history would have proved immune to either the bureaucratic influences of the past or the bureaucratic imperatives of modern political and economic forces. The traditional Confucian bureaucracy which disintegrated along with the breakup of traditional society in the modern era was replaced by a variety of new bureaucratic structures as notorious for their oppression as for their corruption and inefficiency. If the Communist victory of 1949 largely removed bureaucratic corruption and inefficiency, it did not remove bureaucracy. Indeed, in the wake of the Revolution, as in the case of all modern revolutions, there came a massive process of bureaucratic centralization, a phenomenon that was both the producer and the product of national unification and the drive for rapid economic development. The new Communist bureaucracy grew rapidly in the 1950s. It was an eminently modern bureaucracy in both its "rational" nature and the efficiency with which it functioned—and it was far larger and penetrated society far more deeply than any previous bureaucracy in Chinese history. The process of bureaucratic proliferation and routinization was temporarily halted during the Great Leap Forward era, but the process resumed with renewed vigor in its aftermath.

It is very much in the mainstream of contemporary Western social thought to view bureaucratization not only as an inevitable historical development in the modern world but also as generally desirable, at least insofar as modern bureaucracies function with precision and with honesty and serve to maintain sociopolitical "equilibrium." At the very least, bureaucracy is widely regarded as a necessary evil for the functioning of complex societies. Thus most Western scholars of contemporary China have viewed with relative favor the periods in the history of the People's Republic that have seen the growth of modern-style bureaucratic structures (such as the early and mid-1950s and the early 1960s) and have condemned as abnormal and aberrant such Maoist-inspired eras as the Great Leap and the Cultural Revolution for having violated the dictates of "bureaucratic professionalism" and "instrumental rationality."

Yet if bureaucracy in its modern and "rational" form is something of a virtue in much of contemporary Western scholarly thought, it is seen in Marxist theory as a principal historical vice in any form and wholly incongruous with socialism, particularly in the Maoist variant of Marxism. Rejecting the Hegelian premise that the state, as the moral ideal, is distinct from civil society and that bureaucracy is the mediator between the two, Marx viewed the state as the product of the contradictions of society and bureaucracy as its typical and representative organizational form. Marx saw state and bureaucracy as reflections of man's alienated "prehistory" and as alien powers that rise above society to usurp human social powers. The bureaucratic state is rooted in what Marx called "the unsocial nature" of social life, in "private property, trade, industry, and the mutual plundering of different civil groups . . . this dismemberment, this debasement, this slavery of civil society is the natural foundation on which the modern state rests, just as the civil society of slavery was the foundation of the state in antiquity. The existence of the state and the existence of slavery are indivisible."[1] And socialism, for Marx, demanded the abolition of state and bureaucracy, just as it presupposed the abolition of the class-based society from which they arose. The Marxist notion of the "withering away" of the state under the dictatorship of the proletariat is based on the early Marxist premise that when the "organizing activity [of socialism] begins, where its own aim and spirit emerge, there socialism throws the political hull away."[2] For Marx, human emancipation would be realized "only when man has recognized and organized his own powers as social powers so that social force is no longer separated from him as political power."[3]

While Marxist theory sets forth the general historical rule that state and bureaucracy serve as instruments of the economically dominant class —a proposition that receives its simplest and best-known expression in Marx's characterization of the modern state as merely "a committee for managing the common affairs of the whole bourgeoisie"[4]—Marx also was concerned with historical situations where the bureaucratic state acquired relative independence from particular social classes and imposed its own political dominance over society in general. To a lesser degree (and an inadequate one in historical retrospect), he also was concerned with the possibility of the restoration of bureaucratic power in the wake of a socialist revolution.

Put in brief and schematic form, Marx identified three general types of sociohistorical situations that fostered the autonomy of the bureaucratic state. The first is a situation where all social classes are weak and undeveloped, a phenomenon he saw as universal in traditional societies characterized by the so-called Asiatic mode of production, for which precolonial India was the classic example and where a despotic state and ruling bureaucracy rested on the social basis of presumably unchanging, isolated, and self-sufficient village communities.[5] To a lesser extent, it was the case in czarist Russia, where neither the old feudal nobility nor the modern bourgeoisie was sufficiently strong to exercise state power, and where, consequently, a despotic bureaucracy was able to achieve and maintain dominance. Another (and vastly different) situation conducive to bureaucratic independence is characterized by a relative balance between two equally strong social classes. Such was the situation in much of Western Europe when the decaying yet still powerful feudal aristocracy was engaged in a long-term struggle with the emergent bourgeoisie. It was to this stalemate in the class struggle that Marx attributed the power and relative autonomy of the absolutist monarchies and their bureaucracies in the seventeenth and eighteenth centuries. Finally, in the case of a relatively economically advanced society, Marx pointed to the persistence of a massive class of individual peasant cultivators as providing the social foundation for the power and independence of the bureaucratic state presided over by Napoleon III following the failure of the revolution of 1848. The French case, as Marx put it, was one where "the political influence of the allotment farmer finds its ultimate expression in an Executive power that subjugates the commonweal to its own autocratic will."[6]

But if Marx recognized that under certain sociohistorical conditions the bureaucratic state could achieve a large measure of autonomy and independence, he did not believe such conditions would prevail in the aftermath of a socialist revolution. He remained convinced, as he had so optimistically predicted in the *Manifesto*, that when "class distinctions have disappeared and all production has been concentrated in the hands of a vast association of the whole nation, the public power will lose its political character."[7] To be sure, Marx was not wholly oblivious to the possibility of the persistence and revival of bureaucracy in the postrevolutionary period. In his analysis of the Paris Commune of 1871, he emphasized the need for the working class to destroy, and not simply take over, "the centralized State power, with its ubiquitous organs of standing army, police, bureaucracy, clergy, and judicature." He praised, and established as Marxist principles, the antibureaucratic safeguards introduced by the Communards. In order to restore political power to society, the producers were to be organized in working, rather than parliamentary, bodies, which combined executive and legislative functions. Whatever administrative functions were socially necessary were to be performed not by appointed officials but by simple working men (or their acknowledged representatives), who were to be elected by the masses, remain directly responsible to them, and be subject to immediate popular recall. Moreover, those performing public service were to do so at ordinary workingmen's wages and were not to be granted special status or privileges.[8] This essentially was Marx's remedy for the problem of bureaucracy in postrevolutionary society. Elsewhere, Marx said little more about the problem, and classical Marxist theory rested on, and conveyed, the comforting assumption that the abolition of state and bureaucracy inevitably would accompany the abolition of social class divisions.

It is, of course, one of the ironies of the history of Marxism in the modern world that where successful Marxist-inspired revolutions have taken place they have resulted not in the reduction of bureaucratic power, much less any process of the withering away of the state, but rather in the growth of bureaucracies more massive in scale, more powerful in function, and more independent in nature than those they replaced. That Marx, and Marxists generally, gravely underestimated the threat that bureaucracy might pose in the wake of a socialist revolution is a matter that often has been noted. But then, equally well noted, is the fact that Marx never anticipated the possibility of socialist revolutions in the economically and socially backward lands where they have in fact occurred in the twentieth century—indeed, precisely those historical situations that Marx himself viewed as those likely to foster the emergence of powerful bureaucratic states. The problem materialized soon after the first successful socialist revolution. Less than five years after the Russian Revolution, Lenin pondered the reasons why the new Soviet order had so quickly become so bureaucratic and so oppressive. On his deathbed he somberly concluded that he had witnessed the resurrection of the old czarist bureaucracy to which the Bolsheviks "had given only a Soviet veneer." Lenin's worst fears were soon to be realized with the massive bureaucratization of Soviet state and society during the Stalinist era, and the unleashing of what Isaac Deutscher once termed "an almost permanent orgy of bureaucratic violence."[9]

The objective sociohistorical conditions that prevailed in China at the time of the Communist victory provided even more fertile soil for the growth of an independent bureaucracy than had been the case in Russia. China was (and remains) a far more economically backward land, a much more eminently peasant country, and one with a far weaker social class structure. The Chinese proletariat was smaller and less politically mature than its Russian counterpart, and a class that had only the most tenuous links to the ruling Communist Party. Moreover, it was a country that lacked a democratic tradition and was burdened by a long and deeply ingrained bureaucratic tradition. The revolution itself took place in a profoundly nationalist environment; it almost entirely lacked any genuine internationalist dimension either in objective historical reality or in the mentality of its leaders. China in 1949, in short, suffered from a total absence of the historical conditions that Marx and Marxists traditionally assumed would guarantee a postrevolutionary society ruled by the masses of producers rather than by a new bureaucracy: a mature working class, conditions of relative economic abundance, a prior bourgeois–democratic tradition upon which to build new forms of popular democracy, and an international revolutionary process and spirit. The conditions favoring bureaucratization were intensified by the imperatives of political centralization demanded by the need for national unification and economic development in a country so long racked by political fragmentation and poverty. Furthermore, the destruction of the propertied classes—the gentry–landlord elite and what remained of the bourgeoisie, however socially progressive and socially necessary—removed the last limitations to the growth of a powerful and autonomous bureaucracy. Chinese society after the revolution was less divided by social class differences than by the more elemental distinction between the rulers and the ruled, what Mao Tse-tung referred to as the contradiction between "those in positions of leadership and the led."[10] And with the nationalization of the key means of production, "those in positions of leadership" not only wielded political power but controlled the national economy as well.

Given these conditions, it is hardly surprising—indeed it was inevitable—that a vast bureaucratic apparatus would rise above society and come to be the dominant force. The only cause for surprise is that bureaucratic power and privilege in China did not grow to the extent and to the extremes that it did in the Soviet Union, that the separation and conflict between rulers and ruled has been comparatively less sharp and less severe. A new bureaucracy arose in the People's Republic, but from the beginning its power and independence were relatively restrained. The restraints were imposed by two factors. One was the enormous personal authority and prestige of Mao Tse-tung, whose deep hostility to bureaucracy and bureaucrats, coupled with the special relationship with the masses he enjoyed, served to counter the routinization and institutionalization of bureaucratic power. More pervasive has been the Chinese revolutionary heritage, with its profoundly egalitarian spirit and values forged during the bitter struggles of the 1930s and 1940s, and its guiding principle of the mass line dictating intimate relationships and common bonds between cadres and masses, between the leaders and the led.

While these restraints were themselves restrained during the early years of the People's Republic, the years between 1955 and 1960 saw their partial revival. When Mao launched the collectivization drive in 1955, he did so in the populist spirit of the revolutionary years, by going over the heads of party bureaucrats and bypassing much of the formal bureaucratic structure of the new state. The Hundred Flowers campaign posed an explicit threat to the privileges and independence of entrenched bureaucratic interests, especially when Mao pointed to "the bureaucratic practices of certain state functionaries in their relations with the masses" as a principal contradiction in Chinese society and demanded that "we must stamp out bureaucracy."[11] And the egalitarian and populist thrust of the Great Leap Forward had profound antibureaucratic implications—and encountered powerful bureaucratic resistance. The revolutionary revivalism of the late 1950s did not stamp out either bureaucracy or bureaucratism, but it did serve to inhibit the actions of bureaucrats and mitigate the power of a bureaucracy separated from, and standing above, society.

However, the retreat from the Great Leap in 1960, and Mao's retreat from the center of the political stage, led to the reassertion of the power of party and state bureaucracies. Faced with what was becoming a struggle for sheer survival, the mood of the masses turned sullen and apolitical. Maoist ideological appeals fell on deaf ears. A demoralized and politically apathetic population is a condition on which bureaucracy always thrives, and such was the condition of China in the aftermath of the Great Leap. The sharp decline in both agricultural and industrial production, the shortages in food and supplies, the dislocations in the systems of transportation and distribution, the breakdown of national planning, and the generally chaotic conditions of economic and social life all demanded the reintroduction of centralized economic and political controls. The demand reflected itself in a renewed Leninist emphasis on the virtues of discipline, order and organization. And there was a general aversion to Maoist-style mass campaigns in favor of economic stability and sociopolitical order. A return to order was the order of the day and the mood of the times. Thus both powerful objective and subjective factors were at work to bring about the restoration of bureaucratic rule.

Bureaucratization marked and molded virtually all facets of Chinese economic, social, and political life in the early 1960s, but it was a phenomenon that had its primary locus in the Chinese Communist Party itself. There is, to be sure, a distinction to be made between the party and the formal state administration in the People's Republic, but the distinction is a thin one. Most of the higher officials of the state, as well as most functionaries who held administrative positions of any significance, were members of the party and subject to its discipline—while the state administrative apparatus in general was an instrument that carried out the policies decided upon in the higher councils of the party. The party itself had grown into a huge organization with a membership of 17,000,000 by 1961, and was growing at the rate of almost 1,000,000 additional members per annum. Closely attached to the party, indeed its auxiliary arm, was the Comminist Youth League with a membership of approximately 25,000,000 in the early 1960s. And such mass associations as the Federation of Trade Unions (20,000,000 members), the Women's Federation (75,000,000) and the Students' Federation (4,000,000) were, in effect, organizations of the party. The renewed bureaucratization of state and society centered in the Chinese Communist Party, and emanated from it.

The history of the Chinese Communist Party from 1960 to 1965 was above all dominated by the reaffirmation of firm Leninist principles of political organization, particularly the cardinal Leninist principle of the crucial role of the vanguard party. The party was to be a highly centralized apparatus presided over by a revolutionary leadership possessing a true socialist consciousness and functioning with military-like precision; a disciplined organization in which the party center (or the "general staff," as Lenin had phrased it) exercised the appropriate discipline over its cadres (or what Lenin called "the shock troops"), who, in turn, disciplined and organized the masses for effective action. This Leninist conception of the nature of the party was naturally accompanied by a typical Leninist hostility towards the "spontaneity" of the masses. Nothing better describes the mentality of those who were in control of the party apparatus during those years, and their conception of the relationship between the party and the people, than Lenin's own dictum that "the party exists for the very purpose of going ahead of the masses and showing the masses the way."[12] Just as the leaders of the party were to train and discipline their cadres, the latter were to train and organize the masses.

It was precisely the "spontaneity of the masses," the virtue so prized by Maoists, that was seen as having undermined the stability of the postrevolutionary socioeconomic order in general, and the organization and authority of the party in particular. By the end of the Great Leap the organizational structure of the party had been gravely weakened, and much of its membership had become demoralized. The leaders of the party, who now began to look more to the leadership of Liu Shaoch'i than Mao Tse-tung, were first and foremost intent on reestablishing the Leninist authority and legitimacy of the party, restoring firm lines of command within it, and restoring its command over society in general.[13] From the prevailing Leninist perspective, this was the immediate and essential prerequisite for dealing with the economic crisis and for restoring social order.

One of their first acts was to blame the disasters of the Great Leap on lower-level party cadres (mostly Maoist-inspired rural cadres), who were accused of a vast array of Marxist–Leninist ideological deficiencies and charged with failing to understand and carry out the policies of the party. They also were accused of the sin of "commandism"—ignoring the desires, wishes, and complaints of the masses. It was an easy enough charge to make at a time when the masses had lost their taste for radical social action and the popular mood of an impoverished population favored order and stability. Many local cadres were dismissed, and those who remained were instructed to act strictly in accordance with the directives passed down from higher levels of the party hierarchy. It was therefore not the party as such that was to be faulted for the difficulties and problems plaguing Chinese society but rather the faults and errors of some of its individual members. It was thus that the myth of the infallibility of the Leninist party was maintained for the time being.

The downgrading of the role and function of basic-unit cadres (those who were in direct contact with the masses in factories, communes, schools, and residential organizations in cities and towns) was naturally accompanied by an increase in the power and authority of the middle and higher organs of the party hierarchy, especially the authority of provincial, regional, and urban party committees. The latter were headed by party secretaries, usually members of the central committee and directly responsible to it, who became the most powerful figures in their respective areas of jurisdiction. The centralization of the party apparatus was reinforced by the establishment in 1960 of new regional party bureaus directly attached to the central committee and a new emphasis on the role of control commissions, which hitherto had played only a relatively limited role in party life. New party schools for the training of disciplined cadres were established, and party directives stressed more strongly than ever the Leninist virtues of a tightly knit organizational structure, strict adherence to formal Party rules and procedures, and the obedience of lower- to higher-level organs—and ultimately obedience to the central committee and its politburo, which stood at the apex of the ultra-centralist structure of command. A 1961–1962 campaign to restore the Leninist spirit of the party stressed the principle of "democratic centralism," with the emphasis clearly on centralism. In view of the firm control exercised by the party over the key organs of the state, and indeed the very considerable overlapping in key personnel, the increasingly centralized and bureaucratic character of the party meant the increasing bureaucratization of the formal state administrative structure. It also meant increased centralized control over the rural communes by out-

side party organs and the restoration of the authority of economic ministries in Peking over urban factories and other large enterprises.

These tendencies toward bureaucratic centralization and professionalism were reflected in the party's recruitment patterns and personnel
policies in the post–Great Leap period. While the role of radical rural
cadres who had spearheaded the communization movement was downgraded and circumscribed, many officials and cadres purged in the antirightist campaign of 1957–1958 were reinstated. New recruits tended to
be people who possessed technical and administrative expertise; such
matters as class background and ideological commitment were factors
of decidedly lesser concern in recruitment and promotion. It was an environment in which the party tended to attract opportunists rather than
revolutionaries, one that reinforced the latent careerist tendencies already
present in the party. This was hardly a new phenomenon. Bureaucratic
opportunism and careerism had been among the more prominent objects
of attack by the critics whom Mao briefly had invited to "bloom and
contend" in the spring of 1957. In the early 1960s the tendency merely
was more pronounced than it had been a half-decade earlier. Indeed, the
bureaucratization of party and state in the post–Great Leap years was
largely a continuation, perhaps at an accelerated pace, of a trend that
had dominated the 1950s and had been interrupted only temporarily by
the utopianism and populism of the Great Leap. It took the form of the
institutionalization of a system of thirty formal ranks for state and party
cadres, the introduction of a differentiated system of wage payments
corresponding to the hierarchy of cadre ranks, and the growth of functional specialization among cadres in both governmental and party
organs. The transformation of revolutionary cadres into bureaucratic
functionaries and administrators, the development of a bureaucratic caste
enjoying special privileges, the growth of bureaucratic professionalism
and occupational specialization, and the general growth of a bureaucracy
increasingly separated from, and standing above, society—all were phenomena that had their roots in the pre–Great Leap era and flourished in
the post–Great Leap years.

If the Chinese Communist Party was in the process of being transformed from a revolutionary organization into a professional bureaucratic
apparatus with strong vested interests in its own self-preservation and
perpetuation, it had an equally strong interest in preserving the society
from which it had sprung and which it ruled. And preservation, in the
first instance, required overcoming the grave economic crisis into which
the Great Leap Forward campaign had degenerated. Whatever the evils
of bureaucracy, the party demonstrated the virtues of bureaucratic organization and efficiency in rescuing China from its plight and reestablishing a viable national economy. Through a combination of the restoration
of centralized control over the means of production and a renewed em-

phasis on material incentives for the producers, the leaders in Peking, relying primarily on the organizational effectiveness of a reinvigorated Leninist party, succeeded in reviving the national economy in a remarkably short time. The ministries in Peking reestablished centralized control and planning over the modern industrial sector of the economy, and the authority of managers and technocrats (acting according to the guidance of the party) was greatly strengthened. Higher party organs imposed central direction over the operation of the communes and over the rural economy in general. Centralization of economic life was coupled with a policy that allowed wide latitude for authorities in local productive units to offer financial incentives to workers and peasants in order to raise popular morale and spur production. In industrial enterprises this meant increasingly differentiated wage rates and a system of bonuses and prizes. In the rural areas it meant the encouragement of private peasant plots, the reappearance of private markets, and toleration of a growing tendency toward a market economy. By the end of 1961 conditions in both town and countryside were largely stabilized, and production began to increase after three successive years of decline. The rapidity of the recovery from near-disastrous economic conditions and the renewal of growth must be attributed in large measure to the organizational effectiveness of the Chinese Communist Party and the bureaucratic precision with which it functioned.

During the early 1960s Mao Tse-tung occupied a most ambiguous position in the political life of the People's Republic. Mao remained the chairman of the party, but he did not control its apparatus or determine its policies; indeed, the policies the party pursued were increasingly repugnant to him. Maoist slogans and quotations were widely propagated, but they were used less to achieve radical Maoist social aims than to promote national unity, maintain social order, and spur production. Due homage was paid to Mao as the leader of the revolution and the Party, but he did not, and could not, assume leadership of the nation. When Mao appeared at party gatherings, his speeches were greeted with the customary "enthusiastic applause" (according to the official transcripts), but the import of his words were largely ignored by most party leaders. The gap between Chinese Communist theory and practice widened, and the conflict between radical Maoists and party bureaucrats grew increasingly sharp and eventually irreconcilable.

Shortly after his victory over P'eng Te-huai at the Lushan meeting of August 1959, Mao removed himself from the day-to-day affairs and operations of the party. The withdrawal was perhaps voluntary, or at least graceful, but it was certainly motivated by Mao's awareness that P'eng's criticisms of the Great Leap were widely shared by party leaders, even if they did not share P'eng's bluntness, by a recognition that he could not command a majority of the central committee to continue the socially radical policies of the Great Leap (even assuming that he might have been inclined to do so), and that a collapsing economy and a demoralized peasantry did not provide favorable circumstances for any attempt to override the central committee in the fashion he had followed in the past. Thus control over the party and its policies fell into the hands of organization men, the "Thermidoreans" who were less interested in social change than in social stability, political order, and economic efficiency. The most prominent of the Thermidoreans was Liu Shao-ch'i— the formal head of state of the People's Republic, the senior vice-chairman of the party, Mao's informal heir apparent, and certainly the most orthodox Leninist among Chinese Communist leaders. Another was Teng Hsiao-p'ing who, as the Secretary-General of the Party, wielded vast power over its organizational apparatus. The ascendency of Liu and Teng was accompanied by the restoration of the authority of party bureaucrats whose power had been eclipsed during the Great Leap era— such leading party officials as Lu Ting-yi, P'eng Chen, and Lo Jui-ch'ing; and the economic planners who had been the architects of the First Five Year Plan, such as Ch'en Yün, Li Fu-chun and Po I-po. All had been critical of the policies of the Great Leap (although hitherto mostly silent critics), and they now proceeded to dismantle those policies and to return China to a condition of "normalcy."

The early 1960s were undoubtedly the most frustrating years in Mao's long political life. He was the acknowledged and still celebrated leader of the revolution, but he was no longer able to determine the direction in which the new society was moving. His attempts to inaugurate new revolutionary campaigns were repeatedly thwarted, distorted or ignored. Having taken the fateful decision to withdraw from active leadership in late 1959, Mao found it impossible to regain the reins of control over an increasingly bureaucratized and routinized party machine. They were years in which he was "treated as a dead ancestor," as he later charged. "Teng Hsiao-p'ing never came to consult me," he complained in 1966; "from 1959 to the present he has never consulted me over anything at all."[14]

With the disintegration of the Great Leap and his consequent isolation from the center of political power, Mao began to suffer from an uncharacteristic loss of confidence in the future and fate of the revolution. He no longer entertained any hope of an imminent transition from socialism to communism. The vision of a "leap" from "the realm of necessity" to "the realm of freedom" was no longer conceived as a sudden qualitative change, but rather now was characterized by Mao as a gradual process of indeterminate length. The Great Leap Forward promise of an economic miracle vanished in similar fashion. Whereas in 1958 Mao

had declared that it would take only fifteen years for China to reach the
economic levels of the industrialized West, in 1962 he somberly concluded that "it will be impossible to develop our productive power so
rapidly as to catch up with, and overtake, the most advanced capitalist
countries in less than one hundred years." He observed that Western
capitalism had developed over a period of three centuries and implied
that the development of socialism and communism would take place over
an equally lengthy historical era.[15]

Not only did visions of communism fade, but so did confidence in the
continued viability of the existing system. Mao began to brood over the
possibility that the work of the revolution would be destroyed and that
he might be forced to begin anew. He speculated that the revolutionary
order might "perish" and be replaced by a nonrevolutionary state. He
became increasingly obsessed with the possibility of historical regression.
New bourgeois elements are produced in a socialist society, he insisted
much more forcefully than ever before; classes remain, the class struggle
persists, and "this class struggle is a protracted, complex, [and] sometimes even violent affair."[16] Nor was it by any means assured that this
"protracted" class struggle would have a favorable outcome. In the autumn of 1962 Mao raised the possibility of "the restoration of the reactionary classes" and warned that "a country like ours can still move
toward its opposite."[17] In the years preceding the Cultural Revolution
the sense of historical indeterminateness that generally characterizes the
Maoist mentality—and which hitherto generally reflected itself in a deep
faith that determined revolutionaries could mold history in accordance
with their ideas and ideals—began to assume darkly pessimistic overtones
and implications.

While Mao was less confident about the future of the People's Republic than he had been, he did not fall into a state of political paralysis. He
was unwilling to play the role of a "dead ancestor" to which he claimed
he had been assigned. If he had lost faith in the party as a reliable revolutionary instrument, or at least in the party as it was, he remained
confident in his own abilities to rekindle the flames of revolution through
other means. If Mao could not control the party bureaucracy, the party
bureaucrats were unable to control Mao. They could not physically remove him from the political scene or even from his formal position as
chairman of the Party without risking a massive political struggle and
very possibly a violent civil war. Mao still enjoyed enormous personal
prestige in Chinese society (which he and his followers undertook to
cultivate through the form of the "Mao cult") and he retained a wide
following among the party rank and file, most of whom were probably
unaware of the conflict among their higher leaders. Most importantly, he
apparently commanded the loyalty of much of the People's Liberation
Army (PLA) largely through the efforts of Lin Piao. Mao had lost control over the party, but he hardly was powerless.

Nor is it likely that those who came to dominate the party and state bureaucracies in the early 1960s were inclined to remove Mao as titular head of the party. The "Thermidoreans," after all, were above all men of order who were intent on reestablishing social, economic, and political stability. They were not about to compound the chaos they inherited by precipitating a new political crisis with unpredictable consequences. They preferred to use Mao for their own ends rather than attempt to bury him. They invoked his name as a symbol of national unity and his slogans to promote the non-Maoist order they were attempting to build. Yet by invoking the authority of Mao and his "thoughts," the "Thermidoreans" were unwittingly contributing to their own political demise. In the meantime, they were determined to avoid an open clash. It was Mao who was to pose the political challenges and force the political confrontations.

In the years 1960 and 1961 Mao apparently took little or no part in the work of the party. His energies were turned to fortifying his political and ideological control over the PLA. He emerged from relative political seclusion in January of 1962, with a speech delivered to a national party work conference attended by some 7,000 provincial and district party functionaries. The speech was a wide-ranging and harshly critical attack on the bureaucratic methods and practices that had come to dominate party life in the post–Great Leap years. Mao focused on the Leninist principle of democratic centralism, a formula much emphasized by Liu Shao-ch'i and other party leaders over the previous two years. Liu had interpreted and applied the principle in a super-Leninist and ultra-centralist fashion, perhaps best described in Rosa Luxemburg's prophetic critique of the Leninist scheme of party organization and the "bureaucratic straitjacket" it threatened to impose; writing in 1904, she characterized it as a scheme that demanded "blind subordination" to "the party center, which alone thinks, guides, and decides for all," and meant "the rigorous separation of the organized nucleus of revolutionaries" from the mass movement.[18] No better words can be found to describe the character and methods of the Chinese Communist Party in the early 1960s. Mao for his part affirmed the validity of the principle of democratic centralism, but gave it a far different interpretation. In effect, he equated the Leninist notion with his own principle of the mass line, which, he strongly implied, the party had abandoned. Charging that "some of our comrades still do not understand the democratic centralism which Marx and Lenin talked of," he defined it for them in the fashion of a formula: "First democracy, then centralism; coming from the masses, returning to the masses; the unity of leadership and the masses."[19] The issue was not "democracy" in the conventional sense, but rather whether the impulses leading to policy decisions were to come primarily from the bottom up or to be dictated from the top down. By emphasizing democracy over centralism, Mao was expressing his abiding faith in the revolutionary spontaneity and initiative of the masses—the mass spontaneity so much distrusted in orthodox Leninist theory, and at the same time condemning party leaders who lacked that faith. For Mao, democracy meant that the masses were to speak first, even though they were not necessarily to have the last word.

The absence of a proper Maoist understanding of "democratic centralism" was reflected in party officials whom Mao chastised as being

> afraid of the masses, afraid of the masses talking about them, afraid of the masses criticizing them. . . . There are some comrades who are afraid of the masses initiating discussion and putting forward ideas which differ from those of the leaders and leading organizations. As soon as problems are discussed they suppress the activism of the masses and do not allow others to speak out. This attitude is extremely evil.[20]

Among the practitioners of this evil were the first secretaries of provincial, district, and county party committees—the pillars of the party bureaucracy—whom Mao called "tyrants" and against whom he directed some of his most bitter and sarcastic barbs.

Another proposition Mao pursued was that class struggles persist in a socialist society. It was not a new notion, but he now presented it in a qualitatively new way. The class struggle in China was no longer seen in the relatively benign form of mostly nonantagonistic contradictions that took place primarily "in the ideological field," as Mao had characterized it in 1957. "The reactionary classes which have been overthrown are still planning a comeback," he now warned. "In a socialist society, new bourgeois elements may still be produced." But it was not the fear that old reactionary classes or the bourgeoisie as such might regain state power that concerned Mao but rather the state of the party: "There are some people who adopt the guise of Communist Party members, but they in no way represent the working class—instead they represent the bourgeoisie. All is not pure within the Party." And with his own minority position in the higher councils of the party no doubt very much in mind, he defended the rights of a minority: "Very often the ideas of a minority will prove to be correct. History abounds with such instances." He concluded his remarks with a warning and a threat: "let other people speak out. The heavens will not fall and you will not be thrown out. If you do not let others speak, then the day will surely come when you are thrown out."[21]

Mao's speech, according to the official transcript, was greeted with the usual "enthusiastic applause." But it had no noticeable effect on the policies and practices of the Party.

Mao spoke again in September 1962 at the central committee's tenth plenum. Mao's speech at the plenum (and his talks at the informal sessions which preceded it) largely repeated the views he had presented in his "7,000-cadres" speech in January, stressing particularly the necessity and inevitability of class struggle to combat the growing danger of "revisionism."[22] Mao also called for a massive ideological education campaign for both party cadres and masses to be conducted in accordance with the principles of the Yenan rectification movement of 1942–1945. This was duly approved by the central committee and, in various forms and through a variety of instrumentalities, was to proceed over the next three and one-half years under the name of the "Socialist Education Movement." For Maoists, the aims of the new campaign were to revolutionize the party and the thought and behavior of its cadres, raise the ideological consciousness and socialist spirit of the masses, and reverse what were seen as "capitalist" and "revisionist" tendencies in the social and economic life of the country—and particularly the countryside. The Maoist thrust of the movement was to be blunted, and its aims were to be subverted, by an entrenched party bureaucracy, which wanted neither the leadership of Mao nor the disruptions of Maoist mass campaigns.

As the Socialist Education Movement foundered on bureaucratic resistance and popular apathy, the frustrations and fears of Mao and Maoists grew. Mao's own frustrations were certainly, in part, political ones; he hardly could have been anything less than deeply bitter that he was unable to control the party that he had built and guided through more than two decades of bitter revolutionary struggle, the party of which he was still the formal (but only the formal) leader a decade and a half after the revolutionary victory. All the more galling was that he had lived to witness, and was powerless to prevent, the transformation of the party from a revolutionary instrument into a conservative bureaucratic apparatus, a party that had succumbed to all the bureaucratic practices he had so long fought against. For Mao, bureaucracy had always been among the greatest of all evils. He viewed bureaucracy not so much, in a Marxist sense, as a reflection and product of the evils of society, but rather more, in an anarchist sense, as an evil that is visited upon society, as a principal source of social vices and inequities. And while Marxists traditionally have been reluctant to assign a social class status to bureaucratic strata, Mao was not. As he put it in 1965:

> The bureaucratic class is a class in sharp opposition to the working class and the poor and lower-middle peasants. How can these people who have become or are in the process of becoming bourgeois elements sucking the blood of the workers be properly recognized? These people are the objectives of the struggle, the objectives of the revolution.[23]

For Mao, then, "the bureaucratic class" was virtually synonymous with "the bourgeoisie," and bureaucratic dominance was equated with the dominance of capitalism, or at least considered the main force leading to a "bourgeois restoration." That the leaders of "the bureaucratic class" to which Mao referred were the leaders of the Chinese Communist Party is, of course, self-evident. But the Maoist concern was more than a concern with political power, pure and simple. That Mao was struggling for political power, that he was determined to regain political supremacy, and that he was determined to remove the bureaucratic obstacles that stood in his way are all matters that may be taken for granted. But if Mao regarded bureaucracy as evil, he also viewed as evil the socio-economic policies that Party bureaucrats were pursuing. If he found intolerable his own loss of power, he found no less intolerable the direction in which Chinese society was moving.

Notes

1. Karl Marx, "Critical Notes on 'The King of Prussia and Social Reform,'" in *Writings of the Young Marx on Philosophy and Society,* trans. Loyd Easton and Kurt Guddat (New York: Anchor, 1967), p. 349.

2. *Ibid.,* p. 357.

3. Karl Marx, "On the Jewish Question," in *Writings of Young Marx,* p. 241.

4. "Manifesto," Karl Marx and Frederick Engels, *Selected Works* (Moscow: Foreign Languages Publishing House, 1950), 1:35.

5. See especially, Karl Marx, "The British Rule in India," Marx and Engels, *Selected Works,* 1:312–318.

6. Karl Marx, *The Eighteenth Brumaire of Louis Bonaparte* (Chicago: Kerr, 1919), p. 146.

7. Marx and Engels, *Selected Works,* 1:51.

8. Karl Marx, "The Civil War in France," in Marx and Engels, *Selected Works,* 1:468–481.

9. Isaac Deutscher, *Marxism in Our Time* (San Francisco: Ramparts Press, 1971), p. 201.

10. Mao Tse-tung, *On the Correct Handling of Contradictions Among the People* (Peking: Foreign Languages Press, 1957), p. 9.

11. *Ibid.,* pp. 10, 61.

12. As Lenin put it at the Second Comintern Congress meeting at Petrograd in 1921. The concept of the vanguard party is, of course, most fully set forth in Lenin's 1902 treatise "What Is to Be Done?" See V. I. Lenin, *Selected Works* (Moscow: Foreign Languages Publishing House, 1952), 1, Part 1:203–409.

13. As Franz Schurmann has noted, it was during the years of Liu Shao-ch'i's dominance that the writings of Lenin were most widely propagated. Franz Schurmann, *Ideology and Organization in Communist China* (Berkeley University of California Press, 1966), p. 520.

14. Mao Tse-tung "Talk at the Report Meeting," October 24, 1966, in Schram ed. *Mao Tse-tung Unrehearsed,* pp. 266–267.

15. Mao Tse-tung, "Talk at an Enlarged Central Work Conference," January 30, 1962, in Schram, ed., *Mao Tse-tung Unrehearsed,* pp. 170–175.

16. *Ibid.,* p. 168.

17. Mao Tse-tung, "Speech at the Tenth Plenum of the Eighth Central Committee," September 24, 1962, in Schram, ed., *Mao Tse-tung Unrehearsed,* p. 189.

18. Rosa Luxemburg, "Organizational Questions of Social Democracy," in *Rosa Luxemburg Speaks* (New York: Pathfinder Press, 1970), p. 118.

19. Mao, "Talk at Enlarged Central Work Conference," pp. 158–160.

20. *Ibid.,* pp. 160–162.

21. *Ibid.,* pp. 168–187.

22. The text of Mao's formal speech to the plenum is translated in Schram, ed., *Mao Tse-tung Unrehearsed,* pp. 188–196.

23. "Selections from Chairman Mao," JPRS 49826, p. 23.

16

The New Economic Policy 1961–1965

DURING THE CULTURAL REVOLUTION OF 1966–1969, the economic policies of the preceding half-decade were condemned for leading China on a retreat from "socialism" to "capitalism," and the party leaders, especially Liu Shao-ch'i, responsible for formulating and implementing those policies were purged as "capitalist-roaders" who allegedly had exercised a "bourgeois dictatorship." This, in brief, was the Maoist Cultural Revolution perspective on the developments of the early 1960s, or at least the dramatic picture of a "life-and-death struggle" between capitalism and socialism that Maoists presented to the world.

Yet viewed from other historical perspectives, the differences between what came to be known as the Maoist and Liuist roads do not appear to be nearly so sharp. It is instructive to compare the economic policies pursued by Liu Shao-ch'i in the early 1960s with those adopted by Lenin in the Soviet Union forty years earlier. In 1921 Lenin introduced the New Economic Policy in an effort to rehabilitate the Russian economy after the ravages and disruptions of World War I, the revolution, and the ensuing civil war. The new policy was presented explicitly as a retreat from the radical socialist policies of the period of War Communism and involved a widespread reintroduction of capitalist forms of economic activity, as Lenin frankly acknowledged. The NEP, as the program came to be called, established what was in effect a "mixed economy," partly socialist and partly capitalist. While large industrial and other enterprises remained in the hands of the Bolshevik state, private enterprise was permitted (and indeed encouraged) in smaller industries and in commerce. Except for standard forms of agricultural taxation, the countryside was largely left to itself, that is to say, left free for the development of small-scale capitalist farming and the normal workings of a free market. The import of foreign capital for industrial development was encouraged—and eminently capitalist methods of management and the organization of work (such as Taylorism) were adopted even in state-owned industrial enterprises. Lenin's immediate aim was national economic recovery; his long-range expectation was that the socialist sector gradually would expand and eventually prove victorious in a process of essentially peaceful economic competition.

The economic policies adopted by Chinese leaders forty years later were in some respects similar to Lenin's NEP. They constituted a large-scale retreat (in fact if not in name) from the radicalism of the Great Leap Forward in an attempt to deal with the grave economic crisis of 1960–1961. In agriculture, concessions were made to "petty capitalism," primarily through permitting an extension of the private plots worked by individual peasant households. In industry, greater emphasis was placed on the criterion of "profitability" in the operation of enterprises, and the authority of managers and technocrats was strengthened. In general, wider scope was given to the free play of market forces and prices, and material incentives were stressed over moral ones. Yet, as an alleged "retreat to capitalism," the Chinese program was but a pale reflection of its earlier Soviet counterpart. Agricultural production remained basically collectivized; no more than 12 percent of the tillable land was allowed to be restored as private plots. Industries, both large and small, remained under state ownership, and commerce in general remained under fairly strict centralized government control. No invitations were extended for foreign capitalist investment. If Liu Shao-ch'i was a "capitalist-roader," he walked a far more narrow and cautious path in the early 1960s than did Lenin in the early 1920s. Nonetheless, the differences between what came to be known as "the two roads," between "Liuism" and "Maoism," were profound, and the policies dominant in the early 1960s had significant social consequences—and ones which Maoists found repugnant and intolerable.

The Chinese version of NEP began as a series of *ad hoc* emergency measures in 1960 and 1961 to deal with the immediate crisis of widespread food shortages and the threat of famine. Part of the problem was one of distribution, and that part was handled with dispatch by a reinvigorated centralized state apparatus through an efficient system of rationing and transport. Famine was avoided. But the larger problem was the sharp decline in agricultural production over three successive years (1959–1961). Production was revived through a combination of the reimposition of centralized party control over the countryside, the virtual removal of communal controls over individual peasant producers, and urban assistance to the countryside. Hundreds of thousands of party cadres were sent to the villages, displacing (and criticizing) the Maoist-inspired local rural cadres. They were reinforced by soldiers, students, and millions of unemployed urban dwellers who were directed to the countryside to engage in agricultural work. The small private plots were restored to individual peasant families, the free market in rural areas was reopened, "communized" personal and household belongings were returned, and peasants were permitted to reclaim uncultivated lands and till them on their own. From the cities came emergency aid in the form of insecticides, chemical fertilizers, and small farm tools. By the end of 1962 the agrarian economy was stabilized.

These measures proceeded under the policy of taking "agriculture as the foundation of the economy and industry as the leading sector," formally adopted at the ninth plenum of the party central committee in January 1961. The slogan reflected a recognition upon the part of all Communist leaders of the central importance of a viable and developing agricultural economy for the national economy in general. It meant giving priority to the agrarian sector and accepting a slower rate of industrial development than had been envisioned both in the First Five Year Plan and the Great Leap. It was a slogan that could be accepted by both Maoists and non-Maoists alike, and there was to be no attempt to return to a Stalinist strategy, which subordinated agriculture to the development of heavy industry.

Yet the slogan was not without ambiguities. For if agriculture was now to be granted a certain priority, it was by no means clear how agricultural production was to be socially organized. Also left ambiguous was the question of the relationship between agriculture and industry, between town and countryside, and the fate of the Maoist program of industrializing the rural areas. What "taking agriculture as the foundation" meant in terms of concrete policies was dependent upon who was determining and implementing policy.

The Decline of the Communes

The post-1960 reaction against the Great Leap did not result in the abolition of the rural people's communes, although it did result in a drastic reduction in their size. The 24,000 communes were broken down into approximately 74,000 units, each with about 1,600 households, and each corresponding roughly to the old *hsiang* structure and, it has been argued, to the traditional rural marketing area.[1] The communes remained as the basic administrative units in the countryside, but operated under the direction of full-time and salaried state functionaries who were responsible for the implementation of centrally determined policies.

But while the communes remained as political units, their original socioeconomic functions were largely emasculated. Party directives of the early 1960s denounced "egalitarianism" in the distribution of the agricultural product and encouraged the use of material incentives to promote production. Not only were private plots returned and peasants encouraged to engage in "sideline" occupations and to trade on the reopened free market, but the operation of commune industries was discouraged in favor of peasants purchasing goods produced in urban factories. Furthermore, the basic work unit was progressively reduced from the commune as a whole to the production brigade and finally to the production team. By the beginning of 1962 the team, consisting of about twenty or thirty households (the equivalent of the former "lower" agricultural producer cooperative), was established as the principal unit for the organization of labor and production.[2]

The autonomy of the commune was reduced further by transferring control of its commercial and financial affairs—and the function of collecting taxes from the production teams—to the *hsien* (county) governments, organs of the centralized state administrative apparatus. The *hsien* administration also assumed control of the commune militia and its educational institutions and health services. The tractors and other large-scale farm machinery distributed to the communes during the Great Leap were now returned to Soviet-style state tractor stations. By 1964, there were more than 2,000 such stations renting tractors to the communes, with the profits from the rentals going to the state.

The policies of the period facilitated the growth of capitalism in the countryside and the appearance of a nascent class of rich peasants, although on a far smaller scale than Lenin and other Russian leaders had been willing to tolerate in the Soviet Union forty years earlier. Nevertheless, the retreat from collective forms of life and production was by no means insignificant. Although private family plots officially were limited to 6 percent of the arable land, they actually came to constitute twice that percentage. Given the relatively high prices for fruits, vegetables and domestic animals that could be commanded on the free market (and even higher prices on a flourishing black market in the cities), most peasants naturally were disposed to devote more time and energy to their private holdings than to collective work. By the mid-1960s, private production probably accounted for about one-third of peasant income. Moreover, collective labor on the production team was by no means conducted along egalitarian lines. Complex workpoint systems were introduced to remunerate peasants according to their individual productivity rather than according to the amount or time of labor they contributed.

Both the workpoint system in collective production and the new opportunities for sideline production on private plots inevitably benefited the more productive, physically stronger, more experienced, and more entrepreneurial-minded peasants. The result was increasing income differentiations among the rural population. Although it would be going much too far to speak of the emergence of a new "kulak class," there did emerge quasi-class distinctions between richer and poorer peasants, and the former were often the rich peasants of the precollectivization era. The problem of growing inequality was exacerbated by the far greater problem of widespread corruption among rural party cadres. During the early 1960s, the communes were plagued by local leaders who engaged in the embezzlement of communal funds and the outright theft of resources. Even more widespread was collusion between lower–level team cadres and peasants (often members of the former village elite) in the allocation and misallocation of workpoints, to the economic advantage of both.

The differences between the "Maoist" and "Liuist" lines in dealing with these problems of corruption and inequality in the countryside were not as great as they later were portrayed during the Cultural Revolution. Liu Shao-ch'i was no less intent than Mao in eliminating cadre corruption and blunting spontaneous tendencies towards rural capitalism. The differences centered more on the methods to be employed than on the goals to be achieved. Whereas Liu and most party leaders were inclined to use the direct force of the central bureaucratic party and state apparatus to rectify the rural situation, Mao and Maoists were insistent upon building a popular grass roots movement based on the ideological and political mobilization of the poorer peasants.

The Reorganization of Industry

As in the rural areas, the new policies in the cities initially took the form of emergency measures to alleviate a critical and rapidly deteriorating economic situation. In 1960 and 1961, some factories had closed and many were operating at reduced capacities for want of adequate raw materials and supplies. A large number of small industrial enterprises and shops, hastily established during the Great Leap, were grossly inefficient and wasteful of scarce resources. By 1962, industrial production had declined by about 40 percent from the 1958–1959 levels. The cities were filled with an enormous number of unemployed and underemployed, their ranks swollen by millions of peasant migrants from the more depressed rural areas.

The first step taken by the government to rationalize production and reestablish a viable urban economy was a stringent policy of financial retrenchment. Thousands of small and economically inefficient factories and shops were closed and most of the workers in larger enterprises hired during the Great Leap years were dismissed. A freeze was placed on new employment. In all, the total industrial work force was cut by half. A second measure was to send the excess, economically redundant urban population to the countryside, a drive that reached its peak in the spring of 1962 in what was called the "return to the village" (*hui-hsiang*) movement. The "return to the village" campaign was not motivated by any populist spirit, nor was it conducted in the manner of earlier Maoist-inspired *hsia-fang* movements. It was dictated by the economic necessity to relieve the strain on a precarious urban food supply, just as the industrial cutbacks were dictated by a shortage of raw materials and a scarcity of state investment capital. It was accompanied by the frail hope that unemployed urban dwellers could find a productive place in agricultural work.

The long-term problem of reviving and developing the modern industrial sector was approached through the reintroduction of centralized economic planning from Peking combined with a degree of economic autonomy to individual enterprises and a consequent reliance on semi-market forces, the strengthening of managerial authority, a renewed emphasis on technological and scientific expertise, and a heavy stress on financial incentives for the workers to spur productivity and raise the quality of what was being produced. Direction over the economy in general was returned to the economic ministries in Peking, and the architects of the First Five Year Plan were restored to prominence. Managerial authority in individual factories and enterprises, which had virtually disappeared during the Great Leap, was reestablished. Managers and technological experts, who were closely linked to district and provincial party organizations, regained control over the operations of industrial enterprises, although now under a more flexible and autonomous system called "independent operational authority." The traditional distinction between managers and workers reemerged, and the new emphasis clearly was on technical "expertise" rather than political "redness." If industrial workers were once again subjected to the authority of managers, they were compensated through the revival of a system of financial incentives for increased productivity and promises of a better material life. Increasing economic differentiations among the working class came about less through revisions in the formal wage structure than through the widespread introduction of piece rate work and the use of prizes and bonuses to reward workers for their individual productive performances and for contributing technological improvements and inventions. The reliance on material incentives was justified on the grounds of economic efficacy—the pressing need to raise productivity in a still economically backward land—and ideologically justified by the traditional Marxist principle that in a socialist (but not yet communist) society the distribution of goods necessarily would be guided by the principle "to each according to his work" rather than the communist principle "to each according to his needs."

While the new industrial policies marked the reappearance of many of the features and tendencies of the First Five Year Plan, they were by no means a wholesale return to the "Stalinist model." The policy of "taking agriculture as the foundation" was in fact taken seriously. The policy found concrete expression in a significant shift of capital investment from urban industrial development to agriculture. Important sectors of modern industry were refashioned to increase production of chemical fertilizers and modern farm tools. Scientific institutes were established for the development and application of improved seeds, and a program for rural electrification was undertaken. While the principal formulators of the First Five Year Plan had been restored to their posts, they now envisaged a much more modest pace of industrial development than the ambitious targets they had set in the previous decade, and now gave priority to the development and modernization of agricultural production. In this economic sense, the Liuist period marks a fundamental departure from the Stalinist strategy of subordinating all other economic considerations to the heavy industrial push.

In light of the disastrous conditions confronting the government in 1960-1961, the rapidity of the recovery and the renewal of economic growth were quite remarkable accomplishments. Agricultural production began to revive in 1962 and increased at a steady, if not spectacular rate, over the following years. According to scanty official reports, grain output rose from a low of 193,000,000 tons in 1961 to 240,000,000 tons in 1965.[3] And the nation's food supply was augmented by large wheat purchases from Canada and Australia. The modern industrial sector was stabilized by the end of 1962. Between 1963 and 1965 industrial production grew at an average annual rate of approximately 11 percent, industrial employment 7 percent, and labor productivity 5.5 percent.[4] Moreover, there were substantial gains in areas not easily quantified: education, public health, scientific research, development of new products, and the introduction of new and more complex technology.

While the policies of Liu Shao-ch'i brought economic recovery and renewed growth, the social and ideological results were less salutary. There was a social price to be paid for economic progress—and the price was the emergence of new forms of inequality. The tolerance of market forces and the ever present "spontaneous" tendencies toward capitalism in the countryside gave rise to a new stratum of relatively rich peasants who, often in cooperation with local cadres and officials, began to develop a vested interest in the new economic policies and the government that presided over them. In the cities there emerged a relatively privileged stratum of more experienced and skilled industrial workers who benefited from the system of piece rate work and incentive bonuses, measures that encouraged productivity but also induced workers to compete with one another and worked against the development of a sense of collective class solidarity. The absence of a collective consciousness among the workers facilitated, in turn, an increasing differentiation between the working class as a whole and a rising technological–bureaucratic elite fostered by the emphasis on material rewards for professional competence and technical skills.

Perhaps the most glaring manifestation of inequality was a growing social, economic and cultural gap between the cities and the rural areas. If a minority of peasants prospered under the new policies, the countryside as a whole remained backward and fell further behind the modernizing cities. The Great Leap Forward policy of industrializing the countryside was abandoned and most local rural industrial undertakings were closed or atrophied, thus firmly reestablishing the sharp distinctions between industrial and agricultural production and between workers and peasants. The prices of industrial goods sold to the peasants (such as chemical fertilizers, agricultural machinery, cloth, salt, kerosene, matches, and, for those few who could afford them, radios and bicycles) were kept artificially high, to the benefit of the urban economy and in contradiction to the Maoist policy of encouraging peasant consumption by maintaining only a narrow differential between the prices of industrial and agricultural products.[5] Moreover, since productivity in industry rose far more rapidly than in agriculture, the bonus system served to further increase the already considerable differential between worker and peasant incomes. Further widening the gap between town and countryside were urban-oriented educational policies and an inequitable distribution of medical and social services. Just as during the years of the First Five Year Plan, the countryside was being exploited for the benefit of the cities.

The growth of new forms of socioeconomic inequality was alluded to by Chou En-lai in his report to the Third National People's Congress, which met in Peking in late December of 1964 and reelected Liu Shao-ch'i as chairman of the People's Republic. After lauding the economic gains of the previous two years, Chou observed:

> For quite a long period the landlord class, the bourgeoisie and other exploiting classes which have been overthrown will remain strong and powerful in our Socialist society; we must under no circumstances take them lightly. At the same time, new bourgeois elements, new bourgeois intellectuals and other new exploiters will be ceaselessly generated in society, in Party and government organs, in economic organizations and in cultural and educational departments. These new bourgeois elements and other exploiters will invariably try to find their protectors and agents in the higher leading organizations. The old and new bourgeois elements and other exploiters will invariably join hands in opposing Socialism and developing capitalism.[6]

Who were the "new bourgeois elements" to which Chou referred? Obviously they were not people distinguished by the ownership of property, but rather those who enjoyed economic privileges, social prestige, and political power within the existing "socialist" order. They were privileged not by virtue of property but by virtue of function and income. The new rich peasants and the more highly paid industrial workers hardly could be described as "new exploiters." However undesirable, such economic differentiations among the masses were no more than symptoms of a deeper social disease. The nature of the disease was hinted at (and partially diagnosed) in Chou's statement that the "new exploiters" are "generated" in "party and government organs." Implicit was the suggestion that the party–state bureaucracy itself was the source and site of "new bourgeois elements."

What Chou En-lai left implicit, Mao Tse-tung soon made bluntly explicit. By 1965 he began to charge that "the bureaucratic class" was the oppressor of the masses of workers and peasants, and it was this view of bureaucracy as constituting a new exploiting class (or at least the belief that a substantial portion of Communist leaders and state functionaries were becoming transformed into such a "new class") that lay behind Mao's increasingly strong insistence that China was racked by a sharpening conflict between "the bourgeoisie" and "the proletariat," a growing emphasis on the need for "class struggle," and the belief that the contest between "socialism" and "capitalism" was approaching a decisive stage. No doubt these Maoist perceptions were influenced by the deepening conflict with the Soviet Union—and, consequently, a heightened awareness that the pursuit of "revisionist" policies portended a regression to "capitalism." But the Maoist fears of the time grew primarily out of the concrete realities of the internal Chinese situation. For Mao, the economic policies pursued during the post–Great Leap years posed the question as to whether socialist ends could be achieved through non-socialist means. From the sense of historical indeterminateness that characterizes the Maoist mentality—that is, the absence of any confidence in the historical inevitability of socialism—flowed the belief that men are free to choose their ends and thus the moral injunction that they must choose means which are consistent with the ends they seek. In the eyes of Mao, the means most Party leaders had chosen to employ were seen as incompatible with socialism; instead, they were seen as leading to what Maoists chose to call "the road back to capitalism."

Of no less concern to Maoists than the tendencies towards social inequality and bureaucratic elitism were the processes of ideological decay which accompanied them. Due homage was paid to the "Thoughts of Mao," but mostly in ritualistic fashion. If Mao was treated politically as a "dead ancestor," his ideas and ideals fared little better. The leaders who presided over the party and state apparatus were preoccupied with social order, administrative efficiency, technological progress and economic development. The popular mood was dominated by a longing for security and a quest for a better material life. Between the party leaders and the mostly politically apathetic masses, stood a technological intelligentsia and the cadres of state and party who increasingly ignored the Maoist political ethic in favor of a bureaucratic vocational ethic. It was a tendency that was in harmony with the dominant policies and the general temper of the times, as was the conversion of the "red and expert" notion from a universalistic Maoist ideal of the future "all-round" communist man into a formula that gave priority to the acquisition of professional and technological competence over political and ideological considerations. The urban masses, it was observed, responded with a most non-Maoist enthusiasm to state appeals to increase production—and thus to increase income—in order to purchase "the four good things": watches, bicycles, radios, and sewing machines. And in the countryside, Maoists observed, and condemned, such "unhealthy tendencies" among the peasants as the revival of traditional religious festivals, money marriages, superstitious cults, extravagant spending on holidays, and gambling; and they also observed a sharp decline in the political zeal and ideological morale of rural cadres.[7]

Education

In a society where stratification is based primarily on income and function, rather than on property, the educational system is a particularly powerful force for promoting either socioeconomic equality or inequality. The educational policies adopted in the early 1960s tended to promote the latter.

The previous decade had witnessed an enormous expansion of educational facilities and opportunities. Between 1949 and 1957 the number of primary school students increased from approximately 26,000,000 to 64,000,000, while university enrollment almost quadrupled, from 117,000 to 441,000. The early educational policies and practices of the People's Republic, like its economic policies, were largely patterned on the Soviet model, especially in institutions of higher education. The overwhelming emphasis was on scientific and technological education to produce specialists and experts necessary for carrying out the industrial goals of the First Five Year Plan. There was a wholesale borrowing of Russian pedagogical methods, forms of organization, and textbooks. Thousands of college graduates went to the Soviet Union for advanced training in modern science and technology.[8]

While great progress was made in the 1950s in expanding educational opportunities to a much wider section of the population than under the old regime, the opportunities remained limited and unequal. Although the stated purpose of the new educational system was to serve workers and peasants, the criterion of formal academic achievements for admission to middle schools and universities favored both the old and new privileged groups in Chinese society—the sons and daughters of the remnant urban bourgeoisie, higher party and government officials, and the technological intelligentsia. Moreover, educational opportunities were unevenly distributed between the cities and the rural areas. Universities were located in the cities, urban oriented in curricula, and drew most of their students from the urban classes. While children who lived in the cities were afforded the opportunity of at least a primary school education, many rural children were not, or received only a most rudimentary education.

The educational policies of the Great Leap Forward campaign had been designed to correct these inequities through the introduction of new programs of mass education, particularly in the countryside. A vast variety of "half-work, half-study" programs, "red and expert universities," and part-time evening schools for peasants and workers were hastily established in accordance with the Great Leap goals of permitting "the masses to make themselves masters of science and technology" and eliminating the distinction between mental and manual labor. Regular six-year primary schools and three-year middle schools were expanded in the rural areas and turned over to the direct administration of the communes in order to orient education to serve particular local needs and realize the aim of combining education with productive activities.

In the early 1960s these egalitarian policies were reversed in favor of practices and procedures which had prevailed in the early and mid-1950s. Financial retrenchment forced many of the poorer schools to close, thus restricting educational opportunities for children from lower-income families in both town and countryside. Many of the half-study and part-time schools and programs were abandoned or discouraged. Primary and middle schools in the rural areas were removed from communal control and returned to the administration of the *hsien* education departments, thus restoring control over the rural educational system to the central state apparatus. A renewed emphasis on standardized admissions criteria for middle schools and universities, on formal examinations, and on the quality of education in urban schools worked to the advantage of the children of the more privileged social groups and to the advantage of urban over rural youth. What was in effect a two-track educational process emerged, roughly divided between town and countryside. In the rural areas, children who received a primary school education (and not all of them did[9]) advanced, if they did at all, mostly to what were called "agricultural middle schools" for vocational training rather than to regular full-time middle schools. In the cities, special schools of high quality were favored to produce a small minority of highly trained experts to replenish and expand the ranks of the technological intelligentsia and the administrative–bureaucratic elite. The first duty of students was to study and acquire professional ability, it was emphasized, and in the better schools and in the universities political education and productive-labor requirements tended to become ritualistic observances. In all, the educational system in the early 1960s was probably more elitist than it had been a decade earlier, reinforcing the growing socioeconomic differences and fortifying the new patterns of social stratification.

Just as inequalities in the educational system reflected and perpetuated social and economic differentiations, so too was this the case in other state-financed and -operated services—most notably in the realm of medicine and public health. In the years since 1949 striking progress had been achieved in the elimination or control of the infectious and parasitic diseases endemic in old China and in the building of a nationwide modern medical system which had been so lacking. Beginning with an emphasis on preventive medicine and popular campaigns to raise the levels of sanitation and public hygiene, the new government soon was able to claim credit for the virtual elimination of smallpox, cholera, typhus, typhoid fever, plague, and leprosy, as well as venereal disease and opium addiction; tuberculosis and most parasitic diseases were reduced to at least tolerable levels. Huge state investments funded modern medical training and hospitals, hitherto largely dependent on foreign philanthropic efforts. Between 1949 and 1957, over 800 Western-type hospitals were built, adding some 300,000 beds to the 90,000 available when the People's Republic was established. The number of doctors trained in modern Western medicine increased from 40,000 in 1949 to 150,000 in 1965, supplemented by 170,000 paramedics; by the early 1960s, medical schools were graduating about 25,000 new doctors each year.[10] The achievements were impressive by any standard of judgment, but the benefits were unevenly distributed. Urban inhabitants enjoyed access to modern medical services to a disproportionate degree, and the differences between town and countryside in this area (as in so many other areas in the early 1960s) were glaring and growing. It was a matter that brought forth some caustic comments from Mao Tse-tung in June of 1965:

> Tell the Ministry of Public Health that it only works for fifteen percent of the total population of the country and that this fifteen percent is mainly composed of gentlemen, while the broad masses of the peasants do not get any medical treatment. First they don't have any doctors; second they don't have any medicine. The Ministry of Public Health is not a Ministry of Public Health for the people, so why not change the name to the Ministry of Urban Health, the Ministry of Gentlemen's Health, or even to the Ministry of Urban Gentlemen's Health? . . . The methods of medical examination and treatment used by hospitals

nowadays are not at all appropriate for the countryside, and the way doctors are trained is only for the benefit of the cities. And yet in China over five hundred million of our population are peasants.[11]

The economic successes of the time, based on the use of non-Maoist methods and means, thus produced social and political results that were incongruous with the Maoist vision of China's future. The price for economic progress was bureaucratic and technocratic elitism, the decay of the spirit (if not the rhetoric) of Maoist ideological precepts, the emergence of new forms of inequality in both the cities and the rural areas, and an ever-widening gap between town and countryside. The price was not one which Mao was willing to pay, and the Maoist-inspired Socialist Education Movement, launched in 1963, was the first attempt to reverse the course that the "Thermidoreans" were following.

Notes

1. The argument that *hsiang* boundaries were drawn to generally correspond to the traditional "standard marketing area," consisting of a dozen or so villages economically and socially oriented to a market town, is presented in G. William Skinner "Market Town and Social Structure in Rural China," *Journal of Asian Studies*, 24, 1 (November 1964):32–43.
2. These measures were officially carried out in accordance with the "Urgent Directive on Rural Work" (the "Twelve Articles") and the "Draft Regulations Concerning Rural Communes," respectively issued by the central committee in November 1960 and March 1961.
3. Chao Kang, *Agricultural Production in Communist China, 1949–65* (Madison: University of Wisconsin Press, 1970), pp. 242–60. Chao's reconstructed data give the figures of 160,000,000 tons in 1961 and 200,000,000 tons in 1965 but nonetheless reflect a similar rate of increase.
4. Barry Richman, *Industrial Society in Communist China* (New York: Random House, 1969), p. 615.
5. Mao's views on the issue were set forth in his 1956 speech "On the Ten Great Relationships": "The peasants' burden of taxation is too heavy while the price of agricultural products is very low, and that of industrial goods very high. While developing industry, especially heavy industry, we must at the same time give agriculture a certain status by adopting correct policies for agricultural taxation, and for pricing industrial and agricultural products. . . . In the exchange of industrial and agricultural products we adopt in our country a policy of reducing the 'scissors' gap, a policy of the exchange of equal or near-equal values, a policy of low profit and high sales in industrial products, and a policy of stable prices." Stuart R. Schram, ed., *Mao Unrehearsed: Talks and Letters, 1956–71* (Middlesex, England: Penguin, 1974), pp. 64, 71.

6. Chou En-lai, "Report on the Work of the Government," December 30, 1964, *Peking Review,* 8, 1 (January 1, 1965):6–20.

7. "Report to the Hsien Three Level Cadre Meeting," February 9, 1963, Appendix A in Richard Baum and Frederick C. Teiwes, *Ssu-Ch'ing: The Socialist Education Movement of 1962–1966* (Berkeley: University of California Press, 1968), pp. 49–57.

8. Generally reflective of the heavy emphasis on scientific and technological education is the composition of college and university graduates for the year 1962. According to official data, only 7,000, or 4 percent, of the 170,000 graduates majored in the social sciences and humanities; 59,000 of the 1962 graduates were engineers; 11,000 were graduates in science; 20,000 in agriculture and forestry; 17,000 in medicine and public health; and the remaining 56,000 were graduates of teachers' or normal colleges, where a similar technological orientation was present, as it was in the primary and middle schools.

    Of the 170,000 graduates in 1962, only 1,000 passed examinations to become research students (graduate students). Prior to 1949, it might be noted, there was not a single graduate school in China, save for a small number of medical and professional schools. Postgraduate education developed only very slowly after 1949, but on a high and rigorous academic level. Most Chinese students who went on for postgraduate study did so in the Soviet Union, and to a lesser extent in the Eastern European countries.

9. In 1965 it was reported that 30,000,000 primary-school-aged children, mostly in the rural areas, were not receiving formal education of any sort. *People's Daily,* May 18, 1965 (SCMM, No. 3475, p. 14.).

10. Victor W. Sidel, "Medicine and Public Health," in Michel Oksenberg, ed., *China's Developmental Experience* (New York: Praeger, 1973), pp. 110–120. For a particularly perceptive account of the development of medical care in the People's Republic, see Joshua Horn, *Away with All Pests* (New York: Monthly Review Press, 1969).

11. "Directive on Public Health," June 26, 1965, in Schram, ed., *Mao Tse-tung Unrehearsed,* pp. 232–233.

17

The Socialist Education Movement, 1962–1965

IN LATE 1962, with the economic situation stabilized, Mao Tse-tung emerged from political seclusion to launch what came to be known as the "Socialist Education Movement." The new campaign was an attempt to counter the bureaucratization of Chinese political life, reverse socio-economic policies that Maoists condemned as "revisionist" and believed were creating new forms of capitalism, and revitalize a collectivistic spirit and consciousness both within the party and in society at large. It was to prove to be Mao's last attempt to implement his vision of radical social transformation through existing party and state institutions.

The campaign had its origins in the September 1962 speech to the tenth plenum of the central committee when Mao had set forth the thesis that classes and class struggles necessarily exist in socialist societies, stressed that the class struggle in China would continue for a prolonged period, and raised the spectre that the outcome of the struggle could be a "restoration of the reactionary classes." "A country like ours can still move toward its opposite," he warned. To wage the struggle between "Chinese revisionism" and "Marxism–Leninism," Mao proposed a Yenan-style movement, based on the model of the rectification campaign of 1942–1944.[1]

While Mao was no longer in control of the party apparatus, he was not without the power to influence formal party policies. He still commanded enormous personal prestige and, no less important, seemed to command the People's Liberation Army as well. Thus the central committee duly promulgated resolutions officially endorsing the major points made by Mao. With copious quotations from Mao, the resolutions re-affirmed the view that the entire historical period of "the transition to communism" would be characterized by a continuing class struggle between the proletariat and the bourgeoisie, condemned revisionist tendencies within the party, and called for strengthening the socialist life of the rural people's communes.[2] The practical (and rather pale) expression of these resolutions was a limited ideological rectification campaign to improve the work of rural party cadres and raise the consciousness of the masses in selected rural areas during the winter of 1962–63. It was not until May 1963 that the "Draft Resolution of the Central Committee on Some Problems in Current Rural Work" concretely stated the purposes and methods of the Socialist Education Movement and launched the campaign on a nationwide basis.

The May 1963 resolution, or the "First Ten Points" as it came to be known, was an eminently Maoist document, written either by Mao or under his direction. The document expressed the two major concerns around which the Socialist Education Movement initially focused. One was the virtual dissolution of the communes and the disintegration of collective farming in general, accompanied by the appearance of quasi-capitalist socioeconomic relationships and the resurgence of traditionalist attitudes and practices in the countryside. The second concern was the increasingly bureaucratic character and methods of the Communist Party in general and the widespread corruption which pervaded local rural party organs and cadres in particular. Accordingly, the original aims of the movement were to restore collectivism in the rural areas and re-establish the communes as functioning socioeconomic units, and to cleanse the party of corruption and mitigate bureaucratic elitism.

The most visible and concrete measure inaugurated by the "First Ten Points" was the "four cleans" (*ssu-ch'ing*) campaign, an investigation of how cadres determined workpoints, kept accounts, distributed supplies, and handled warehouses and granaries. The aim was not only to root out corrupt practices but to expose the collusion between party cadres and rich peasants and their exploitation of the majority of the rural population. The method to carry out the campaign was "to set the masses in motion" through the organization of "poor and lower-middle peasant associations." The new associations, to be composed of the masses of ordinary peasants, were to "oversee" the "four cleans" and the work of commune and brigade administrative organs.

To combat bureaucracy and the growing separation between leaders and masses, the resolution stressed the need for officials and cadres to labor in the fields on a regular basis to demonstrate that "the cadres of our Party are ordinary laborers... and not overlords who sit above the heads of the people." And to overcome the political apathy of both masses and cadres, the resolution called for new ideological reeducation campaigns and a renewed emphasis on "self-education."[3]

What marked the "First Ten Points" as distinctively Maoist was not so much the goals it announced—for all party leaders shared the concern with the problems of cadre corruption and the growth of "spontaneous" capitalist tendencies—but rather the means by which Maoists proposed to restore socialist principles in the countryside. The document was permeated by populist and antibureaucratic impulses phrased in characteristically Maoist terms, stressing a far greater reliance on the grass-roots organization and initiative of the peasant masses than on the organizational apparatus of the party. Time and again it was emphasized that the success of the movement was dependent on a faith in the "poor and lower-middle" peasant masses to judge and rectify the errors of the party. Erring cadres and officials were to "wash their hands and bodies and shed their burdens, so that they may come face to face with the masses and settle the problem of abnormal relations that have existed between cadres and masses for many years." The masses were to supervise the administrative work of officials, and they were to have "the opportunity fully to express their views, to make criticism of errors and shortcomings, to expose bad people and evil deeds." Party cadres were not to lead the masses but rather were to "merge" with them. Indicative of the populist tone of the resolution was the inclusion of Mao's 1941 statement that, "We must clearly understand that the masses are the real heroes, while we ourselves are often childish and ignorant." And the document concluded with a lengthy passage from a more recent directive by Mao, where he warned that the Chinese Communist Party was not only in danger of turning to revisionism but to "fascism" as well, and where he described the Socialist Education Movement in terms that foreshadowed the chiliastic fervors of the Cultural Revolution:

> This is a struggle that calls for the reeducation of man. This is a struggle for reorganizing the revolutionary class armies for a confrontation with the forces of feudalism and capitalism which are now feverishly attacking us. We must nip their counterrevolution in the bud. We must make it a great movement to reform the bulk of elements in these counterrevolutionary forces and turn them into new men. With cadres and masses joining hand in hand in production labor and scientific experiments, our Party will take another stride forward in becoming a more glorious, greater, and more correct party; our cadres will be versed in politics as well as in business operations, become red as well as expert. They will then no longer be toplofty, no longer bureaucrats and overlords, no longer divorced from the masses. They will then merge themselves with the masses, becoming truly good cadres supported by the masses.[4]

Although party leaders generally shared Mao's concern over cadre corruption and the retreat from collectivism, they viewed the new Maoist calls for the mass mobilization of the peasantry and an intensified class struggle as threats to maintaining agricultural productivity and to the organizational viability of the CCP—and as a threat to their own control over the party and state apparatus. Bureaucratic resistance to carrying out the measures proposed in the "First Ten Points" was fortified by the appearance of two additional party directives on the Socialist Education Movement; the first came to be called the "Later Ten Points" and was drafted by the Party's Secretary-General Teng Hsiao-p'ing in September 1963, while the second (known as the "Revised Later Ten Points") was issued by Liu Shao-ch'i in September 1964.[5] Both offered detailed instructions on implementing the policies set forth in Mao's original directive of May 1963. Both borrowed much of the language and phraseology of the latter and duly quoted the writings of Mao. But the real purpose was to blunt the radical thrust of the movement, limit its scope, and, most importantly, keep the movement under the centralized control of the party. The device for accomplishing this was the dispatch of "work teams" (small groups of outside cadres organized by higher party organs) to villages and communes to supervise local cadres and the masses. The work team was an old Communist organizational method, widely employed during the land-reform campaigns. The method was revived to replace and to negate the Maoist demand that the Socialist Education Movement proceed on the basis of the initiative and mobilization of the peasant masses themselves. Whereas the original Maoist directive emphasized that the first step was "to set the masses in motion," Liu Shao-ch'i insisted that "to launch the Socialist Education Movement at any point requires the sending of a work team from the higher level. The whole movement should be led by the work team."[6] Neither version of the "Later Ten Points" made mention of the peasant associations that figured so prominently in the "First Ten Points;" instead, it was decreed that "meetings should first be convened within the Party."[7] Rather than the peasants having their own organizations, as Mao had proposed, Teng and Liu emphasized the central importance of the organizational structure of the party, with higher organs rectifying the errors of local-level cadres and then proceeding to lead and educate the masses: "[T]o consolidate over 95 percent of the cadres is a prerequisite to the consolidation of over 95 percent of the masses. When the question of the cadres is properly handled, the question of consolidating the masses will also be solved."[8]

Operating from orthodox Leninist perspectives, most party leaders— and most notably, Liu Shao-ch'i and Teng Hsiao-p'ing—believed that what was crucial for successful political and economic work was the organizational and ideological soundness of the CCP and the quality and discipline of its members and cadres. This firm Leninist belief in the party as the sole bearer of a true socialist consciousness (and thus the only institution capable of correct political action) was epitomized in the crucial role assigned to the work team, the agency of the centralized party apparatus that would discipline lower-level party organs and cadres and guide the masses from above.

Mao Tse-tung, by contrast, never had arrived at so firm a Leninist belief in the revolutionary and ideological infallibility of the party as an institution. His faith in the party as the repository of "proletarian consciousness" always had been mitigated by an equally strong faith that the true sources of revolutionary creativity resided in the masses themselves, and particularly in the peasantry. For Mao, the party was as much the "pupil" of the masses as it was their "teacher," and particularly so in the early 1960s when his trust in the party as a reliable instrument of revolution had all but vanished. In the Socialist Education Movement, he looked primarily to the peasant masses themselves, to a more or less spontaneous upsurge from below. From this essentially populist faith in the people flowed the strong Maoist insistence that the movement to restore collectivism and revive a socialist spirit was to be based on associations comprising a majority of the peasantry, and not on "work teams" controlled by higher party organs.

The differences were made explicit in January 1965 when Mao convened a "national work conference" (ostensibly under the auspices of the politburo of the party's central committee) and from that forum issued a new directive known as the "Twenty-three Articles."[9] Beginning with the proposition that the struggle between "socialism" and "capitalism" in society at large was reflected within the party in particular, the document redirected the focus of the movement away from cadres in rural localities to "those people in positions of authority within the Party who take the capitalist road." Some such "capitalist-roaders" (as they soon came to be called) remained concealed, it ominously was warned, and some were operating at the highest levels of the party, including the central committee itself. It was, in effect, a declaration of political war against the party bureaucracy and its top leaders. And the war was to be waged through a radical implementation of the principles of the mass line. "We must boldly unleash the masses," Mao declared, and he added (reviving a metaphor made famous in his collectivization speech of a decade earlier), "we must not be like women with bound feet." There was a renewed call for the establishment of peasant associations and an injunction that specific problems arising during the course of the movement were to "be judged and decided by the masses" and "not be decided from above." While local cadres were to be supervised from both "above and below," it was stipulated that "the most important supervision is that which comes from the masses." And the "four cleans," hitherto confined to correcting specific economic and political irregularities in the countryside, was now broadly redefined as "clean politics, clean economics, clean organization, and clean ideology," thus making no one immune to the campaign for purification. The document left little doubt that Maoists regarded the party itself, particularly its highest leaders, as the primary source of political and ideological impurities, and it left little room for compromise.[10] With the Socialist Education Movement now turned against "those people in positions of authority within the Party who take the capitalist road," the battle lines for the Cultural Revolution inexorably were being drawn.

In the end, the Socialist Education Movement did little to change socioeconomic relationships in the rural areas or to reverse the general tendencies that Maoists labeled "revisionist" and "capitalist." Most of the countryside remained largely untouched by the movement, while in the "target" areas entered by outside work teams, the party apparatus generally managed to channel Maoist demands for class struggle and mass mobilization into rather benign ideological education campaigns. In the cities, where the central organs of the Party exercised the most direct control, the "five antis" campaign, the announced urban counterpart of the rural "four cleans" movement, apparently never materialized even in benign form. The party, in any event, demonstrated that it had little taste to "set the masses in motion," nor is there much evidence that the masses were inclined to mobilize themselves. Indeed, the most tangible results of the Socialist Education Movement were in many respects precisely the opposite of what Maoists hoped the movement would bring. Where party work teams entered local rural areas, the usual result was a massive purge of the rural cadres, who were potentially the most amenable to Maoist calls for radical social action. While this no doubt mitigated corruption in cadre ranks, the overall effect was to strengthen the centralized authority of the party in the countryside—the very organizational apparatus that Maoists were now convinced was led by those "taking the capitalist road."

The Role of the Army

As Maoists grew increasingly disillusioned with the party, they began to look more and more to the People's Liberation Army as the primary institutional repository of revolutionary values, as a model for refashioning society according to Maoist precepts, and as a political instrument to combat the conservatism of the party bureaucracy. It is, of course, paradoxical that a standing army, generally the most bureaucratic and hierarchical organ of the state machine, should have been seen as an instrument to serve antibureaucratic and egalitarian ends. This apparent contradiction between Maoist means and ends seems less glaring (although it by no means vanishes) in light of the rather unique history and character of the People's Liberation Army (PLA). During the revolutionary years, the Red Army was less a professional military organization than a highly politicized and egalitarian popular force of peasant guerilla fighters. In a situation where revolutionary struggle primarily took the form of military struggle over a period of two decades, the function of the army could not be confined to fighting alone but necessarily encompassed political organization, economic production, and the ideological education and mobilization of the masses. The party may have commanded the gun, as the Maoist maxim went, but the distinction between military and civilian functions, between army and party, was a thin one or, perhaps more precisely, an overlapping one. The army was led not by professional soldiers but by eminently political men, the leaders of the CCP. The situation gave rise to the perception, and particularly on the part of Mao, that the army no less than the party was a revolutionary organization and the bearer of the values and conscience of the revolution. The perception remained, even as the PLA increasingly took on the characteristics of a professional standing army in the years after 1949, a development well in tune with the general post-revolutionary tendencies toward functional differentiation and bureaucratic specialization in society as a whole. Under the leadership of P'eng Te-huai, commander of Chinese forces in the Korean War and minister of defense through most of the 1950s, the PLA became both modernized and professionalized, largely on the pattern of the highly professional Soviet army. Yet the political values and egalitarian traditions which were forged during the revolutionary years remained the PLA's heritage, and it was this heritage that Maoists began to revive and cultivate in the late 1950s. The tensions between the requirements of a professional military force and Maoist demands to preserve the revolutionary traditions of the army came to a head in the clash between Mao and P'eng Te-huai at the Lushan meeting in 1959. What was at issue, at least as far as the PLA was concerned, was not the technical modernization of the army—for Mao had no intention of reverting to bands of peasant guerilla fighters—but rather the question of the dominance of a professional officer corps divorced from the Maoist political ethic and the issue of the army's reliance on the Soviet Union. P'eng's dismissal and the subsequent rise to power of Lin Piao set the stage, in the early 1960s, for a massive intra-army campaign to reverse the trend towards professionalism. The followers of P'eng were purged and massive efforts were undertaken to instill the troops with Maoist values and ideals—a process that Lin Piao called "living ideological indoctrination."

The army, now presumably refashioned and revolutionized according to Maoist precepts, first appeared on the civilian political scene early in 1963 with the launching of the "learn from the PLA" campaign. Its role, initially, was largely confined to propaganda efforts, which primarily took the form of popularizing the heroic and self-sacrificing deeds of revolutionary soldiers; the first and most celebrated of these model soldier-heroes who exemplified all the proper Maoist moral virtues and life orientations was the perhaps legendary Lei Feng, typically described as "one of Chairman Mao's good warriors." By 1964 military intervention in civilian affairs became more direct when the PLA's General Political Department assigned army personnel to work in schools and a variety of government and economic organizations, while civilian cadres and professionals were assigned to the army for training and learning. In the countryside, the influence of the PLA was exercised mainly through its control over the local militia, organizations composed of army veterans and young peasants, which were now revived after having fallen into disarray with the collapse of the Great Leap.

The political effects of military intervention are difficult to measure, except to note that the intervention was limited and its nature unique. While the growing involvement of the army in society no doubt served as a Maoist instrument to press the party bureaucracy to pursue the Socialist Education Movement more vigorously than it otherwise would have been inclined to do, the PLA did not take over either the functions of the party or the running of the government. The operations of both party and state remained in the hands of their officially designated civilian leaders. Nor did the PLA prove decisive in the outcome of the Socialist Education Movement, the final results of which, from a Maoist point of view, were meager at best. What made the process of military involvement unique was that the impetus for intervention came not from within the army but rather from without, from the civilian political sector itself. The army did not intervene in civilian life on its own but was called into the political arena by party politicians or, more precisely, by the Maoist faction of the party. And it was the latter who defined and limited the role of the army. The call was intended partly to assist Maoists in an intra-party conflict, but perhaps in greater part to present the PLA as a model for emulation in various areas of political, economic, and ideological life. The political results, in any event, were inconclusive. In 1965 the "Liuists" remained in control of the party and state apparatus, while the Maoist minority within the party remained in increasingly hostile opposition, backed by the apparent support of the army.

The Mao Cult

Perhaps the most important political role played by the army during these years was the glorification of both the person and the thought of Mao Tse-tung. The cult of Mao was by no means an entirely new phenomenon, for he long had occupied a semi-sacred position in the eyes of his more devoted followers and among much of the peasantry. But prior to the 1960s it was a position and perception that developed more or less naturally and spontaneously, largely corresponding to the enormous personal role Mao played in the history of the revolution. As early as the early Yenan days, Edgar Snow reported in 1937, legends that Mao led "a charmed life" already were widespread in the Soviet areas.[11] The popularization of Mao's writings and the veritable canonization of his "thought" during the rectification campaign of the early 1940s contributed to the rapidly growing "personality cult," and perceptions of him as a "savior" and "the star of salvation" undoubtedly were reinforced by the victory of 1949. While the revolutionary triumph served to magnify Mao's vast personal power and prestige, in the early years of the People's Republic he did not attempt to use that power to go beyond the rules of the party and state institutions he headed—although there was no lack of public praise for the creativity of his thought and the wisdom of his leadership. It was not until 1955, when Mao found it necessary (or at least expedient) to place himself above the party leadership in the agricultural collectivization campaign, that he began to foster the political conditions that demanded a supreme leader and a political climate conducive to the flourishing of the cult that was to grow up around him. Those political conditions, briefly put, amounted to the demonstration of the ability of a popular leader to overcome bureaucratic resistance to his policies by standing above established political institutions and by speaking to and for society as a whole. Implicit in that demonstration was the message that political wisdom resided not in the institution of the party but in its leader and his thought.

The growth of the Mao cult was temporarily retarded by the impact of Khrushchev's 1956 speech denouncing Stalin and his "cult of the personality." While the official Chinese response duly denounced "personality cults," it did not truly reflect Mao's own views on the matter. In a secret speech delivered early in 1958, Mao distinguished between "correct" and "incorrect" forms of political cults: "The question at issue is not whether or not there should be a cult of the individual, but rather whether or not the individual concerned represents the truth. If he does, then he should be revered."[12] Mao's belief that he possessed the truth and that he deserved reverence was amply demonstrated during the Great Leap Forward campaign, when he appeared on the historical scene as a utopian prophet speaking and appealing directly to the people, partly bypassing and transcending the regular institutions of party and state. The failure of the Great Leap gravely undermined the semi-sacred posture Mao had come to assume—and indeed led to the publication of a rash of bitter satirical attacks against him, mostly in the form of historical allegories. The reassertion of the power of party and state bureaucracies in the early 1960s, in turn, created a new and urgent political need to reestablish the personal and ideological supremacy of Mao. It was a task that now fell to the People's Liberation Army.

In contrast to its earlier incarnations, the Mao cult fashioned in the

1960s was a very deliberate effort and rather contrived affair, although, as the events of the Cultural Revolution were soon to demonstrate, no less real a political phenomenon because of that. Following his campaign, launched in 1960, to turn the PLA into a "great school of Mao Tse-tung Thought," Lin Piao proceeded to use that school to educate the entire nation—and to deify Mao and his "thought" in the process. It was the Political Department of the army that published the first edition of *Quotations from Chairman Mao* in May of 1964. In his introductions to the various editions of that soon to be famous—and fetishized—"little red book," Lin Piao made increasingly extravagant claims for the universal validity and extraordinary powers of Mao's thoughts. "Comrade Mao Tse-tung is the greatest Marxist–Leninist of our era" whose genius had raised the doctrine to "a higher and completely new stage," Lin proclaimed. The masses of the people as well as cadres and intellectuals were advised to "study Chairman Mao's writings, follow his teachings, act according to his instructions and be his good fighters," for, once grasped by the masses, Mao's thought was no less than "an inexhaustible source of strength and a spiritual atom bomb of infinite power," Lin wrote shortly after China's first successful nuclear test in October 1964. The campaign to study Mao's writings, to the virtual exclusion of all other writings, was conducted largely by the PLA, who printed nearly a billion copies of the *Quotations* along with some 150,000,000 copies of Mao's *Selected Works* over the next three years. And the heroic figures popularized as models for emulation were mostly PLA soldiers, all of whom attributed their miraculous deeds to the inspiration of Mao's thought.

By 1965 the cult was becoming all pervasive. It was not only the "thoughts" that were being deified but their producer as well. When Edgar Snow visited the People's Republic in the winter of 1964–1965, he was puzzled by the "immoderate glorification" of Mao. "Giant portraits of him now hung in the streets," Snow observed:

> . . . busts were in every chamber, his books and photographs were every-where on display to the exclusion of others. In the four-hour revolutionary pageant of dance and song, *The East Is Red,* Mao was the only hero. As a climax in that performance—presented, with a cast of 2,000, for the visiting King Mohammed Zahir Shah and the Queen of Afghanistan, accompanied by their host, Chairman Liu Shao-ch'i—I saw a portrait copied from a photograph taken by myself in 1936, blown up to about thirty feet high. It gave me a mixed feeling of pride of craftsmanship and uneasy recollection of similar extravaganzas of worship of Joseph Stalin seen during wartime years in Russia. . . . The one-man cult was not yet universal, but the trend was unmistakable.[13]

Mao apparently had few reservations about the cult. Not only had he distinguished between "good" and "bad" personality cults, but in an interview with Edgar Snow (held in January 1965) he suggested that such cults were political assets. Candidly acknowledging the existence of the phenomenon in China, Mao went on to suggest that Khrushchev's fall from power, which had occurred only three months earlier, might be attributed to the fact that the former Russian leader "had had no cult of personality at all."[14]

Revolutionary Successors

One of the major themes of the forthcoming Cultural Revolution was first heard in the spring of 1964: the need to train "revolutionary successors." The Maoist call was of course directed to the youth of China, for the youth were not only the bearers and builders of the future society, they also were (it was assumed) less corrupted by the traditions of the past and the pernicious "revisionist" influences of the present, and thus more amenable than their elders to acquiring the proper consciousness and values to ensure that revolutionary goals would continue to be pursued. It is thus hardly surprising that the problem of training "worthy successors" was first publicly discussed at a Communist Youth League congress, held in June 1964, although there was to be some historical irony in the fact that the youth organization (along with its parent party) was to be dismantled little more than two years later in the name of removing one of the obstacles to continuing the revolution. And it was wholly appropriate that the five criteria for revolutionary successors that Mao laid down were first published in the most comprehensive Chinese critique of Russia in the increasingly bitter Sino–Soviet dispute—the document entitled "On Khrushchev's Phoney Communism and Its Historical Lessons for the World"[15]—for the Soviet Union (in Maoist eyes) now had become a wholly negative example of postrevolutionary social development. In that document Mao made public his fears that China was following the same revisionist path to capitalism as Russia and his warnings (hitherto confined to Party councils) that China was threatened with the danger of "a counterrevolutionary restoration," that the Chinese Communist Party was in danger of becoming transformed into a revisionist and even a fascist party, and that the struggle between socialism and capitalism in China would span a lengthy historical era of a century or longer. The criteria Mao set forth for training "millions of successors who will carry on the cause of proletarian revolution" are not especially noteworthy, and we shall not pause to note them here.[16] What is worth noting about the campaign is that it reflected not only Mao's fears about the future and fate of the revolution but also his distrust of the Communist Party. Implicit in the campaign was the assumption that the party could not be relied upon to continue the work of the revolution. True successors were to be trained not by the party but directly through the study and the practice of the thought of the Chairman. Here the movement to train revolutionary successors merged with "the learn from the PLA" campaign and the growing Mao cult, the two main carriers of revolutionary values and the revolutionary alternatives to a conservative party and state apparatus.

Mao's concern with the overriding need for ideological purity among the youth was reflected in his growing dissatisfaction over China's educational system, where, he complained, "book-learning" divorced from social reality and revolutionary practice was corrupting both the minds and the bodies of young people. The remedy he proposed in 1964 was to reduce the period of formal education and to "put into practice the union of education and productive labor."[17] While Mao long had held a certain enmity toward formal education (and especially to institutions of higher education), he had never expressed his views in so extreme a form as he did in the years immediately preceding the Cultural Revolution. "At present," he complained, "there is too much studying going on, and this is exceedingly harmful." From the history of traditional China he drew the lesson that, "when the intellectuals had power, things were in a bad state [and] the country was in disorder," and thus the conclusion, "It is evident that to read too many books is harmful." True knowledge came from the practical experiences of real life and not from formal education, a point demonstrated by the fact that Confucius

> ... never attended middle school or university. ... Gorki had only two years of primary school; his learning was all self-taught. Franklin of America was originally a newspaper seller, yet he discovered electricity. Watt was a worker, yet he invented the steam engine. Both in ancient and modern times, in China and abroad, many scientists trained themselves in the course of practice.

From this flowed the conclusion that, "if you read too many books, they petrify your mind in the end," and demands to reform the existing school system, their curricula, and methods of teaching and examination—all of which Mao condemned as "exceedingly destructive of people."[18]

Debates on History and Dialectics

If Mao was concerned about the education of the youth of China—and whether they would be educated as bearers of the Maoist revolutionary ethic—his doubts and fears about the future probably deepened as he heard the views and theories then being put forward by many of China's most prominent intellectuals. Between 1962 and 1965 Marxist theoreticians, scholars, and writers engaged in debates on such subjects as the inheritability of traditional Chinese culture, the role of the peasantry in Chinese history, the nature of human nature, historical materialism, Marxist literary theory, and Marxian dialectics. The debates and discussions were erudite, for the most part, and were conducted in a relatively free and open atmosphere—and many of the views and arguments that emerged were decidedly anti-Maoist in their theoretical content and political implications.[19]

The noted philosopher Feng Yu-lan and the historian Wu Han (vice-mayor of Peking as well as a professor at Peking University) suggested, for example, that traditional Confucian thought, especially the concept of *jen* ("humanism"), offered a universally valid system of ethical and moral values and a rich cultural legacy that could and should be inherited and appropriated by contemporary socialist society. It was not a suggestion that conformed with the increasingly antitraditionalist posture Maoism had assumed or with Maoist demands for a radical break with the vestiges of the feudal traditions of the past. At the same time other presumably Marxist historians, such as Liu Chieh (as well as Wu Han), were arguing that the laws of class struggle had not governed Chinese history as they had the history of the West, and this had resulted in a distinctively Chinese evolutionary rather than revolutionary process of historical development; also invoking the concept of *jen*, which allegedly had mitigated class conflict in the past, it was argued that the principle might be applied to serve the same purpose in the present. The argument appeared at the very time Mao was insisting that the survival of the revolution was dependent on intensifying class struggle. Other scholars took issue with the Maoist thesis that peasant rebellions were the motive force of historical development in traditional society, some suggesting that the peasantry constituted a social force no less conservative in the present than it allegedly had been in the past, whereas Maoists, in the Socialist Education Movement, were hailing the revolutionary energies and the spirit of struggle they believed to be latent in the peasant masses.

These profoundly non-Maoist historical views were echoed in the appearance of unorthodox literary theories. In a remarkably explicit refutation of the Maoist emphasis on class struggle and the accompanying Maoist insistence that all forms of consciousness, including all literature and art, were expressions of particular class interests, some literary theorists (most notably, Chou Ku-ch'eng) set forth an "historicist" position to the effect that in a given historical era various forms of consciousness inevitably merged into a "spirit of the age." From this proposition it followed that such revolutionary and nonrevolutionary elements in contemporary Chinese society were more or less united in a general national spirit and consciousness, and with contradictions thus naturally reconciled, there was no need to artificially foster ideological and political struggle. Other writers and critics challenged the Maoist precept that the function of literature and art in a socialist society was to popularize heroic revolutionary examples and condemn counterrevolutionary villains. Instead, it was argued, realism demanded that the masses be portrayed as they really were rather than as Maoists wished them to be—as mostly what were termed "middle people," caught up in the whirlwinds of revolutionary change, who stood ambiguously between the forces of the new and the persistence of the old. Such, in reality, was the position of the peasants in particular, who were to be realistically portrayed as essentially nonrevolutionary or politically ambivalent. It was not a very Maoist portrait of the peasantry, needless to say.

The controversies that emerged over these and other subjects eventually came to focus on two Marxist theoretical issues: the proper interpretation of historical materialism and the proper understanding of dialectical materialism. On the first, the non-Maoist participants generally held to an orthodox Marxist view, invoking, often in rather deterministic fashion, the Marxist proposition that "being determines consciousness"— as opposed to the voluntaristic Maoist emphasis on the decisive role of the superstructure (and particularly consciousness) in transforming objective historical and social reality. The political implications of these differences were made rather explicit in the course of the debates. Mao, with an excessive reliance on subjective historical factors, his critics suggested, had gone beyond the bounds of objective historical possibilities in the Great Leap Forward campaign, and was attempting to do so again with the Socialist Education Movement. In brief, he had violated the dictates of the objective laws of historical development as taught by Marxist theory. For Maoists, by contrast, it was a prime article of faith that "the subjective can create the objective," and they never tired of quoting Marx's statement that "once theory is grasped by the masses, it itself becomes a material force" and Marx's injunction that hitherto "the philosophers have only interpreted the world, in various ways; the point, however, is to change it." The critics of Mao were charged with failing to recognize the dynamic role of the masses in sociohistorical development, with attempting to dampen their revolutionary enthusiasm, and indeed with propagating theories designed to prevent the masses from changing the world in accordance with socialist goals.

The theoretical debates culminated in a bitter ideological controversy on dialectical materialism in 1964 which centered on the views of Yang Hsien-chen, head of the Higher Party School for the training of upper level cadres and a theoretician widely regarded as an ideological spokesman for Liu Shao-ch'i. While the debates on dialectics produced a voluminous and rather obtuse body of literature on epistemology and other philosophical problems, the differences were popularized and oversimplified in Yang's mathematical formula that "two combine into one" constitutes the fundamental law of dialectics, as opposed to Mao's insistence that "one divides into two." Whereas Mao held that the unity of opposites was temporary while the struggle between them was absolute and eternal, Yang and his disciples stressed the mutuality of opposites and the unity of contradictions as the principal law of dialectical materialism and sociohistorical development. Yang's views provided theoretical support for the then still politically dominant Liuists and their policies of an orderly and more or less evolutionary pattern of development, whereas the views of his Maoist protagonists lent support to Mao's emphasis on the necessity of revolutionary transformations through class struggle in the present and to the Maoist notion of the inevitability and ceaselessness of contradictions and struggles in the future. Yang's ideological heresies were compounded, in Maoist eyes, by his proclivity to find more precedents for modern dialectics in traditional Chinese thought than in the thought of Marx or Mao. Nor was Yang Hsien-chen's reputation enhanced by the fact that he had spent many years studying and working in the Soviet Union, from where it was alleged his revisionist theories partly derived.

The question of dialectics was a particularly sensitive ideological and political issue for Maoists, and especially for Mao personally, and they brought forth as Yang's main protagonist the most venerable of Maoist theoreticians, Ai Ssu-ch'i. In the earlier debates they had been content to leave the defense of the Maoist position to younger theoreticians and scholars, such as the radical Shanghai writer and critic Yao Wen-yuan.

The ideas and theories advanced by many of the intellectuals in the years 1962–1964 were seen by Maoists as ideological reflections of the "revisionist" tendencies that had come to dominate the party and indeed Chinese society as a whole; in part, they were attributed to the persistence of traditional Chinese values among the intelligentsia and the equally pernicious influences of contemporary Soviet and East European intellectual sources. But for Mao ideas were more than simply reflections of social reality; consciousness was an historical force in its own right in determining the direction of social and political development. And more than purely academic debates were required to remedy the situation. The remedy Mao first proposed (in February 1964) was both simple and drastic: "We must drive actors, poets, dramatists, and writers out of the cities, and pack them off to the countryside."[20] In June 1964 he called for a "rectification" campaign along the lines of the antirightist movement of the latter half of 1957. For the past fifteen years, he complained, the intellectuals:

> . . . have acted as high and mighty bureaucrats, have not gone to the workers, peasants, and soldiers, and have not reflected socialist reality

and socialist construction. In recent years, they have slid right down to the brink of revisionism. Unless they remold themselves in real earnest in the future, they are bound to become a group like the Hungarian Petofi Club.[21]

If Mao was concerned over the revisionist tendencies of the intelligentsia, he probably was even less happy about the feeble efforts of the party to reverse those tendencies. The task of conducting the rectification movement in the latter half of 1964 naturally fell to the Party's Propaganda Department, headed by Lu Ting-yi and Chou Yang. It was a perfunctory and pale affair compared to previous ideological campaigns, and largely kept within the boundaries of polite academic debate. It was not that Lu Ting-yi or Chou Yang had become recent converts to the cause of intellectual freedom—for Chou Yang in particular had long established himself as the fountainhead of orthodoxy in literary and cultural affairs, and had a well-deserved reputation as a witch-hunter of considerable ruthlessness. Rather, it was their intention to insulate the Party and the state Ministry of Culture from Maoist and PLA influences. It was hardly to be expected, in any event, that the leaders of the party apparatus would prove especially ardent in "remolding" the thoughts of those who were providing ideological justification and theoretical support for their policies. Nor is it likely that Mao expected much more than the little that was done. Indeed, his opinion of the party had fallen so low that he no longer refrained from such sarcastic comments as the one he made in August of 1964: "At present, you can buy a party branch secretary for a few packs of cigarettes, not to mention marrying a daughter to him."[22] The rectification campaign, along with the historical and philosophical debates, quietly petered out early in 1965, as did the Socialist Education Movement as a whole.

The more heretical and heterodox voices were stilled by 1965, but the theoretical and ideological issues remained unresolved, just as the political struggle between Maoists and the Party bureaucracy remained at a stalemate. Only in one limited area of the cultural realm did Maoists gain a symbolic victory, and that involved the curious spectacle of the army, assisted by Mao's wife Chiang Ch'ing, involving itself in the reform of the traditional Peking opera. Otherwise, Maoism was dominant only in the realm of formal ideology. While appropriate lip service was paid to the "thought of Mao," real power over the party and state remained in non-Maoist hands and basically conservative socioeconomic policies continued to be pursued under the cover of radical rhetoric. Maoist attempts to revolutionize thought and society were frustrated at every turn by the resistance of entrenched bureaucracies and the apparent political inertia of the masses. At no time in the history of the People's Republic was the gap between theory and practice so wide.

The sense of activism—and the impatience—that continued to characterize Mao's mentality during those years were reflected in the well-known lines of his poem entitled "Reply to Kuo Mo-jo," written in 1963: "Seize the day, seize the hour! . . . Our force is irresistible." These activist impulses were soon to find real political expression, and on a vast and momentous scale. If the half-decade following the Great Leap can be seen as a variant of the "Thermidorean reaction," then the events that began to unfold in early 1966 marked the beginning of Mao's revolution against the "Thermidoreans."

Notes

1. Mao Tse-tung, "Speech at the Tenth Plenum of the Eighth Central Committee," in Stuart R. Schram, ed., *Mao Tse-tung Unrehearsed: Talks and Letters, 1956–71* (Middlesex, England: Penguin, 1974), pp. 188–196.

2. Of the three main resolutions which emerged from plenum, only the general communiqué was made public at the time. *Documents of Chinese Communist Party Central Committee* (Hong Kong: Union Research Institute, 1971), pp. 185–192. The other two were secret documents circulated through interparty channels. *Documents of the Chinese Communist Party Central Committee*, pp. 193–205, 695–725.

3. "Draft Resolution of the Central Committee of the Chinese Communist Party on Some Problems in Current Rural Work," May 20, 1963. Text translated in Richard Baum and Frederick C. Teiwes, *Ssu-Ch'ing: The Socialist Education Movement of 1962–1966* (Berkeley: University of California Press, 1968), Appendix B, p. 68 and pp. 58–71, *passim*.

4. *Ibid.*, pp. 62–71.

5. Both documents were titled "Some Concrete Policy Formulations of the Central Committee of the Chinese Communist Party in the Rural Socialist Education Movement." (See Baum and Teiwes, *Ssu-Ch'ing*, Appendixes C and E, pp. 72–94, 102–117.)

6. "Revised Later Ten Points," Baum and Teiwes, *Ssu-Ch'ing*, Appendix E, p. 105.

7. "Later Ten Points," Baum and Teiwes, *Ssu-Ch'ing*, Appendix C, p. 91.

8. "Later Ten Points," p. 85. Liu Shao-ch'i's revised version elaborated on, and emphasized even more strongly, the point that the rectification of the cadres was the key to the proper development of the mass movement; "In short," he concluded, "to educate the masses we must first educate the cadres; and to solve the problems of the masses we must first solve the problems of the cadres." ("Revised Later Ten Points," p. 108.)

9. The document was formally titled "Some Problems Currently Arising in the Course of the Rural Socialist Education Movement." Baum and Teiwes, *Ssu-Ch'ing*, Appendix F, pp. 118–126.

10. In late 1964, Liu Shao-ch'i apparently was willing to compromise his differences with Mao, or at least paper them over, through the device of combining Mao's original directive on the Socialist Education Movement with his own "Revised Later Ten Points" and calling them the "Double Ten Points." Mao refused the offer and issued his twenty-three-point directive of January 1965. Liu, in turn, refused to accept the latter, which was aimed against the party bureaucracy over which he still wielded firm control.

11. Snow's own impressions of the forty-four-year-old Mao in 1937, when Mao's name was hardly known outside of China and little known within China save for the still limited Soviet areas, were uncannily perceptive and prophetic: "You feel a certain force of destiny in him. It is nothing quick or flashy, but a kind of solid elemental vitality. You feel that whatever extraordinary there is in this man grows out of the uncanny degree to which he synthesizes and expresses the urgent demands of millions of Chinese, and especially the peasantry—those impoverished, underfed, exploited, illiterate but kind, generous, courageous and just now rather rebellious human beings who are the vast majority of the Chinese people. If these demands and the movement which is pressing them forward are the dynamics which can regenerate China, then in this deeply historical sense Mao Tse-tung may possibly become a very great man." Edgar Snow, *Red Star Over China* (New York: Random House, 1938), p. 67.

12. Mao Tse-tung, "Talks at the Chengtu Conference," March 10, 1958, in Schram, ed., *Mao Tse-tung Unrehearsed*, pp. 99–100.

13. Edgar Snow, *The Long Revolution* (New York: Random House, 1971), pp. 68–69.

14. *Ibid.*, p. 205.

15. The lengthy treatise first appeared on July 14, 1964 as editorials in the *People's Daily* and the Party theoretical journal *Red Flag*. It was the ninth and final Chinese reply to the "open letter" of the central committee of the Soviet Party, published July 14, 1963. An English translation published in pamphlet form by the Foreign Languages Press (Peking, 1964) is reproduced in A. Doak Barnett, *China after Mao* (Princeton, N.J.: Princeton University Press, 1967), pp. 123–195.

16. The five criteria, briefly, were that "worthy successors" must be genuine Marxist–Leninists, revolutionaries who serve the majority of the people, "proletarian statesmen" capable of uniting with the vast majority of the masses, models in applying the principles of democratic centralism and the mass line, and people who were "modest and prudent." *Ibid.*, pp. 193–194. Mao elaborated on the criteria in a revealing discussion with his nephew Mao Yüan-hsin; for a transcript of the talk, see Schram, ed., *Mao Tse-tung Unrehearsed*, pp. 242–250.

17. Mao Tse-tung, "Remarks at the Spring Festival," February 13, 1964, *Mao Tse-tung Unrehearsed*, p. 206.

18. *Ibid.*, pp. 203–211.

19. For an excellent survey of the debates and the issues involved, see Merle Goldman, "The Chinese Communist Party's 'Cultural Revolution' of 1962–64," in Chalmers Johnson, ed., *Ideology and Politics in Contemporary China* (Seattle: University of Washington Press, 1973), pp. 219–254.

20. Mao, "Remarks at the Spring Festival," p. 207.

21. Mao Tse-tung, "Instructions Concerning Art and Literature," June 27, 1964, in *Mao Tse-tung Ssu-hsiang Wan-sui* (Taipei; n.p., 1967). Translated in *Current Background*, No. 891.

22. Mao Tse-tung, "Talk on Questions of Philosophy," August 18, 1964, *Mao Tse-tung Unrehearsed*, p. 217.

Part Five

The Cultural Revolution and Its Aftermath

18

The Political History of the
Cultural Revolution, 1966–1969

THE FIRST PUBLIC RUMBLINGS of what was to be baptized the "Great Pro-
letarian Cultural Revolution" were heard in November 1965, when the
Maoist theorist Yao Wen-yuan published a critique of the popular play
Hai Jui Dismissed from Office. Written five years earlier by the historian
Wu Han (who was also vice-mayor of Peking), the drama was set in the
Ming Dynasty and celebrated the heroism of a virtuous official deposed
by a tyrannical emperor for having protested the confiscation of peasant
lands by landlords and corrupt bureaucrats. It took little imagination on
the part of the politically informed Chinese reader to know that the tyrannical emperor was Mao Tse-tung, the virtuous official P'eng Te-huai,
and that the confiscation of land referred to the communization campaign,
which P'eng had so vehemently opposed, resulting in his political downfall in 1959. Wu Han's play was only one of many anti-Maoist historical
allegories and political satires written during the "bitter years" following
the collapse of the Great Leap Forward campaign. Others appeared in
several series of essays entitled "Evening Chats at Yenshan" and "Notes
from Three-Family Village," where, among other things, it was suggested
that Mao was an amnesiac who had forgotten to keep his promises and
suffered from a severe mental disorder.[1]

Most of the satirical attacks ceased with Mao's tenth plenum speech
of September 1962 and the inauguration of the Socialist Education Movement. At the time Mao sarcastically remarked that "the use of novels for
anti-Party activity is a great invention," and entirely without sarcasm went
on to observe that "anyone wanting to overthrow a political regime must
create public opinion and do some preparatory ideological work."[2] If the
direct literary attacks on Mao ended in 1962, they were not forgotten,

despite Mao's alleged amnesia. It was at Mao's personal direction (and with the assistance of Mao's wife, Chiang Ch'ing, it was said) that Yao Wen-yuan published his critique of Wu Han in November 1965. Not only did Wu Han distort the Ming historical record, Yao charged, but the play's theme of "returning the land" to the peasants offered contemporary ideological support to those who wanted to "demolish the people's communes and to restore the criminal rule of the landlords and rich peasants," all of which was "the focal point of bourgeois opposition to the dictatorship of the proletariat."[3]

While Maoists now date the beginning of the Cultural Revolution with the appearance of Yao's article, it seemed a matter of little significance at the time. Nor was there anything particularly revolutionary, or even exceptional about the literary debates and discussions that ensued over the following six months. If the Cultural Revolution was under way, it seemed a largely academic and narrowly cultural affair.

The problem, for Maoists, was that the established party apparatus was little inclined to cleanse the cultural realm in the fashion Mao wished, much less unleash the forces of social and political struggle that Maoists saw lurking beneath the symptoms of ideological and cultural decay, especially since Mao already had found the principal enemy to be "those people in authority *within the party* who are taking the capitalist road." At the January 1965 politburo meeting, from which Mao had emerged with this remarkable and politically prophetic thesis, he had prevailed upon party leaders to begin a "cultural revolution." Appointed to plan and implement this still vague and seemingly innocuous concept was a "Five-Man Group" chaired by P'eng Chen, the fifth-ranking member of the politburo, head of the Peking party organization and Mayor of Peking.[4] The "Five-Man Group" remained dormant until Mao by-passed party channels to launch his own version of the "Cultural Revolution" in the form of Yao Wen-yuan's article—and then P'eng Chen's group was moved to action, but only to blunt the political thrust of the attack. In his "February Theses" of 1966, P'eng censured Yao and other radical Maoists for "treating a purely academic question in political terms." Despite the obvious political issues and implications involved, P'eng and the party apparatus managed to keep the debate confined to largely academic and historical questions well into the spring of 1966. In the meantime, Mao had disappeared from the public scene, embarking in November 1965 on a six-month tour of the provinces to rally support for his policies.

With Mao's return to Peking in the spring and the simultaneous entry of the army into the political arena, events began to unfold at a dizzying pace. The attacks against Wu Han and other literary-political foes of Mao—the "Black Gang," as they were called—became more shrill and increasingly political. The army, now more firmly under the command of

Lin Piao following the purge of its Chief of Staff, Lo Jui-ch'ing, earlier in the year (the former head of the secret police had been accused of having given priority to military affairs over the thoughts of Mao), announced itself as "the mainstay of the dictatorship of the proletariat" and said it would play an important role in the developing Cultural Revolution. Editorials in *Liberation Army Daily* in late April and early May demanded not only a thorough purge of "anti-socialist elements" in the cultural and ideological sphere but the elimination of "right-opportunist elements within the Party." On May 16 a directive drafted by Mao and issued in the name of the central committee dissolved the "Five-Man Group," condemned P'eng Chen for having obstructed the Cultural Revolution, charged that "representatives of the bourgeoisie" had infiltrated the party at all levels (including the Central Committee itself), and warned that such "counterrevolutionary revisionists" were preparing to "seize political power and turn the dictatorship of the proletariat into a dictatorship of the bourgeoisie." "Persons like Khrushchev," the document ominously concluded, "are still nestling beside us."[5]

The Cultural Revolution was thus quickly turning political, and the first of the high-ranking party leaders to fall was P'eng Chen. Early in June it was revealed that P'eng and his followers had been dismissed from their official posts and that the Peking party committee and municipal government had been reorganized around loyal Maoists, headed by Li Hsüeh-feng. A wholesale purge of the central organs of propaganda and culture in the capital immediately followed; the most notable victims were Lu Ting-yi, head of the party's propaganda department (who also controlled the authoritative *People's Daily*), and Chou Yang, China's long-time literary and cultural czar. Under the direction of the newly appointed Cultural Revolution Group (headed by Ch'en Po-ta, Chiang Ch'ing, and K'ang Sheng), Maoists now controlled Peking and the principal central organs of communication.

But the Maoist purpose was not simply to achieve ascendancy in Peking, however strategically important that was. They aimed at the total reorganization and reformation of the political structure and social life of the nation—and, moreover, the spiritual transformation of its people. Indeed, it was precisely the factors of revolutionary spirit and consciousness that were regarded as decisive in determining the eventual political and social outcome. For the Maoist assumption underlying the Cultural Revolution was the belief that the existing state and party apparatus was dominated by "bourgeois ideology" and thus was producing, and would continue to produce, capitalist-type socioeconomic relationships. Only by raising the political consciousness of the masses, revitalizing the socialist spirit and ideals of the revolution, and refashioning a state structure guided by "proletarian ideology" could the danger of a regression to capitalism be forestalled. And by both Maoist preference and objective political necessity, these aims could be accomplished only by the ideological and political mobilization of the masses for Mao-ist-inspired revolutionary action. In the course of revolutionary struggle, it was believed, the masses would spiritually transform themselves while transforming the objective world in which they lived. What Mao called for was no less than a "profound" revolution "that touches people to their very souls." If Marx believed that social being determines conscious-ness, Mao believed that it was consciousness as such (mediated through political action and the state apparatus) that ultimately determined social being.

The spontaneous mass movement from below was not long in forth-coming, although it came with the generous encouragement of Lin Piao's army and Mao's Cultural Revolution Group. University students were the first to respond to the Maoist call to rebel against established authority. On May 25 young Maoists at Peking University led by a philosophy instructor, Nieh Yuan-tzu, put up a big-character poster denouncing university president Lu P'ing for having suppressed student political meetings and discussion of the Wu Han affair, and calling upon "all revolutionary intellectuals . . . to go into battle." A week later, when Mao hailed the poster as "the manifesto of the Peking commune of the 1960s" (predicting that China soon would see "a wholly new form of state struc-ture") and had it published in the *People's Daily* and broadcast by Pe-king radio, rebel student groups sprung up with extraordinary rapidity and in bewildering variety. Encouraged by a June 18 decree that uni-versity entrance examinations were to be postponed for six months in order to refashion the entire educational system (and to ensure that "the revolutionary fervor of the leftist students does not cool off"), student rebels became locked in battle with school administrators, teachers, and party functionaries—and also with rival student groups organized by work teams dispatched by the established party apparatus to keep the new movement under its own organizational control. From the chaotic and often violent struggles which ensued between vaguely Maoist and Liuist student groups (during what was later condemned as "the fifty days of White Terror") there emerged the Red Guards, the first group of which was organized at a middle school attached to Tsinghua University in Peking. Over the summer months the Red Guard movement spread to virtually every university and middle school in the country. Rallying under the slogans "it is justified to rebel" and "destruction before con-struction," rebellious youth swept the country spreading their Maoist messages to destroy the "ghosts and monsters" of the past and present. They flocked to Peking to receive Mao's personal blessings, which came dramatically on August 18 when hundreds of thousands of Red Guards crowded into the square below the Gate of Heavenly Peace. Mao ap-peared atop the gate at sunrise in an almost godlike presence and solemnly donned a red armband, thereby becoming the "Supreme Commander" of the Red Guards. A month earlier the seventy-two-year-old Mao had performed another dramatic act in his deification, announcing his politico-ideological supremacy as well as demonstrating his physical virility by taking a much-publicized swim in the Yangtze, allegedly covering a distance of nine miles in sixty-five minutes.

Both the deified presence of an aging Mao and the rebellious energies of the youthful Red Guards were essential for carrying out the program of the Cultural Revolution, for the latter were the chosen instrument to implement the various "directives" and "instructions" issued by the former. The program itself was set forth in the form of a "sixteen-point decision" approved by an August 1–2 meeting of the central committee—from which most non-Maoist party leaders were excluded, although it was reportedly attended by several Red Guard representatives. The "sixteen-point decision" explicitly defined the purpose of the movement as the overthrow of "those within the Party who are in authority and taking the capitalist road."[6] A second, and closely related, purpose was to uproot and destroy what soon was to become known as "the four olds." "Although the bourgeoisie has been overthrown," the document read, "it is still trying to use the old ideas, culture, customs, and habits of the exploiting classes to corrupt the masses, capture their minds, and endeavor to stage a comeback." The "bourgeoisie" was thus to be identified with those deemed to be the carriers of "old ideas," and it was made abundantly clear that the danger of a "bourgeois restoration" resided primarily within the party itself and emanated from among its highest leaders. Thus the tasks of cleansing the party and eliminating bourgeois influences in society as a whole were not to be left to the party in the fashion of earlier rectification campaigns. Rather, the cultural revolutionary means was "boldly to arouse the masses." Time and again it was emphasized that "the only method is for the masses to liberate themselves, and any method of doing things in their stead must not be used." It also was emphasized that the main agency for stimulating and organizing the mass movement from below was to be the Red Guards, who were referred to as those "large numbers of revolutionary young people, previously unknown [who] have become courageous and daring pathbreakers." Moreover, it was by no means entirely clear that the ultimate political result of the revolution from below would be simply a rectified Communist Party in its old Leninist form. It was hinted that in the future political power should be reorganized more in accordance with Marx's description of the Paris Commune than with Lenin's concept of the vanguard party. The new political organizations which spontaneously had come into being during the first phases of the upheaval, the "cultural revolutionary groups, committees, and congresses," it was declared, "should not be temporary organizations but permanent, standing mass organizations." They were suitable organizational forms not only for schools and economic enterprises but also for governmental organs in both cities and villages. It was further stated that "it is necessary to institute a system of general elections, like that of the Paris Commune." Indeed, Mao personally endorsed the original Marxist model of the dictatorship of the proletariat, having proclaimed in July that Nieh Yuan-tzu's big-character poster was the "manifesto of the Chinese Paris Commune of the sixties of the twentieth century, the significance of which surpasses the Paris Commune."[7]

While the leaders of the Cultural Revolution left ambiguous the question of the precise nature of the new political order they envisioned—and the place of the party in it—there was nothing ambiguous (although there was much that was astonishing) about Mao's call for the masses to rebel against the existing party and its organizations, albeit a call made in the name of the party and by its official chairman. On August 5 Mao had posted his own ta-tzu-pao on the door of the room where the central committee was meeting, calling upon the youth to "bombard the headquarters" of his party opponents who, he alleged, were exercising a "bourgeois dictatorship." Three days later the "sixteen-point decision" formally was promulgated as the charter of the Cultural Revolution. And on August 18 the Red Guards, guided by the thoughts of Mao and acting in accordance with his personal instructions, were officially sanctioned as the vanguard to stimulate the revolution of the masses against the established institutions of state and party. At the same time Lin Piao, now described as Mao's "closest comrade in arms," was anointed his successor. Henceforth, the attack was directed against the entire party apparatus and its highest leaders, especially Liu Shao-ch'i, now variously referred to as "the leading person in authority taking the capitalist road" and "China's Khrushchev," and Teng Hsiao-p'ing, the Party Secretary-General, now known as "the second leading person in authority taking the capitalist road." In official publications, Liu Shao-ch'i was not to be referred to by name (although he was named on wall posters) until he was formally expelled from the party and branded as a "counterrevolutionary" in the autumn of 1968. But after November 1966 he was no longer seen in public, having been apparently placed under house arrest, and the ceremonial functions of head of state were performed by Soong Ch'ing-ling, widow of Sun Yat-sen and vice-chairman of the People's Republic.

What makes all this such a remarkable phenomenon in the history of postrevolutionary societies is that the impetus for the rebellion against the established state and party organizations came from among those who had been most prominent in building and leading that party and state. It came from the veterans of the revolution—and Mao was certainly the most venerable and venerated of the veterans—who had created political institutions they now had come to regard more as obstacles to than as instruments of revolutionary social change.

Following the August 18 rally, the Red Guards took to the streets in a militant crusade against the "ghosts and demons" of the past and the present. And they did so in a far more indiscriminate fashion than their elders wanted or anticipated. Although the "sixteen points" had enjoined them to "put daring above everything else," it had also stressed that "contradictions among the people" were to be resolved "by reasoning, not by coercion or force," and that even the "anti-socialist rightists" who were to be "fully exposed, refuted, overthrown and completely discredited" were to "be given a chance to turn over a new leaf." And it was stipulated that "both the cultural revolution and production [should be carried on] without one hampering the other;" indeed, it was emphasized that one of the aims of the movement was to revolutionize the people's consciousness in order to increase production, not disrupt it. But in their initial assaults, the Red Guards paid little heed to such distinctions and restraints. The young rebels acted more in the spirit of the initial Red Guard manifesto, which proclaimed that the "supernatural powers" and "magic" derived from "Mao Tse-tung's great invincible thought" was to be used "to turn the old world upside down, smash it to pieces, pulverize it, create chaos and make a tremendous mess, the bigger the better!"[8] During the chaotic latter months of 1966 millions of Red Guards, carrying portraits of Mao and waving copies of his "little red book" (to which they often attributed semimagical properties), marched through the streets of the cities and traveled over the country in an iconoclastic campaign against the symbols of the feudal past and bourgeois influences of the present. Museums and homes were ransacked; old books and works of art destroyed; everything from old Confucian texts to recordings of Beethoven were sought out and thrown into the dustbins; new revolutionary names were pasted on streets and buildings along with the face and the sayings of the Chairman. Hapless citizens wearing Western-style clothes or Hong Kong-style haircuts were attacked and humiliated along with those possessing old Buddhist and Taoist relics; Party officials and school administrators were "arrested" and paraded through the streets in dunce caps and forced to confess their "crimes" at public rallies. And sometimes bloody battles ensued when the Red Guards entered factories and communes and were confronted by rival rebel groups of workers and peasants.

The older cultural revolutionaries in Peking variously attempted to restrain and encourage the actions of their youthful "pathbreakers." They were exhorted not to use force; ordered not to interfere with the productive activities of workers and peasants; admonished for indiscriminate attacks on regional and provincial party organizations rather than on individual "capitalist-roaders"; and criticized for fomenting differences among the masses of working people rather than uniting with them in common struggle. Ineffective attempts were made to bring the swelling (and increasingly factionalized) movement under some form of centralized control and direction. On the other hand, the PLA was ordered to facilitate the movement and activities of the Red Guards, who were given free use of railroads and other forms of public transport, and provided with food and lodging wherever they went. Such privileges hardly were conducive to dampening the wanderlust and rebelliousness of the Red Guards. Nor was the announcement at the end of October that middle-schools and universities would remain closed for the remainder of the academic year. Before the year was out, it was reported that some 11 million Red Guards had come to Peking to see (and be seen by) Chairman Mao. The massive rallies beneath the Gate of Heavenly Peace (the eighth and last of which was held November 25–26), and the magnetic presence of Mao did nothing to undermine the movement, especially since the speeches of Lin Piao and others did more to praise the Red Guards for their revolutionary zeal than criticize their "leftist" excesses. The Red Guards continued to embark on "long marches" through the countryside to steel themselves as "revolutionary successors;" traveled across the land to "exchange revolutionary experiences;" and continued to "bombard the headquarters" of local and regional party organizations.

By the end of 1966 the Red Guards had performed their assigned role as the vanguard of the Cultural Revolution, and in the eyes of most members of the Cultural Revolution Group in Peking they had outlived their political usefulness. They had more than fulfilled the aim to "expose" party leaders "taking the capitalist road," and indeed had put the entire party apparatus on the defensive, but their totalistic attacks on all authority threatened anarchy and was hardly in accord with the Maoist goal to "achieve the unity of more than 95 percent of the cadres." They had carried out the Maoist injunction to "boldly arouse the masses," but their intrusions into factories and communes had aroused many workers and peasants not for revolution but to organize for battles against the youthful and often arrogant interlopers in defense of the existing order of things. Moreover, the almost total lack of discipline, the bitter and sometimes violent factionalism, and the often outright hooliganism that characterized the movement led the leaders in Peking to the conclusion that the Red Guards had become a political liability. In 1967 various and increasingly stringent measures were taken to remove them from the center of the political stage. But the Red Guards were not to be dispersed as easily as they had been called into being.

The Cultural Revolution was not to end with the attempts to end the political life of the Red Guards. In 1967 the Great Proletarian Cultural Revolution moved to a new stage—the move to "seize power" from local, provincial, and regional party authorities—and new political actors moved to the center of the political arena: workers and soldiers. The new stage was to prove far more turbulent than that of the previous six months, when the Red Guards had dominated the stage.

The Rise and Fall of the Shanghai Commune

As the Cultural Revolution spread from Peking to other urban centers and the provinces in the summer and fall of 1966, it became apparent to Maoist leaders in the capital that they had underestimated both the disorders that the movement would bring and the power of local and provincial party organizations to resist the movement. At a central committee work conference in Peking in late October, Mao Tse-tung acknowledged that "the Great Cultural Revolution wreaked havoc after I approved Nieh Yuan-tzu's big-character poster" and that "I myself had not foreseen that as soon as the Peking University poster was broadcast [on June 1], the whole country would be thrown into turmoil. . . . Since it was I who caused the havoc, it is understandable if you have some bitter words for me."[9] At the same time, Ch'en Po-ta, head of the central Cultural Revolution Group, addressed himself to the question of why the mass organizations had failed to achieve unity and fashion a new political structure; he attributed the failure to local party leaders who were "afraid of losing their positions and prestige" and thus had "instigated workers and peasants to fight against the students."[10]

There was a third factor Maoists had underestimated—the spontaneous social and political radicalism of the urban working class, which, as events were soon to demonstrate, was to acquire a momentum of its own that was not to spend itself until well into 1968. But at the end of 1966 the Maoist concern was with the resilience of the old party bureaucratic structures in the cities and the provinces, which had managed to maintain themselves by playing upon and manipulating the divisions within the growing mass movement. As a functioning national political organization, the CCP virtually had ceased to exist. In Peking, Mao and the Cultural Revolution Group held sway, issuing directives and speaking in the name of the old central committee. But in the provinces, districts, and cities, local party organizations persisted within their own spheres of jurisdiction. Everywhere the old bureaucratic apparatus was under attack, but everywhere the separate parts of the old structure remained more or less intact, their leaders paying due homage to the thoughts and directives of Mao while fending off the onslaughts of the Chairman's local supporters. To break the political stalemate, the leaders in Peking called for the immediate and literal implementation of one of the aims announced in the "sixteen points": the "seizure of power by proletarian revolutionaries." The first attempt was made in Shanghai, and the events in that city of 11,000,000 in the early months of 1967 were to prove decisive in determining the future course of the nationwide struggle, revealing both the objective limits that the Cultural Revolution confronted and the subjective limitations of the cultural revolutionaries.

Shanghai is not only the most populous city in China, it is also the most highly industrialized. In the huge and modern factories of the sprawling metropolis there labors the largest and most concentrated section of China's proletariat, heir to a militant working class tradition forged in the bloody revolutionary struggles of the 1920s. Shanghai is the most cosmopolitan of Chinese cities and also the most politically radical, the home of a mature working class and long the center of modern China's radical intelligentsia. The CCP was born in Shanghai in 1921 and Mao Tse-tung called upon members of its intelligentsia to begin the Cultural Revolution in 1965. If China was to have a "proletarian cultural revolution," Shanghai was its natural base. Indeed, the events which unfolded in the city in late 1966 and early 1967 presaged what was to occur in other urban areas, albeit on a smaller scale.

Inspired and influenced by the developments in Peking, the Cultural Revolution in Shanghai began in the summer of 1966 with university students organizing Red Guard groups much like their counterparts in the capital. As elsewhere, the Red Guards were rent by bitter internal disputes from their inception, both of their own making and manufactured by party officials. But however factionalized, the movement grew and acquired an increasingly radical momentum, rapidly escalating from verbal attacks on wall posters and at mass rallies to physical attacks on government offices; moving from the criticism and ouster of "bourgeois" authorities in individual schools and institutes to a massive challenge to the authority of the established party–government bureaucracy headed by the mayor of the city, Ts'ao Ti-ch'iu, and the secretary of the party's East China bureau, Ch'en P'ei-hsien.

A particularly explosive issue that arose early in the Shanghai movement, as it did elsewhere, and revealed the latent hatreds of the masses against those who were governing them, was the matter of the so-called "black files," political dossiers on citizens compiled over the years by party authorities in schools, factories, and mass organizations. The very existence of the files inhibited the actions of those who were responsive to the Maoist call to "dare to rebel," and this was particularly true of the workers, for it was feared that the files would be used to take political and economic retribution against those who participated in the movement should the party be restored to its old preeminence. The student rebels demanded that the files be destroyed, and they were en-couraged by an October 5 "urgent directive" from Peking ordering the "black files" be burned in public. But Party officials refused to turn over materials they labeled "state secrets," and in early November some of the more militant Red Guard groups staged nocturnal raids on party offices to seize and destroy the files, resulting in violent clashes with party cadres and their supporters. A new directive from Peking on No-vember 16 again called for the destruction of the files, but stipulated that the matter should be settled by "persuasion" and not by force. Party authorities proved less than amenable to persuasion; and the end result was not the elimination of the political dossiers but a legacy of increased hostility and distrust between rebel masses and party cadres that was to prolong the Maoist attempt to bring about a reconciliation between the two.

While the prestige and authority of the Shanghai party apparatus was undermined by the struggle over the "black books," the power of the apparatus was destroyed by Shanghai's working class. By mid-au-tumn the rebellion against established authority had spread from the schools to the factories, thus marking the appearance of the actual proletariat in the drama of the "Great Proletarian Cultural Revolution." But the working class did not join the battle as a united entity. It was a class divided between older and more skilled workers who benefited from the old wage and bonus system and younger and relatively under-paid workers who were the first to rebel. A far greater gap separated regular workers who were permanent state employees and a massive semiproletariat consisting of contract workers, day laborers, and peas-ants employed in the cities on a seasonal basis; these "temporary" work-ers lived on the barest margins of subsistence, not only suffering from meager wages but lacking even the most elementary social welfare bene-fits and job security enjoyed by regular workers. And the ranks of the Shanghai proletariat expanded when workers who had been involun-tarily dispatched to the countryside in earlier years returned to the city, demanding jobs and housing. From these various and disparate sectors of the working class came different and often conflicting socioeconomic demands, which found expression in separate (and sometimes rival) political organizations and factions. What was remarkable was not the conflicts among them but the extraordinary degree of political unity they were able to achieve in early 1967 and the spirit of revolutionary egali-tarianism that grew spontaneously in the course of the movement. For what they shared was a general antipathy to an overbearing bureau-cratic apparatus that controlled their lives but over which they had no control, latent hostilities that were released when the Cultural Revolu-tion temporarily brought them the freedom to establish their own orga-nizations and throw off old organizational restraints. Even relatively privileged workers harbored deep resentments against the often oppressive and arbitrary practices of party cadres and factory managers, and they were particularly resentful of the official trade unions, which functioned less as representative institutions of the workers than as bureaucratic appendages of party and state to control workers and spur productivity.

In early November workers' groups from a number of factories established a citywide organization called the Headquarters of the Revolutionary Revolt of Shanghai Workers. The Workers' Headquarters was in every sense the self-creation of the workers themselves, owing its existence neither to local student Red Guards nor to instructions from Peking. Indeed, Maoist leaders in the capital were then emphasizing more the productive than the revolutionary role of the workers, instructing them to fulfill their eight-hour working day before participating in the Cultural Revolution. What was vaguely envisioned was a peaceful transformation of productive relationships within individual factories, with new workers' committees (created during spare-time hours) cooperating with managerial cadres. It was not until the beginning of the new year that Peking was to call upon workers to organize themselves as "revolutionary rebels."

But events in Shanghai moved more rapidly. On November 8 the Workers' Headquarters presented its demands to the Shanghai Municipal Committee—and they clearly pointed to the replacement of the old bureaucratic administration by new popular organs of government. The workers demanded that the Headquarters be recognized as a legal organization under "the dictatorship of the proletariat"; that the workers be provided with the means to organize in all factories of the city; and that the municipal government give a public accounting of its administration. When the demands were ignored, the workers were determined to take them to Peking and on November 11 attempted to do so by commandeering a train bound for the capital. Party authorities had the train halted at Anting, a small town on the outskirts of Shanghai, but the workers refused orders to return to the city and defiantly settled in for what was to be a three-day siege.

The leaders in Peking responded to the crisis at Anting with hesitation and uncertainty. First came a telegram from Ch'en Po-ta, head of the Cultural Revolution Group, warning: "it is a serious matter to disobey Party instructions. . . . As workers, their main job is to work. Joining in the Revolution is only secondary. They must therefore go back to work."[11] But before the Shanghai authorities could implement the order, new instructions arrived from Peking in the person of Chang Ch'un-ch'iao, who had been Secretary of the Shanghai Party Committee until July when he had departed to become a leading member of the Cultural Revolution Group in the capital. On November 14, Chang declared the Workers' Headquarters a legitimate revolutionary organization, signed their demands in the name of the central committee, and forced Mayor Ts'ao to grudgingly sign as well. The Maoist leaders in Peking apparently had concluded that the time had come to allow the proletariat, or at least the proletariat of Shanghai, to fully participate in what was hailed as a "proletarian" revolution.

From this point on, the power of the Shanghai party and government apparatus disintegrated rapidly as rebel groups freely roamed the city to organize the working masses. The mass movement grew at a frantic pace and on a vast scale as several working-class organizations, loosely allied with Red Guard groups, competed for popular support and for power, each proclaiming more loudly than the other their loyalty to Chairman Mao and his thought. By the end of the year, the city was roughly divided into two huge and rival coalitions, one led by the original Workers' Headquarters and the other known as the Scarlet Guards, generally thought to be the more "moderate" of the two and also the larger, claiming some 800,000 working-class members. The rivalry erupted into large-scale violence at the end of the year, virtually halting production in the factories and disrupting municipal services. Yet the factional struggles that threatened chaos and civil war in the early days of 1967 soon gave way to a remarkable display of working-class solidarity. And the officials of the old party apparatus, having failed in various attempts to use the Scarlet Guards for their own ends, stood by helplessly observing the rise of the popular movement that was preparing to overthrow them. On January 5, a dozen rebel organizations, headed by the Workers' Headquarters, published the "Message to All the People in Shanghai" in the city's leading newspaper *Wen-hui-pao*, which had been seized by insurgents two days before. The "Message" condemned the divisions within the revolutionary movement (and condemned the Scarlet Guards and party authorities for creating them), called upon the workers to return to the factories, and appealed for the unity of workers, revolutionary students, intellectuals, and cadres. That call for unity received dramatic expression the next day, January 6, when more than a million workers gathered to hold a massive meeting in the central city square (the proceedings were televised to millions of other citizens), where Mayor Ts'ao and other high party officials were denounced, removed from their positions, and forced to make public confessions of their political sins. Over the next few days lesser officials and cadres were similarly humiliated at other public meetings and paraded through the streets wearing placards and dunce caps. The old regime had fallen.

The political and ideological maturity of the Shanghai working class was further demonstrated in the way its members went about restoring order in the huge metropolis where administrative and police organs virtually had ceased functioning and where the economy was in a state of paralysis. One of the last acts of the old bureaucracy, in a desperate attempt to stem the popular revolutionary upsurge, was to expend the financial resources of the city and its factories in an effort to bribe the workers into political passivity. Bonuses, retroactive wage increases, and cash handouts were offered to encourage workers and technicians to leave the factories and leave the city, and attempts were made to organize a general strike for purely economic demands. What later was condemned as "the ill wind of economism" served to gravely compound an already chaotic situation. But in the hectic weeks following the January 6 seizure of power, teams of workers and students managed to reestablish the more or less normal economic and administrative functioning of the city, appealing to workers to return to their jobs and often successfully appealing for them to return the unearned collective funds.

Power was now in the hands of the workers, and for a brief time in Shanghai the much celebrated Cultural Revolution aim to achieve a "great alliance of proletarian revolutionaries" was a reality. But the Shanghai workers were soon to lose the power that they had acquired on their own, or, more precisely, they were to freely surrender it to a "higher authority."

Chang Ch'un-ch'iao had arrived from Peking to head the victorious "January Revolution," which was being hailed throughout the country. His political base was the original Workers' Headquarters, the nucleus of what remained a reasonably unified mass movement. What kept the movement united was the promise that the new order would be built in accordance with the principles of the Marxist model of the Paris Commune, principles loudly proclaimed since the beginning of the Cultural Revolution and, indeed, personally endorsed by Chairman Mao. Factional differences and bickerings continued, but most revolutionary organizations coalesced around Chang's efforts to create a Shanghai Commune. "All power to the Commune" was the slogan heard throughout the city.

The Shanghai People's Commune was formally proclaimed on February 5 and its birth was accompanied by a massive rally of a million workers who came to celebrate "the greatest day in the history of proletarian and revolutionary Shanghai." But the attempt to establish a "proletarian dictatorship" in accordance with the principles Marx set forth in his analysis of the Parisian events of 1871 was flawed from the outset. Whereas the Marxist model demanded a "self-government of the producers" where officials were to be democratically elected and subject to mass supervision and immediate popular recall, the leaders of the Shanghai Commune—Chang Ch'un-ch'iao and his assistant Yao Wen-yuan—were appointed by Peking. Such authority and legitimacy as Chang and Yao possessed derived not from the workers of Shanghai but ultimately from the supreme authority of Chairman Mao. Yet the Commune and its principles had been proclaimed in Shanghai, and, given the opportunity and freedom, the embryonic organization might have functioned and grown to maturity on its own base of popular support and participation.

But such was not to be the case. While the revolutionaries in Shanghai waited for Peking to hail the creation of their Commune with the same measure of enthusiasm that the January Revolution had been celebrated, Mao (if not necessarily all Maoists) now was looking to very different political models. During the month of January, two other "power seizures" had taken place, one in Shansi Province and the other in the city of Harbin, capital of Heilungkiang Province in northern Manchuria. In both cases, a most prominent element in the revolutionary movement had been units of the People's Liberation Army. And in both areas the political outcome of the overthrow of the old provincial party leaders were not communes but rather "revolutionary committees" based on what was to be called the "triple alliance" of mass revolutionary organizations, pro-Maoist Party cadres, and the army—with the last clearly the dominant partner. Within a month, the leaders in Peking were to proclaim the "revolutionary committee" the only appropriate form for the reorganization of political power. In the meantime, nothing was said publicly about the Shanghai Commune. But the decision was conveyed privately to Chang Ch'un-ch'iao and Yao Wen-yuan when Mao summoned them to an audience in Peking in mid-February. Having heard that some Shanghai revolutionaries were demanding the abolition of all "heads," Mao informed Chang and Yao that, "This is extreme anarchism, it is most reactionary.... In reality there will still always be heads." On the Shanghai Commune itself, Mao doubted that its radical principles could be implemented in any other place in the land but Shanghai and also doubted whether it was a form of political power that could exercise the necessary revolutionary vigilance and discipline even in Shanghai: "Communes are too weak when it comes to suppressing counterrevolution. People have come and complained to me that when the Bureau of Public Security arrest people, they go in the front door and out the back." Thus Mao suggested—and a suggestion from the Chairman at the time was no less than a supreme command from on high—that the Shanghai Commune transform itself into a "revolutionary committee."[12] And in what was a prophetic pointer to the future course of the Cultural Revolution, Mao wondered whether the Commune left any place for the party, insisting that China would require the party and its experienced cadres for the foreseeable future.[13]

Upon his return to Shanghai on February 24, Chang Ch'un-ch'iao was faced with the task of explaining to the people of the city why their Commune had ceased to exist, no easy assignment in view of the widely publicized claims of Maoist theorists that Mao had not only inherited but also "developed and enriched" the experience of the Paris Commune, not to speak of Mao's own lavish praise of the Marxist model of proletarian dictatorship. In any event, the Shanghai Commune, after a brief nineteen-day existence, became the "Revolutionary Committee of the Municipality of Shanghai." The decision was made in Peking, not by the workers of Shanghai. Plans to establish communes in other cities immediately were abandoned in favor of the "triple alliance," and the Shanghai Commune itself became a non-event; nowhere is either its birth or its death to be found in official accounts of the "Great Proletarian Cultural Revolution."

More than a change of names was involved in the demise of the Shanghai Commune. It involved an abandonment of principles and the crushing of hopes. For the "revolutionary committees," in Shanghai as elsewhere, were not organs of popular democratic rule but essentially bureaucratic instrumentalities; initially dominated by the army, they eventually were to come under the control of, and merge with, a refashioned but still very Leninist Communist Party.

The events of February 1967 signaled the first of a long series of Maoist retreats from the original aims and promises of the Cultural Revolution. They also revealed that all political power in China ultimately resided in, and was attributed to, one man and his "thought," a phenomenon akin to that once described by Marx as one where the political power of the people "finds its ultimate expression in an Executive power that subjugates the commonweal to its own autocratic will."[14] For the "cult of Mao" had now become so pervasive that the Chairman could decide not only the fate of individuals but determine the fate of mass movements. The Cultural Revolutionary right "to dare to rebel" was not a right inherent in the people but one given them by the authority of the deified Mao, and thus one that could be revoked by him. For the workers of Shanghai, in February of 1967, Mao defined the limits of rebellion and determined its political outcome.

Power Seizures, the Army, and the Phenomenon of the "Ultra-left"

The pattern of events in Shanghai which culminated in the "January Revolution" was repeated elsewhere in China in 1967. But in most other cities and provinces the power of local party organizations was greater and the mass movement was weaker and even more factionalized than in Shanghai, although this by no means lessened the degree of disorder and turmoil. Moreover, the movements to "seize power from below" were now conditoned, if not restrained, by two new factors. First, by late February it clearly had been laid down that the only acceptable political outcome was a revolutionary committee resting on the "triple alliance"; in practice there were to be no more radical experiments with the model of the Paris Commune, even though its principles might still be hailed in theory. Second, on January 23 Lin Piao, on orders from Mao, had instructed the People's Liberation Army to enter the political struggles to support "the revolutionary left" in the drive to "seize power" and to maintain order at the same time.

The decision in favor of military intervention was both momentous and incongruous, for now the army, the most bureaucratic agency of the state apparatus, was called upon to promote what was supposed to be a popular revolutionary movement against bureaucratic elitism. Yet for Mao, if not necessarily for all Maoists, this fateful step perhaps did not appear as inconsistent as it does to later observers—and indeed as it did to many Chinese involved in the battle at the time. Mao probably looked upon an army made up mostly of peasants as a more reliable and certainly a more effective revolutionary force than the urban masses who seemed utterly incapable of self-discipline and unity. Moreover, he always had regarded the army as the main repository of the revolutionary heritage of struggle and egalitarianism. And, thanks to Lin Piao, the PLA had undergone the process of "living ideological indoctrination" in the "thought of Mao Tse-tung" in the years prior to the Cultural Revolution and was therefore, it was thought, fully prepared to play its appointed revolutionary role. These views were not shared by all of the Chairman's followers.

Perhaps the most remarkable aspect of military intervention was not that the army became the arbiter of the struggles of the Cultural Revolution, but that it displayed so great a degree of self-restraint in view of the chaotic situation into which it was thrust and the provocations to which its highest leaders were to be subjected. Mao did not call on the PLA to impose a revolution from above, nor did the army attempt to do so on its own. On the whole, the army remained obedient to the "civilian" authority of Mao and Lin Piao, if not to the Cultural Revolution Group as a whole; it neither rallied to defend the party that was under attack nor attempted any military takeover in the name of "law and order." Yet in a situation where the party had ceased to function as a national political organization and the mass movement was hopelessly divided into rival factions, it was inevitable that political power, at least on the local and provincial levels, would fall into military hands. And as conditions became more chaotic, the army came to play an increasingly prominent role not only in the political but also economic life of the nation. Soldiers entered factories and communes, and it was largely due to the discipline and assistance provided by the PLA that production in both the cities and the countryside was maintained during these turbulent years. Where revolutionary committees were established, it was usually the military that assumed the dominant position in the tripartite alliance, or at least held the balance of power, more often than not siding with the old cadres rather than the more radical representatives of mass organizations. Faced with the dilemma of determining who was "the revolutionary left" among a multitude of groups all claiming to be the true followers of Chairman Mao's thought, the army usually supported the less radical of the rebel organizations in the interests of political and economic stability. Charged with the often conflicting tasks of assisting the revolutionary efforts of the masses and maintaining social and economic order, army commanders usually preferred order.

If military intervention generally served to blunt the radical thrust of the Cultural Revolution, the actions of the PLA were largely in accord with the relatively moderate course Mao (if not all Maoists) was pursuing in the early spring of 1967. Having declared in February that the slogan "doubt everything and overthrow everything" was reactionary, Mao moved to eliminate the more anarchistic tendencies in the movement. Nationwide organizations of contract workers, apprentices, demobilized soldiers, and students who had been sent to the countryside in earlier years—now deemed excessively radical and violent—were branded as "counterrevolutionary" and officially banned. New efforts were made to restrain the activities of Red Guards, if not to remove them from the political scene entirely. Students were urged to return to their schools, which, it was prematurely announced, were to reopen in March. Draconian punishments were decreed for attacks on government offices, seizures of official files, and physical assaults on state and party cadres. In April, a new drive was launched against the already silenced Liu Shao-ch'i, now accused (although still not yet by name) of being a national traitor as well as a capitalist-roader. The purpose was to unify the factionalized movement by "narrowing the target." More significant was the attempt to reestablish the functioning of the state apparatus headed by Chou En-lai, and to a lesser extent, the legitimacy of the party, excepting, of course, those still very large and numerous segments headed by alleged followers of Liu Shao-ch'i. The effort centered on the rehabilitation of party cadres, the overwhelming majority of whom, it was said, were good and loyal revolutionaries, or at least amenable to rectification. Cadres, it increasingly was emphasized, were to be included among "the core of the leadership" of the revolutionary movement and were described as the "backbone of the struggle to seize power." Chou En-lai made Herculean efforts to persuade the mass organizations to end their indiscriminate attacks on cadres and to unite with them in common struggle.

Despite the efforts to unify the mass movement and the presence of the PLA on the political scene, the drive to "seize power" and establish revolutionary committees proved to be a slow and arduous process. Many attempts failed and others were denounced as "false power seizures," cases where existing party committees simply changed their names. At the end of April 1967, apart from Shanghai and Peking,[15] only four of China's twenty-seven provinces and autonomous regions had set up officially approved revolutionary committees: Shansi, Heilungkiang, Kweichow, and Shantung. Elsewhere the old party organizations remained entrenched, besieged by a variety of rebel organizations. The latter, in turn, were in conflict with each other as well as with the army units that had been dispatched to support them. The struggle seemed to have reached a stalemate, and the Cultural Revolution seemed to be grinding to an inconclusive end.

The revolutionary flames soon were reignited by radical Maoist leaders and organizations who later were to be condemned as "ultra-leftists." Hostility to the army grew in the spring of 1967 as local military commanders came down on the side of "order," which in most places meant protecting what remained of the old party machine and preserving the political *status quo*. Popular resentments over the intrusion of the army were exacerbated by a concurrent campaign for the restoration of cadres, orchestrated from Peking by Chou En-lai. The opposition was by no means confined to a few radical extremists, for the whole history of the Cultural Revolution clearly reveals that workers, students, and peasants long had harbored the most bitter feelings against party cadres in general, and not simply against the mere "handful" officially termed "anti-socialist rightists."

Opposition to military intervention and to the resurrection of old cadres meant, of course, an implicit rejection of the revolutionary committees, the now orthodox Maoist political formula. The rejection was more than implicit, for fears that the masses would be excluded from the triple alliance soon were expressed in charges that this in fact was becoming the case. The complaints were not groundless, for most everywhere political power was gravitating into the hands of the army, which in turn increasingly relied on the experienced cadres to maintain administrative order and production.

In May these resentments burst forth against what was called the "blackwind" of the previous months and soon exploded into a frenzy of popular violence against all authority. In Peking, where wallposters denouncing Chou En-lai as the leader of the "red capitalist class" had begun to appear in late April, the leftist attack centered on the state bureaucracy and its ministries, particularly the Ministry of Foreign Affairs. Red Guard organizations conducted a series of raids on its offices, seized and destroyed secret documents in its archives, and demanded the ouster of the foreign minister, the veteran Red Army Marshal Ch'en Yi. From provincial cities there came a growing and increasingly ominous stream of reports of armed struggles between contending mass organizations in factories, schools, and streets. Despite orders from the Cultural Revolution Group in Peking forbidding violent struggles, acts of destruction, illegal arrests, and the seizure of arms from PLA arsenals, the scale and scope of the battles escalated. By July, amidst a background of nationwide violence and chaos, there were new demands to implement the old Maoist call for a "Commune of China."

In an attempt to bring an end to the violence and reconcile the warring factions, high government and military leaders were sent from Peking to critical areas in the provinces to achieve "great revolutionary alliances." A particularly perilous situation existed in Wuhan, a major industrial center and the heart of China's railroad system. From the beginning of July, much of the paralyzed city on the Yangtze had become a battleground for two huge rival mass organizations. One, the "Million Heroes" (made up of some 500,000 skilled industrial workers, state office employees, and militiamen), was supported by the local party organization and by the regional military commander, General Ch'en Tsai-tao, who long had ignored official instructions to refrain from attacking rebel organizations. The other, an alliance of more radical (and younger) workers and student Red Guard organizations, the Wuhan Workers' General Headquarters, was besieged by the Million Heroes, who had been supplied with weapons and troops by General Ch'en. When Ch'en refused to obey orders from Chou En-lai to lift the siege, two of the more prominent members of the Cultural Revolution Group, Wang Li and Hsieh Fu-chih, were dispatched to Wuhan. Wang and Hsieh arrived in Wuhan on July 16 and three days later ordered Ch'en and other local commanders to withdraw their support of the Million Heroes in favor of the Workers' Headquarters and make public self-criticisms of their errors. The response of the Wuhan military leaders was swift; in the early morning hours of July 20, soldiers of the mutinous PLA division arrested the emissaries from Peking. Hsieh, who was Minister of Public Security, was held under house arrest while Wang Li was taken to a military headquarters and brutally beaten. The response from Peking was equally swift when the news reached the capital—and after Chou En-lai failed in an attempt to mediate the dispute, his plane unable to land at an airfield surrounded by hostile troops and tanks. Three infantry divisions and an airborne unit converged on Wuhan, along with navy gunboats sailing up the Yangtze. It was only under the threat of superior military force that Ch'en Tsai-tao capitulated. Wang Li and Hsieh Fu-chih returned to Peking to receive a hero's welcome at a massive rally held at T'ien-an-men Square on July 25. The Wuhan military leaders were arrested and returned to the capital in disgrace. No one could have foreseen that within a few months Wang Li would be removed from the political scene, branded as a "counterrevolutionary," whereas a year later the leader of the mutiny, General Ch'en, would be standing on public podiums alongside the highest leaders of the People's Republic, as if he had been a loyal supporter of the Cultural Revolution all along. It was an ironic turn of events, yet perhaps not out of keeping with the inexorable political logic of the retreat from the principles of the Cultural Revolution that had begun in February.

The Wuhan mutiny raised the specter of civil war, for it revealed that the one apparently cohesive force that remained in the country, the PLA, was something less than a monolithic entity. That specter loomed ominously larger during the critical month of August 1967, as leftist leaders vociferously questioned the revolutionary credentials of the army and rebel masses attacked it physically, thus threatening to bring to the army the same political differences that already had torn the party asunder and had divided the mass movement into a multitude of warring factions. While Chairman Mao remained publicly silent for the time being, Madame Mao did not. Referring to the Wuhan incident, she advised Red Guards to "attack with words, but defend yourselves with weapons."[16] An editorial in the July 31 issue of *Red Flag*, entitled "The Proletariat Must Firmly Grasp the Barrel of the Gun," called for the overthrow of "persons in authority taking the capitalist road" in the army as well as in the party. On August 9, Lin Piao criticized unspecified military commanders for "suppressing the masses," demanded that they make public self-criticisms, and advised them to take "revolutionary rebels" as their teachers.[17] Wang Li and other leaders of the Cultural Revolution Group made public speeches demanding the ouster of the "handful of revisionists" who had usurped power in the army, just as their counterparts had done in the party.

Individual army leaders had been criticized earlier in the Cultural Revolution, not excluding Chu Teh, the "father of the Red Army," who on one occasion was characterized as "a big warlord who has wormed his way into the Party." But this was the first time that leading luminaries of the movement suggested that the model Maoist instrument as a whole, the "pillar of the dictatorship of the proletariat" itself, was suffering from "bourgeois" and "revisionist" infections and therefore should be subjected to the same processes of cultural revolutionary purification as all other organizations and institutions.

In Peking, the new leftist offensive of August, fueled by the passions aroused over the Wuhan affair and the fiery speeches of left-wing leaders, focused more on the central state apparatus than the PLA as such. The Gate of Heavenly Peace Square was occupied for a week by hundreds of thousands of demonstrators demanding that Liu Shao-ch'i be turned over to the masses for public trial. Angry crowds besieged the offices of Chou En-lai, apparently intent on seizing the files of the central committee. And in one of the more spectacular and bizarre episodes of the Cultural Revolution, the Foreign Ministry was actually taken over by rebels for two weeks. Installed as *de facto* foreign minister in place of Ch'en Yi was Yao Teng-shan, the diplomat who had won popular acclaim for his heroics in attempting to defend the Chinese embassy in Jakarta when it had been sacked in April. Chinese foreign policy had been largely dormant since the beginning of the Cultural Revolution, but now a new "revolutionary internationalist" program was proclaimed, based on a literal reading of Lin Piao's 1965 treatise, "Long Live the Victory of People's War." Cables bearing new "revolutionary" instructions flowed from Peking to Chinese embassies abroad; foreign diplomats were harassed in the Chinese capital; and an ultimatum was presented to the British government demanding the release of Communist journalists imprisoned in Hong Kong. The brief era of "proletarian internationalism" in foreign policy culminated—and ended—with the burning of the British Chancery in Peking on August 22.

The functioning of the regular central government in Peking soon was restored, but in other cities and provincial centers the situation was far more serious and difficult. Mass rebel organizations, armed with weapons seized from military depots—and in some cases from convoys of war materials bound for Vietnam—were locked in pitched battles with PLA soldiers throughout much of the country. In some areas, armed peasants marched into cities and towns to attack government buildings. The PLA now not only had to defend itself against the masses who had "dared to rebel," but had to protect, willing or not, such civilian administrations that still functioned in the local areas, whether they were new revolutionary committees or old party organizations. The battles, often bloody and usually inconclusive, were spreading and threatened total economic and political chaos.

In late August China seemed to be hovering on the brink of anarchy. Mao, having returned to Peking from an "inspection tour" of the provinces, was now convinced that to continue the Cultural Revolution as a movement based on the initiative of the masses was to run the risk of plunging the country into a massive and perhaps fatal civil war. He opted for order and, in effect, the end of the Cultural Revolution.

The Thermidor of the Cultural Revolution

On September 5, 1967 the army was instructed to restore order. The masses were ordered to turn in their arms and forbidden to interfere with the mission of the PLA, which was hailed as a "peerless people's army" that was "personally formed and led by our great leader Chairman Mao and commanded by Vice–Supreme Commander Lin Piao." Lest there be any question that the order was definitive, the directive was jointly issued by the Party central committee, the Cultural Revolution Group, the State Council of the central government, and the Central Military Affairs Committee of the PLA—and signed by Mao Tse-tung. The directive was addressed to all mass rebel organizations the Cultural Revolution had produced as well as to all governmental and military organs. The restoration of order under PLA direction was accompanied by efforts to rebuild the party and the reestablishment of the authority of the central state bureaucracy under the leadership of Chou En-lai. The process was protracted and difficult, but it proceeded with an inexorable logic which dictated that the political power that had fallen to the army would eventually pass to a revived and revitalized Leninist party.

The whole process of this "return to normalcy" was decorated with an abundance of revolutionary rhetoric—and the retention of many of the forms, slogans and battle cries of the Cultural Revolution—but it was made abundantly clear that the right of the masses to rebel had been withdrawn. The task of publicly announcing that decision had fallen to Chiang Ch'ing, who took advantage of the occasion to hastily renounce her own past views and leftist comrades, declaring that it was no longer permissible to attack either the army or the government and that even verbal criticisms would be considered counterrevolutionary. Attacks were now to be directed against the "ultra-leftist" plotters with whom she had so recently been intimately associated, but which she now had discovered were really members of "a very typical counterrevolutionary organization" to whose machinations all the factionalism and violence of the summer months were to be attributed.[18]

The message that order was now the order of the day was forcefully conveyed by public executions of alleged instigators of violence. That the army was now inviolable, at least as far as the masses were concerned, was symbolically demonstrated on National Day, October 1, 1967, when most of the old generals and PLA commanders denounced so vehemently earlier in the year stood prominently alongside Mao atop the Gate of Heavenly Peace. That the Red Guards were no longer needed or wanted was made clear two weeks later in a directive ordering the immediate reopening of all schools and universities and ordering the youth to return to their studies. And the demise of the central Cultural Revolution Group itself was signaled in November, when *Red Flag*, the Party theoretical journal which had become the radical voice of the Cultural Revolution, was ordered to suspend publication.

According to later official versions, the chaos of the "hot summer" of 1967 resulted from "plots" hatched by a small group of leaders in Peking who had formed a clandestine organization known as the "May 16 Corps," the name taken from the famous secret circular that had launched the Cultural Revolution and was published on its first anniversary. The "plotters," we are told, playing on the divisions within the revolutionary movement (especially among the gullible Red Guards), instigated the violence for the ultimate purpose of overthrowing the "proletarian head-quarters" of Mao Tse-tung and seizing state power. Once uncovered, they were duly disposed of and variously denounced as "anarchists," "neo-Trotskyists," and "ultra-leftists." But in the Orwellian world of offi-cial mythology, and aided by a bit of dialectical magic, the "ultra-leftists" were converted into counterrevolutionary rightists, who, subsequent in-vestigations presumably revealed, were really tied to Liu Shao-ch'i. "Ultra-left in form, but ultra-right in essence" was the official verdict.[19]

The leaders of the alleged conspiracy turned out to be most of the leading members of the central Cultural Revolution Group, especially those who in the years before and during the Cultural Revolution were most closely identified with Mao Tse-tung. Initially they included such eminently Maoist leaders and theoreticians as Wang Li, Kuan Feng, and Ch'i Pen-yü—and eventually, some years later, even Ch'en Po-ta and Lin Piao.[20]

Revolutionary movements typically produce extremists and radical excesses, and the Cultural Revolution certainly produced more than its fair share. In mid-1967 there was no lack of "cultural revolutionaries" who were literally practicing the slogan Mao had condemned some months earlier—"Doubt everything and overthrow everything." But this nihilistic tendency had been present in the Cultural Revolution from the beginning, from the time of the inception of the Red Guards a year before. More important for understanding the events of the summer of 1967 is another common phenomenon in the history of revolutions: lead-ers who adhere to the original aims and vision of the revolution appear as "extremists" when higher leaders compromise those aims and moder-ate the radical thrust of the movement. For the fact of the matter is that in February Mao had embarked on a more moderate course—perhaps more because of what he perceived to be objective limitations than be-cause of natural inclination—and those who were to be branded as "ultra-leftists," for the most part, were those who did not move as rapidly as the Chairman or who were unwilling to do so. And no less important is the fact that the mass movement that Mao had called into being had acquired a radical life of its own, and much of it was no longer under anyone's control or direction.

To be sure, the Cultural Revolution Group was deeply divided by the spring of 1967, and the divisions at the top no doubt reflected and perpetuated the factionalism that plagued the mass movement below. And it may very well have been the case that the radical faction at the center had loosely organized itself, using the name of "May 16" as sym-bolic of their commitment to the original goals and spirit of the Cultural Revolution. In the streets of Peking in late May, it was observed, there marched young militants calling themselves the "May 16 Armed Corps," and they may well have taken their inspiration (if not necessarily their direction) from the more radical leaders in the capital, including, it might be noted, Mao's wife Chiang Ch'ing, who was particularly noted for her inflammatory speeches to young rebels. But there is no evidence of any organized "plot" to seize state power, much less to overthrow Mao. Even less credible is the view that a few "ultra-radical" leaders in Peking, entirely lacking an organizational structure of any sort, could have provoked and directed the massive violence that appeared virtually everywhere over the vast land during the summer. A far more plausible explanation for the events of the "hot summer" is that they were largely spontaneous reactions, among leaders and rank and file alike, to widespread fears that the promises and ideals of the Cultural Revolution were being betrayed.

The construction of the post–Cultural Revolution order and the preservation of such gains as could be salvaged from the wreckage of the upheaval required both a united leadership at the top and the obedience of the masses below. Neither was easy to achieve. Some of the more prominent of the radical leaders of the Cultural Revolution Group, such as Wang Li and Kuan Feng, were arrested at the end of August. But the counter–Cultural Revolution thrust against the ever reappearing "ultra-left" became an almost permanent purge that continued until virtually all the original leaders of the Cultural Revolution (save Mao himself) were removed from the political scene, for as Mao moved to the right, or at least to the center, most of his disciples found themselves too far to the left.

Not even the highest leaders of the PLA were immune to political purges. In March 1968 it was revealed that Yang Ch'eng-wu, acting chief of staff of the army since the dismissal of Lo Jui-ch'ing in 1965, had been arrested and replaced, along with the commander of the Peking garrison and the political commissar of the air force. Reportedly, Lin Piao personally arrested Yang in the presence of 10,000 Army officers meeting in the Great Hall of the People in Peking, despite the fact that the two men had been the closest of comrades since the days of the Long March. At the time, Lin vaguely explained the affair as a factional dispute within the PLA. It was also rumored that the three generals were involved in a rightist plot against Mao's "proletarian headquarters." More recently we have been told that Yang was really a member of the ubiquitous "ultra-left," that he was involved with the infamous "May 16" group in a plot against Mao, and that his "hidden master" was none other than Lin Piao himself.[21] The latter seems the least plausible of all explanations. It is more likely that Mao had ordered the arrests, fearing that the army was moving too rapidly and acquiring too large a share of power. However that may be, the incident suggested that the army was not necessarily the most stable pillar of "the dictatorship of the proletariat" and thus provided impetus to a campaign, now being quietly promoted by Mao and Chou En-lai, to reestablish the supremacy of the party and the central state apparatus as the most appropriate institutions to guide the country eventually into a new era of consolidation and stability.

While continuing political differences and intrigues among the leaders in Peking hindered the stabilization of the post–Cultural Revolution order, the state of the mass movement posed more formidable barriers. The desired Maoist resolution presupposed a "great alliance" of the mass revolutionary organizations whose members harmoniously and enthusiastically would integrate themselves into the "triple alliance." But there was little real unity among the masses and even less enthusiasm. By the spring of 1968 most of the working class, having grown weary of the strife and struggles of a movement whose goals and meaning they could no longer easily define, turned politically passive, and many of their organizations disintegrated or became dormant. The mood of the urban populace that had begun to set in earlier in the year was noted in Peking in the summer by two American teachers who had perceptively observed the Cultural Revolution:

> a pall hung over the capital city of the revolution. As we took long walks down the back lanes of Peking and rode the buses from here to there, silently observing the people who had learned about revolution by making it, there could be no question that the joy had gone out of the movement. The spirit of adventure had been replaced by a grimness reflected in the faces of a people who still marched behind crimson banners and portraits of the Chairman, but who did so out of habit.[22]

The political activists who remained from what was left of the mass revolutionary organizations remained distrustful of the party cadres and the PLA soldiers with whom they were enjoined to unite. The reconciliation was difficult and more often than not was enforced by the army, which bore the ultimate responsibility for establishing the tripartite revolutionary committees from provinces down to factories and neighborhoods. And some of the more militant elements of the remnant mass movement continued to fight battles of a war that was over. Well into the summer of 1968 old factional disputes flared into sporadic and purposeless outbursts of violence in various areas of the country, particularly between rival Red Guard groups. In Canton the fighting was so intense that the army was forced to impose a dusk-to-dawn curfew in June. But the last battles of the Cultural Revolution were fought where they had begun two years before—on university campuses in Peking. For three months the campuses were turned into bloody battlegrounds by student rebels, partly repeating the factional struggles of the previous summer, partly in inchoate rebellion against the new authoritarian order being imposed from above. Finally, at the end of July, Mao summoned the student leaders to a personal audience and gently informed them (with tears in his eyes, it was reported) that the time had come for the Red Guard movement to pass from the historical scene.[23] Less gently, PLA–directed "Workers' Mao Tse-tung Thought Propaganda Teams" were sent to the campuses to end the fighting and discipline the students. Throughout the country, where Red Guard groups failed to dissolve themselves, they were swiftly crushed by the army, and not without further bloodshed. The death of the Red Guard movement thus came at the hands of the force that had assisted its birth. Many student rebels were dispatched to the countryside to be "reeducated by the poor and lower-middle peasants," while those permitted to remain in school continued their studies under the supervision of soldiers and workers.

Also sent to the countryside—to balance the political ledger, as it were—were hundreds of thousands of party officials and cadres who had been among the more intransigent in their resistance to the Cultural Revolution. Tilling virgin lands and living a spartan life for several years, it was hoped, would cure them of their bureaucratic habits before they were returned to their official posts. The "May Seventh Cadre Schools," as they were called, were to become a prominent feature of Chinese political life in the years after the Cultural Revolution and a celebrated remedy for bureaucratism. At the time, in 1968, the removal of the more conspicuous bureaucrats from the cities was a way to ease tensions between masses and cadres—and to ease the way for the reappearance of a presumably more egalitarian party.

However, before the supremacy of the party could be fully reestablished it was necessary to complete what was called the "phase of broad unity," now the desired political result of the Cultural Revolution. Progress toward unity was measured by the establishment of officially approved provincial revolutionary committees, which in turn were responsible for setting up similar "three-in-one" committees at the district, county, and municipal levels of administration. The process went more slowly than was anticipated, but it was finally completed in September 1968, when revolutionary committees had been established in the southwestern provinces and finally in Sinkiang and Tibet. In all cases, the committees (which presumably united the army, the party, and the masses) were formed largely under the auspices of the army, and indeed most provincial committees were headed by military commanders or PLA political commissars.[24] The masses or, more precisely, those selected as their representatives, participated, but the representatives were drawn less from the vital and spontaneous mass organizations that had come into being during the Culural Revolution than from what could be salvaged from the ruins of the mass movement. The revolutionary committees were hardly the "permanent mass standing organizations" instituted by "a system of general elections" that had been promised in 1966.

With the political situation more or less stabilized, and with the radicalism of the mass movement tamed, the central committee convened its twelfth plenum in October, and did so in customary secrecy. The main business was the formal expulsion of Liu Shao-ch'i from the CCP, a decision publicly announced at the end of the month. Also announced was that Liu had been removed from all his official posts, including that of chairman of the People's Republic (a position he formally owed not to the party but rather to the National People's Congress). Liu's excommunication was based on not only the charge he had followed a "capitalist road" but also the accusation that he was a "renegade, traitor, and scab"—and, moreover, a secret agent of the Kuomintang who had consistently betrayed the party since 1922. The purpose of these absurd accusations, so reminiscent of those leveled at the Old Bolsheviks by Stalin during the purge trials of the 1930s, was painfully obvious—to restore the revolutionary image of a more or less infallible Leninist party. For now it could be suggested to the more gullible that the Liuist deviation was not one that grew naturally within the party, but rather was an alien intrusion. The struggle between the "two lines" could now be reduced to a struggle between revolutionaries and counterrevolutionaries, between a proletarian party that on the whole had maintained its revolutionary purity and enemy agents who had infiltrated its ranks from without.

As the Cultural Revolution waned in 1968, the cult of Mao, paradoxically, grew to more extravagant proportions. The writings of the Chairman were printed and distributed in ever greater volume. Portraits, statues, and plaster busts of Mao increased both in size and number. But whereas in the early days of the Cultural Revolution the cult had inspired, and had flourished on the basis of, the genuine and spontaneous revolutionary fervors of the masses, it now manifested itself more in the form of the established rituals of an orthodox church. It was observed, for example, that "PLA teams fostered group therapy sessions all over Peking, at which members of opposing factions sat together and embroidered portraits of the Chairman."[25] In households there were often "tablets of loyalty" to Mao's thought around which family members gathered to pay reverence. Schoolchildren no longer began the day by saying "good morning" but by chanting, "May Chairman Mao live ten thousand times ten thousand years." Throughout the land exhibition halls were built to chronicle and commemorate the life and deeds of the Chairman, and to them came people on organized pilgrimages to pay homage at what the official press termed "sacred shrines." The test of loyalty to Mao was no longer measured by revolutionary acts inspired by his thought but more by the ability to recite his sayings and by the size of portraits that were carried in the streets or hung in homes. In 1966 the Mao cult had stimulated iconoclasts; in 1968 it produced icons.

Both Mao and the cult were probably essential for the birth of the Cultural Revolution, but the cult reached its strange apogee as the movement was being buried. It was perhaps inevitable that the masses, having surrendered the power they briefly had grasped, should now subordinate themselves to the all-embracing wisdom of one man.

The Cultural Revolution came to its anti-climactic end when the CCP opened its Ninth Congress on April 1, 1969, the first held since 1958 and the first to which observers from foreign Communist parties were not invited. Lin Piao, now at the height of his political power and popular prestige, delivered the main political report, generally assessing the Cultural Revolution and the international situation. At the time, there seemed nothing exceptional about his remarks. The congress' resolutions stressed the need to study "Mao Tsetung Thought" (as it was officially canonized) as the sole guide for correct revolutionary action; the need to emphasize agriculture in economic development; and especially the need to rebuild the party, which now was to be fully restored to its customary vanguard position. Mao underscored the latter point in a talk delivered shortly after the close of the congress, adding that the party should continue to be "rectified" by the masses in the process of its reconstruction. He also added that "after a few years maybe we shall have to carry out another revolution."[26]

The predominant role that the army had assumed in the political life of the People's Republic was reflected in the composition of the new central committee elected at the Ninth Congress. Of the 170 full and 109 alternate members named to the now enlarged body, 40 percent were PLA soldiers while the remainder were equally divided between old party officials and representatives of mass organizations. The five-member standing committee of the politburo, the locus of power, included, in addition to Mao and Lin Piao, Chou En-lai, Ch'en Po-ta and K'ang Sheng. And, perhaps reflecting doubts that even a rebuilt and rectified party would remain faithfully Maoist, it was written into the new Party constitution that "Comrade Lin Piao is Comrade Mao Tsetung's close comrade-in-arms *and successor*."[27] The public communiqué released at the conclusion of the closed-door meeting on April 24 duly condemned Liu Shao-ch'i as a "counterrevolutionary revisionist," hailed the "great victories" of the Great Proletarian Cultural Revolution, and proclaimed that it had been "a congress of unity and a congress of victory."

Yet unity was to prove an elusive goal and the nature of the victory was difficult to define. The Cultural Revolution had begun with a wholesale attack on the Leninist party; it ended with the resurrection of the party in its orthodox form, albeit shorn of Mao's more prominent opponents. In 1966–1967 a massive popular movement had flourished on the basis of the principle that "the masses must liberate themselves"; by 1969 the mass movement had disintegrated and its selected remnants had been absorbed by old bureaucratic apparatuses. What had changed? That question must have been on the minds of many Chinese in the spring of 1969.

Notes

1. Besides Wu Han, the best known satirists were Teng T'o and Liao Mo-sha, both leading officials in the Peking Party Committee. The essays, including Teng's "Special Treatment for Amnesia," originally appeared in leading Peking newspapers, one of which, *Frontline,* was edited by Teng.

2. Mao Tse-tung, "Speech at the Tenth Plenum of the Eighth Central Committee," September 24, 1962, in Stuart R. Schram, ed., *Mao Tse-tung Unrehearsed: Talks and Letters, 1956–71* (Middlesex, England: Penguin, 1974), p. 195.

3. Yao Wen-yuan, "On the New Historical Play 'Dismissal of Hai Jui,'" Shanghai, *Wen-hui-pao,* November 10, 1965. For an English translation, see *The Case of Peng Teh-huai, 1959–68* (Hong Kong: Union Research Institute, 1968), pp. 235–261.

4. Of the members of the group charged with implementing a "cultural revolution," only one, K'ang Sheng managed to politically survive *the* Cultural Revolution.

5. The May 16 Circular was not published until a year later, on May 16, 1967. For an English translation of the text, see *Peking Review,* No. 21, 1967, pp. 6–9.

6. *Decision of the Central Committee of the Chinese Communist Party Concerning the Great Proletarian Cultural Revolution* (Peking: Foreign Languages Press, 1966), pp. 1–13.

7. Mao Tse-tung, "Talk to Leaders of the Centre," July 21, 1966, in Schram, ed., *Mao Tse-tung Unrehearsed,* p. 253.

8. "Long Live the Revolutionary Rebel Spirit of the Proletariat," *Peking Review,* September 9, 1966, pp. 20–21.

9. Mao Tse-tung, "Talk at Central Work Conference," October 25, 1966, in Schram, ed., *Mao Tse-tung Unrehearsed,* p. 271.

10. "A Summary of the Last Two Months of Progress in the Cultural Revolution," *Tung-feng chan-pao* (East Wind Combat News), December 11, 1966, JPRS No. 40488, p. 13.

11. Quoted in Neale Hunter, *Shanghai Journal* (Boston: Beacon Press, 1969), pp. 139–140.

12. Mao Tse-tung, "Talks at Three Meetings with Comrades Chang Ch'un-ch'iao and Yao Wen-yüan," in Schram, ed., *Mao Tse-tung Unrehearsed,* pp. 277–278.

13. SCMP, No. 4147.

14. Karl Marx, *The Eighteenth Brumaire of Louis Bonaparte* (Chicago: Kerr, 1919), p. 146.

15. Peking, Shanghai, and Tientsin are classified as autonomous cities administered directly by the central government rather than by provincial governments.

16. Chiang Ch'ing's celebrated speech was delivered in Peking on July 24 and widely disseminated among rebel groups throughout the country, who promptly proceeded to seize such weapons as they could.

17. Lin Piao's speech was delivered to a meeting of high military and political leaders in Peking. For a translation, see *SCMP* No. 4036, pp. 1–6.

18. For an English translation of the text of Chiang Ch'ing's speech, see *SCMP*, No. 4069, pp. 1–9.

19. For a rendition of the official version, see William Hinton, *Turning Point in China* (New York: Monthly Review Press, 1972), especially pp. 71–78.

20. The fall of Ch'en Po-ta in 1970 and of Lin Piao in 1971 is discussed in Chapter 20.

21. The official version of the still rather mysterious episode—at least the version of 1972—is dutifully recited in Hinton, *Turning Point in China*, pp. 76–77 and footnote pp. 39–40. The mystery was not unraveled when Yang Ch'eng-wu reappeared on the military and political scene after the fall and death of Lin Piao in 1971.

22. David Milton and Nancy Dall Milton, *The Wind Will Not Subside: Years in Revolutionary China—1964–1969* (New York: Pantheon Books, 1976), p. 330.

23. The text of the tape-recorded talk, "Dialogue with the Capital Red Guards," widely distributed in China at the time, is translated in *JPRS* document No. 61269-2, February 20, 1974.

24. Civilian leaders chaired revolutionary committees only in the provinces of Hopei and Shensi.

25. Milton, *The Wind Will Not Subside,* p. 335.

26. Mao Tse-tung, "Talk at the First Plenum of the Ninth Central Committee of the Chinese Communist Party," April 28, 1969, in Schram, ed., *Mao Tse-tung Unrehearsed,* pp. 282–289.

27. "The Constitution of the Communist Party of China" (adopted April 14, 1969), text in *Peking Review*, April 30, 1969. (italics added).

19

Social Results of the Cultural Revolution

IN 1969 IT APPEARED that the Cultural Revolution had come full circle, returning the People's Republic to its pre–Cultural Revolution starting point. Political power resided where it had been three years before—in the closely intertwined trinity of party, army and state bureaucracy. The party was being rebuilt on its traditional Leninist foundations and was being restored to its old preeminence. To be sure, new revolutionary committees had come into being at all levels of political administration and economic life, and, while as an organizational innovation they were by no means insignificant, it took little political foresight in 1969 to know that such committees soon would become instruments to carry out policies decided upon within the councils of the party, whose supreme authority was now clearly being reestablished.

Yet the Cultural Revolution did bring important changes in the social character and political climate of life in China, even if not so much in its formal institutions. One change that was immediately apparent in 1969 was that the reins of political power were firmly in Maoist hands. More precisely, it should be said, they were in the personal hands of Mao in large measure, for many of the most eminent "Maoists" had fallen by the wayside in the course of the upheaval, and others were soon to follow them to political oblivion. That power now rested with Mao, in any event, was an elemental political fact and one with enormous social consequences in an historical situation where political power was so crucial in determining the direction of social development. And the power that Mao derived from the Cultural Revolution was employed to bring about far-reaching social changes in the late 1960s and the early years of the new decade. The changes were not as revolutionary as they have been officially advertised. They do not represent the victory of "socialism" over "capitalism," have not brought about a fundamental transformation in the social division of labor, and have not given rise to a new system of social relationships, as we have been told by both Chinese and foreign ideologists.[1] But the changes were important, nevertheless, vitally affecting the lives of the vast majority of the Chinese people, even though the ultimate social results cannot yet be predicted. The Cultural Revolution delivered far less than its leaders originally promised and its remaining leaders claim, but the turbulent three years that make up its history cannot be dismissed as simply another case of "plus ça change, plus c'est la même chose."

The Peasantry and the Relationship between Town and Countryside

The Cultural Revolution was an eminently urban movement. Its great political battles were fought in the cities and its main revolutionary actors were urban workers, students, and intellectuals. But, paradoxically, most of the social gains it yielded were to go to the countryside.

During the years that the cities were in turmoil, the countryside remained politically quiescent for the most part. Villages on the outskirts of cities sometimes were drawn into the struggles of the Cultural Revolution. Old party organizations and new rebel groups both attempted to recruit peasants to participate in the urban battles. In the relatively few cases in which peasants acted on their own, they did so for mostly conservative and "economist" ends, marching into the cities and towns to demand an extension of private family plots and free markets. But the vast majority of the peasantry never became directly involved in the Cultural Revolution. It was a situation in keeping with the desires of the leaders in Peking, whose policy was to insulate the countryside from the urban battles. Red Guards were forbidden to enter the villages, and although the prohibition was not always heeded, the student radicals rarely found peasant audiences responsive to revolutionary appeals. Directives issued from Peking, to be sure, called for poor peasants to wage their own "class struggle" and to struggle against the "four olds"; but above all the directives emphasized the need to maintain and increase productivity. For, while temporary disruptions in the factories could be tolerated, this clearly was not the case with agriculture. When token forces of PLA soldiers were sent to the countryside in the summer of 1967 to "aid agriculture" and assist the "poor and lower-middle peasants," they found that many villagers had never heard of the Cultural Revolution, while most of the remainder were rather indifferent to the battles being waged in the urban areas. The task of the soldiers, in any event, was less to promote class struggle than to ensure that such struggles as there were did not hinder production.

Only when the Cultural Revolution was waning and dying in the cities was the movement extended to the countryside. There was a struggle between the "two lines" in the villages, but it was a rather benign one, largely confined to ideological campaigns against Liu Shao-ch'i and the organization of sessions for the study of the thoughts of Mao. For once the Maoist line was victorious on the basis of the great urban battles, the Liuist line could be defeated in the rural areas without any great political struggles.

Thus the social transformation of the countryside proceeded slowly and systematically, and without the utopian revolutionary fervors that had characterized the Great Leap Forward campaign. But many of the abandoned programs of the Great Leap were reintroduced in more moderate fashion and many of the Socialist Education Movement policies were finally implemented. The process typically began, the impetus often provided from above by PLA soldiers, with the revival of the poor-peasant associations and the formation of revolutionary committees to administer the communes, brigades, and production teams. The revolutionary committees—composed of poor and middle peasants, cadres, and demobilized soldiers or members of the militia (rather than representatives of the PLA as such)—replaced the old party-controlled management committees. However, the long-term significance of these presumably democratic institutional changes has become increasingly problematic. With the reestablishment of the party apparatus in the years since 1969, it would seem to be the general case that local party committees have overshadowed the revolutionary committees. Indeed, the membership of the two are usually identical; more often than not, the secretary of the party committee is also the chairman of the equivalent revolutionary committee. Moreover, since the early 1970s it has been reported that the peasants' associations convene only if called upon to do so by the party committees.[2] Nevertheless, the changes are by no means insignificant. By all accounts, the peasant masses, and particularly the poorer peasants, have a far greater voice in the making of local economic and social decisions than they did before the Cultural Revolution. And cadres and officials, tempered and sometimes humiliated during the upheaval, perhaps are more responsive to the masses than they had been and adhere more closely to the principles of the "mass line." The Cultural Revolution certainly did not result in peasant control over the institutions that govern their lives, but it has permitted a far greater degree of mass participation and popular initiative in the socioeconomic life of the countryside.

At the same time, effective measures were taken to halt the "spontaneous tendencies toward capitalism" which were developing so rapidly in the early 1960s. The limitation of private plots to 5 percent of the area under cultivation is the rule that appears to be generally enforced. Free markets for privately produced goods remain but are counterbalanced by strong political and ideological pressures for the sale of such products to state commercial organizations. And perhaps most beneficial to the great majority of peasants has been the apparent elimination of cadre corruption in the allocation of workpoints for collective labor, practices that were fostering greater socioeconomic inequalities in the years prior to the Cultural Revolution. But the workpoint system remains the same, resting on the socialist principle (at least ideally) of "to each according to his labor," perhaps modified in some cases by an emphasis on moral and political incentives. Moreover, the responsibility for determining workpoints and income has remained with the production team. Experiments in 1969 to make brigades and communes "the unit of account," which presumably would bring greater equality by amalgamating teams of unequal wealth, proved abortive and since have been denounced as a form of "ultra-leftism."

The realities of rural life are far different from the principles presumably governing the much publicized Tachai brigade, which epitomizes the higher Maoist ideal of the total triumph of moral over material incentives. Here, in a remote and relatively barren area of Shansi province, it is said that a group of self-reliant and selfless peasants spontaneously organized and built a model agrarian community from the fruits of the earth. Rejecting private plots from the outset, they evolved a new system of collective work and distribution inspired by the teachings of Mao. Although the social product is not divided in accordance with the communist principle of "to each according to his need," distribution is collectively determined, based on such criteria as political consciousness, honesty, and a spirit of dedication to work performed for the good of the community. The Tachai experiment first was set forward as a model by Mao in 1964, and post–Cultural Revolution campaigns to emulate the example no doubt have had their effect on peasants elsewhere, perhaps promoting more collectivistic attitudes and depreciating the importance attached to private plots. But Tachai remains a model, the example of the spartan and egalitarian social organization that Maoists believe Chinese rural life ought to be, not what it really is or necessarily is becoming. Indeed, in recent years calls for the total abolition of private plots and the abolition of the system of payment according to the amount of work done have been condemned as manifestations of the "ultra-left" line in the countryside.

Certainly the most striking and probably the most historically significant social result of the Cultural Revolution has been the emergence of a new relationship between town and countryside. This has been effected by several innovative policies which have involved a substantial shift of resources from the cities to the rural areas. One such policy, whose implications for the present and future of Chinese social development hardly can be overestimated, has been the massive revival of programs for rural industrialization.

The industrialization of the countryside was announced as one of the goals of the Cultural Revolution at the outset of the movement. In a May 7, 1966 letter to Lin Piao, Mao wrote: "While the main task of the peasants in the communes is agriculture . . . they should at the same time study military affairs, politics and culture, [and] where conditions permit, they should collectively run small plants. . . ."[3] The goal was not a new one. Many local rural industries were established during the Great Leap Forward campaign, but most proved abortive or atrophied, and the effort largely was abandoned. In the aftermath of the Cultural Revolution, the program was revived and since has thrived as one of the principal features of the Maoist developmental strategy. Its aims are both social and economic: social, insofar as it serves to lessen inequalities between urban and rural areas in the short term and holds the long-term promise of abolishing the distinction between town and countryside; and economic, insofar as it is a program that utilizes local labor and resources that otherwise would go to waste, thus contributing both to rural development and the national economy in general.

The major purpose of developing small and medium-sized industrial enterprises in the countryside, official publications emphasize, is to promote agricultural production. The purpose is served in many forms: the production and repair of farm machinery and tools; the manufacture of chemical fertilizers; the establishment of local industries for processing locally produced agricultural products for the market; and the establishment of a network of small scientific–technical institutes for the development and popularization of improved seeds and agricultural techniques. By the early 1970s, most of China's rapidly growing output of farm machinery and chemical fertilizer was being produced by local rural industries—and in a fashion eminently well suited to meet widely different local conditions and needs. These innovative achievements, together with scientific improvements, are largely responsible for the steady increases in agricultural productivity and in yields per acre that China has enjoyed in recent years.

But rural industries are by no means confined to production strictly in support of agriculture. Many small- and medium-sized factories produce cement, pig iron and steel, construction materials, electricity, chemicals, pharmaceuticals, and a vast variety of small consumer products. Indeed, it is no longer untypical for a single county (*hsien*) to have more than a hundred such factories producing many hundreds of different products. By initially taking low-level and intermediate technologies which can be learned relatively quickly and are adaptable to local conditions, rural industries have grown and flourished on the basis of the utilization of the vast surplus labor power of the peasantry and the particular (and hitherto largely untapped) raw materials in local areas. The results have been a significant amelioration of the chronic problem of rural underemployment; the transformation of many peasants into full or part-time industrial workers; a substantial increase in the purchasing power of the rural inhabitants; and the generation of new capital for further investments in both rural industry and agriculture.

The cities have provided the countryside with the essential technology and technicians for the development of the new rural industries.[4] But the rural enterprises are not under the control of urban political and economic structures. Rather, and this is one of their essential and unique features, they are managed locally by brigades, communes, and *hsien* administrations that utilize local human and natural resources to the best advantage of the local community. The program of rural industrialization has been one of the principal factors in the regeneration of the people's communes, which have reemerged as vital socioeconomic organizations in the years since the Cultural Revolution. Furthermore, the rural industries themselves have become mini-technological centers, disseminating scientific knowledge and technical skills to surrounding agricultural areas.

The Chinese countryside has thus achieved a remarkably high degree of self-sufficiency. On the basis of the technology and capital that has been extracted from the cities, the rural areas are now far less dependent on overpriced urban goods and materials than in earlier years. Wages in rural industries, and income in the countryside in general, remain far lower than in the cities, but the gap is narrowing and the age-old exploitation of the countryside by the towns has been greatly mitigated, even though not eliminated. Indeed, China may well be experiencing an unprecedented historical phenomenon: rapid industrialization that does not entail rapid urbanization. For while the modern capital-intensive industries of the large cities continue to grow, the population of the cities do not. The development of the urban economy has been accompanied by programs to send millions of underemployed and unemployed urbanites to the countryside where their labor potential might be more efficiently utilized. As a result, the population of the large cities in the years since the Cultural Revolution appears to have been reduced, or at least stabilized, and the drive to industrialize the countryside appears to be gathering momentum. In general, the dominant socio-economic tendencies of the post–Cultural Revolution era are largely in accord with the dictum Mao set forth in 1961:

> Don't crowd into the cities. Vigorously develop industry in the countryside and turn peasants into workers on the spot. This is a very important question of policy; and that is that rural living standards must not be lower than in the cities. They can be more or less the same or slightly higher than in the cities. Every commune must have its own

economic center and its own institutions of higher learning to bring up its own intellectuals. Only in this way can we truly resolve the problem of excessive population in the rural areas.[5]

The Cultural Revolution also has resulted in a significant shift of resources, and a very large shift of emphases, from the cities to the countryside in two other vitally important areas of Chinese life—medical care and education. In 1965 Mao Tse-tung, complaining that doctors were being trained "only for the benefit of the cities" in a country where the vast majority of the population lived in the rural areas, proposed some radical measures to remedy the situation:

> In medical education there is no need to accept only higher middle school graduates. . . . It will be enough to give three years [of medical training] to graduates from higher primary schools. They would then study and raise their standards mainly through practice. If this kind of doctor is sent down to the countryside, even if they haven't much talent, they would be better than quacks and witch doctors, and the villages would be better able to afford to keep them.

He also suggested a greater emphasis be put on preventive medicine and on the treatment of "commonly seen, frequently occurring and widespread diseases" rather than the study of what he called "rare, profound, and difficult diseases at the so-called pinnacle of science." And he concluded, "We should leave behind in the city a few of the less able doctors who graduated one or two years ago, and the others should all go into the countryside. . . . In medical and health work put the emphasis on the countryside!"[6]

The policies pursued since 1969 have followed these proposals, by and large. When medical schools resumed normal functioning after the disruptions of the Cultural Revolution, the program of formal study was reduced from six to three years in order to graduate doctors to meet immediate needs, and the curriculum revised to deal with the problems that, as Mao had put it, "the masses most need solutions." The new classes admitted for study in 1971 included a far greater number of students from the rural areas, many of them younger "barefoot" doctors who lacked formal education but who possessed a wealth of practical knowledge and experience. The entire national health-care system was radically decentralized, with urban hospitals and medical schools establishing clinics and local teaching institutes on the rural communes and providing doctors to staff them. More mobile medical teams were dispatched to the countryside by urban medical centers and the PLA (which has its own system of medical schools and hospitals), and all city medical personnel were required to serve on such teams or at commune medical centers on a rotating basis. In 1969 the training program of barefoot doctors was greatly accelerated and systematized. Today over a million such paramedics (the number having increased more than fourfold since 1965) are engaged in preventive medicine; providing health education and birth-control information and devices; and treating common illnesses while referring more seriously ill patients to commune or city hospitals. After a six-month period of training by professional doctors in commune or town hospitals, the barefoot doctors return to the local community that selected them for training in the first place and are paid as ordinary peasants on the prevailing work-point system, usually supplementing their medical duties with agricultural work. Periodically, they have the opportunity to receive more advanced and specialized training at professional centers and then again return to the rural community.

The financing of the new, and still evolving, rural health care system is marked by considerable local variations. On some communes, cooperative medical plans have been established, covering the costs of most services; members pay a nominal annual premium of one to two yuan (forty to eighty cents), supplemented by contributions from collective commune, brigade, or production team funds. Elsewhere, the individual "fee-for-service" system remains, although the fees are low and often paid from commune or brigade collective welfare funds. The construction of rural hospitals and clinics has been financed by the state in some areas, and by communes in others. The general emphasis in financing is on local self-support and self-reliance, but central government support has been essential for developing a viable rural health-care system. Professional medical personnel working in rural areas, for example, are on state salaries, the mobile medical teams are state financed, and the costs of training barefoot doctors are largely borne by the state. In all, this has involved a considerable transfer of resources from urban to rural areas, although, by all accounts, the level of medical services in the cities remains far higher than in the countryside.

The radical restructuring of the educational system during and after the Cultural Revolution has benefited the countryside much in the same fashion as the reforms in the realm of health care. The deficiencies and inequities in the system that prevailed in the years prior to 1966 were glaring and growing. Educational resources were concentrated in the urban areas, not only in universities and middle-schools but in the quantity and quality of primary schools as well. Entrance exams and a grading system based upon formal academic qualifications and achievements, the enforcement of rigid age limits for attendance, and the imposition of tuition fees, severely limited educational opportunities for the urban poor and even more so for rural youth. In very large measure, the system and the content of the education it imparted was oriented to train students for professional and official careers in the cities, and, intentionally or not, it served to perpetuate the privileges of urban elites. Moreover, the system was both costly and inefficient. Universities produced an abundance of specialized graduates for already overstaffed government and urban industrial bureaus, but few with the requisite technological skills so much needed in the countryside. The universities and middle–schools were graduating a good many frustrated youth unable to obtain positions in the cities. And under the prevailing party *hsia-fang* system, the less academically promising students (most of whom came from worker and peasant families) were sent off to the villages where they neither wished to go nor where they had much to contribute.

The educational system had come under strong criticism in the years prior to 1966. The severest critic was Mao Tse-tung, who in 1964 concluded that "the present method of education ruins talent and ruins youth." He condemned the prevailing school curriculum and methods of teaching and examination, which he described as "exceedingly destructive of people." He advocated that the period of formal schooling be shortened and that a new system based on "the union of education and productive labor" replace the old system of book learning divorced from real life. Mao emphasized his long-held belief that the best and most creative form of education is that which comes from self-teaching in the course of practice. To support the latter point, he novelly converted Confucius into a poor peasant, an "all-round" man, and even an early practitioner of the mass line:

> Confucius was from a poor peasant family; he herded sheep, and never attended middle school or university either. He was a musician, he did all sorts of things. . . . He may also have been an accountant. He could play the *ch'in* [lute] and drive a chariot, ride a horse and shoot with bow and arrow. He produced seventy-two sages, such as Yen Hui and Tseng-tzu, and he had 3,000 disciples. In his youth, he came from the masses, and understood something of the suffering of the masses.[7]

But significant educational reforms did not come until the Cultural Revolution destroyed the established party apparatus, which had controlled the schools. When schools reopened, after having largely ceased to function during the 1966–1967 academic year (and for longer periods of time in the case of many areas and institutions), they did so in accordance with new Maoist educational policies. Certainly the most striking feature of those policies was the expansion and development of education in the rural areas. State aid to relatively well-off districts was reduced (and sometimes eliminated), as was the educational administrative staff and the number of full-time teachers; and funds were redirected to the poorer areas, primarily to the countryside and particularly to its most backward parts. While local self-reliance is proclaimed as the guiding principle in education, as in most other areas of social and economic life, state financial aid nonetheless remains a critical factor in determining how and where education is provided. The new policies have placed an absolute priority on the development of primary schools—and since primary education was already universal in the cities, the effect has been to provide at least five years of primary school education in even the more remote rural areas. Whereas prior to the Cultural Revolution rural schools were administered by *hsien* governments in accordance with standardized national policies, the new policies favor decentralization and a large measure of local community control. Primary schools are now generally managed by production brigades and middle-schools by communes, thus allowing the peasants a greater voice in selecting teachers and teaching materials, in recommending students for admission to middle-schools and universities, and in refashioning the curriculum to fit particular local economic needs.[8] In addition, tuition fees, entrance examinations, and age limits for student attendance have been abolished. Many of the spare-time and work-study educational programs introduced during the Great Leap Forward were revived and have become an established feature of rural life. Changes in admissions criteria and curricula in middle-schools and universities have enhanced opportunities in higher education for rural youth. For admission to universities, entrance examinations have been downgraded in favor of a system of recommendation from local production units and selection on the basis of political criteria as well as academic ability, with priority given to poorer peasants, workers, soldiers, and lower-level cadres. University students are admitted only after having completed several years of productive labor in industry or agriculture and are expected to return to work in their home areas after graduation.

Universities were slower to recover from the effects of the Cultural Revolution. Emptied of their students at the end of the upheaval, they began to resume functioning on only a limited basis in the years 1970–1972. By the mid-1970s, university enrollments were only about one-third of what they were a decade before, and reports from virtually all foreign visitors suggest that the campuses are not only politically quiescent but largely devoid of intellectual life and in a state of academic semi-paralysis. With the notable exception of medical schools, the government apparently does not deem it urgent to remedy the languor. Official statements calmly report that the universities are undergoing a long-term process of experimentation and reform. In the meantime, the lifelessness of the urban universities stands in striking contrast to the vigor with which the new rural education programs are being pursued.

The gap between the cities and the countryside in educational opportunities and facilities remains wide, as it does in most other areas of life, but it is a narrowing gap and it would not be going too far to say that the Cultural Revolution has yielded what several observers have termed "a policy of positive discrimination . . . to ensure that those who are the most deprived get their share."[9]

The Working Class and the Division of Labor in Industry

If the Cultural Revolution brought substantial socioeconomic benefits to the peasantry, and perhaps the beginnings of a fundamental change in the relationship between town and countryside, it brought only relatively minor gains for the urban workers who had been principal actors in the revolutionary dramas of 1966–1968. There are, to be sure, official Maoist claims (echoed by several eminent "neo-Maoist" foreign observers), that the Cultural Revolution resulted in the introduction of a new system of social relations and a revolutionary transformation in the industrial division of labor, changes that presumably are finding expression in what one writer has termed "the gradual elimination of the distinction between performance tasks and administrative tasks [and] between manual labor and intellectual labor."[10] Evidence to support these rather grandiose claims is lacking, and recent tendencies suggest that the basic structure of productive relationships in the factories remains much the same as it was in the years prior to 1966.

During the Cultural Revolution there was a wholesale attack against the existing system of industrial organization launched by rebel workers' groups and sometimes supported by the more radical leaders in Peking. Demands were heard for the immediate producers to assume effective control over the means of production; for the elimination of wage differentials and bonuses in favor of a more or less egalitarian system of remuneration; for the abolition of the system of temporary and contract workers; for freedom for workers to work in factories and enterprises of their own choosing; and for the abolition of the party-controlled trade unions.

These demands did not go wholly unheeded in the new industrial policies pursued after the Cultural Revolution. The trade union bureaucracy, having collapsed along with the disintegration of local party organizations between 1966 and 1968, was formally abolished along with the central Ministry of Labor. Individual bonuses and piecework rate wages were eliminated as part of a general policy that aimed to establish the primacy of moral–political incentives over material ones. The bureaucratic and hierarchical character of enterprises was mitigated by reductions in administrative personnel and the abolition of "unreasonable rules" governing work organization and factory operations—the "10,000 rules" which proliferated over the years and which were attributed to the bureaucratic practices of the Liuist regime. Attempts to reduce the status and functional differences between workers and administrators, and between manual and mental labor, were implemented through the revival of the old revolutionary tradition of cadre participation in productive labor and new forms of worker participation in management. Whereas administrative cadres and technicians were instructed to spend at least a third of their time on the factory benches, elected workers' management teams were to play a role in planning and decision-making at basic-level production units as well as oversee managerial practices in general. The central responsibilities for managing enterprises were lodged in factory revolutionary committees (based on the "three-in-one" combination of workers' representatives, cadres, and soldiers) that replaced the old one-man management system.

But many of these innovations either proved abortive or were partially reversed in the early 1970s, or were far less than they seemed to be. And the more fundamental demands that emerged from the Cultural Revolution were either ignored or denounced as "ultra-leftist." Indeed, the most striking feature of industrial organization in the post–Cultural Revolution era is not the changes introduced but what has remained the same. The strict external controls over the movement of laborers—more stringent than those ever practiced in the Soviet Union—remain in force. The policy is justified on the grounds that it is essential to control peasant migrations to the cities, while the notion of freedom of job choice is regarded as a Liuist heresy.[11] The highly exploitive system of temporary and contract workers, who constitute about 35 percent of the non-agricultural work force, has been maintained, despite the fact that it was widely denounced as a particularly pernicious capitalist form of exploitation during the Cultural Revolution and the expansion of the system in the early 1960s was attributed to the "capitalist" policies promoted by Liu Shao-ch'i. The basic wage system has remained intact, mitigated only by the elimination of individual bonuses and prizes (some of which, in fact, had been abolished prior to 1966) and politico-ideological campaigns denouncing monetary incentives and celebrating the moral virtues of selfless and collectivistic work in behalf of the people. Salary differentials for employees in state enterprises are approximately the same as before the Cultural Revolution, with a national 8-grade wage system for factory workers ranging from 30 to 108 yuan per month (excluding apprentices and temporary and contract workers whose wages fall below the minimum), a 15-grade system for technicians, and a 24-grade system for administrative cadres. In 1972 at a model factory in Peking, for example, workers' wages ranged from 30 to 102 yuan, with an average of 54 yuan, whereas the average for technicians, engineers, and cadres was about 150 yuan.[12] Proposals for a more egalitarian restructuring of the wage system are officially condemned as a form of "ultra-leftism."

Moreover, the drive to reestablish labor discipline in the factories after the disruptions of the Cultural Revolution (particularly among the younger workers who had been the most politically active), was followed in the early 1970s by the gradual revival of many of the old factory rules

and regulations previously abolished and by a growing emphasis on specialist administrators and technical criteria.[13] Radical critiques of prevailing factory work regulations are now considered to be manifestations of
the unbiquitous "ultra-left line."[14] Even the demise of the trade unions has
proved to be temporary. By mid-1973, new union organizations had
emerged on the provincial level,[15] replacing the "workers' representative
congresses" organized during the Cultural Revolution, and the reappearance of a national federation has followed. It remains to be seen whether
the functions of the new trade unions will be significantly different from
the old ones.

However, crucial for measuring changes in industrial organization is
the question of the nature and role of the factory revolutionary committees. The revolutionary committees, after all, are hailed as the major
organizational achievement of the Cultural Revolution and the main
institutions for the working masses to participate in the making of economic and political decisions. Here the obvious and essential fact is that
factory revolutionary committees have come under the effective control
of the party. With the 1969 decision to rebuild the party, the reestablishment of the authority of provincial and municipal party organizations
was quickly followed by the reestablishment of party committees in the
factories. It was clear in 1969—and it has become even clearer since—
that factory revolutionary committees would be subordinated to factory
party committees, which, in turn, are ultimately responsible to higher
levels of the party. The majority of the members of factory revolutionary
committees are party members (who are subject to the discipline of the
party) and there is considerable overlapping in the membership of the
two committees. It is almost invariably the case that the secretary of the
party committee is also the head of the revolutionary committee and,
simultaneously, the director of the factory as well. That the power to
make economic and managerial decisions resides, in the final analysis, in
the party committees, and that the revolutionary committees are instruments to carry out those decisions, are matters that are as much emphasized in official theory as they are apparent in fact. As Charles Bettelheim
approvingly notes: "The revolutionary committee is an administrative
body under the political leadership of the factory party committee and
is in charge of the implementation of established policy." And, lest the
point be lost, he adds, "In every factory the revolutionary committee
implements the revolutionary line as defined by the party committee."[16]

It may well be the case that the revolutionary committees, which
continue to exist (albeit now largely as appendages of the party), provide an important institutional means through which workers are able
to express their views and grievances—and even perhaps express some
of the more egalitarian ideals of the Cultural Revolution. It is probably
true, as many foreign visitors' reports suggest, that Chinese factories are

now characterized by a more collectivistic spirit conducive to experimentation, innovation, and participation on the part of rank-and-file workers. It is no doubt true that administrative and managerial cadres, having gone through the trials of the Cultural Revolution, have abandoned many of their more bureaucratic habits and are now more inclined to consult workers in a more meaningful fashion than in the years before the great upheaval. And there certainly is at least symbolic significance in the fact that administrators and technicians leave their desks and engage in productive labor. But consultation, participation, and a collectivistic spirit are no substitutes for producers' control over the productive process. And it seems abundantly clear that control over and within the factories resides ultimately with the party committee and the factory director, just as it did in the years prior to the Cultural Revolution. The factory director (or the chairman of the revolutionary committee, if one prefers) who periodically descends to work on the factory bench (and who even listens to the views of the workers while performing the ritual) still remains the director. In the end he is less responsible to the workers he directs than to the state and party apparatus that employs him and of which he is an integral part. A comment made to Joan Robinson, when the famed economist visited the People's Republic in 1972, perhaps captures the essence of the matter: "As one director said with a wry smile: 'The achievements of our enterprise are due to collective work, but if anything goes wrong, it is my responsibility.' "[17]

In China, as elsewhere, collective work is not yet under collective control. There may be a new climate in Chinese factories, but the basic structure of productive relationships remains the same. The claim that the Cultural Revolution wrought a fundamental change in the division of labor will not stand the test of serious scrutiny.

The Cultural Revolution thus had the ironical result of yielding the most social benefits to those who had been the least politically involved. The urban student radicals who spearheaded the movement were, at the end, shipped off to the countryside and removed from the political scene. For the urban workers, who manned the battalions of "revolutionary masses," things have remained much the same. The real beneficiaries were the masses of poor peasants who had been on the political sidelines. Perhaps it was only a matter of elemental historical justice. In 1949 the cities and the politically passive urban proletariat were liberated by peasants who had won the crucial battles in the countryside. Since 1969 the countryside has reaped most of the socio-economic fruits of the political battles fought in the cities. It was, in many respects, an eminently Maoist resolution.

Political Power and Social Classes: The Dominance of State over Society

The great failing of the Great Proletarian Cultural Revolution was not that it did not bring fundamental changes in the social division of labor. Under prevailing conditions of economic scarcity, any attempt radically to transform the existing division of labor and abolish all class distinctions surely would have resulted in economic chaos. The real failure of the Cultural Revolution was that it did not produce popular and democratic political institutions that might have permitted the working masses to acquire control over the means of production and eventually, as they developed modern productive forces, bring about their own socio-economic emancipation and the emancipation of society as a whole.

At the beginning, the Cultural Revolution seemed to promise fundamental political changes. The "sixteen points" of August 1966 had called for the establishment of "permanent, standing mass organizations" as "organs of power" at all levels of political, social, and economic life and, moreover, for the institution of "a system of general elections like that of the Paris Commune." At the same time, Mao himself had predicted that China would soon see the emergence of a "wholly new form of state power" and implied that it would be organized in accordance with the principles of the Marxist model of the Commune. But the history of the Cultural Revolution was in part a history of retreats from these socialist ideals. The retreat began with Mao's rejection of the Shanghai Commune in February 1967 in favor of military-dominated revolutionary committees and concluded in 1969 with the restoration of the authority of the party, which soon turned the revolutionary committees into bureaucratic organs to carry out its policies. Whatever may have been Mao's intentions at the beginning of the Cultural Revolution, in the end he settled for the reestablishment of a presumably ideologically rectified party and a presumably reformed state bureaucracy.

The failure of the Cultural Revolution to produce new political institutions is particularly striking in view of the Maoist emphasis that it is precisely the political superstructure that is the crucial arena for the struggle between "socialism" and "capitalism." Maoists began the Cultural Revolution with the assumption that the existing party–state apparatus was leading China on the road back to capitalism. The assumption was based on two propositions. The first was that officials in the upper echelons of the party bureaucracy, by virtue of their power and prestige in the state apparatus, were acquiring material privileges and exploiting society as a whole; in effect they were becoming a functional bourgeoisie, albeit one whose privileges derived from political power rather than from property. The Cultural Revolution attacks against "the bourgeoisie" were of course directed not primarily at the remnants of the old national bourgeoisie—which lingered on only in the form of a small and dwindling number of elderly pensioners collecting paltry dividends on state bonds —but rather against what Mao called "the bureaucratic class." The second proposition was that an entrenched bureaucracy had acquired a vested interest in preserving the social order over which it ruled and from which it derived its privileged position, and thus was opposed to radical social changes and willing to tolerate (and perhaps even promote) capitalist forms of socio-economic relations and ideologies in society at large.

Yet the end result of the Cultural Revolution was the restoration of the very political structure that presumably is the main source for the forces that lead a socialist society on the road back to capitalism. To be sure, the political structure underwent reforms in the wake of the Cultural Revolution, but the changes do not appear to be qualitatively different from earlier attempts to rectify and control the bureaucracy. In accordance with the Maoist ideal of "simple administration," the number of government organizations and functionaries was reduced, at least at the central and provincial levels. In late 1970 Chou En-lai claimed that 90 central government bureaus had been consolidated into 26, and their administrative personnel reduced from 60,000 to 10,000. Yet at the same time Chou reported that 95 percent of Party officials had been reinstated,[18] suggesting that the old bureaucratic apparatus emerged from the Cultural Revolution largely intact, albeit with some changes in personnel and organization. There were new campaigns against bureaucratic arrogance and bourgeois habits and life styles, as well as a renewed emphasis on the virtues of the mass line. However, there was no change in the formal system of cadre salaries based on a hierarchy of 24 official ranks, which remain far higher than wages paid to workers and peasants. Nor is there any evidence of the elimination of informal benefits traditionally enjoyed by those occupying official positions, such as free meals and expenses provided in the performance of official duties; and for higher officials, cars and servants as well, although such material benefits and rewards may not be as conspicuously displayed as they were in the past.

The most radical Maoist remedy for bureaucratism, although hardly new, is the insistence that officials and all "brain workers" regularly participate in productive labor so that they do not become "divorced from the masses." The Cultural Revolution produced a more or less institutionalized means for this practice in the form of "May Seventh" cadre schools. It is estimated that three million officials and cadres found themselves in these newly built communes during the first year of their existence (the first was established on May 7, 1968), and many millions more have undergone this process of "ideological revolutionization" in subsequent years. Dividing their day between self-sufficient productive labor and intensive study of Marxism–Leninism and the thoughts of Mao for periods ranging from six months to two years, officials are allegedly cured of their bureaucratic proclivities by "learning from the peasants" and "integrating themselves with the masses." Yet, however admirable it may be to have bureaucrats depart from their offices to labor in the fields, particularly in a country where the separation between mental and manual labor traditionally was so sharp, the system leaves something to be desired as a cure for bureaucratism, much less as a remedy for bureaucracy. If the purpose is to teach officials to "integrate themselves with the masses," it is strange that the "May Seventh" schools are physically separated from neighboring communes of peasants who remain peasants. The officials, moreover, remain officials. During the period that they engage in work and study in the countryside (for which, it is claimed, they volunteer and regard as an honor), they retain their official titles and continue to receive the salaries appropriate to their rank. And after having taken the cure, they usually are returned to their original posts. Even if the experience has the salutary effects on the behavior and attitudes of cadres in their relations with the masses that is so much celebrated in official publications, it leaves untouched the basic structural and functional distinction between rulers and ruled—the distinction between "leaders and led" that Mao identified as early as 1957 as the main "contradiction" in Chinese society.

If the political reforms that resulted from the Cultural Revolution mitigated some of the more glaring manifestations of bureaucratic elitism, they did not fundamentally alter the relationship between state and society. And that relationship, bluntly put, is one where the state (and the bureaucrats who are its representatives) exercise an overwhelming dominance over society. Paradoxically, it is a form of domination that has increased as China has become more "socialist," and one which the Cultural Revolution may very well have served to intensify, despite the intentions of its leaders. For in a society in which private property is abolished, the political power of the state bureaucracy is reinforced by the fact that it also becomes the economic manager of society. And it is precisely the reduction of social class differences that increasingly makes the remaining distinction between state and society, between leaders and led, the central and essential social division. Insofar as the Cultural Revolution served to reduce and minimize social inequalities, it also served to make the contradiction between bureaucrats and masses all the more crucial, at least insofar as the state apparatus remains relatively autonomous and is not subject to popular control. The failure to produce institutions whereby the masses of producers might exercise democratic control over state and bureaucracy thus suggests that the egalitarian social results of the Cultural Revolution potentially have very nonegalitarian political implications.

The phenomenon of the dominance of political over social power is of course hardly a new one. It has characterized the whole history of the People's Republic and indeed modern Chinese history in general; to greater or lesser degrees, it is a universal historical phenomenon. But rarely has it manifested itself so forcefully as it did during and after the Cultural Revolution, and rarely has the problem cried out so urgently and so obviously for a solution. In Marxist terms, although such are not the terms preferred by Maoists, it is the age-old phenomenon of "alienated social power," that is, the phenomenon by which the state, the product of society, rises above society, becomes estranged from it, and comes to dominate social life. The Cultural Revolution yielded no solution to the problem, but only perpetuated it.

It is of course widely argued that there is no solution; bureaucracy, we are told time and again, is an inevitable and necessary feature of modern societies and bureaucrats will forever remain a more or less autonomous and privileged group. And Marxists will argue that in "the lower phase of Communism," where all are paid according to their work rather than their needs and where society is still stamped by "bourgeois right," it is "utopian" to expect either the elimination of bureaucracy or equality of distribution. But it is hardly utopian to expect that those who profess to be engaged in carrying out "the transition to socialism" under "the dictatorship of the proletariat" would recognize that the historical task is a process whereby (as Marx put it) man "organizes his own powers as social powers so that social force is no longer separated from him as political power." The process, which demands that political power take the form of what Marx called "the self-government of the producers," is not only a central feature of socialism but an essential precondition for its emergence; it lies at the very heart of the Marxist conception of the dictatorship of the proletariat and its "transitional" tasks. But it is not a process that has ensued from the Cultural Revolution, however ardently and frequently Maoists may proclaim the existence of "the dictatorship of the proletariat." Instead of new institutional forms built in accordance with the principle of "the self-government of the producers," the Cultural Revolution offered only palliatives such as "May Seventh" cadre schools.

The Cultural Revolution not only failed to produce permanent institutions of popular self-government but also failed to resolve the more immediate problems of political succession. One of the original aims of the Cultural Revolution was to "train revolutionary successors." But in the summer of 1968, when Mao summoned Red Guard leaders to his "proletarian headquarters" to inform them that the time had come to end their rebellions (and then dispatched most of their followers to the countryside), it was a tacit admission that the young generation had failed to pass the political test. Nor did the Cultural Revolution yield an answer to the short-term question of political succession at the top—in effect, the question of who would (or who possibly could) succeed Mao. If the masses were politically quiet after 1968, this was not the case in the politburo, where the unresolved issues of the Cultural Revolution were to erupt into fierce political struggles in the 1970s and throw its partici- pants into a Byzantine world of political intrigues.

Yet the Cultural Revolution may have had long-term effects that might well facilitate a future process whereby political power is reappro- priated by society and is no longer permitted to stand high above it. Beneath the apparent political passivity of the masses in the years since the Cultural Revolution, one suspects the ideals and battle cries of the great upheaval still echo and that the political consciousness of the peo- ple is far different from what it was. For two years the people of China enjoyed an unprecedented freedom to criticize society, rebel against exist- ing political authorities, establish their own political organizations, and express their grievances and hopes in public forums, on wall posters, and in newspapers. This vast (even though aborted) experiment in freedom of speech, assembly, and press was so widespread and so intense an ex- perience, at least in the urban areas, that it must have wrought profound changes in attitudes toward authority, especially among the youth. Only Mao himself was above criticism during those years, and it is difficult to believe that the hundreds of millions who were his faithful followers during the period of "mass democracy" will prove to be so obedient in following the directives of his successors. Nor is it likely that the Chinese Communist Party can easily reclaim its mantle of Leninist infallibility after so many had so ardently heeded the Maoist call to rebel against it, and after so many of its leaders had been branded as "counterrevolution- aries" or worse. Whatever the failings of Mao, he did instill in the popu- lar consciousness the notion that the essence of Marxism is the right to rebel. As the Chinese people come more fully to recognize that right as their own, and not one to be granted or revoked by higher authorities, they perhaps again will practice what the charter of the Cultural Revo- lution originally preached: that "the only method is for the masses to liberate themselves, and any method of doing things in their stead must not be used."

Notes

1. The most sophisticated argument that the Cultural Revolution was a social revolution is presented by Charles Bettelheim, *Cultural Revolution and Industrial Organization in China* (New York: Monthly Review Press, 1974).
2. Marianne Bastid, "Levels of Economic Decision-Making," in Stuart Schram, ed., *Authority, Participation and Cultural Change in China* (Cambridge, England: Cambridge University Press, 1973), p. 185.

3. Text translated in *Current Background*, No. 891, p. 56. The following discussion on the industrialization of the countryside is partially drawn from Jon Sigurdson's excellent article, "Rural Industry and the Internal Transfer of Technology," in Schram, ed., *Authority, Participation and Cultural Change*, pp. 199–232.

4. Urban assistance takes many forms: the transport of small plants and thus capital to the countryside; the dispatch of technicians, scientists, and industrial managers from the cities to the rural areas; the distribution of technical knowledge through books and teachers; and the training of rural people in urban factories and universities.

5. "Reading Notes on the Soviet Union's 'Political Economy,'" *Mao Tse-tung Ssu-hsiang Wan-sui* (Taipei: n.p. 1969), pp. 389–399.

6. Mao Tse-tung, "Directive on Public Health," June 26, 1965, in Stuart R. Schram, ed., *Mao Tse-tung Unrehearsed: Talks and Letters, 1956–71* (Middlesex, England: Penguin, 1974), pp. 232–233.

7. Mao Tse-tung, "Remarks at the Spring Festival," (February 13, 1964), in Schram, ed., *Mao Tse-tung Unrehearsed*, pp. 197–211.

8. Local autonomy and flexibility are counterbalanced by a national policy that demands that the curriculum at all levels must include political education, and particularly the study of "Mao Tse-tung Thought," military training, and participation in productive manual labor on a regular basis.

9. John Gardner and Wilt Idema, "China's Educational Revolution," in Schram, ed., *Authority, Participation and Cultural Change*, p. 261.

10. Bettelheim, *Cultural Revolution and Industrial Organization*.

11. Among the accusations made against Liu Shao-ch'i was that he favored Soviet-style "Libermanism" and thus planned to introduce a capitalist-type free labor market. See Christopher Howe, "Labor Organization and Incentives in Industry, Before and After the Cultural Revolution," in Schram, ed., *Authority, Participation and Cultural Change*, p. 242.

12. Bettelheim, *Cultural Revolution and Industrial Organization*, pp. 15–16. Similar and sometimes wider differentials have been reported from other factories in different parts of the country. Inequalities in formal wages are somewhat reduced by subsidies provided for canteens, day-care centers, and health services, but probably no more so than in the more advanced capitalist countries.

13. For concrete examples of these tendencies, see Howe, "Labor Organization and Incentives in Industry," pp. 248–250.

14. As laboriously explained by Bettelheim, for example, in *Cultural Revolution and Industrial Organization*, pp. 114–115.

15. As noted by Joan Robinson, *Economic Management in China* (London: Anglo-Chinese Educational Institute, 1975), p. 38 footnote.

16. Bettelheim, *Cultural Revolution and Industrial Organization*, pp. 35, 39.

17. Robinson, *Economic Management in China*, p. 35.

18. Edgar Snow, *The Long Revolution* (New York: Random House, 1972), pp. 13–14.

20

China in the Aftermath of the
Cultural Revolution, 1969–1976

THE MAOIST ARGUMENT that the Cultural Revolution really was a revolution rests on the twin propositions that a bureaucratic caste had transformed itself into a "new bourgeoisie" in the early 1960s and that this "bourgeoisie" was overthrown by a victorious "proletariat" in the course of the great upheaval. There is a large measure of truth in the proposition that a "new class" (in the sense that Milovan Djilas and Mao Tse-tung similarly used that term to designate the elite of a bureaucratized Communist Party) was gaining ascendancy in the years prior to the Cultural Revolution. But in view of the wholesale restoration of the party and state bureaucracies (and virtually all of their leaders with the notable exception of Liu Shao-ch'i) in the years since 1969, it is difficult to accept the claim that this putative new ruling class was removed from power, much less replaced by the proletariat—unless, of course, one is willing to accept the additional Maoist proposition that the dominance of the proletariat is to be equated with the dominance of what is deemed to be "proletarian ideology."

Yet the outcome of the Cultural Revolution was certainly a political victory for Mao and thus for Maoist socioeconomic policies. While this was something less than a "revolution," it was sufficient to forestall, at least temporarily, the bureaucratic institutionalization of postrevolutionary society and the ritualization of Marxist goals. It was sufficient to reverse many of the social, political, and economic tendencies of the "Thermidorean" years when China seemed to be moving closer to a more orthodox Soviet-type pattern of development. It resulted in the revival of many of the Great Leap Forward policies, which focus on the countryside as the main site and source for China's socialist regeneration.

These are no small achievements, even though the gap between the promises and the results of the Cultural Revolution remains a wide one, and is perhaps widening. Mao himself was aware of some of the movement's limitations, and he certainly did not regard it as a definitive solution. As early as 1967 he warned that: "The Great Proletarian Cultural Revolution presently going on is only the first of its kind. In the future other such revolutions will necessarily take place at several occasions. . . . All Party members, and the population at large, must refrain from thinking that all will be smooth after one, two, three, or four Cultural Revolutions."[1]

The demand for future periodic "cultural revolutions" is now part of official Chinese doctrine, although it is difficult to imagine one occurring without Mao as its prophet and leader. But whatever will prove to be the ultimate results of the Cultural Revolution that did take place, the traumatic experiences of those extraordinary years have largely molded the history of the People's Republic in the years that followed. No sooner had the Ninth Party Congress of April 1969 closed, proclaiming the slogan of "unity and victory," than new political struggles erupted to shatter that "unity," and the struggles revolved around the issues that the Cultural Revolution had raised (and left unresolved) and the political passions it continued to arouse.

Two issues dominated Chinese political life in the years after the Ninth Congress seemingly had written the closing chapter on the Cultural Revolution. One was the question of the place of the People's Republic in a hostile international arena presided over by two imperialist "superpowers," the United States and the Soviet Union. The other was the question of the place of the party in the internal post–Cultural Revolution order. The two questions were curiously interrelated, for both were derived from (and framed in the context of) the experience of the Cultural Revolution, an experience whose meaning was perceived differently by its surviving leaders.

At first sight, it is difficult to see any significant relationship between the Cultural Revolution and questions of foreign policy. Between 1966 and 1969 China seemed to withdraw into herself, her own leaders reinforcing the national isolation first imposed by a hostile United States and then by an equally hostile Soviet Union. Preoccupied with internal conflicts, Maoist leaders seemed content to allow China's foreign relations to remain dormant, even recalling virtually all Chinese ambassadors in 1967. Indeed, when the Cultural Revolution was launched in 1966, United States military intervention in Vietnam was being massively escalated, bombs were being dropped very near the Chinese border, and the United States was threatening to extend the war to China itself. But the Cultural Revolution was undertaken not because of the threat posed by American intervention in Vietnam, as some observers speculated at the time,[2] but rather in spite of it. For the Maoist belief was that, as far as the "world revolution" was concerned, the internal class struggle in China was far more important than the struggle then raging in Vietnam. It had been Liu Shao-ch'i, not Mao, who had issued the strongest warnings that China was prepared to come to the assistance of the Vietnamese people in their resistance to American imperialism. In fact, Mao candidly told Edgar Snow in 1970 that one of the major reasons he had been determined to depose Liu Shao-ch'i was because Liu proposed reviving the Sino–Soviet alliance to ward off the American threat in Vietnam, and thereby delay the Cultural Revolution.[3]

There was an enormous measure of national egoism involved in this Maoist belief in the absolute primacy of developments within China over all developments elsewhere in the world, but it was not purely national self-interest that was involved. In the minds of Maoists, the fate of the world revolution was inextricably linked to the fate of the Chinese revolution. What the Chinese took to be "proletarian internationalism" received its fullest expression in Lin Piao's 1965 treatise "Long Live the Victory of People's War," a then eminently Maoist document that projected the Chinese revolutionary experience into a global vision of a worldwide revolutionary process where the "revolutionary countryside" of the economically backward lands of Asia, Africa, and Latin America would surround and overwhelm the advanced "cities" of Europe and North America. This, to be sure, was more a description of the world situation (and the way it was thought to be moving) than a prescription for Chinese action in the world, but it was the revolutionary world view held by the leaders of the Cultural Revolution. It was assumed that the success of socialism in China, to be ensured and demonstrated by the success of the Cultural Revolution, would serve as the model and stimulus for successful socialist revolutions elsewhere. A socialist China would thus become the "revolutionary homeland," replacing a morally bankrupt and capitalist Soviet Union, where revisionism at home and opportunism abroad were leading the forces of world revolution astray. Insofar as the Chinese practiced national isolation during the Cultural Revolution, they did so in what they perceived to be the interests of "proletarian internationalism." From Peking during these years there came fervent declarations of solidarity with popular revolutionary movements throughout the world,[4] accompanied by wholesale denunciations of reactionary governments and leaders everywhere, from the "fascist" Ne Win in Burma to de Gaulle in France, and of course Lyndon Johnson and Leonid Brezhnev. In 1967 Mao not only called China "the political center of world revolution" but also proposed that it become "the military and technical center of the world revolution."[5]

Before the Cultural Revolution came to an end, however, the actions of the Soviet Union rudely intruded on this "internationalist" revolutionary vision. In August 1968 Soviet armies invaded Czechoslovakia, an action more harshly denounced in Peking than in any other of the world's capitals. While the Chinese Communists had precious little sympathy for Dubcek's experiment in democratic socialism, they did (and do) insist on the right of national sovereignty, both as a matter of principle and a matter of national self-interest. The occupation of Czechoslovakia raised the specter of war with the Soviet Union, for along with it came the infamous "Brezhnev doctrine" of "limited sovereignty" for socialist countries, that is, the "right" of Soviet military intervention in the countries that made up what was once known as the "Communist camp." For China the threat was ominous and immediate, for the Russians already had been making thinly veiled warnings about a "preemptive" attack (preferably in concert with the United States) against Chinese nuclear installations.[6] More than a million Russian troops were being deployed along the 5,000-mile Sino–Soviet border, hundreds of Soviet nuclear missiles were targeted against Chinese cities, and border clashes were growing in frequency and intensity. When the CCP's Ninth Congress opened in April 1969, Chinese and Soviet troops had just concluded bloody battles on the frozen Ussuri River in northern Manchuria.

It was at that congress, through the medium of Lin Piao's main report, that the Chinese Communists first placed Soviet "social imperialism" on an equal footing with American imperialism, both principal enemies of the oppressed nations and of China. While American imperialism was typically denounced as "the most ferocious enemy of the peoples of the world," Lin had even harsher words for the Soviet Union. The "new czars," he charged, were establishing colonies "on the model of Hitler's 'New Order'" and were engaged in "fascist acts of banditry." But both imperialism and social imperialism, Lin optimistically concluded, would inevitably meet their doom at the hands of the popular forces of world revolution.[7]

But for Mao, and particularly for Chou En-lai, merely condemning the Soviet Union and the United States as equally evil and relying on the *deus ex machina* of world revolution were insufficient to deal with the peril from the north. Chou, undoubtedly with the strong support of Mao, was advocating a new global diplomatic strategy based on the rather traditional principles of national sovereignty, peaceful coexistence, and the establishment of friendly relations "between states with different social systems"; it was a strategy that defined the Soviet Union as the principal enemy, and one, correspondingly, that dictated a tactical accommodation with the United States. As it happened, it was a strategy that coincided with American interests, one that soon was to bring Henry Kissinger and Richard Nixon to Peking. This new diplomacy was of course a negation of the spirit of "proletarian internationalism" (or what might better be called a spirit of messianic revolutionary nationalism) that briefly had held sway—and to Lin Piao it seemed no less than a betrayal of the principles of the Cultural Revolution. On the question of China's foreign policy and, particularly, the policy of rapprochement with the United States, one of the battle lines between Mao and his "designated successor" was drawn.

Another battle line was drawn on a second and closely related question: the pace and manner that Mao and Chou proposed for rebuilding the party and reestablishing its authority. What was at issue was not whether the party would and should be rebuilt—for the Cultural Revolution had produced no viable institutions to take its place—but rather whether it would be rebuilt on its old Leninist foundations, reassume its former monopolistic position, and incorporate most of its pre–Cultural Revolution leaders and personnel. For Mao, and especially for Chou En-lai, the rapid restoration of the party was the first and most essential domestic order of business, particularly to correct the anomalous political result of the Cultural Revolution, which had made the army the dominant force in the political life of the nation. No matter how much proletarian virtue the PLA might possess, the prevailing situation was one that gave rise to Bonapartist fears, and Mao began to criticize the rule of the military commanders as "arrogant." Moreover, the growing preoccupation with the Russian menace made all the more urgent the fashioning of a stable internal political order. The Maoist emphasis was on national unity and reconciliation under the leadership of a revived and rebuilt party, and Mao now was openly sanctioning the return of most former party leaders and the wholesale rehabilitation of its cadres who had been so harshly attacked (and often "overthrown") during the Cultural Revolution. Indeed, Mao told Edgar Snow in December 1970 that from the beginning of the Cultural Revolution he had disapproved of the "maltreatment" of party members and pointed to this unhappy legacy as a major factor still impeding the rebuilding of the party.[8]

To Lin Piao and other surviving radical leaders, most notably Ch'en Po-ta, old "capitalist-roaders" were being returned to prominence with unseemly haste, and new leaders (who mostly were old leaders) were being selected less in accordance with the criterion of political virtue than on the basis of administrative competence. At the Ninth Congress, Lin Piao proposed that the central Cultural Revolution Group, which had been headed by Ch'en Po-ta since its inception three years earlier, should continue to function—perhaps partly as a symbolic affirmation of the goals of the revolution, perhaps partly to serve as a counterweight to the party politburo. The proposal, in any event, was unsuccessful, and in December 1969 the Cultural Revolution Group formally was abolished.

The political struggles that ensued after the Ninth Congress, or at least the conflict between Lin Piao and Mao Tse-tung, cannot easily be interpreted as simply a struggle between military and civilian authority, between army and party, however tempting it might be to do so to dispose of an episode that still remains so enshrouded in mystery and ambiguity. As that secret struggle unfolded between 1969 and 1971, it is unlikely that Lin spoke in the name of the army or that he perceived himself as its spokesman. For Lin had become identified with the radical civilian leadership of the Cultural Revolution and in fact was closely associated with many of those who attacked the PLA during the most turbulent and radical phases of the upheaval. For this he had earned the wrath of a good many army commanders. It was Chou En-lai, not Lin, who had come to the defense of the PLA during the time it was under attack. To be sure, Lin had his followers among PLA leaders, but probably they were far fewer in number and power than those who owed their loyalty to Mao and Chou. Lin's challenge to Mao was not a military challenge to civilian authority but the challenge of the ideals of the Cultural Revolution that Lin had come to champion and Mao had partly abandoned.

The issues that were dividing Mao and Lin, party rebuilding and foreign policy, resulted in an open confrontation between the two when the central committee of the Ninth Congress convened its second plenum at Lushan in late August 1970. Or more precisely, the conflict was openly revealed to the members of the central committee; the Chinese people were not to be told of the struggle until two years later, and then only the victors' version of the events and issues involved, for, in contrast to the days of the Cultural Revolution, public debate of public policy no longer was in fashion.

According to Mao's later account, Lin Piao and Ch'en Po-ta (who were at least tactically allied at the time along with other powerful members of the politburo) carried out a "surprise attack" at the Lushan meeting. And Mao described the "program" of his opponents as twofold: first, the appointment of a state chairman to fill the post from which Liu Shao-ch'i had been removed, and second, the addition of a provision in the draft of the new state constitution extolling Mao as a "genius."[9] The "surprise attack" consisted of speeches critical of the foreign and domestic policies of Chou En-lai, surprising only because their content was not discussed with Mao beforehand. The proposal to appoint a state chairman was in opposition to Mao's decision of several months earlier to omit mention of the position in the new constitution of the People's Republic then being drafted, in effect, to abolish the office, probably because he did not want his "successor" Lin Piao to obtain it or inherit it for fear of undermining Premier Chou En-lai's supremacy over the state administration. The proposal to canonize Mao formally as a "genius" was a somewhat more enigmatic matter. Mao later called it a "theoretical question." At the time, it would seem that it was an eminently practical political question. To praise Mao as a genius was very much in the spirit of the

Cultural Revolution, when Mao stood high above all institutions as supreme leader and utopian prophet with direct links to the masses. And to celebrate the genius of Mao officially in 1970 was an attempt to recreate the Cultural Revolution situation when all political wisdom and authority resided in Mao and his thought rather than in the party, and thus to attempt to blunt the current drive to restore the party to its pre–Cultural Revolution Leninist preeminence. Mao was quick to recognize the political implications of this belated attempt to use the cult of Mao against his policy on the party. He refused the accolade and later commented on its political import: "Genius does not depend on one person or a few people. It depends on a party, the party which is the vanguard of the proletariat."[10]

The central committee neither appointed a chairman of the Republic nor proclaimed Mao a genius. Instead, Lin Piao and Ch'en Po-ta were criticized for obstructing the process of party rebuilding. Moreover, after apparently considerable and heated debate, the new foreign policies designed by Chou En-lai were endorsed. The official communiqué that issued from the two-week closed-door meeting announced that China's foreign policy was based on the principle of "peaceful coexistence between countries with different social systems."[11] It was the first time in more than five years that this phrase had been heard in public.

The Lushan plenum also marked the downfall of Ch'en Po-ta, Mao's long-time personal secretary, confidant, and Maoist theoretician par excellence. The Cultural Revolution had elevated Ch'en to the apex of political power as one of the five members of the standing committee of the politburo, standing alongside Mao, Lin Piao, Chou En-lai, and K'ang Sheng. He now became the victim of a brief campaign of vilification. Accused of various "ultra-leftist" deviations, allegedly committed both during and after the Cultural Revolution, he soon was excommunicated as "China's Trotsky."

The problem of deposing Ch'en's ally Lin Piao was a far more formidable task. For Lin was not only Mao's official heir apparent, he emerged from the Cultural Revolution with a popular prestige second only to the Chairman himself. From the time of the Nanchang uprising of 1927, he had been one of the great heroes and leaders of the Chinese Revolution and, since their first meeting in 1928, one of Mao's closest comrades in arms. Moreover, the extent of military support Lin could command was still an unknown factor in the fall of 1970. The strategy that was to bring about his downfall was to take a year to unfold.

The conflict between Mao and Lin was of course totally hidden from public view. To the Chinese people, Lin still appeared to be Mao's closest comrade and chosen successor. He continued to make public speeches, presided at official gatherings, and his picture was displayed in newspapers almost as prominently as Mao's. On May Day 1971 Lin and Mao stood together on the reviewing stand above T'ien-an-men Square. But under the facade of public unity, the political struggle was intensifying. While the fall of Lin Piao was being prepared, the policies against which he had fought, and which he continued to oppose, were being implemented. The process of rebuilding the party machine was greatly accelerated. For eighteen months after the party's Ninth Congress it had proved impossible to establish provincial party committees. The Lushan plenum served to remove the obstacles. Between December 1970 and August 1971, party committees were set up in all provinces, effectively subordinating the provincial revolutionary committees. In the meantime, Chou En-lai's new diplomacy was beginning to bear its anticipated fruits. In November 1970 Chou told Edgar Snow that the Chinese government had responded affirmatively to overtures from Washington to resume the Sino–American discussions that had been suspended in Warsaw a year before, although preferably at a different site.[12] The new site was to be Peking. In December, Mao told Snow that Richard Nixon would be welcomed in China as either tourist or president.[13] The invitation was quickly relayed to Washington and Snow received permission to publish his interview with Mao. It appeared in *Life* magazine in April 1971, at the very time Lin Piao and his supporters were making their final appeal before the politburo to reverse the course of Chinese foreign policy. But the era of "ping-pong diplomacy"[14] already had begun, and it soon gave way to the era of *realpolitik*. On July 11 came the startling announcement that Secretary of State Kissinger had been in Peking for two days of discussions with Premier Chou En-lai, preparing the way for President Nixon's dramatic visit the following February. It was a diplomatic triumph for both sides.

In September, two months after Kissinger's visit, Lin Piao vanished from the public scene. No explanation for his absence was forthcoming for ten months. Finally, on July 28, 1972, there was issued the first official account of what is now called "the tenth major struggle between the two lines in the history of the Communist Party of China." Lin Piao, it was said, had plotted a coup d'etat that involved an attempt to assassinate Mao Tse-tung. When the plot failed, he attempted to flee to the Soviet Union on a jet aircraft along with his wife and son and other accomplices. But the plane crashed in the People's Republic of Mongolia, killing all aboard.

There is, of course, no way to either verify or disprove the official story. As in most such cases, one is left with little more than such versions and documents that the survivors and victors choose to provide. All that can be said with any reasonable degree of certainty is that a major political crisis took place in September 1971, which involved a wholesale purge of the upper echelons of both the military and civilian administrations, including the dismissal of eleven of the twenty-one members of the politburo, and that Lin Piao perished in the process, whether on the Trident jet that crashed in Outer Mongolia on September 13 or by other means at another time.[15]

Perhaps more revealing about what had been involved in the political struggle was the host of "ultra-leftist" charges leveled against Lin shortly after his fall. In addition to allegations that he had conspired to establish a military dictatorship, had conducted "illicit relations" with the Soviet Union, and had opposed Mao's policy on the rehabilitation of party cadres and his "revolutionary line" in foreign policy, Lin and his followers also were accused of having exaggerated the spontaneity of the masses; overemphasized the human and spiritual factor in production; undermined rural stability by attempting to universalize the Tachai model and by advocating a more or less immediate transition to communism; and having fostered the Mao cult and the rote memorization of the Chairman's sayings rather than the serious study of his works. In 1972 it appeared to a number of pro-Maoist foreign observers that Lin Piao had been unmasked as the most prominent of the "ultra-leftists."[16] Indeed, high officials told visitors to the People's Republic at the time that Lin had been the "backstage boss" of the May Sixteenth group.[17]

In recent years volumes of "revelations" about Lin Piao have issued from Peking, but they have revealed little more about the crisis of September 1971 than was known in the summer of 1972. The most conventional of explanations (held by most Western observers and partly supported by the darkly conspiratorial tales told in Peking), that what was essentially involved was a struggle for supreme power, is certainly the least plausible. For over forty years Lin had been the most loyal of Mao's followers, and in 1969 he had been rewarded for that loyalty by being officially designated as the Chairman's successor. Had Lin been motivated purely by considerations of personal power, it seems hardly likely that he would have jeopardized that position by quarreling with Mao on matters of either principle or tactics. Yet on the basis of the scanty evidence that is available—and without the benefit of any evidence from the losing side—it would appear to be the case that it was precisely the principles of the Cultural Revolution that lay at the heart of the controversy, or more precisely, Lin's belief that Mao had embarked upon a course that constituted a wholesale betrayal of those principles. There were limits to Lin's loyalty to Mao, and those limits were reached with the drive to restore the party in its pre–Cultural Revolution form and by the rapprochment with the United States.

There were plots and no doubt counterplots in the year following the Lushan plenum, but it cannot be taken for granted that Lin and his supporters were the original plotters. Equally plausible is that Mao, determined to eliminate Lin and his faction, took the political initiative. When Mao embarked on a tour of the provinces in August 1971, he clearly was gathering political support in the campaign against Lin and preparing for the denouement that was to take place in September. At the time he claimed that he had been shielding Lin and following the policy of "curing the disease to save the patient." "We still want to protect Lin," he is reported to have said. "After I return to Peking I must seek them [i.e., Lin and his associates] out again to have a talk. . . . Some of them may be saved, others it may not be possible to save. This depends on their actions. They have two possible futures: they may reform or they may not." But he ominously added: "It is difficult for someone who has taken the lead in committing major errors of principle, errors of line or direction, to reform. Looking back, did Ch'en Tu-hsiu reform? Did Ch'ü Ch'iu-pai, Li Li-san, Lo Chang-lung, Wang Ming, Chang Kuo-t'ao, Kao Kang, Jao Shu-shih, P'eng Te-huai or Liu Shao-ch'i reform? They did not reform."[18]

Clearly, Mao intended to bring the struggle to a decisive conclusion, with little expectation that Lin Piao would prove amenable to "reform." Lin may or may not have responded to this threat with the abortive coup d'etat and assassination attempt that Chinese authorities allege were planned by the conspirators a year earlier and set forth in a document entitled "Outline of the '571 Project.'" It is interesting to note, however, that Chou En-lai later implicitly acknowledged (in an interview with a group of visiting American newspaper editors) that the "571 Project" was never even attempted. There apparently was no attempt on the Chairman's life and no effort to carry out the alleged coup; instead, fearing the plot had been discovered, Lin simply and hastily fled on the ill-fated plane that crashed in Mongolia.[19]

But whatever Lin Piao's motives and activities may have been, he was the last important figure who continued to voice the original ideals and aims of the Cultural Revolution. His demise, and the purge of his supporters from the party, army, and revolutionary committees, removed the last barriers to the consolidation of the post–Cultural Revolution order as Mao and Chou wished to have it.

The deradicalization of the Cultural Revolution accelerated in the years after the fall of Lin Piao. It was a process above all marked by the reestablishment of the authority and organizational apparatus of the Chinese Communist Party, which soon was no less dominant and pervasive in the political and economic life of the nation than in the years before the Cultural Revolution. It was not only the institution that was restored but also the great majority of its old leaders. Officials and cadres denounced and overthrown as "capitalist-roaders," "demons," and "monsters" were returned to positions of power and prominence in ever increasing numbers—and without official explanation, save for charges that the "excesses" of the Cultural Revolution were largely due to the evil machinations of Lin Piao. Most of the old provincial party leaders and their deputies were reappointed to high offices, although it was politically less embarrassing to station them in provinces other than those they had governed in 1966.[20] In general, the older and more conservative cadres prevailed over the younger and more radical ones who had risen to prominence during the Cultural Revolution. The process of "rehabilitation" did not exclude such prominent "monsters" as Ch'en Tsai-tao and Chung Han-hua, the leaders of the 1967 Wuhan mutiny, who reappeared at public forums in 1972 and were assigned new military commands. There also reappeared the old party-controlled mass organizations; a reorganized Communist Youth League replacing the Red Guards, and a reconstructed trade-union federation replacing the workers' congresses.

As the party was rebuilt, the political role of both the revolutionary committees and the army declined. In a sense, the revolutionary committees had become anachronistic, for their purpose in large part had been to represent the popular mass organizations which now had disappeared. They nevertheless continued to exist, partly as an administrative convenience, partly as a politico-ideological necessity, lest their formal abolition be taken as a renunciation of the Cultural Revolution. At the same time, the PLA, purged of leaders who were alleged supporters of Lin Piao, gradually withdrew from the dominant political position it had been called upon to assume during the Cultural Revolution. That the party again would command the gun was a point that Mao had made clear in the course of his 1971 provincial tour, advising army commanders: "You should pay attention to military affairs. . . . It would be putting the cart before the horse if matters already decided by regional party committees were later turned over to army party committees for discussion."[21] A decade earlier Maoists had established the PLA as the model for universal emulation; by 1973 the slogans of the day enjoined the PLA to learn from "the fine work style" of the party and from the masses.

The rebuilding of the party was logically accompanied by the partial dismantling of the cult of Mao. This had been a Janus-faced phenomenon. On the one hand, it was an extreme expression of the alienation of the social power of the people, for it was not simply a matter of the masses worshiping the authority of a state that stood above them but totally subordinating themselves (and their power) to the higher authority of a single man, perceived as the embodiment of their collective will and the source of all wisdom. Yet during the Cultural Revolution the cult had been the major instrument that encouraged the masses to strike at the bureaucratic apparatus which ruled over them and to legitimize that rebellion against authority. Mao was certainly acutely aware of the political utility and functions of the cult, even if not of its alien and alienating character. In his December 1970 talk with Edgar Snow, he again candidly acknowledged the existence of a "cult of personality" (as he had in 1965) and, moreover, argued that it had been a necessary weapon to dismantle a party bureaucracy that was no longer under his control. Now that the situation had been rectified, the time had come for the cult to be "cooled down," although Mao implied that this might take some time, for he went on to observe that it was difficult for people to overcome the habits of "3,000 years of emperor-worshiping tradition."[22] The cult was in fact "cooled" in the years after 1971 and although neither Mao nor his thought suffered any lack of public and official adulation, the emphasis was now on the supreme authority (if not necessarily the absolute infallibility) of the party. The party itself, of course, was still led by Mao and presumably guided by his thought. The excesses and more irrational aspects of the cult were blamed on Lin Piao. Lin, to be sure, had been the most ardent promoter of the cult, just as he was the most severe critic of the party bureaucracy. But there is no evidence that Mao had any objections to the efforts of his one-time "closest comrade in arms" before 1970.

In the years after Lin Piao's death, the new foreign policy designed by Chou En-lai began to pay great nationalist dividends, but at an enormous cost for China's proclaimed principles of "proletarian internationalism." In October 1971 the People's Republic triumphantly entered the United Nations, the United States no longer willing or able to continue the obstructionist policies it had pursued for more than two decades. The "Shanghai Communiqué" that concluded President Nixon's celebrated visit of February 1972 essentially endorsed the positions the Chinese had been setting forth since 1949; it promised the eventual normalization of diplomatic relations between the two countries, called for the progressive withdrawal of United States military forces from Taiwan, and recognized that the future of Taiwan was an internal Chinese matter. The implementation of these agreements was to be long delayed by the inscrutabilities of American domestic politics. In the meantime, the policy of "peaceful coexistence between countries with different social systems" was practiced with a vengeance elsewhere. Entirely "peaceful relations" were maintained with the government of Pakistan during the Bengali revolt and with Madame Bandaranaike during the revolutionary uprising in Ceylon in 1971. The notorious "Christmas bombings" of North Vietnam in 1972 brought forth verbal protests from Peking, but they were sufficiently restrained to preserve cordial relations with Henry Kissinger and Richard Nixon. All manner of feudal monarchs and military dictators (many formerly denounced as fascist or worse) embarked upon pilgrimages to Peking and were received with all due honors. Normal diplomatic and trade relations were established with the Franco regime in Spain and the fascist military junta in Greece. In recent years China has emerged as one of the great champions of the North Atlantic Treaty Alliance and is one of the few countries in what was once known as "the socialist bloc" to maintain formal relations with the Chilean militarists who so brutally overthrew the Marxist government of Allende. And in early 1976 China was to find itself involved in Angola on the same side as the United States and South Africa.

These more embarrassing developments which have followed from China's new diplomacy and her entrance into the world of international power politics have flowed from a policy that subordinates all other considerations to the overriding struggle against "Soviet social imperialism." The tactics motivated by considerations of national self-interest in general, and by the very real threat of the Soviet Union in particular, have been elevated to the level of a doctrine proclaiming that the interests of revolutionary movements everywhere are identical with the national interests of "socialist China." It is a doctrine that bears the imprint of Stalin's doctrine of "socialism in one country" as well as one that reflects the profoundly nationalist content of Maoism. And what is hailed as "Chairman Mao's revolutionary line in foreign policy" probably holds the same ominous implications for foreign revolutionary movements as its Stalinist counterpart.

The foreign and domestic policies Mao and Chou were pursuing received formal ratification at the Tenth National Congress of the Chinese Communist Party held in Peking from August 24 to 28, 1973. The Congress met without prior public announcement and was convened with more than the usual secrecy. But it had the eminently public purpose of attempting to demonstrate to party members and nonparty masses alike that, despite the demise of Lin Piao, the remaining leaders remained true to the spirit and principles of the Cultural Revolution—and to show that Lin had not adhered to those principles and, indeed, never had represented them. The concern to document continuity with the Cultural Revolution doubtless was largely responsible for the decision to have one of the two major reports to the Congress delivered by Wang Hung-wen, a former Shanghai factory worker and youthful party activist whom the Cultural Revolution had catapulted to a position of national political leadership. The other report was presented by Chou En-lai. Mao presided over the Congress but apparently did not address the gathering.

Both Chou and Wang took pains to emphasize the correctness of the general political lines laid out at the Ninth Congress, and from there the lines that linked the present leadership to the Cultural Revolution. Both emphasized the total supremacy and indispensable vanguard role of the party. "We should further strengthen the centralized leadership of the Party," Chou stressed. "Of the seven sectors—industry, agriculture, commerce, culture and education, the army, the government, and the Party —it is the Party that exercises overall leadership."[23] Wang Hung-wen presented an even more fundamentalist conception of the Leninist party. "The Party must exercise leadership in everything," he insisted. Moreover, "as regards the relationship between various organizations at the same level . . . the Party is not parallel to the others and still less is it under the leadership of any other [and] as regards the relationship between higher and lower levels, the lower level is subordinate to the higher level, and the entire Party is subordinate to the Central Committee." To be sure, Wang also stressed the old Maoist maxim that party cadres must accept "criticism and supervision from the masses." And he struck a faintly cultural revolutionary note when he declared that "a true Communist must act without any selfish considerations and dare to go against the tide, fearing neither removal from his post, expulsion from the Party, imprisonment, divorce nor guillotine."[24] However, in the wake of the Lin Piao affair, it was most unlikely that there were many eager to take up the challenge. The main thrust of the Congress, in any event, was to sanction the reestablishment of the party in its orthodox Leninist form; in the documents that emerged from the meeting in the Great Hall of the People, it was stressed time and again (and always in bold block characters) that "it is the Party that exercises overall leadership."

This full restoration of the system of total party dominance, now fully laid down in theory as well as in fact, required a partial rewriting of the history of the Cultural Revolution. Thus the revised party constitution solemnly declared that the "great victories in the Great Proletarian Cultural Revolution" had occurred under the leadership of the Chinese Communist Party.[25] And Wang Hung-wen proclaimed that the Cultural Revolution had been a "Party consolidation movement."[26]

Chou En-lai discussed the international situation (which he described as "one characterized by great disorder on the earth"[27]) in general and familiar terms, but his specific policies of *realpolitik* received concrete approval with the election to the central committee of Foreign Minister Chi P'eng-fei and his chief deputies. At the same time, the number of PLA representatives in the central committee was significantly reduced.

The most difficult matter confronting the congress was to explain—and explain away—the demise of Lin Piao. In 1972 Lin and Ch'en Po-ta had been depicted as "ultra-leftists." It was soon realized, however, that such accusations against two of the most prominent leaders of the Cultural Revolution might create doubts about the validity of the whole enterprise or doubts about whether the present leaders truly represented its now canonized principles and spirit. Thus Lin and Ch'en hastily were converted into "ultra-rightists," and both formally expelled from the party —Lin, posthumously, as a "bourgeois careerist, conspirator, counter-revolutionary double dealer, renegade and traitor;" and Ch'en as a "principal member of the Lin Piao anti-Party clique, anti-Communist Kuomintang element, Trotskyite, renegade, enemy agent and revisionist." Chou En-lai went to fantastic lengths to connect Lin with Liu Shao-ch'i. Lin was charged with opposing the doctrine of "continuing the revolution under the dictatorship of the proletariat," holding that the major contradiction in Chinese society was between "the advanced socialist system and the backward productive forces" (rather than the Maoist thesis that it was between the "proletariat" and the "bourgeoisie"), and therefore advocating the heinous view that the main task was to "develop production." His aim was no less than to turn the CCP into "a revisionist, fascist party. . . . subvert the dictatorship of the proletariat and restore capitalism, . . . institute a feudal-compradore-fascist dictatorship, . . . [and] capitulate to Soviet revisionism and social imperialism." As if this was not enough, Chou (in good Stalinist fashion) charged that Lin's crimes were not only of recent vintage but could be traced back to his earliest days as a Communist. Mao, it was claimed, had been "trying seriously and patiently to educate" Lin since 1929, but, as matters turned out, "Lin Piao's bourgeois idealist world outlook was not at all remolded. At important junctures of the revolution he invariably committed Right opportunist errors and invariably played double-faced tricks, putting up a false front to deceive the Party and the people."[28] Why it took more than forty years for Mao to uncover the false front was not explained. Such was the verdict of a congress that proclaimed its faith and trust in the masses—but the masses certainly were not to be trusted with the truth about their leaders.

The party constitution was revised, most notably of course by deleting that most embarrassing paragraph which declared Lin Piao to be Mao's chosen successor. The new constitution also took a further step in the "cooling" of the Mao cult by omitting some of the more grandiose statements on the powers of Mao Tsetung Thought which had appeared in the 1969 document and were identified with the attack on the party during the Cultural Revolution. However, continuity with the Cultural Revolution was expressed in retaining the Maoist thesis that class struggles persist in a socialist society, the theory of "continued revolution under the dictatorship of the proletariat," and the promise that other cultural revolutions would take place "many times in the future." While the long-term sociopolitical implications of these propositions have yet to reveal themselves, in 1973 they were glaringly incongruous with the Maoist emphasis on political unity, centralization, and consolidation.

Finally, the congress duly confirmed the political leadership of the Party which had emerged after the fall of Lin Piao, emphasized the urgency of training revolutionary successors, and, in the interim, established a system of more or less collective leadership under Mao by appointing five vice-chairmen: Chou En-lai, Wang Hung-wen, K'ang Sheng, Yeh Chien-ying, and Li Teh-sheng.[29]

Soon after the Tenth Congress closed—after an unusually brief five-day session—it became apparent that the problem of burying the dead Lin Piao was a far more difficult task than it had been to politically bury Liu Shao-ch'i during the Cultural Revolution. Liu had been the principal target and victim of the Cultural Revolution, while Lin had been one of its principal leaders and heroes. The difficulties in providing a credible explanation for the fall of Lin Piao were compounded when it was decided to add to the long list of charges already made the fantastic allegation that he also had been a disciple of Confucius.

In mid-1973 articles attacking Confucius and Confucianism had begun to appear in Chinese newspapers and magazines. The origins and purposes of the campaign remain obscure. At the time, it variously was interpreted as simply an ongoing effort to combat the persistence of traditional ideas and attitudes, a veiled attack on the "pragmatism" of Chou En-lai promoted by more radical elements in the party (most notably, Chiang Ch'ing), or even the ideological harbinger of another cultural revolution. But whoever the original promoters may have been, and whatever their motives, soon after the Tenth Congress the campaign was seized upon by Chou En-lai and his supporters to justify their post–Cultural Revolution policies—and to consign Lin Piao to an even lower level in the "dustbin of history." The "P'i Lin, P'i K'ung" (criticize Lin, criticize Confucius) campaign dominated the official press and public political life for more than a year. The major thrust of this strange campaign, so filled with complex and obtuse historical allusions and allegories, was to celebrate the historically progressive character of the Ch'in Dynasty (which had unified China in 221 BC), its first emperor (Ch'in Shih Huang Ti), and its authoritarian Legalist doctrines; and to condemn as historically reactionary the Confucian opposition which represented the interests of the dying slave-owning aristocracy, clinging to ancient political and territorial divisions. The contemporary political message, simply put, was that Mao and Chou, the contemporary Shih Huang and his loyal minister Li Ssu, recognized and acted upon the objective forces of progressive historical change by promoting national unity, centralization, and modern economic development. On the other hand, Lin Piao was the modern personification of the old Confucian scholars—particularly the traitorous official Lü Pu-wei—who set themselves against the progressive forces of history, promoting political factionalism, separatism, and outmoded ideas. Lin thus was portrayed as the heir of a reactionary 2,000-year-old ideological tradition.

Perhaps the most noteworthy aspect of the anti-Confucian campaign was a new and untypically Maoist emphasis on the objective, determining laws of historical development, and a consequent deemphasis on "subjective factors" and the ability of men to shape historical reality in accordance with their will. This more deterministic historical world view by no means precluded change; indeed it demanded socioeconomic change (and human activity to effect change) in accordance with the progressive movement of history. Yet it also demanded that the pace, if not the nature, of change was to be restrained by a recognition of objective historical limitations. It was a far cry from the spirit of the Cultural Revolution when the masses were portrayed as continually surging forward and scaling ever new heights, but it was entirely in harmony with the current drive for political consolidation and economic development. Against the conservatism of Liu Shao-ch'i, Mao had employed his usual highly voluntarist interpretation of historical materialism. Against the radicalism of Lin Piao, and in reaction to the "excesses" of the Cultural Revolution, Mao (or those who now spoke in his name) fell back on more orthodox Marxist historical perspectives and a newly found faith in the objective laws of history.

At the end of 1974 the anti-Confucian campaign was fading, and its promoters would have been hard pressed to explain what it had accomplished. A simultaneous campaign to encourage cadres and masses to read the original writings of Marx and Engels continued, probably serving to reinforce the more deterministic interpretation of Marxist theory that now seemed to be gaining ascendancy. It was accompanied by a new movement, beginning in February 1975, to study the Marxist concept of the dictatorship of the proletariat; leading theoreticians stressed that carrying out the tasks of this lengthy transitional period between socialism and communism demanded "unity and stability." Unity and stability were certainly the main political watchwords of the time.

The final consecration of the post–Cultural Revolution order came with the long-delayed convening of the Fourth National People's Congress, which met in Peking January 13–17, 1975. This was the first meeting since 1964 of what is officially "the highest organ of state power" in the People's Republic. The more than 2,800 deputies now gathered to ratify the enormous changes that had taken place in the decade since they last had met and to promulgate a new state constitution. Chou En-lai, dying of cancer, left his hospital bed to deliver the report on the work of the government, summing up the accomplishments of the past twenty-five years (for which Chou could rightly claim a good share of the credit), and expressing his hopes for the future, for a China that would be a "powerful modern socialist country." Mao did not attend, remaining in his native province of Hunan, underscoring his withdrawal from the political stage.

Chou En-lai's report emphasized China's economic progress and revealed that the disruptions of the Cultural Revolution had not had any adverse long-term effects on the program for industrialization. Total industrial output for 1974, he noted, was 190 percent greater than in 1964, including a 120 percent increase in steel production, 91 percent in coal, 650 percent in petroleum, 200 percent in electric power, 330 percent in chemical fertilizers, and a 520 percent increase in the production of tractors. Agricultural production in 1974 was estimated to be 51 percent higher than in 1964. And Chou claimed that since the founding of the

People's Republic, grain production had increased by 140 percent while the population had grown by 60 percent.[30] These claims are generally supported by the estimates made by most foreign economic specialists,[31] supporting the more or less conventional wisdom about China: that the People's Republic has achieved the remarkable feat of becoming self-sufficient in food production while simultaneously rapidly becoming a modern industrial power. These economic accomplishments, together with continuing progress in such areas as health care and education, stand in striking contrast to the political instability that reigns at the upper levels of power. Indeed, in the mid-1970s, China is marked by a deep incongruity between socio-economic progress and a political life (at least at the top) that has regressed to a succession of Byzantine-like palace intrigues.

The most spectacular political event of the Fourth Congress was the full public resurrection of Teng Hsiao-p'ing. The former Secretary-General had appeared at official banquets in the spring of 1973, no one noting, at least not publicly, that a few years before he had been "the second leading person in authority taking the capitalist road." At the Tenth Party Congress in August 1973, Teng had been reelected to the politburo, and in the spring of 1974 headed the Chinese delegation to a special session of the United Nations to announce that the post–World War II socialist bloc no longer existed and that China was a member of the Third World. At a party meeting held a few days before the opening of the People's Congress Teng was elevated to the politburo's standing committee. At the Congress itself, Teng seemingly became Premier Chou's heir apparent, appointed as the first of twelve new vice-premiers —and, as it was revealed a few weeks later, chief of staff of the army as well. But his tenure was brief. The strange apotheosis of Teng was apparently more than Mao and others could countenance. Mao had not forgotten that the old Secretary-General had arrogantly treated him as a "dead ancestor" during the years of the Liuist regime. When Chou En-lai died on January 8, 1976 at the age of 78, he was succeeded as Premier not by Teng, as he apparently had planned, but by Hua Kuo-feng, a man little known outside of China, but nevertheless a high-ranking member of the politburo (although not of its standing committee) who had been appointed Minister of Public Security a year earlier. Teng Hsiao-p'ing was again branded "China's second Khrushchev" and once more cast into political oblivion.

The new state constitution, replacing the one of 1954 was significantly revised to take into account the vast political, social, and economic transformations of the preceding twenty years. Reflecting the assumption that the bourgeois stage of the revolution was completed, the People's Republic no longer was described as a "people's democratic State" but as "a socialist State of the dictatorship of the proletariat." The total supremacy of the party over the state administration was now made a matter of law as well as of fact. Whereas the 1954 constitution stated that "All power ... belongs to the people," the new document added: "The Communist Party of China is the core of the leadership of the whole Chinese people. The working class exercises leadership over the state through its vanguard, the Communist Party of China." Further, it explicitly was laid down that the National People's Congress and state power in general was under the leadership of the Party. Also written into the constitution was the dictum that "Marxism–Leninism–Mao Tsetung Thought is the theoretical basis guiding the thinking of our nation." The rural communes were formally institutionalized as the basic form of both economic and political organization in the countryside, although the production team was to remain "the basic accounting unit" and the right of commune members to farm small private plots for personal needs was recognized. The local revolutionary committees were made permanent institutions, although they were defined more as administrative bodies than as policy-making organs. The celebrated "three-in-one" principle, upon which the revolutionary committees presumably rested, was redefined as the "combination of the old, the middle-aged, and the young," a formula doubt-lessly reflecting concerns over problems of political stability and succession. The problem of filling the position of Chairman of the Republic, vacated by the purge of Liu Shao-ch'i, was resolved by simply abolishing the office. Some of the freedoms formally granted in the 1954 constitution were deleted from the 1975 document, most notably "the freedom of citizens to engage in scientific research, literary and artistic creation, and other cultural pursuits" and the "freedom of residence and freedom to change their residence." One new freedom was added at the personal direction of Mao: the right to strike.[32] It remains to be seen whether this right will be practiced and honored any more fully than other constitu-tionally guaranteed rights such as freedom of speech, press, assembly, association, and demonstration.

On October 1, 1974 celebrations were held throughout the land to mark the twenty-fifth anniversary of the founding of the People's Republic. An editorial in the *People's Daily* proudly proclaimed: "Earth-shaking changes have taken place in China in the past twenty-five years. Old China, poor and backward, has changed into socialist New China with the beginnings of prosperity." Yet the generation of revolutionary leaders who had brought about those changes—the generation of men who had grown to intellectual and political maturity during the time of the May Fourth Movement—were rapidly passing from the historical scene at the time of the twenty-fifth-anniversary celebrations. The Cultural Revolu-tion and its traumatic aftermath already had taken an enormous toll of the country's leadership, first among the "capitalist-roaders" against whom the movement originally was directed, and then among those Maoist leaders who originally directed the movement and then fell victim to the purge of "ultra-leftists." For very different reasons, neither of Mao's putative successors, Liu Shao-ch'i nor Lin Piao, survived the upheaval. Age and illness removed the other old revolutionaries who survived a revolutionary process that consumed so many of its leaders and children. Tung Pi-wu, one of the few remaining founders of the Chinese Communist Party died in April 1975. In December, death took K'ang Sheng, one of Mao's closest comrades since the revolutionary years. Chou En-lai, having valiantly conducted affairs of state from his hospital bed for a year, succumbed in January 1976, and his accomplishments and his statesmanship were lauded in the Western press as his death was mourned in China. The ninety-year-old Chu Teh, the father of the Red Army, died six months later.

Among the original revolutionary leaders, only Mao Tse-tung remained. He made his last official appearance at the party's Tenth Congress in 1973 and then retired to the seclusion of his study. Ailing and increasingly feeble, he confined himself to brief meetings with visiting foreign dignitaries in his residence located in the old imperial section of Peking once called the Forbidden City. In the summer of 1976 it was announced that the Chairman could no longer receive foreign visitors. Mao Tse-tung died on September 9, 1976 at the age of 82.

The leaders of China's political and military bureaucracies, which had arisen phoenix-like from the ashes of the Great Proletarian Cultural Revolution, wasted little time in severing such tenuous links as remained with the radical Maoist tradition, although invoking the name of Mao and his slogans while doing so. Early in October, with the period of mourning for Mao barely concluded, the politburo purged itself of its radical members who had risen to prominence during the Cultural Revolution. The "Gang of Four" were arrested and accused of having conspired to seize state power, among a vast variety of other accusations. They included Wang Hung-wen (whom the Tenth Congress of 1973 had placed second only to Mao in the party hierarchy), Chang Ch'un-ch'iao (the leader of the abortive Shanghai Commune), Yao Wen-yuan (whose celebrated article had announced the opening of the Cultural Revolution), and Mao's widow, Chiang Ch'ing.[33] Selected to replace Mao as chairman of the Chinese Communist Party was the relatively obscure Hua Kuo-feng, who appeared on the contemporary political stage less as a revolutionary leader than as a caretaker for the bureaucracy.

The year 1976 thus marks the close of the Maoist era and also the final departure from the historical scene of the first generation of Chinese Marxist revolutionaries. For over half a century they had been the carriers of the most modern of revolutionary doctrines in the oldest of nations.

Historians surely will record them as among the most remarkable and important of revolutionary intelligentsias, for they were the leaders of the greatest and most dynamic revolution in the history of the modern world and the leaders who presided over the modern transformation of the world's most populous country—and also one of the most backward. Their victory of 1949 earned them power, but in a country that was utterly destitute and with a population racked by wretched poverty and despair. On the basis of the most meager of material resources they fashioned a China that Sun Yat-sen once called "a loose sheet of sand" into a unified and modern nation-state. The basic foundations for a modern industrial economy have been laid, and without the brutalities and the extremes of social inequality that accompanied the process in the Soviet Union. Once the most backward of countries, China now ranks sixth among the nations of the world in total industrial production. Among the "underdeveloped" countries, the People's Republic is one of few that is self-sufficient in food production, and the Maoist strategy of agricultural development is now universally praised and likely to be widely emulated. Once inhabiting the very homeland of famine and starvation, the Chinese people, by all accounts, are adequately fed and enjoy a slow but steadily rising standard of living, and opportunities for education and medical care that cannot be matched by any nation outside the advanced industrialized world. China is still a poor country, as her leaders constantly emphasize, but her people are no longer impoverished either materially or spiritually. And China, long "the sick man of Asia" has emerged as one of the three great powers in the world, even though its leaders eschew the title of "superpower" that is likely soon to be conferred upon it.

The material—and indeed moral-spiritual—accomplishments of the People's Republic, although belatedly discovered by foreign observers, have been widely reported and celebrated in the West in recent years, and there is no need to continue the celebration in these pages. What does need to be emphasized is that the aim of the old revolutionaries was to make China both modern *and* socialist. However bitterly they became divided in their later years over means and methods, the first generation remained firmly committed to achieving the Marxist goals they adopted in their youthful days. The new generation of leaders undoubtedly will continue to promote the modern economic and political development of China, but the historical question is whether they will continue to strive to realize socialist goals as ardently as did their predecessors. It is a question about which Mao, at the end, had the gravest doubts and he poignantly expressed them in a poem he wrote to the dying Chou En-lai in 1975:

> Loyal parents who sacrificed so much for the nation
> never feared the ultimate fate.

> Now that the country has become Red,
>   who will be its guardians?
> Our mission, unfinished, may take a thousand years.
> The struggle tires us, and our hair is gray.
> You and I, old friend, can we just watch our efforts
>   being washed away?

And there is another question, and that is just how socialist is the legacy that the old revolutionaries bequeathed to their successors? While they were eminently successful in realizing those long elusive and eminently nationalist goals of "wealth and power," their success in building a socialist society, or even one moving in that direction, is far more problematic. It is a problem about which a few concluding remarks might be made.

Notes

1. Cited in Jean Daubier, *A History of the Chinese Cultural Revolution* (New York: Vintage Books, 1974), p. 265.

2. Most notably, Schurmann. See Franz Schurmann, "What Is Happening in China: An Exchange," *New York Review of Books,* January 12, 1967.

3. Edgar Snow, *The Long Revolution* (New York: Random House, 1972), pp. 17–20.

4. Chinese support for armed revolutionary struggles was of course largely verbal, and it was also selective; the death of Che Guevara, for example, was not so much as even mentioned in the Chinese press.

5. From remarks made by Mao in the summer of 1967 and widely disseminated throughout China in pamphlet form. For a translation of the text, see Jean Daubier, *A History of the Chinese Cultural Revolution,* Appendix 4, pp. 307–313.

6. China had tested its first hydrogen bomb in 1967.

7. Lin Piao, "Report to the Ninth Congress of the Communist Party of China," *Collection of Important Documents of the Great Proletarian Cultural Revolution* (Peking: Foreign Languages Press, 1970), pp. 94–107.

8. Snow, *Long Revolution,* p. 174.

9. Mao Tse-tung, "Summary of Chairman Mao's Talks with Responsible Comrades at Various Places during his Provincial Tour," August–September 1971, in Stuart R. Schram, ed., *Mao Tse-tung Unrehearsed: Talks and Letters, 1956–71* (Middlesex, England: Penguin, 1974), pp. 292–293.

10. *Ibid.,* p. 293.

11. "Communiqué of the Second Plenary Session of the Ninth Central Committee of the Communist Party of China," *Peking Review,* September 11, 1970.

12. Snow, *Long Revolution,* pp. 10–12. Chinese and American ambassadors had held more than one hundred fruitless meetings in Warsaw from the mid-1950s.

13. *Ibid.,* pp. 171–172.

14. In early April a Chinese table-tennis team in Japan invited a touring American team to visit the People's Republic. They were accompanied by a large number of American journalists.

15. A Chinese Trident jet did crash near Under Khan in Mongolia on September 13, but Chinese and Russian accounts differ on the identity of the victims.

16. See, for example, Charles Bettleheim, *Cultural Revolution and Industrial Organization in China* (New York: Monthly Review Press, 1974), pp. 118–122, and William Hinton, *Turning Point in China* (New York: Monthly Review Press, 1972), pp. 39–40 footnote.

17. For example, see Parris H. Chang, "Political Rehabilitation of Cadres in China: A Traveller's View," *China Quarterly,* April–June, 1973, p. 333.

18. Mao, "Summary of Chairman Mao's Talks," p. 294. Here Mao listed the principal figures involved in the first nine of the "major struggles" in the history of the Party. Lin Piao, of course, was to be the tenth of the principal opponents.

19. *New York Times,* October 12, 1972, p. 3.

20. On a visit to the People's Republic in the autumn of 1972, one observer was able to identify at least fifty Party secretaries and deputy secretaries who had been returned to office. The number since has grown. Chang, "Political Rehabilitation," p. 335, note 11.

21. Mao, "Summary of Chairman Mao's Talks," p. 296. The new slogan Mao set forth at the time was: "Let the PLA learn from the people of the whole country." (p. 297).

22. Snow, *Long Revolution,* pp. 18–19, 169–170. That Mao connected his own "cult of personality with "3,000 years of emperor-worshiping tradition" suggests that he was aware of the social basis of the cult, aware that the cult flourished because China is a basically peasant country and still dominated by old peasant traditions and superstitions, and that he took advantage of this condition of backwardness by mystifying his own authority in order to demystify the authority of the Chinese Communist Party.

23. Chou En-lai, "Report to the Tenth National Congress of the Communist Party of China," August 24, 1973, in *The Tenth National Congress of the Communist Party of China (Documents)* (Peking: Foreign Languages Press, 1973), p. 34.

24. Wang Hung-wen, "Report on the Revision of the Party Constitution," August 24, 1973, in *ibid.,* pp. 48–54.

25. "Constitution of the Communist Party of China," in *ibid.,* p. 61.

26. Wang Hung-wen, "Report," p. 44.

27. Chou En-lai, "Report," p. 21. The more picturesque and literal translation of the phrase—much favored by Mao at the time—is "great disorder under Heaven."

28. *Ibid.*, pp. 5–20.

29. Yeh Chien-ying (1898–), an instructor at the Whampoa Academy in the mid-1920s, became one of the principal leaders of the Red Army after 1927, serving under Chu Teh and P'eng Te-huai as chief of staff of the main Communist army during the Yenan era. After the fall of Lin Piao in 1971, he emerged as the most powerful military figure in the People's Republic. Li Teh-sheng (1916–) joined the Red Army in 1935 at the age of 19. Primarily a professional soldier, he rose rapidly through the ranks to become a divisional commander in the post-revolutionary years. An unwavering supporter of Mao Tse-tung during the Cultural Revolution, he was elected an alternate member of the Party's politburo in April, 1969.

30. Chou En-lai, "Report on the Work of the Government," January 13, 1975, *Peking Review*, January 24, 1975, pp. 21–25.

31. On economic development since the Cultural Revolution, see, for example, Thomas G. Rawski, "Recent Trends in the Chinese Economy," *China Quarterly*, No. 53 (January–March 1973), pp. 1–33; and Robert Michael Field, Nicholas R. Lardy, and John Philip Emerson, "Industrial Output by Province in China, 1949–73," *China Quarterly*, No. 63 (September 1975), pp. 409–434. The data compiled by Field et al. suggest that industrial production is increasing at a current rate of about 10 percent per annum.

32. For an English translation of the text of the 1975 constitution, see *Peking Review*, January 24, 1975, pp. 12–17.

33. All four victims of the purge were members of the politburo of the Party's Central Committee elected at the Tenth Congress of 1973, while Wang Hung-wen and Chang Ch'un-ch'iao were members of the politburo's all-important standing committee as well. Of the nine men who made up the latter in 1973, only two remained at the end of 1976; death had taken Mao Tse-tung, Chu Teh, Chou En-lai, K'ang Sheng, and Tung Pi-wu before the post-Maoist purge removed Wang Hung-wen and Chang Ch'un-ch'iao.

Conclusion: Maoism and Socialism

WHEN THE CHINESE COMMUNISTS came to power in 1949 they promised not one revolution but two—a bourgeois revolution and a socialist one. The former, left unfinished by the old regime, was accomplished swiftly by the new one. In the early 1950s the Communists rapidly fashioned China into a modern nation-state and instilled her people with a strong sense of national identity and purpose. The long-delayed agrarian revolution was completed with the conclusion of the land-reform campaign in 1952, liberating the great majority of the Chinese people from the most inhumane forms of economic exploitation and social oppression imposed by the modern persistence of traditional rural social class relationships. Territorial unification, the establishment of a strong centralized state and a national market, and the abolition of precapitalist relations in the countryside created, in turn, the essential preconditions for the development of modern productive forces; the enormous human and material resources latent in the vast land soon were harnessed to bring about the modern industrial and technological transformation of a backward and hitherto stagnant economy.

What was accomplished during the early years of the People's Republic was essentially the program that Sun Yat-sen had set forth at the beginning of the century: national unification, "land to the tiller," and a plan for modern industrial development. And the Communists, to whom the task of implementing that program fell, justly can claim to be the true heirs of that most eminent of modern China's bourgeois revolutionaries. The fruits of that now-completed bourgeois revolution are apparent. China, long (and not long ago) among the most wretched and impoverished of lands, today stands in the world as a powerful, independent, and rapidly modernizing nation.

The bourgeois phase of the Chinese revolution did not resemble any classic model of that process, at least not any model that can be derived from Western historical experience. In China it was carried out under the auspices of a Marxist political party proclaiming socialist and communist goals. What remained of the Chinese bourgeoisie were neither its leaders nor its beneficiaries. Moreover, the distinguishing feature of Western bourgeois revolutions—the creation of conditions conducive to the flourishing of private property and capitalist economic development —hardly distinguished the Chinese version. The era of "national capitalism" in the cities and individual peasant proprietorship in the countryside was both limited and brief. The limitations were imposed by a state presided over by Marxists who aimed to abolish private property and capitalism. And when those Marxist leaders determined that the essential "bourgeois" tasks had been accomplished, they were determined to bring about the second of the two revolutions they had promised. The era of the "transition to socialism" officially began in 1953.

More than two decades have passed since the Chinese Communists announced the inauguration of the socialist phase of the revolution. Have they succeeded in creating a socialist society, as they claim? Is the People's Republic, as its leaders declare, a state under "the dictatorship of the proletariat," a country in the "transitional" stage between socialism and communism? The close of the Maoist era is an appropriate time to ask these questions, although it is perhaps still too early to provide any definitive answers. Nonetheless, some tentative observations might be offered.

The socio-economic changes that have transformed China in the years since 1949 cannot easily be subsumed under the rubric of "the modernization process," however broadly one may choose to define that rather vague term. "Modernization," after all, does not typically entail the abolition of private property. Yet it is precisely the absence of private ownership over the means of production that crucially characterizes contemporary Chinese society. The nationalization of the urban economy and the collectivization of agriculture in the 1950s have proved to be irreversible measures, and they are necessary (if not necessarily sufficient) conditions for socialism.

The abolition of private property was accompanied by an intensive drive for industrialization, and the latter of course lies at the heart of anyone's concept of modernization. But industrial development has proceeded under state direction and ownership, and the process was conceived not simply as an end in itself but as a means to achieve socialist ends, as the essential means to build the material base upon which any future socialist society inevitably must rest. Indeed, perhaps the most unique and noteworthy feature of that process has been the Maoist attempt to reconcile the means of modern industrialism with the ends of socialism. In China, as in the Soviet Union, rapid industrialization rapidly produced new forms of social inequality: the growth and stratification of new bureaucratic and technological elites; the exploitation of the rural areas for the benefit of the industrializing cities; and a tendency for the industrial values of economic rationality and bureaucratic professionalism to become the dominant social values, subordinating the socialist values and goals which industrialization originally was intended to serve.

What has been distinctively "Maoist" about the Maoist era has been an effort to avoid (or at least mitigate) the social and ideological consequences of industrialization by attempting to pursue modern economic development in a fashion consistent with the achievement of Marxist goals. Rejecting the comfortable but illusory Soviet orthodoxy that the combination of nationalization and industrialization automatically guarantees the arrival of a socialist society, Maoists have demanded that modern economic development must be accompanied by (and perhaps preceded by) a "continuous" process of the revolutionary transformation of social relationships and popular consciousness, a demand that socialist organizational forms and communist values must be created in the very process of constructing the material prerequisites for the new society. That demand, expressed in its most pristine form in the ill-fated Great Leap Forward campaign, since has found more lasting expression in such policies as those which aim to combine industrial with agricultural production, combine education with productive labor, and oblige officials and intellectuals to periodically engage in work on farms or in factories— and perhaps most importantly, in the program for the industrialization of the countryside. These policies were conceived not only (or even primarily) for their economic efficacy but with classic Marxist aims in mind: the reduction of the age-old distinctions between mental and manual labor, between workers and peasants, and between town and countryside. At the close of the Maoist era, China is far from realizing these ultimate goals, but the striving to achieve them has served to narrow the range of socioeconomic inequalities, to prevent the differentiation of a professional vocational ethic from the Maoist political ethic, and to forestall the stratification of bureaucratic elites separated from the masses. In general, the thrust of Maoist policies pursued over the past quarter-century has been specifically socialist and not generally "modernistic."

Yet if the Maoist era established many of the socioeconomic preconditions for socialism, it did not create its no less essential political preconditions. For socialism involves more than the abolition of private property and more than a general social leveling. Socialism means, if it is to have any genuine meaning, a system where political power is exercised by the masses of the producers themselves, permitting them to control the conditions and the products of their labor. The dictatorship of the proletariat, as socialism, or the "lower phase of communism," is defined in Marxist theory, is a time marked by a process whereby the social

powers usurped by the state are returned to society as a whole; more specifically, it is a period when the state, both as a repressive instrument
and in its constructive functions, takes the form of what Marx termed
"the self-government of the producers." In what has passed for "the dictatorship of the proletariat" in Maoist China, these socialist political conceptions and forms have been absent in both theory and practice. If
Maoism is a doctrine that has confronted the dilemma of reconciling the
means of modern economic development with socialist ends, it is not a
doctrine that recognizes that popular democracy is both the means and
the end of socialism.

There were two crucial periods in the history of the People's Republic
when the critical problem of the relationship between state and society
was raised and presented for solution. During the Hundred Flowers
campaign Mao himself posed the question of the contradiction between
"the leadership and the led," and from the movement itself there came
widespread demands for political democracy and intellectual freedom.
But the demands were suppressed and the contradiction between rulers
and ruled remained unresolved. The Cultural Revolution launched a
wholesale attack against party and state bureaucracies and at first seemed
to promise the reorganization of political power in accordance with the
Marxist principles of the Paris Commune. But the promise was aborted
and the Cultural Revolution concluded with the total reestablishment
of the rule of the Leninist party. If Mao can be credited with initiating
the Hundred Flowers campaign and the Cultural Revolution, he also
must bear the historical responsibility for their failure to initiate processes
to transform the state from the master of society into its servant.

Maoists long have pointed to the Soviet Union as a "negative example" for the building of socialism. Yet they have not derived from the
Soviet historical experience the obvious lesson that socialism is impossible without freedom and popular democracy—and that conditions of
economic backwardness and a hostile international arena cannot indefinitely be used to justify their absence. The old Marxist dream of the
"withering away" of the state may be a "utopian" demand in the present
historical situation, but there is nothing at all utopian about the demand
that the Chinese people should enjoy such elemental democratic liberties
as freedom of expression and association. Without that modest beginning
"the dictatorship of the proletariat," however ardently proclaimed, will
remain a hollow ideological rationalization for the continued domination
of state over society. It was not a beginning that was made during the
Maoist era.

The legacy of Mao is thus an ambiguous one, for it is marked and
marred by a deep incongruity between its progressive socio-economic
accomplishments and its retrogressive political features. On the one hand,
Maoism has thrown off Stalinist orthodoxies and methods in forging a
new pattern of economic development which has, on balance, moved

Chinese society in a socialist direction. On the other hand, it has retained
essentially Stalinist methods of bureaucratic political rule, generated its
own cults, orthodoxies and dogmas, and consistently suppressed all forms
of intellectual and political dissent. Mao, to be sure, regarded bureaucracy
as the greatest of evils, but his weapon to combat the phenomenon was
to rely on his personal prestige and the forces he could rally under his
own banner. Neither in theory nor practice does the Maoist legacy include institutional safeguards against bureaucratic dominance.

The new rulers of the People's Republic, whoever they ultimately may
turn out to be, will surely wrap themselves in the mantle of Maoism;
they will certainly continue the modern economic development of China,
and they even may do so through Maoist methods, although the latter
can by no means be taken for granted. But the question that will determine the future course of China's social development is not simply
whether Mao's successors will inherit his legacy, for as a socialist legacy
it is politically deficient. The real question, at least insofar as the possibility of socialism is concerned, is whether new and future generations
of Chinese will enrich and develop that legacy in a manner that will
make China politically democratic and intellectually free. For the absence of political and intellectual freedom precludes the possibility that
political power will take the form of "the self-government of the producers," the only form that will permit the Chinese people to bring about
their own emancipation, the form that is both the essential condition of
socialism and the essential precondition for its genuine emergence and
development.

The prospects for such a democratic evolution are hardly promising,
for not only are the necessary political prerequisites absent in Chinese
Communist reality but the need for them is unrecognized in Chinese
Communist theory. Indeed, at the close of the Maoist era, Chinese sociohistorical conditions powerfully favor the further growth of an autonomous bureaucratic state standing ever higher above society. First and
foremost among those conditions is the absence of a dominant social class
capable of restraining the independent power of the state. In original
Marxist theory it was assumed that political power in a postrevolutionary
society would be exercised by the proletariat and would be employed
for universalistic ends, the creation of a classless and stateless society. In
lieu of a politically active proletariat (or its functional equivalent), the
socially egalitarian results of the Chinese Revolution, far from initiating
a process leading to the "withering away" of the state, ironically have
created conditions for the state to become all the more powerful. The
postrevolutionary history of China offers abundant contemporary evidence
to support Max Weber's proposition that "every process of social leveling
creates a favorable situation for the development of bureaucracy."[1]

To this general condition there must be added several specific factors
conducive to bureaucratic autonomy and supremacy: the persistence of

old Chinese bureaucratic traditions and habits; the bureaucratic elites and mentalities fostered by modern industrialism; the elitist implications of Leninist principles of party organization, now fully restored; and, what has gone hand in hand with the latter, the political apathy of the masses since the Cultural Revolution. And perhaps the passing of Mao has removed the last and greatest barrier to the bureaucratic institutionalization of the Chinese Revolution.

Thus China finds itself in that misty historical realm of socioeconomic orders that are neither capitalist nor socialist and are sometimes simply labeled, for want of any better term, "postcapitalist." The People's Republic is not simply capitalist because it is a society which has abolished the essential condition of capitalism—private property and private ownership of the means of production. And it is not genuinely socialist because the masses of producers do not have the means to control the products of their labor, nor do they control the state that has become the economic manager of society and that stands above them. It is as if China is

> ... Wandering between two worlds, one dead,
> The other powerless to be born. . . .[2]

If China is unlikely to go back to the old world, it is not necessarily the case that she will move forward to a new socialist world. "Wandering" can become a more or less permanent state of affairs and "postcapitalist" societies can crystallize into new forms of bureaucratically dominated social orders, as the history of the Soviet Union demonstrates. During the Maoist era, the impetus for socialism and the struggle against bureaucracy came from the top, principally from Mao himself. That impetus struck responsive chords in Chinese society and Maoist goals were pursued through the mobilization of the masses for radical social change. It is highly improbable that any similar impetus will come from the leaders of the post-Maoist order, for they are men who are essentially the managers of a powerful party–state bureaucracy that has a strong interest in its own self-preservation, and thus a vested interest in the political apathy of the masses. If much of the Maoist era was guided by the principle of "permanent revolution," it is likely, at least for the foreseeable future, that the post-Maoist era will be marked by the permanence of bureaucracy and its dominance over society.

Notes

1. Max Weber, *The Theory of Social and Economic Organization* (New York: The Free Press, 1964), p. 340.
2. *The Poems of Matthew Arnold* (London: Oxford University Press, 1930), p. 272.

Selected Bibliography

MUCH OF THE BEST LITERATURE on the history of Chinese Communism and the People's Republic of China is to be found in periodicals, most notably the *China Quarterly* (London). Other periodicals of special interest are *Asian Survey* (Berkeley), *Bulletin of Concerned Asian Scholars* (San Francisco), *Far Eastern Economic Review* (Hong Kong), *Journal of Asian Studies* (Ann Arbor), *Modern China* (Los Angeles), and *Pacific Affairs* (Vancouver). The relevant articles that have appeared in these and other journals are too numerous to list individually in this bibliography. The titles listed below include only works cited in the text and other works that have been considered in preparing this book. While the bibliography is thus far from complete, it might prove to be of some help to readers who wish to pursue particular topics in greater depth or who seek different interpretations from those offered in the preceding chapters.

BARENDSON, R. D. *Half-Work Half-Study Schools in Communist China.* Washington, D.C., 1964.

BARNETT, A. DOAK. *Cadres, Bureaucracy and Political Power in China.* New York: Columbia University Press, 1967.

——. *China on the Eve of Communist Takeover.* New York: Praeger, 1963.

——. *China After Mao.* Princeton, N.J.: Princeton University Press, 1967.

——. *Communist China: The Early Years 1949–55.* New York: Praeger, 1964.

——, ed. *Chinese Communist Politics in Action.* Seattle: University of Washington Press, 1969.

BAUM, RICHARD. *Prelude to Revolution: Mao, the Party and the Peasant Question.* New York: Columbia University Press, 1975.

——, and FREDERICK C. TEIWES. *Ssu-Ch'ing: The Socialist Education Movement of 1962–1966.* Berkeley: University of California Press, 1968.

BENNETT, GORDON A., and RONALD H. MONTAPERTO. *Red Guard: The Political Biography of Dai Hsiao-ai.* New York: Doubleday, 1971.

BETTELHEIM, CHARLES. *Cultural Revolution and Industrial Organization in China.* New York: Monthly Review Press, 1974.

BODDE, DERK. *Peking Diary.* New York: Henry Schuman, 1950.

BOWIE, ROBERT R., and JOHN K. FAIRBANK, eds. *Communist China 1955–1959: Policy Documents with Analysis.* Cambridge, Mass.: Harvard University Press, 1962.

BRANDT, CONRAD. *Stalin's Failure in China, 1924–1927.* Cambridge, Mass.: Harvard University Press, 1958.

————, BENJAMIN SCHWARTZ, and JOHN K. FAIRBANK, eds. *A Documentary History of Chinese Communism.* Cambridge, Mass.: Harvard University Press, 1952.

BRINTON, CRANE. *The Anatomy of Revolution.* New York: Vintage, 1965.

CHANG, KUO-T'AO. *The Rise of the Chinese Communist Party.* 2 vols. Lawrence: University of Kansas Press, 1971–72.

CHANG, PARRIS. *Radicals and Radical Ideology in China's Cultural Revolution.* New York: Research Institute on Communist Affairs, Columbia University, 1973.

CHAO, KANG. *Agricultural Production in Communist China, 1949–1965.* Madison: University of Wisconsin Press, 1970.

CHAO, KUO-CHÜN. *Agrarian Policies of Mainland China: A Documentary Study (1949–1956).* Cambridge, Mass.: Harvard University Press, 1957.

Che-hsüeh Yen-chiu (Philosophical research). Peking.

CH'EN, JEROME. *Mao and the Chinese Revolution.* London: Oxford University Press, 1965.

CH'EN, THEODORE H. E. *Thought Reform of the Chinese Intellectuals.* Hong Kong: Hong Kong University Press, 1960.

CHENG, CHU-YUAN, *Communist China's Economy 1949–1962: Structural Change and Crisis.* South Orange, N.J.: Seton Hall University Press, 1963.

CHENG, PETER. *A Chronology of the People's Republic of China.* Totowa, New Jersey: Littlefield, Adams & Co., 1972.

CHESNEAUX, JEAN. *The Chinese Labor Movement, 1919–1927.* Stanford, Calif.: Stanford University Press, 1968.

Chinese Law and Government. Edited by International Arts and Sciences Sciences Press, White Plains, N.Y.

Chinese Studies in History and Philosophy. Edited by International Arts and Sciences Press, White Plains, N.Y.

CHOW, TSE-TSUNG. *The May Fourth Movement: Intellectual Revolution in Modern China.* Cambridge, Mass.: Harvard University Press, 1960.

Chung-kuo Ch'ing-nien (Chinese youth). Peking.

CLARK, ANNE B., and DONALD W. KLEIN, *Biographic Dictionary of Chinese Communism, 1921–65.* Cambridge, Mass.: Harvard University Press, 1971.

COHEN, JEROME ALAN. *The Criminal Process in the People's Republic of China, 1949–63.* Cambridge, Mass.: Harvard University Press, 1968.

Collection of Important Documents of the Great Proletarian Cultural Revolution. Peking: Foreign Languages Press, 1970.

Committee of Concerned Asian Scholars. *China, Inside the People's Republic.* New York: Bantam, 1972.

COMPTON, BOYD, ed. *Mao's China: Party Reform Documents, 1942–44.* Seattle: University of Washington Press, 1966.

CROIZIER, RALPH C., ed., *China's Cultural Legacy and Communism.* New York: Praeger, 1970.

CROLL, ELISEBETH, ed. *The Women's Movement in China: A Selection of Readings.* London: Anglo-Chinese Educational Institute, 1974.

CROOK, DAVID, and ISABEL CROOK. *Revolution in a Chinese Village: Ten Mile Inn.* London: Routledge & Kegan Paul, 1959.

Current Background. U.S. Consulate General, Hong Kong.

DAVIN, DELIA. *Woman-Work: Women and the Party in Revolutionary China.* London: Oxford University Press, 1976.

DAUBIER, JEAN. *A History of the Chinese Cultural Revolution.* New York: Vintage, 1974.

Decision of the Central Committee of the Communist Party of China Concerning the Great Proletarian Cultural Revolution. Peking: Foreign Languages Press, 1966.

DEUTSCHER, ISAAC. *Ironies of History.* London: Oxford University Press, 1966.

DITTMER, LOWELL. *Liu Shao-ch'i and the Chinese Cultural Revolution: The Politics of Mass Criticism.* Berkeley: University of California Press, 1974.

DOMES, JURGEN. *The Internal Politics of China, 1949–1972.* London: C. Hurst, 1973.

DONNITHORNE, AUDREY. *China's Economic System.* London: George Allen & Unwin, 1967.

DUNAYEVSKAYA, RAYA. *Philosophy and Revolution.* New York: Dell, 1973.

DUNN, JOHN. *Modern Revolutions.* London: Cambridge University Press, 1972.

ECKSTEIN, ALEXANDER, WALTER GALENSON, and TA-CHUNG LIU, eds. *Economic Trends in Communist China.* Edinburgh University Press, 1968.

ENCAUSSE, HÉLÈNE CARRERE, and STUART R. SCHRAM. *Marxism and Asia.* London: Allen Lane, 1969.

The Eighth National Congress of the Communist Party of China (Documents). Peking: Foreign Languages Press, 1956.

ESMEIN, JEAN. *The Chinese Cultural Revolution.* New York: Anchor, 1973.

FAIRBANK, JOHN K. *China: The People's Middle Kingdom and the U.S.A.* Cambridge, Mass.: Harvard University Press, 1967.

———. *China Perceived: Images and Policies in Chinese-American Relations.* New York: Knopf, 1974.

FEI, HSIAO-T'UNG. *China's Gentry.* Chicago: University of Chicago Press, 1953.

FEUERWERKER, ALBERT, ed. *History in Communist China.* Cambridge, Mass.: MIT Press, 1968.

FOKKEMA, D. W. *Literary Doctrine in China and Soviet Influence, 1956–60.* The Hague: Mouton, 1965.

FRASER, STEWART E., ed. *Education and Communism in China.* Hong Kong, 1969.

FRIEDMAN, EDWARD. *Backward Toward Revolution: The Chinese Revolutionary Party.* Berkeley: University of California Press, 1974.

———, and MARK SELDEN, eds. *America's Asia.* New York: Vintage, 1971.

GITTINGS, JOHN. *The Role of the Chinese Army.* New York: Oxford University Press, 1967.

————. *Survey of the Sino-Soviet Dispute, 1963–67.* London: Oxford University Press, 1968.

————. *The World and China, 1922–72.* New York: Harper & Row, 1974.

GOLDMAN, MERLE. *Literary Dissent in Communist China.* Cambridge, Mass.: Harvard University Press, 1967.

GRAMSCI, ANTONIO. *Selections from the Prison Notebooks.* New York: International Publishers, 1971.

GRAY, JACK, and PATRICK CAVENDISH, *Chinese Communism in Crisis: Maoism and the Cultural Revolution.* London: Pall Mall, 1968.

GRIFFITH, WILLIAM E. *The Sino-Soviet Rift.* Cambridge, Mass.: MIT Press, 1964.

GUILLERMEZ, JACQUES. *A History of the Chinese Communist Party, 1921–1949.* New York: Random House, 1972.

HARRISON, JAMES P. *The Communists and Chinese Peasant Rebellions.* New York: Atheneum, 1969.

————. *The Long March to Power: A History of the Chinese Communist Party, 1921–72.* New York: Praeger, 1972.

HERZEN, ALEXANDER. *From the Other Shore.* London: Weidenfeld & Nicolson, 1956.

HINTON, WILLIAM. *Fanshen: A Documentary of Revolution in a Chinese Village.* New York: Vintage, 1966.

————. *Hundred Day War: The Cultural Revolution at Tsinghua University.* New York: Monthly Review Press, 1972.

————. *Turning Point in China.* New York: Monthly Review Press, 1972.

HOFFMANN, CHARLES. *The Chinese Worker.* Albany: State University of New York Press, 1974.

HORN, JOSHUA. *Away with All Pests.* New York: Monthly Review Press, 1969.

HOUN, FRANKLIN. *To Change a Nation: Propaganda and Indoctrination in Communist China.* Glencoe, Ill.: The Free Press, 1961.

HOWE, CHRISTOPHER. *Employment and Economic Growth in Urban China, 1949–57.* Cambridge: Cambridge University Press, 1971.

HSIA, ADRIAN. *The Chinese Cultural Revolution.* New York: Seabury Press, 1972.

HSIUNG, JAMES C. *Ideology and Practice: The Evolution of Chinese Communism.* New York: Praeger, 1970.

HSÜEH, CHÜN-TU, ed. *Revolutionary Leaders of Modern China.* New York: Oxford University Press, 1971.

Hung-ch'i (Red flag). Peking.

HUNTER, NEALE. *Shanghai Journal.* Boston: Beacon Press, 1971.

International Journal. Toronto.

ISAACS, HAROLD. *The Tragedy of the Chinese Revolution.* Stanford, Calif.: Stanford University Press, 1951.

JOFFE, ELLIS. *Party and Army: Professionalism and Political Control in the Chinese Officer Corps.* Cambridge, Mass.: Harvard University Press, 1965.

JOHNSON, CHALMERS, ed. *Ideology and Politics in Contemporary China.* Seattle: University of Washington Press, 1973.

————. *Peasant Nationalism and Communist Power.* Stanford, Calif.: Stanford University Press, 1962.

Joint Economic Committee of the United States Congress. *An Economic Profile of Mainland China.* Washington, D.C.: Government Printing Office, 1967.

Joint Publications Research Service (JPRS) (Washington, D.C.).

KAROL, K. S. *China, The Other Communism.* New York: Hill & Wang, 1967.

————. *The Second Chinese Revolution.* New York: Hill & Wang, 1974.

LENIN, V. I. *Selected Works,* 2 vols. Moscow: Foreign Languages Publishing House, 1952.

LEVENSON, JOSEPH R. *Confucian China and Its Modern Fate: A Trilogy.* Berkeley: University of California Press, 1968.

————. *Liang Ch'i-ch'ao and the Mind of Modern China.* Cambridge, Mass.: Harvard University Press, 1959.

LEWIS, JOHN W. *Leadership in Communist China.* Ithaca, N.Y.: Cornell University Press, 1963.

————, ed. *The City in Communist China.* Stanford, Calif.: Stanford University Press, 1971.

————, ed. *Party Leadership and Revolutionary Power in China.* Cambridge: Cambridge University Press, 1970.

LI, CHOH-MING. *The Economic Development of Communist China.* Berkeley: University of California Press, 1959.

LICHTHEIM, GEORGE. *Marxism: An Historical and Critical Study.* New York: Praeger, 1961.

LIFTON, ROBERT JAY. *Revolutionary Immortality.* New York: Random House, 1968.

————. *Thought Reform and the Psychology of Totalism.* New York: Norton, 1961.

LIN YÜ-SHENG. *The Crisis of Chinese Consciousness: Radical Iconoclasm in the May Fourth Era.* Madison: University of Wisconsin Press, forthcoming.

LINDBECK, JOHN, ed. *China: Management of a Revolutionary Society.* Seattle: University of Washington Press, 1971.

LIU, SHAO-CH'I. *Collected Works of Liu Shao-ch'i.* 3 vols. Hong Kong: Union Research Institute, 1968–69.

LIU, T. A., and K. C. YEH. *The Economy of Mainland China: National Income and Economic Development, 1933–59.* Princeton, N.J.: Princeton University Press, 1965.

LUXEMBURG, ROSA. *Rosa Luxemburg Speaks.* New York: Pathfinder Press, 1970.

MACFARQUHAR, RODERICK. *The Origins of the Cultural Revolution, Vol. I: Contradictions Among the People.* London: Oxford University Press, 1974.

————, ed. *China Under Mao: Politics Takes Command.* Cambridge, Mass.: MIT Press, 1966.

————, ed. *The Hundred Flowers Campaign and the Chinese Intellectuals.* New York: Praeger, 1960.

MACCIOCCHI, MARIA ANTONIETTA. *Daily Life in Revolutionary China.* New York: Monthly Review Press, 1972.

MAO TSE-TUNG. *Mao Papers.* Edited by Jerome Ch'en. London: Oxford University Press, 1970.

————. *Mao Tse-tung Ssu-hsiang Wan-sui* (Long live the thought of Mao Tse-tung). 2 vols. Taipei: n.p., 1967 and 1969).

————. *Mao Tse-tung Unrehearsed: Talks and Letters, 1956–71.* Edited by Stuart R. Schram. Middlesex, England: Penguin Books, 1974.

————. *On the Correct Handling of Contradictions Among the People.* Peking: Foreign Languages Press, 1957.

————. *Poems of Mao Tse-tung.* Edited by Wong Man. Hong Kong: Eastern Horizon Press, 1966.

————. *Selected Works of Mao Tse-tung.* 4 vols. London: Lawrence & Wishart, 1954.

————. *Selected Works of Mao Tse-tung.* 4 vols. Peking: Foreign Languages Press, 1961.

MARX, KARL. *Capital*, Vol. I. Chicago: Kerr, 1906.

————. *Selected Writings in Sociology and Social Philosophy.* Edited by T. B. Bottomore and Maximilien Rubel. London: Watts, 1956.

————. *Writings of the Young Marx on Philosophy and Society.* Edited by Loyd D. Easton and Kurt H. Guddat. New York: Anchor, 1967.

————, and FREDERICK ENGELS. *Selected Correspondence.* Moscow: Foreign Languages Publishing House, 1953.

————. *Selected Works.* 2 vols. Moscow: Foreign Languages Publishing House, 1950.

————. *Werke.* Berlin: Dietz, 1964.

MEHNERT, KLAUS. *Peking and Moscow.* London: Weidenfeld & Nicolson, 1963.

MEISEL, JAMES H. *Counter-Revolution.* New York: Atherton, 1966.

MEISNER, MAURICE. *Li Ta-chao and the Origins of Chinese Marxism.* Cambridge, Mass.: Harvard University Press, 1967.

MICHELS, ROBERT. *Political Parties.* Glencoe, Ill.: The Free Press, 1949.

MILTON, DAVID, and NANCY DALL MILTON. *The Wind Will Not Subside: Years in Revolutionary China—1964–1969.* New York: Pantheon, 1976.

MOORE, BARRINGTON. *Social Origins of Dictatorship and Democracy.* Boston: Beacon Press, 1966.

————. *Soviet Politics: The Dilemma of Power.* Cambridge, Mass.: Harvard University Press, 1959.

MYRDAL, JAN. *Report from a Chinese Village.* New York: Pantheon, 1965.

————, and GUN KESSLE. *China: The Revolution Continued.* New York: Pantheon, 1970.

National Programme for Agricultural Development, 1956–1967. Peking: Foreign Languages Press, 1960.

NEE, VICTOR. *The Cultural Revolution at Peking University.* New York: Monthly Review Press, 1969.

New China's Economic Achievements. Peking: Foreign Languages Press, 1952.

OKSENBERG, MICHEL, ed. *China's Developmental Experience.* New York: Praeger, 1973.

On the Historical Experience of the Dictatorship of the Proletariat. Peking: Foreign Languages Press, 1961.

ORLEANS, LEO A. *Professional Manpower and Education in Communist China.* Washington, D.C.: Government Printing Office, 1961.

PECK, JAMES, and VICTOR NEE, eds. *China's Uninterrupted Revolution: From 1840 to the Present.* New York: Pantheon, 1975.

Peking Review (Peking).

People's China (Peking).

People's Daily (Jen-min Jih-pao) (Peking).

PERKINS, DWIGHT H. *Market Control and Planning in Communist China.* Cambridge, Mass.: Harvard University Press, 1966.

PRICE, R. F. *Education in Communist China.* London: Routledge & Kegan Paul, 1970.

RICE, EDWARD. *Mao's Way.* Berkeley: University of California Press, 1972.

RICHMAN, BARRY M. *Industrial Society in Communist China.* New York: Random House, 1969.

ROBINSON, JOAN. *Economic Management in China.* London: Anglo-Chinese Educational Institute, 1975.

RUE, JOHN. *Mao Tse-tung in Opposition, 1927–1935.* Stanford, Calif.: Stanford University Press, 1966.

SCHRAM, STUART R. *Mao Tse-tung.* New York: Simon & Schuster, 1967.

————, ed. *Authority, Participation and Cultural Change in China.* Cambridge: Cambridge University Press, 1973.

————. *La "révolution permanente" en Chine.* Paris: Mouton, 1963.

————. *The Political Thought of Mao Tse-tung.* New York: Praeger, 1969.

SCHURMANN, FRANZ. *Ideology and Organization in Communist China.* Berkeley: University of California Press, 1966.

SCHWARTZ, BENJAMIN. *Chinese Communism and the Rise of Mao.* Cambridge, Mass.: Harvard University Press, 1951.

————. *Communism and China: Ideology in Flux.* Cambridge, Mass.: Harvard University Press, 1968.

————. *In Search of Wealth and Power: Yen Fu and the West.* Cambridge, Mass.: Harvard University Press, 1964.

SELDEN, MARK. *The Yenan Way in Revolutionary China.* Cambridge, Mass.: Harvard University Press, 1971.

SHERIDAN, JAMES E. *China in Disintegration.* New York: The Free Press, 1975.

SIDEL, RUTH. *Women and Child Care in China.* New York: Hill & Wang, 1972.

SIDEL, VICTOR W., and RUTH SIDEL. *Serve the People: Observations on Medicine in the People's Republic of China.* New York: Josiah Macy, 1973.

SMEDLEY, AGNES. *The Great Road: The Life and Times of Chu Teh.* New York: Monthly Review Press, 1956.

Socialist Upsurge in China's Countryside. Peking: Foreign Language Press, 1957.

SNOW, EDGAR. *The Long Revolution.* New York: Random House, 1972.

————. *The Other Side of the River.* New York: Random House, 1961.

————. *Random Notes on Red China, 1936–1945.* Cambridge, Mass.: Harvard University Press, 1957.

————. *Red Star Over China.* New York: Random House, 1938.

SOLOMON, RICHARD H. *Mao's Revolution and the Chinese Political Culture.* Berkeley: University of California Press, 1971.

STRONG, ANNA LOUISE. *Tomorrow's China.* New York: Committee for a Democratic Far Eastern Policy, 1948.

Survey of China Mainland Magazines (SCMM). U.S. Consulate General, Hong Kong.

Survey of China Mainland Press (SCMP). U.S. Consulate General, Hong Kong.

SWEEZY, PAUL M., and CHARLES BETTELHEIM. *On the Transition to Socialism.* New York: Monthly Review Press, 1971.

TAWNEY, R. H. *Land and Labour in China.* London: G. Allen & Unwin, 1932.

Ten Great Years. Peking: Foreign Languages Press, 1960.

The Tenth National Congress of the Communist Party of China (*Documents*). Peking: Foreign Languages Press, 1973.

TERRILL, ROSS. *800,000,000: The Real China.* Boston: Little, Brown & Co., 1972.

TOWNSEND, JAMES. *Political Participation in Communist China.* Berkeley: University of California Press, 1967.

TROTSKY, LEON. *Our Revolution.* New York, 1918.

———. *The Permanent Revolution and Results and Prospects.* New York: Pathfinder Press, 1974.

———. *Problems of the Chinese Revolution.* New York: Pioneer Publishers, 1932.

TUCKER, ROBERT C. *The Marxian Revolutionary Idea.* New York: Norton, 1969.

Union Research Institute, ed. *The Case of P'eng Teh-huai.* Hong Kong: Union Research Institute, 1968.

———, ed. *Documents of the Chinese Communist Party Central Committee.* 2 vols. Hong Kong: Union Research Institute, 1971.

———, ed. *Who's Who in Communist China.* 2 vols. Hong Kong: Union Research Institute, 1969–70.

VAN SLYKE, LYMAN P. *Enemies and Friends: The United Front in Chinese Communist History.* Stanford, Calif.: Stanford University Press, 1967.

VOGEL, EZRA. *Canton under Communism.* Cambridge, Mass.: Harvard University Press, 1969.

WAKEMAN, FREDERIC. *History and Will: Philosophical Perspectives of Mao Tse-tung's Thought.* Berkeley: University of California Press, 1973.

WALICKI, A. *The Controversy Over Capitalism.* Oxford: Clarendon Press, 1969.

WANG, Y. C. *Chinese Intellectuals and the West.* Chapel Hill: University of North Carolina Press, 1966.

WEBER, MAX. *The Theory of Social and Economic Organization.* New York: The Free Press, 1964.

WHEELWRIGHT, E. L., and BRUCE McFARLANE. *The Chinese Road to Socialism: Economics of the Cultural Revolution.* New York: Monthly Review Press, 1970.

WHITING, ALLEN. *China Crosses the Yalu: The Decision to Enter the Korean War.* New York: Macmillan, 1960.

WHITSON, WILLIAM. *A History of Chinese Communist Military Politics, 1927–1961.* New York: Praeger, 1973.

WHYTE, MARTIN K. *Small Groups and Political Rituals in China.* Berkeley: University of California Press, 1974.

WILSON, DICK. *The Long March: The Epic of Chinese Communism's Survival.* London: Hamish Hamilton, 1971.

WITTFOGEL, KARL A. *Oriental Despotism.* New Haven: Yale University Press, 1957.

WOLF, MARGERY and ROXANNE WITKE, eds. *Women in Chinese Society.* Stanford, Calif.: Stanford University Press, 1975.

WONG, JOHN. *Land Reform in the People's Republic of China: Institutional Transformation of Agriculture.* New York: Praeger, 1973.

WRIGHT, MARY C., ed. *China in Revolution: The First Phase, 1900–1913.* New Haven: Yale University Press, 1968.

WU, YUAN-LI. *The Economy of Communist China: An Interpretation.* New York: Praeger, 1965.

YANG, C. K. *The Chinese Family in the Communist Revolution.* Cambridge, Mass.: MIT Press, 1959.

————. *A Chinese Village in Early Communist Transition.* Cambridge, Mass.: MIT Press, 1959.

YAO WEN-YUAN. *On the Social Basis of the Lin Piao Anti-Party Clique.* Peking: Foreign Languages Press, 1975.

YOUNG, MARILYN, ed. *Women in China.* Ann Arbor, Mich.: Center for Chinese Studies, 1973.

ZAGORIA, DONALD S. *The Sino-Soviet Conflict, 1956–61.* Princeton, N.J.: Princeton University Press, 1962.

Index